# Object-Oriented Software Engineering

## A Use Case Driven Approach

## ACM PRESS

| | | |
|---|---|---|
| *Editor-in-Chief* | **Peter Wegner** | Brown University |
| *International Editor* | **Dines Bjørner** | Technical University |
| *(Europe)* | | of Denmark |

### SELECTED TITLES

# Object-Oriented Software Engineering

## A Use Case Driven Approach

### IvarJacobson
### Magnus Christerson   Patrik Jonsson
### Gunnar Övergaard

Objective Systems SF AB
PO Box 1128, S-16422 Kista, Sweden

Objectory Corp.
PO Box 2630, Greenwich, CT 06836, USA

ADDISON-WESLEY

Harlow, England • Reading, Massachusetts • Menlo Park, California
New York • Don Mills, Ontario • Amsterdam • Bonn • Sydney • Singapore
Tokyo • Madrid • San Juan • Milan • Mexico City • Seoul • Taipei

Addison Wesley Longman Limited
Edinburgh Gate
Harlow
Essex, CM20 2JE
England

Cover designed by Chris Eley
Typeset by Columns Design & Production Services Ltd, Reading
Printed in the United States of America
ISBN 0-201-54435-0


First printed 1992. Reprinted 1992 and 1993. Revised fourth printing 1993.
Reprinted 1994 (twice), 1995 (twice), 1996, 1997, and 1998 (twice).

**British Library Cataloguing-in-Publication Data**
A catalogue record for this book is available from the British Library.

**Library of Congress Cataloging-in-Publication Data available.**

# Foreword

Ivar Jacobson is in my opinion one of the foremost methodologists in the field of software engineering. I take great pleasure in writing this, because he is also a close personal friend. He brings a refreshingly pragmatic point of view to a discipline that often seems be so abstract and arcane as to be hopelessly remote from the real world of 'blue collar' programmers. His methodology is based on some really innovative ideas about modeling the software process, presented within a tried and proven engineering framework. It brings to the task of analyzing, designing and constructing complex software intensive products the same disciplined approach that is to be found in other branches of engineering.

Along with many others I have urged lvar for some time to publish his methodology in a textbook, so that it would be accessible to a larger audience. I believe that the concepts in Objectory, the first comprehensive object-oriented process for developing large scale industrial systems, are important and should get wider exposure. This book represents over 20 years of experience building real software based products and a great deal of serious thinking about how such systems should be built. If you have any interest at all in software you will enjoy reading it.

Objectory stands out as being a truly object-oriented methodology, in which both the process and the methodology are themselves represented as objects. While some may find this idea of a reflective or 'meta' architecture to be rather exotic, it is in fact intensely practical and absolutely essential. It makes Objectory an extensible methodology which can be specialized to both the organization and the application domains. Simply put, Objectory provides a software process for building not just software, but also other more specialized software processes.

Another key innovation in Objectory is the concept of use cases, which has now been proved effective in a number of real-world projects. Use cases provide the needed linkage between requirements, development, testing and final customer acceptance. This idea, which originated in Ivar's work on the AXE switch, has been generalized so that it can be applied in application domains as diverse as command and control and business information systems.

Use cases provide a concrete representation of software requirements, which allows them to be both formally expressed and systematically tested. Changes in requirements map directly onto changes in the set of use cases. In this way Objectory provides a solid methodological foundation for rapid prototyping and other forms of incremental software development. Objectory enables managers to move beyond labour intensive hand assembly of software systems, and allows them to transform their organizations into highly automated factories to manufacture software from reusable components.

Many feel that we are in the midst of a software crisis, and I agree. High-quality software has become one of the most sought after commodities in the modern world. We just can't seem to get enough of it, on time and on budget, to meet the demand. This book will help you overcome the software crisis in your own organization, by showing you how to make software construction into a reliable and predictable engineering activity.

One of the more profound insights offered by modern software engineering is that change is inevitable, and that software must be designed to be flexible and adaptable in the face of changing requirements. Objectory, with its reflective architecture, goes one step further, and provides an extensible methodology which can itself adapt to shifts in the business climate or the demands of new technologies. No static text can ever capture all the nuances of such a dynamic software entity but this one comes very close. I strongly recommend it, not only for software managers and designers, but for anyone who wishes to understand how the next generation of software systems should be built.

*Dave Thomas*

# Foreword

Ivar Jacobson has taken the time to create a book that is certain to become essential reading for software developers and their managers. In this book, Jacobson establishes a new direction for the future of software engineering practice. It is a thoughtful and thorough presentation of ideas and techniques that are both solidly proven and, simultaneously, at the leading edge of software engineering methodology. Jacobson is simply a thinker who has been ahead of his time in creating usable methods for building better, more reliable and more reusable large software systems.

Despite the title, this is not 'another book on object-oriented analysis and design', nor yet another standard reworking on the word-of-the-week. Once, of course, the word-of-the-week in software engineering was 'modular', later it was 'structured', and now, as every programmer or software engineer who reads or attends conferences knows, it is 'object-oriented.'

When the word-of-the-week was still 'structured', and I wrote the first edition of *Structured Design*, the very idea of systematic methods for software development was radical. Software engineering was in its infancy, and when I introduced data flow diagrams and structure charts, few recognized either the need for notation or the benefits of well-conceived modeling tools for analysis and design.

But things have changed. Now, new methodologies are created over cocktails, and books spin out of word-processors so fast that revised or 'corrected' editions appear almost before the original has reached the bookstores. Since nearly everyone now recognizes that a methodology must be supported by a notation, notations proliferate. A new object-oriented design notation can be churned out over a weekend so long as the major objective is simply squiggles and icons with a unique 'look and feel', and issues of usability and power in modeling are considered unimportant.

And here we have yet another notation supporting one more methodology? Not quite.

It is true that the serious reader will have to surmount both new terminology and new notation to get to the marrow, but this book is different. It was not conceived and written overnight. The methodology it describes has been in use for years to design and build numerous software systems, and its notation has evolved slowly from both manual and CASE-supported application. It is not the work of a writer or consultant with a long booklist, but comes from a practising software engineer and leader in software engineering who has been doing large-scale object-oriented development for longer than most people even knew that objects existed. Throughout this period, the ideas and methods have been honed by the grindstone of building software and refined by thoughtful reflection and analysis.

What we have here is an approach to object-oriented analysis and design that is fundamentally different from most of the highly touted and more visible methods that clutter the landscape. I believe it is an approach of proven power and even greater promise.

The real power of this approach rests not only in the wealth of experience on which it is based but also in the way in which it starts from a different point of departure and builds an entirely different perspective on how to organize software into objects. Jacobson does not build naive object models derived from simplistic reinterpretations of data modeling and entity object relationship models. He starts from an entirely different premise and set of assumptions uniquely tailored to creating robust, sophisticated object structures that stand the test of time.

His approach centers on an analysis of the ways in which a system is actually used, on the sequences of interactions that comprise the operational realities of the software being engineered. Although it fully incorporates the conceptual constructs, the application and enterprise entities that undergird our thinking about software systems, it does not force the entire design into this rigid pattern. The result is a more robust model of an application, leading to software that is fundamentally more pliant, more accommodating to extensions and alterations and to collections of component parts that are, by design, more reusable.

At the heart of this method is a brilliantly simple notion: the use case. A use case, as the reader will learn, is a particular form or pattern or exemplar of usage, a scenario that begins with some user of the system initiating some transaction or sequence of interrelated events. By organizing the analysis and design models around user interaction and actual usage scenarios, the methodology produces systems that are intrinsically more useable and more adaptable to changing usage. Equally important, this approach analyzes each use case into its constituent parts and allocates these systematically to software objects in such a way that external behavior and internal structure and dynamics are kept apart, such that each may be altered or extended independently of the other. This approach recognizes not one kind of object, but three, which separate interface behavior from underlying entity objects and keeps these independent of the control and coordination of usage scenarios.

Using this approach, it is possible to construct very large and complex designs through a series of small and largely independent analyses of distinct use cases. The overall structure of the problem and its solution emerges, step-by-step and piece-by-piece, from this localized analysis. In principle – and in practice – this methodology is one whose power increases rather than diminishes with the size of the system being developed.

Use case driven analysis and design is a genuine breakthrough, but it is also well-grounded in established fundamentals and connected to proven ideas and traditions in software engineering in general and object-oriented development in particular. It echoes and extends the popular model–view–controller paradigm of object-oriented programming. It is clearly kin to the event-driven analysis and design approaches of Page-Jones and Weiss, as well as to the widely practised event-partitioning methods pioneered by McMenamin and Palmer.

On this ground, Ivar Jacobson has built a work that is nothing short of revolutionary. Rich with specific guidelines and accessible examples, with completely detailed case studies based on real-world projects, this book will give developers of object-oriented software material that they can put into practice immediately. It will also challenge the reader and, I am confident, enrich the practise of our profession for years to come.

*Larry L. Constantine*

# Preface

This is a book on industrial system development using object-oriented techniques. It is not a book on object-oriented programming. We are convinced that the big benefits of object orientation can be gained only by the consistent use of object orientation throughout all steps in the development process. Therefore the emphasis is placed on the other parts of development such as analysis, design and testing.

You will benefit from this book if you are a system developer seeking ways to improve in your profession. If you are a student with no previous experience in development methods, you will learn a robust framework which you can fill with details as you take part in future development projects. Since the focus of the text is on development, the book will be convenient to use in combination with other texts on object-oriented programming. Many examples illustrate the practical application of analysis and design techniques.

From this book you will get a thorough understanding of how to use object orientation as the basic technique throughout the development process. You will learn the benefits of seamless integration between the different development steps and how the basic object-oriented characteristics of class, inheritance and encapsulation are used in analysis, construction and testing. With this knowledge you are in a much better position to evaluate and select the way to develop your next data processing system.

Even though object orientation is the main theme of this book, it is not a panacea for successful system development. The change from craftsmanship to industrialization does not come with the change to a new technique. The change must come on a more fundamental level which also includes the organization of the complete development process. Objectory is one example of how this can be done.

This book does *not* present Objectory. What we present is the fundamental ideas of Objectory and a simplified version of it. In this book we call this simplified method OOSE to distinguish it from Objectory. To use the process in production you will need the complete and detailed process description which, excluding large examples, amounts to more than 1200 pages. Introducing the process into an organization needs careful planning and dedication. It also requires that the process be adapted to the unique needs of the organization. Such process adaptations must of course be carefully specified, which can be done in a development case description, as will later be explained.

It is our hope that we have reached our goal with this book, namely to present a coherent picture of how to use object-orientation in system development in a way which will make it accessible both to practitioners in the field and to students with no previous knowledge of system development. This has been done within a framework where system development is treated as an industrial activity and consequently must obey the same requirements as industry in general. The intention is to encourage more widespread use of object-oriented techniques and to inspire more work on improving the ideas expounded here. We are convinced that using these techniques will lead to better systems and a more industrial approach to system development.

**Part I: Introduction.**   The book is divided into three parts. The first part covers the background, and contains the following chapters:

(1)  System development as an industrial process
(2)  The system life cycle
(3)  What is object-orientation?
(4)  Object-oriented system development
(5)  Object-oriented programming

This part gives an introduction to system development and summarizes the requirements of an industrial process. It also discusses the system life cycle. The idea of object orientation is introduced, and how it can be used in system development and during programming is surveyed.

**Part II: Concepts.**   The second part is the core of the book. It contains the following chapters:

(6)  Architecture
(7)  Analysis
(8)  Construction
(9)  Real-time specialization
(10)  Database specialization
(11)  Components
(12)  Testing

The first chapter in this part introduces the fundamental concepts of OOSE and explains the reason why these concepts are chosen. The following chapter discuss the method of analysis and construction. The next two chapters discuss how the method may be adapted to real-time systems and database management systems. The components chapter discusses what components are and how they can be used in the development process. Testing activities are discussed in a chapter of their own.

**Part III: Applications.**   The third and last part covers applications of OOSE and how the introduction of a new development process may be organized and managed. This part ends with an overview of other object-oriented methods. This part comprises:

(13)   Case study: warehouse management system

(14)   Case study: Telecom

(15)   Managing object-oriented software engineering

(16)   Other object-oriented methods

**Appendix.**   Finally we have an appendix which comments on our development of Objectory.

So, how should you read this book? Of course, to get a complete overview, the whole book should be read, including the appendix. But if you want to read only selected chapters the reading cases below could be used.

If you are an experienced object-oriented software engineer, you should be familiar with the basics. You could read the book as suggested in Figure P.1.

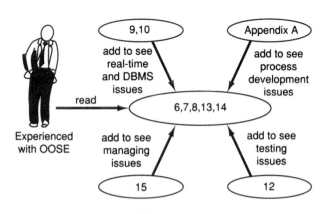

Figure P.1

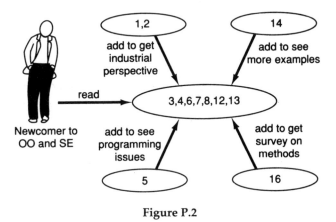

**Figure P.2**

If you are a newcomer to object-orientation and software engineering you could read the book as in Figure P.2.

If you are an experienced software engineer you could read the book as in Figure P.3.

If you are a manager you could read the book as proposed in Figure P.4.

Although the book is not object-oriented, it is written in a modularized way and can be configured in several different ways. Building systems in this way is the theme of the book, and the technique and notation used above is very similar to the technique used in this book.

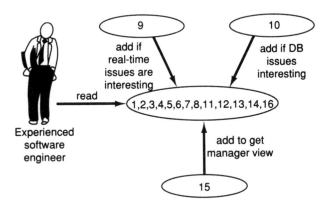

**Figure P.3**

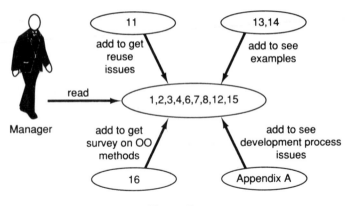

**Figure P.4**

# A short history and acknowledgements

The work presented in this book was initiated in 1967 when I proposed a set of new modeling concepts (notation with associated semantics) for the development of large telecommunication switching systems. The main concepts were signals and blocks. A real-time system is an open system communicating with its environment by signals alone. A signal models the physical stimulus/response communication which a concrete system has when interacting with the outside world. Given a signal as input, a system performs internal actions such as executing algorithms, accessing internal information, storing results and sending output signals to the environment. This view presents the system in a very abstract way – as a black box. A less abstract view on a lower level models the system as a set of interconnected blocks. Blocks are modules which can be implemented in hardware or software or any combination of both. A block communicates with its environment only through signals. Signals between two blocks are internal, whereas signals modeling physical communication, that is, signals between a block and the environment of the system, are external. Internal signals are messengers conveying data from one block to another within the same system. All entries of a block were labelled and constituted the signal interface of that block, to be specified in a separate interface document. Hence the system can now be viewed as a set of interconnected blocks jointly offering the functions of the system. Each block has a program which it obeys on receipt of an input signal, performing internal actions, that is, executing algorithms, storing and accessing block internal information, and sending internal and external signals to the environment.

The proposal can be summarized as an attempt to unify long experience of systems design with the possibilities offered by dramatically new computer technology. Since the two technologies were so different, this was not a self-evident method, neither within Ericsson nor within computer science. There was a rather strong belief that the two represented unrelated technological universes: the new one was so different that it would be meaningless and only a burden to make any attempt to learn from the old one. However, the two techniques were joined and a set of modeling concepts evolved.

The modeling constructs were soon followed by the skeleton of a new design method, the use of which was first demonstrated in the development of the AKE system put into service in Rotterdam in 1971, and more completely demonstrated in the AKE system put into service in Fredhall, Sweden, in 1974. Naturally this experience has guided subsequent work on the development of the successor to AKE, the AXE system, which is now in use in more than 80 countries worldwide. The modeling constructs were very important and, for the AXE system, a new programming language and a new computer system were developed in accordance with these early ideas.

Although it is a neighbouring country, the early development of object-oriented programming and Simula in the 1960s in Norway was done independently and in parallel with our work. It was not until 1979 that we 'discovered' object-oriented programming and then it was in terms of Smalltalk. Although object-oriented ideas have influenced our recent work, basically two separate problems are being solved: 'large-scale' and 'small-scale'.

The modeling constructs introduced during the 1960s were further formalized in research taking place between 1978 and 1985. This research resulted in a formally described language which offered support for object-orientation with two types of object and two types of communication mechanism, send/wait and send/no-wait semantics. The language supported concurrency with atomic transactions and a special semantic construction for the handling of events similar to the use case construct presented later. This work, reported in a PhD thesis in 1985, resulted in a number of new language constructs, initially developed from experience, being refined and formalized. This was a sound basis from which to continue and, taking a new approach, develop the method. The principles of Objectory were developed in 1985–7. I then further refined and simplified the ideas, generalized the technique used in the telecom applications, extended it with the inheritance concept and other important constructs like extensions, and coupled to it an analysis technique and object-oriented programming.

Today these concepts have been further refined. The Objectory process, of which this book describes some fundamental ideas, is the result of work by many individuals, most of whom today work at Objective Systems SF AB, Sweden. Gunnar Övergaard and Patrik Jonsson did much of the writing of the first process description of Objectory analysis and design, respectively. Magnus Christerson did much to condense and rewrite the material into the form of this book. They have all contributed to Objectory; especially the formalization of the concepts. Magnus has also related the ideas of Objectory to other areas as presented in this book. Fredrik Lindström has also been involved in the condensation of the material for this book. Agneta Jacobson, Bud Lawson and Lars Wiktorin have prepared material for some of the chapters.

Marten Gustafsson has substantially contributed to the analysis part of Objectory. Valuable contributions to Objectory have also been made by the following people: Sten-Erik Bergner, Per Björk, Ann Carlbrand, Håkan Dyrhage, Christian Ehrenborg, Agneta Jacobson, Sten Jacobson, Mikael Larsson, Fredrik Lindstrom, Lars Lindroos, Benny Odenteg, Karin Palmkvist, Janne Pettersson, Birgitta Spiridon, Per Sundquist, Lars Wetterborg and Lars Wiktorin. The following users of Objectory have also contributed by feeding back experiences and ideas to enable improvements: Staffan Ehnebom, Per Hedfors, Jörgen Hellberg, Per Kilgren, Håkan Lidström, Christian Meck, Christer Nilsson, Rune Nilsson, Göran Schefte, Fredrik Strömberg, Karin Villers, Stefan Wallin and Charlotte Wranne. The following persons have done a lot to support the technology described in this book: Kjell S. Andersson, Hans Brandtberg, Ingemar Carlsson, Håkan Dahl, Gunnar M. Eriksson, Björn Gullbrand, Lars Hallmarken, Bo Hedfors, Barbara Hedlund, Håkan Jansson, Christer Johansson, Ingemar Johnsson, Kurt Katzeff, Rolf Leidhammar, Jorma Mobrin, Jan-Erik Nordin, Anders Rockström, Kjell Sörme, Göran Sundelöf, Per-Olof Thysselius, Ctirad Vrana and Erik Örnulf. The following people have given me strong personal inspiration and support: Dines Bjørner, Tore Bingefors, Dave Bulman, Larry Constantine, Göran Hemdal, Tom Love, Nils Lennmarker, Lars-Olof Norén, Dave Thomas and Lars-Erik Thorelli. In Sweden we do not normally thank family and friends in these circumstances, but no one believes that results like these can be achieved without exceptional support from them. We are also grateful to the support we have been given from STU (Swedish National Board on Industrial Development, now reorganized to NUTEK) through the IT-4 program which has been part of the financial support and sponsorship for the writing of this book.

Changes to this revised printing, apart from minor general corrections and improvements, are:

- The testing chapter has been restructured and in parts rewritten, also an emphasis on early testing has been added.
- The discussion of robust object structures has been increased and also an example has been added. We hope this will better clarify why such an object structure gives more robust systems.
- The notion of a development case has been introduced as a way to adapt a general process to the specific needs of an organization or a project.
- Some people we would like to thank were unfortunately left out in the first printing and have now been added to the acknowledgement section, particularly Dave Bulman and Nils Lennmarker who have inspired the technology presented in this book.

*The authors*

# Contents

# Part I
# Introduction

# 1 System development as an industrial process

## 1.1 Introduction

The development of software systems is a relatively young industry and has not reached the level of maturity typically found in more traditional branches of industry. Consequently, products developed using software technology often suffer from a lack of the established practices required for their development and exploitation as commercial products. This lack of experience is a result of the emphasis software development has, so far, placed on the creative processes and methods used in the initial development of computer-based systems. This emphasis is found in nearly all of the existing software engineering methods and related tools that have been developed to assist in the realization of software systems. (When we use the word 'system' we not only include software systems, but also systems where hardware and software are integrated.)

In this book, we consider a method which provides support for the creative design of software products, but which also provides an approach for making software development a rational industrial process. Thus the aim is not just to produce well-engineered software systems, but to make them viable 'living' products that can be exploited in an industrial environment.

How do we go about providing the software industry with the methods that enable us to deal with the practicalities of a more global view of software products? Largely, we must understand what goes into making 'industrial processes' successful and then apply this knowledge in an appropriate manner to the software industry. In order to gain the necessary insight, we use an analogy to the industrial processes of another well-established industry. The analogy is useful since it illuminates the scope of the general problem, thus helping us to understand (draw parallels with) several important aspects of Object-Oriented Software Engineering (OOSE) that contribute to making software development an industrial process.

## 1.2  A useful analogy

The building construction industry is one of the most mature branches of industry, having taken advantage of developments since the beginnings of civilized life. Naturally, the advances in this industry have accelerated during the 20th century, which can be regarded as a period in which building construction changed from a craft to refined industrial processes. Since we all use buildings and are accustomed to their properties, the selection of building construction as an analogy provides a useful common denominator. By briefly examining some of the general properties of this industry, we shall be able to understand the need for related properties in the software industry.

Drawing analogies between the construction industry and computer-related processes is not new. Spector and Gifford (1986), via an interview with an experienced bridge designer (Gerald Fox), have documented important analogies between the industrial processes of bridge construction and corresponding computer-related processes.

In order to provide rationality in all phases of building construction, it is essential that a well-established philosophy, or point of view, guides the work of all parties in the various activities of a building project. The philosophy has its concrete realization in the form of an 'architecture' and related activities which establish the 'way of doing business' as shown in Figure 1.1.

By the **architecture** of the construction approach, we mean a foundation of concepts and techniques, selected from a universe of

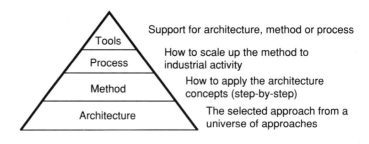

**Figure 1.1**  The constituents of a rational enterprise philosophy.

potential foundations, that defines the characteristic structure of all buildings designed using the approach. As an example, we could consider the selection of an approach based on using building blocks and components. This approach can be compared with other alternatives, for example, an architecture based solely upon customized constructs.

The **method** makes explicit the step-by-step procedures to be followed in applying the architecture to projects.

The **process** allows the method to be scaled up, so that it can be applied to projects with many interacting activities and parties.

**Tools** support all aspects of the enterprise and, explicitly, the activities of architecture, method and process.

The difference between the method and the process will be discussed further in the next chapter, but let us just illustrate some properties here. A method is more basic and is described in the same way as a project, by breaking it down into its various activities. A project ends when the last activity has been performed and the product (or building) has been taken into operation. Operation and maintenance are often described in a simplified way as a single phase. This is not entirely correct since maintenance often involves new projects which encompass all phases. A process, on the other hand, lasts as long as the product lasts and describes how the different activities interact during the whole life of the product.

Note that it is important not to confuse the 'architecture' underlying the method with the architecture of a particular product (that is, 'building') that may be realized by applying the architecture. These 'building' architectures represent 'instances' employing the enterprise philosophy as in Figure 1.2. Hence one architecture may be used for the construction of various buildings, and various architectures may be used for the construction of a specific building.

The architecture may be based solely on using building blocks and components; or solely on using customized constructs made by craftsmen; or any combination thereof. Here building blocks are, for instance, prefabricated sections of a house, and components are off-the-shelf products like windows, doors and bath tubs. Further, the approach may be based on specific materials, for example, bricks or reinforced concrete. For each possible approach, several different methods could be defined to describe how to work with these constructs. This leads to the definition of a variety of step-by-step procedures, namely methods, where for example appropriate combinations of building blocks and components are used. Furthermore, the method must be scaled and also related to other activities, leading to various possible processes for each method defined. These processes could then be supported by various tools.

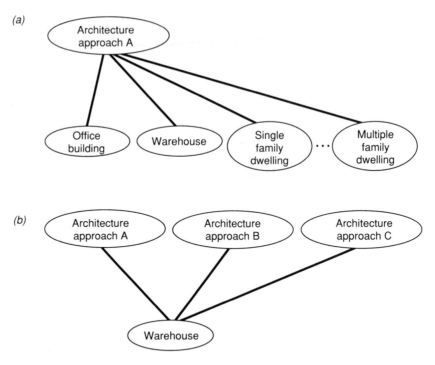

**Figure 1.2**   In (a) one architecture is used for different building products. In (b) we can choose from different architectures for a specific product.

We now consider how various activities of building construction are supported. The model we introduced earlier is applied during each activity of building construction, as illustrated in Figure 1.3. The activities are creative design, construction and long-term support. Of course, well-defined interfaces are needed to make the transition between phases smooth and seamless.

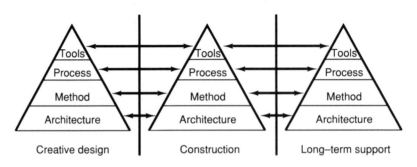

**Figure 1.3**   The constituents of multiple activities of a rational enterprise.

For each activity, there is a philosophy (point of view and related concepts) from which a particular architecture, method, process and tools for the phase are derived. Further, to be successful as a whole, there must be well-defined two-way (seamless) interfaces between these phases. The details of the later activities are directly related to factors in the preceding activities and wherever possible traceability should be applied, enabling us to return to relevant factors in previous activities when problems arise. We will now look at each activity in more detail.

## 1.2.1   Creative design

The transformation from a set of requirements and vague notions of what is desired to a structural plan of the building and a plan of action for its implementation are the creative activities of new development. The requirements for building a house, for example, are expressed in functional terms (an architectural drawing showing the place and function of the rooms) as well as in terms of a construction drawing following specified building standards. Building standards are based on a long tradition of what constitutes a good house (that is, a house that can withstand strong winds, moisture, wear and tear, and so on). With respect to determining what constitutes good software, the software industry is maturing, but still has a long way to go.

In planning for the development of a custom-designed house, the architectural and construction drawings may be the only basis for examining the building prior to its actual production. In some architectural approaches, a miniaturized scale model of the house may be constructed. However, when a series of houses is to be developed, where all the houses have the same basic building architecture, a scale model and usually one or more sample houses (prototypes) are constructed. The prototypes allow potential buyers to evaluate the functionality of the house in terms of their needs, as well as serving as a means of 'debugging' and improving the basic building architecture.

In creating a modern building, in addition to building standards and norms, significant attention is given to approaches which exploit large building blocks based upon sub-assemblies of modules and components. These practices make large-scale building construction economically rational while at the same time insuring quality and safety in the final product.

Creative design thus takes place according to the architectural approach and follows step-by-step method(s) and process(es) (with the assistance of tools) to convert requirements into a viable architectural plan for a building project, including, when desirable, the creation of prototypes.

### 1.2.2 Construction

The first activity in construction is to provide implementation details concerning the architectural and construction plans, that is, to go from the more abstract towards a more concrete plan. After a sufficiently concrete plan has evolved, the production (implementation) takes place. Production is thus the last phase of construction. The number of people involved up to the point of production (even for large-scale projects) is quite small in comparison with the number of people involved in actual production.

Production is the result of manufacturing the more abstract construction plans as well as the detailed construction plan. Further, the production activity may take advantage of any related models and/or prototypes that may have been developed. Here we can differentiate between custom-built houses and houses designed for mass production. In the custom-built case, the implementation is typically performed by artisans who are specialists in their particular field (woodworkers, plumbers, perhaps sculptors, and others). The aesthetic properties of the custom construction are central. In the mass production case, we find the need to employ people who are less skilled, but who can carry out their detailed work in a cost-effective manner. Thus a clear method and process by which the construction plans are followed (with the assistance of appropriate tools) are essential ingredients of successful mass production.

Responsibility for large-scale building projects is most often placed in the hands of an entrepreneur. The entrepreneur takes responsibility for the production according to the building architecture and construction documentation. From this point, the entrepreneur develops the detailed construction plan as well as the process, in preparation for production. The entrepreneur, in turn, enlists the services of subcontractors who take responsibility for portions of the total project. In order to use subcontractors effectively, standards and norms and the usage of building blocks and components become vital, so that the subcontractors can be relied upon to perform their services properly. Further, we find once again the importance of the method, process and tools which explicitly define and document the procedures to be followed by entrepreneur and subcontractors.

### 1.2.3   Long-term support

Building construction projects, custom designed o
must take account of the fact that the products sho
years. Thus the architectural approach of this phase ...
account of 'life-cycle' requirements for maintenance, alteration anu
extension. In the software industry, owing to inherent flexibility of
alteration, a philosophy containing an architecture that permits long-
term support is absolutely essential.

### 1.2.4   Conclusion

During all activities, from the original product requirements,
through the creative design activities to construction, production and
long-term support, documentation is a vital aspect of rational
industrial activity. The documentation must be appropriate
('understandable') for the various parties having a vested interest in
the building project. Documentation must be kept up-to-date
following alterations, variations, experiences and so on, during all
phases of the building project. In this area, computer-aided tools
make a major contribution to their own branch and to all other
branches of industry. The software industry, however, must learn
from the traditions of other branches of industry concerning the
information content and management of appropriate documentation.

The ability to reuse technology that has evolved during
building projects is an essential part of profitability for those
involved in the mass production of housing. Building blocks that
have been identified and exploited must be well documented and
understood so that they can be applied to new projects. In this
regard, we can differentiate between building blocks and
components. Building blocks are typically larger units which have
evolved during specific projects (for example, prefabricated walls);
whereas standard components such as windows and doors may have
been used as parts of the building blocks. The software industry has,
during the 1980s, started to realize the importance of components;
however, to a large extent, the maturity associated with identifying
and exploiting useful building blocks has not yet evolved.

From our characterization of the building process as being
based on an architecture, method, process and tools, we can make
the following observations concerning the results of the scaling-up
process. Direct analogies with the software industry can be drawn
from these observations:

- The process must yield a foreseeable result, irrespective of which individual performed the job.
- The volume of output does not affect the process.
- It must be possible to allocate parts of the process to several manufacturers/subcontractors.
- It must be possible to make use of predefined building blocks and components.
- It must be possible to plan and calculate the process with great precision.
- Each person trained for an operation must perform it in a similar manner.

## 1.3 System development characteristics

Having briefly examined some of the characteristics of a well-established industrial branch, we can better reason about software development and identify the problems and areas in which OOSE provides new solutions. We have, in fact, already identified several aspects of OOSE relating directly to the building construction analogy. As we move on to consider software development, the reader should think from time to time about applying the description of software system development back to the building construction analogy, or draw analogies with other industrial and commercial activities. This bidirectional thinking will be useful in gaining a deeper appreciation of the industrialization of software development. The rational 'architecture' provided in OOSE makes an essential contribution to the long-term support, documentation and reuse of both building blocks and components. Further, OOSE places emphasis on the management of change. It is in providing a rational architecture and related method, process and tools for software development that OOSE makes a contribution to the software industry.

### 1.3.1 Part of a larger activity

System development does not take place in isolation. It is part of a larger activity, often aimed at developing a product in which software is an integrated part. This is the case in large engineering-related industries as well as in commercial enterprises such as insurance companies or banks. In business data processing, the product consists of the administrative services that the data processing department offers to the rest of the company. Figure 1.4 portrays system development as part of the larger activity of a company or department whose products contain software.

The activity viewed as a whole contains at least two other processes besides system development, namely sales and production. The main flow of activity typically passes directly from sales to production. The input consists of new orders from customers and the output consists of systems delivered to customers. (We use the term 'customer' broadly – another department within the same company can also be viewed as a customer.) The sales department orders product configurations for delivery to customers and formulates requirements for new products.

An order should be formulated in such a way that it is immediately possible to identify the configuration of the final product. The production department delivers a complete system to the customer. Further, it should be possible to formulate an order in terms comprehensible to the customer without the aid of the system development department. Thus no programmers should participate in the production process; only persons skilled in duplicating products, assembling and configuring systems and testing them prior to delivery should be involved.

Development of new services is only initiated as a result of the sales department conveying new customer demands to the development department. Again, terminology comprehensible to customers should be employed so that the need for the participation of the development department in customer contacts is minimized. This is possible if products can be described and ordered as sets of

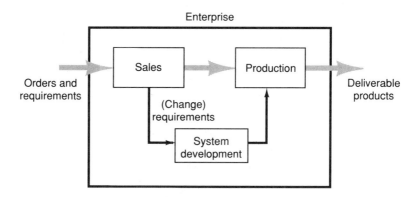

**Figure 1.4** System development is normally an integrated part of an enterprise.

packages of functionality services or, as we will call them in OOSE, **service packages**.

In the development department, new software items (that is, source code and/or other documents for the production of systems) are developed, based on the new product requirements. The sales department can be informed about the new service packages later. Thus service packages play a central role in the development phase.

The staffs of the three subprocesses (sales, production and development) communicate in terms of service packages. In order to achieve a rational return on investment, service packages should be designed so that they can be used in a number of different products. It will then be possible to build a large number of applications from a set of standard service packages.

A customer order corresponds to a product order, specified as a combination of service packages. The production department receives the order and assembles the finished product. To do so, they start from the source code for the service packages and transform the programs into the object code of a particular machine configuration. During these processes, it must also be possible to produce all other forms of documentation that are part of the finished system.

Figure 1.5 illustrates how the sales department passess a customer order, formulated as a combination of service packages, to the production department which assembles the finished product for delivery to a customer. Each service package corresponds to one or more software items which must be configured in the intended combination. Treatment of the list of required service packages represents the initial part of production.

If these processes are to be carried out properly, the service packages must be developed with great care so that they can be configured for a number of product variations. Reuse must be reflected in the way the software is designed. Thus the aim should be to provide software items with substantial reusability both within the system (building blocks) and between different types of system (components). Remember our analogy of the prefabricated wall (building block) and components such as windows and doors.

The building blocks are highly application-related and form the basis for adaptations of the product for different customer categories. A building block corresponds to a service package or part of a service package. Further, the system development department contains a special group of people who are responsible for the development and coordination of general and application-related components. The component developers provide essential support to product developers.

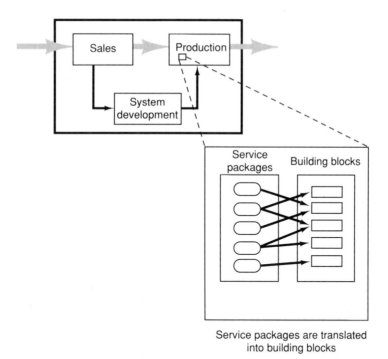

Service packages are translated
into building blocks

**Figure 1.5** Orders from the sales department form the basis for production. Each delivery to a customer consists of a configuration of a number of service packages which together provide the functionalilty.

Reuse occurs in many product-related activities and is not limited to programs. The output of system development is, in fact, a set of descriptions. The descriptions include the source code which can be interpreted by humans and compilers, diagrams, flow charts and so on. All of these **descriptions** must be self-contained (self-explanatory) for reusability. Further, the knowledge of how to organize and manage projects must also be documented in a framed manner and made reusable.

When proper framing is achieved, rationality of software development and product exploitation can be attained. Service packages form the basis for the configuration of a system for a particular customer. Each customer receives their special combination of service packages with relevant documentation which has been assembled from appropriate descriptions. For a new release of a system, it is possible to reuse descriptions from the previous release in a controlled manner so that there is no need to maintain multiple releases of the same document.

### 1.3.2  System development

Let us now concentrate on the system development subprocess. As requirements change, the system changes (see Figure 1.6). The changed system actually consists of altered development information (descriptions) to be used for the production process.

System development is carried out in a number of steps, each of which constitutes a more detailed and concrete development of earlier activities. Thus it can be seen that system development is a gradual transformation of a sequence of models. The first model describes the customer's requirements and the last step is the fully tested program. Between these two end points are a number of other models.

System development can be viewed as a process of producing model descriptions. This is true of all levels – analysis, design, implementation and testing. In this context, the source code is seen as a description that can be understood by programmers and also by the production process (a compiler and linker). The descriptions present models of different degrees of detail. Early models are quite abstract, focusing on external qualities of the system, whereas later models become more detailed and instructional in the sense that they describe how the system is to be built and how it is meant to function.

The aim is to divide the complicated development of a large system into a number of activities and make it possible for several designers to take part at the same time. Each partial model is an abstraction of the system which enables the designer to make the necessary decisions at this level in order to move closer to the final model, the tested source code. Each modeling step adds more structure to the system. Further, each new model is more formal than the previous one. To make the transitions between the different models as simple and faultless as possible, it must be easy to relate the model in one activity to the model in the following activity. We say that two models are seamlessly related to each other if notions

**Figure 1.6** System development is a process of successive changes of systems from new and changed requirements.

which were introduced in one model are represented in the other model in a very simple and straightforward manner.

In essence, system development consists of three distinct phases that follow each other seamlessly – **analysis, construction** and **testing** (see Figure 1.7). In analysis an application-oriented specification is developed to specify what the system offers its users. At this early stage, when changes are still relatively inexpensive, the aim is also to find a good structure for the system, namely a structure that is robust against change and which is divided into clear, comprehensible and indivisible units that can be ordered (that is, service packages). This specification, which we call the analysis model, specifies the functional behavior of the system under practically ideal circumstances and without regard to a particular implementation environment. In other words, initially we disregard any restrictions that might exist in implementation artifacts such as the programming language, the database management system or other surrounding, supporting components. It is important, however, to judge whether the analysis model can actually be realized under the given circumstances, for example, with regard to performance requirements and/or development costs.

During construction, the idealized conditions of the analysis will gradually be replaced by requirements from the chosen implementation environment. This phase defines how the application-oriented analysis model will be realized using such components as system software, database management systems and user interfaces. The construction activities constitute design and implementation. The design activities formalize the analysis model in terms of the implementation environment and specify the identified building blocks. The separate programs (blocks) identified in the design are then coded (that is, implemented).

In testing, the system is checked to make sure that all of the service packages in the analysis model have been correctly implemented and that the performance of the system meets

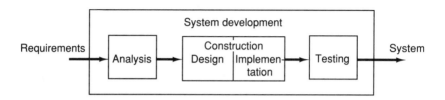

**Figure 1.7**   System development can be divided into three activities.

requirements. Testing takes place at several levels, from specific functions to the system as a whole.

These activities look very similar to a waterfall model. In fact it is, if we are only concerned with a specific project. However, we must raise our vision from the project to the product. This change of view is essential and will be discussed in the next chapter.

### 1.3.3   The transition from analysis to construction

All development methods divide the development work into different stages which may vary from project to project. In one project, a formal analysis model may be required so that different contractors can be asked for bids; the formal analysis model then guarantees that the final design and implementation correspond to what was ordered. In another project, however, it may not be obvious how the implementation environment affects the system requirements. In this case, a less formal analysis model can be chosen in order to make the analysis less implementation-environment-dependent.

At present, formalism during the analysis phase should be restricted to the syntax and semantics of the static structure of the system. We do not know of any sound, practical and strictly formal technique for satisfactory specification of the system's dynamic behavior at this critical phase. A more practical, descriptive technique is therefore preferable to a mathematical, formal method that is not yet fully mature. A formal technique is better used later on, especially during implementation. As the more formal techniques mature, they will probably be preferred.

Even though the boundaries between analysis and construction may seem vague, there are certain guidelines for what should be described during analysis and what should be dealt with during construction (see also McMenamin and Palmer (1984)):

- The analysis must be independent of the implementation environment. Changes in the implementation requirements thus do not affect the analysis result. Even if an important part of the system, such as a database management system, is replaced during implementation, the analysis model is not affected.

- The analysis model must be application-oriented. The work is carried out in an ideal world; memory, performance and fault-tolerance requirements are set aside.

- The analysis model should describe the elements of the application in application-related concepts such as service packages. Given this foundation, the structure of the implementation mirrors the structure of the problem, rather than the other way round.

- The analysis model should not be too elaborate, as some of this work must be adapted to the chosen implementation environment. Such adaptations may be difficult if the analysis model is too formal.

Given the properties of system development that have been described, we conclude that one approach to rational system development is provided by the conceptual framework of OOSE. This is a basic theme of the book.

## 1.3.4   Requirements are input to system development

The primary input for the development of a system is a requirements specification. This will have been developed from facts about the environment that the system is to serve. For 'technical' applications, such as tactical command and control systems, process control systems or telecommunication systems, the role of the system in its environment is identified and the requirements of the system are formulated in terms of the behavior of sensors and actuators. For 'administrative' information systems, such as order-entry systems, personnel administration systems or reservation systems, the work usually begins with an analysis of the needs, problems and development tendencies of the enterprise (see the box on enterprise development at the end of this section). Based on this analysis, a new enterprise model is built where the computer-based information system forms an important part of the enterprise. In fact, the development of a new or changed enterprise is based on the existing enterprise. This is fully analogous to changing an existing information system. Thus the same observations concerning changes which we made concerning the software system are also valid for the enterprise. Although we differentiate here between technical and administrative systems, we do not provide a precise definition of either. In reality, most systems include aspects from both areas.

For administrative systems, the requirement specification is usually developed in a dialogue between customer and producer. It forms the basis for the decision to order the system. When the requirements of the enterprise are less well known, the specification work is preceded by enterprise development (as described below). In some cases, the customers are highly experienced and can provide the specification during the initial contact with the potential producers. In other cases, the customer approaches a producer and solicits assistance in solving his problems. The producer must analyze the customer's situation, try to solve the current problems, and find solutions based upon a new technique. The result is the development of a requirements specification. In administrative system development, developing a requirements specification constitutes a considerable part of the development activity and is often created by the user(s) and the system developer(s) in cooperation.

For technical systems the situation is often somewhat different. A common situation is that the software is to cooperate with other machine or software components in an overall system. The requirements of the software system are then given by the interfaces to the environment (sensors and actuators), where the specification can be derived from a knowledge of required structure and behavior.

There are cases in which an operational system, developed using another (older) technique, is to be modernized. In these cases, the existing system documentation functions as a basis for the development of a requirement specification. This field is often called re-engineering (see Jacobson and Lindström (1991)).

As will be shown, it is practically impossible (for both administrative and technical systems) to foresee all the requirements of a system during the introductory specification work. In the next chapter we will consider incremental development to handle the difficulties of developing a good requirement specification.

**Enterprise development**

Enterprise development can be viewed as a generalization of system development. Instead of a system, a whole enterprise is developed. The company is seen from several different perspectives. The aim is to identify the problem areas and suggest alternative solutions. One result may be to introduce an information system. Enterprise development can be divided into the phases shown in Figure 1.8.

| Establish current state | Enterprise analysis | Change analysis | Enterprise design | Enterprise verification and validation |
| --- | --- | --- | --- | --- |

**Figure 1.8**   The different activities of enterprise development.

The **current state** description is a survey of the framework of the present enterprise including its aims and problems. To begin with, the functionally different activities within the enterprise are separated, and an analysis is made to find out how each activity contributes to the whole. One activity may comprise several parts of the enterprise that are organized separately.

In the **enterprise analysis**, an ideal (analysis) model is made of the present enterprise.

In the **change analysis**, a detailed description is made of current problems and needs, and appropriate changes are suggested. This will result in a changed analysis model.

In the **enterprise design**, the results from the change analysis are given a form which can be 'physically' realized, given the practical conditions of the organization.

During **enterprise verification and validation**, the new enterprise is verified against the initial intentions and also validated in its new context.

The enterprise design result serves, among other things, as input data for system development. For this purpose, it is usually presented as a requirement specification for the information system which is to be developed to support personnel with different roles in the enterprise. This requirement specification thus serves as input data for the development of the supporting information system. Moreover, several aspects of the intended information system which are directly applicable in the system development have been captured during enterprise development.

## 1.3.5   A system is the output from system development

The output from any system development is a set of descriptions, often of considerable number. They function as a basis for production in the production department and for product description in the sales department.

The most obvious result is the program code which constitutes the final, executable model of the system. The result also consists of other related documents which the users need in order to understand and utilize the system in the appropriate manner. In this context, the term 'users' covers not only humans, but also machines that are in contact with the system in any way. Humans include direct users, such as operators in a process industry, as well as personnel involved in error detection and normal maintenance, such as database administrators. For machines, the documents provide interface descriptions to other systems. In other words, there are a number of different users who must all be satisfied by the set of documents which together constitute the final product.

### 1.3.6  Parties interested in system development

The results of system development are used within other related activities of the enterprise, as well as being the products delivered to the customers of the enterprise. We will discuss here two of the parties interested in these products, namely the customer and the departments of the enterprise.

A producer develops a system based on a customer order. A classic problem in all forms of product development is that the orderer and user are different parties. This will lead to conflicts about the aim, as orderers and users seldom come up with the same requirements. The conflict can be diminished, either by making the orderer understand and formulate the users' requirements or by having representatives of the users take part in formulating the requirements. The term 'user-governed' or 'participative' system development is used to classify group work resulting in a shared requirement specification. This work method has been used in the 1980s in the development of administrative systems.

The success of the system is highly dependent upon whether it has been possible to capture and formulate the users' requirements in such a way that the requirements can be formalized and transformed into working programs.

We must not forget that the direct users of the system often work to serve indirect users (see Figure 1.9). For example, policy holders are indirect users of an insurance company's information system, whose direct users are the personnel of the enterprise. If the direct users do not receive the system they need, this will affect the indirect users, namely the policy holders.

In system development, the users obviously play a central role. The system should be specified primarily on the basis of the users and their needs rather than on the orderer's requirements. The system should be validated to determine whether it really functions in accordance with the user requirements and whether it has been documented so that it describes the system from the user's perspective. In other words, we need a development process able to capture and deal with requirements from a user-oriented perspective. Once again, OOSE provides a new solution to this critical aspect.

The department that develops software products is only one

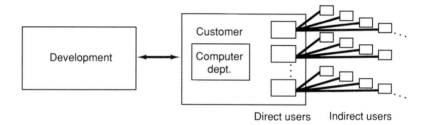

**Figure 1.9**   The interested parties of system development.

of the parties having a vested interest in the development of the system. Other departments within the enterprise, such as sales, production and field service, are parties with an immediate interest in being able to influence the development process.

When the product is an administrative system to be installed in the enterprise to serve its own personnel, the data processing department is typically both the developer and the producer. The users are the personnel of the enterprise.

Other groups, organizations and people that are also interested in the development include various managers, accountants, quality assurance groups, configuration staff, operators and suchlike.

## 1.4   Summary

In this chapter, we have introduced an analogy between the industrial processes of the well-established building construction industry and the software industry. From this analogy, we have been able to compare and understand related aspects. In particular we have introduced the important terms 'architecture', 'method', 'process' and 'tools' and shown how they are related to both branches.

Further, we have introduced the major characteristics of software development. We have identified several important areas where OOSE provides new solutions to existing problems in the software industry, in particular the reuse of all forms of descriptions that are the result of system development. OOSE can be applied to the development of technical and administrative systems. The result of enterprise development provides an important input for the preparation of specification requirements.

The subject of this book has thereby been defined. Finally, it is important to note that the need for an industrial approach to software development was recognized many years ago by, amongst others, Doug McIlroy (1976). In a contribution entitled *Mass-Produced Software Components* he writes:

> 'Software production today appears in the scale of industrialization somewhere below the more backward construction industries. I think its proper place is considerably higher, and would like to investigate the prospects for mass-production techniques in software. [. . .] My thesis is that the software industry is weakly founded, in part because of the absence of a software components subindustry. [. . .] A components industry could be immensely successful.'

# 2 The system life cycle

## 2.1 Introduction

In this chapter, we take a closer look at several important aspects of system development which build on the industrial process thinking described in the introductory chapter. Explicitly, we consider the process of change in system development, reuse of program code and documentation and a deeper examination of methodology.

## 2.2 System development as a process of change

All systems change during their life cycles. This must be borne in mind when developing systems expected to last longer than the first version (that is, practically all systems). Most development methods today focus on new development (see Figure 2.1), treating revision work only briefly, even though it is known that changes constitute the main part of the total life-cycle cost of most systems. An industrial process should therefore focus on system changes.

A system normally develops through changes incorporated in new versions. New development is, from this point of view, only a special case – the first version. That is, new development constitutes a change from nothing into something. New development is nonetheless an important activity. It establishes an architectural philosophy and constitutes the base of the system which must last throughout all subsequent development. A faulty base will have serious consequences for the life cycle of the system.

Let us now relate Figure 2.1 to our earlier presentation of a developing organization or enterprise as part of a larger organization or enterprise. Analysis begins when the sales department sends a requirement specification to the system development department or,

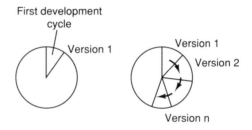

Figure 2.1 The first version of a system represents a minor portion of resource consumption during the life cycle of the system.

more often, when it sends a specification of desired changes to an earlier version. We can call this a **delta requirements specification**.

In Chapter 1, we showed that development work is characterized by the development of a number of models, each increasingly detailed (see Figure 2.2). All of these models are in reality delta models insofar as each model is a changed version of an earlier model at the same level.

In analysis, the delta requirement specification is the starting point from which a delta analysis model is developed. The delta analysis model is then delivered to those responsible for construction, at which point a delta implementation is produced. Each new version of the system is thus a delta version. System development is thus actually a process of progressive change.

It is often difficult to specify which versions of the system descriptions correspond to a particular release of the system. The number of versions is considerable for a sizeable system. For example, different countries need different adaptations for local standards. In this regard, it is not sufficient to describe the system from the designer's perspective; it must also be described for other parts of the enterprise that will use it (for example, marketing, production, installation, operation and maintenance). It is therefore

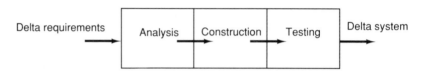

Figure 2.2 For each new version, the same development activities are followed as for the development of a new system. The difference is that the input data comprises requirements for system changes.

vital that the system development enterprise employ an appropriate approach to the handling of successive versions of a system.

To achieve commercial rationality, it is essential to limit the number of versions of a system by using a technique which allows different installations of a particular release of a system to be configured in different ways. Each such configuration must be able to exist independently, and it must be possible to change it independently of other configurations of the same system. This implies that versioning should, at least within the system development enterprise, be on a subsystem or module level as well as on a systems level. Furthermore, it must be possible for different releases of the same system to exist side by side, each with its own installation configuration.

In many cases it is desirable to be able to offer the same system with partially different sets of functions for different customers.[1] Consequently, the arguments we have presented thus far are also valid in this situation. The number of change requirements will increase, leading to the need for strict planning of new releases. The system development process must therefore, by necessity, be framed in such a way that it simplifies the development of several parallel projects.

## 2.2.1   Incremental development

System development is usually regarded as a slow process, which can take several years from beginning to end. Historically, in most computer-related projects, the requirements for the system as a whole are specified. Specification is followed by analysis, construction and testing of the complete system. This method can work if all requirements of the final system are known from the outset. This is, however, rarely the case.

It is the rule, rather than the exception, that the system requirements of both information and technical systems are not fully known at the outset of the project. Knowledge of the system grows

---

[1] We use the word 'functions' here to express some functionality of a system. The word 'function' has a bad reputation since it is sometimes used in opposition to object-orientation. This, we think, is unfortunate since it is a good concept to use in object-oriented systems. The same goes for the word 'structured'. In this book we have tried to avoid these words, but we believe that the words will come back into use when a balance between object-orientation and structural or functional techniques has matured.

progressively as work progresses. When the first version of the system is in operation, new requirements appear and old ones change. Thus the system as a whole cannot be completely developed in the belief that the requirements specification will remain constant during the development period, which can be several years for large systems.

In most cases, it is better to develop the system step by step, beginning with a few of its core functions. As a 'correct' path becomes clear and a better understanding of the system functionality evolves, new functions can be added. In this way, the system is **incrementally** enlarged until the desired level is reached (that is, the finished product is available, normally the first product release as shown in Figure 2.3). Such an incremental strategy also provides faster feedback during the development process. In practice, incremental system development means that we can divide the system into parts, corresponding to customer-requested services.

As can be observed, each new stage extends the system with new functionality up to the finished product which comprises the whole of the desired system. Further, all subsequent releases of the system are developed as a series of incremental stages (see Figure 2.4).

For the sequencing of development stages to be successful, it is essential to define stages which do not necessitate changing the results of earlier stages as the later stages are introduced. Thus early capture of those requirements which form the base of the entire system is important. We will discuss how this can be done later. Each stage is developed as a cycle and is tested before the stage is completed.

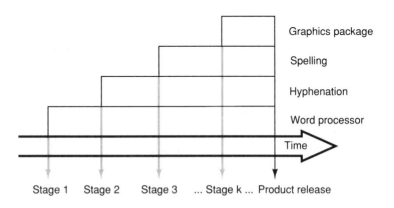

**Figure 2.3**  Systems are developed incrementally in a series of stages.

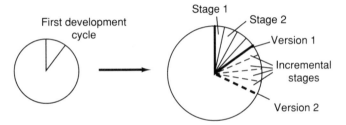

**Figure 2.4**   Every new version is developed incrementally in a series of stages.

## 2.2.2   Prototyping

It is often difficult to determine how a system is supposed to work. The reasons may be technical or functional; they may have to do with efficiency or the user interface. It is helpful in such cases to develop a **prototype** of the intended system. Since a prototype often highlights certain properties of the intended system, other parts can be disregarded, and need only be given in schematic form. The prototype focuses instead on the properties requiring further insight. The prototype allows developers to experiment with a number of different design options. Thus prototyping serves as a complement to incremental system development.

A specific advantage of a prototype is that it can serve as a means of communication between the developer and the customer. It is much easier to express a view about something that can be demonstrated and used, if only partially, than to express an opinion about a specification. A specification cannot capture the dynamics of the system in the same way as a working prototype.

For these purposes, a prototype could be developed in an environment where an acceptable, functioning and easily modified system can be quickly created; this is called **rapid prototyping**. Rapid prototyping is in relatively bad repute today; there are even those who classify it as 'quick and dirty'. This bad reputation has not been earned by the method as such, but results from the way it has been used. In some cases, the prototype has actually been considered so good that it has been kept, and full system development has been deemed unnecessary. This is fine, so long as those involved know what they are doing. Such usage of the prototype may, however, result in malfunctions, or lead to various practical difficulties when modifications are required.

Prototyping is a useful technique for comprehending an application. Furthermore, if the prototype is carefully designed (using the normal development cycle of analysis, construction and testing), it may also prove useful in the final system. Correctly used, prototyping deserves a far better reputation than it has at the moment.

Finally, we can conclude that prototyping is an excellent working method, keeping in mind that it differs from incremental development in that the aim of prototyping is not to create a product, but to emphasize and demonstrate certain properties of the intended system.

## 2.3  System development and reuse

A common desire in all development work is the reuse of results from earlier development work. Reusability has become a buzzword in software engineering, often being seen as the solution to the software crisis (see Cox (1990)). Of course, reusability is very important, but, relative to other engineering branches, we talk a great deal about reuse. In other branches this is not a central issue since it is so obvious and is practiced widely. The reason that there is so much discussion about it in software engineering is that we have been so unsuccessful in reusing existing work. Thus our view of reuse must change into something that is self-evident.

Reusability is of course applicable during coding, since it can influence productivity significantly. This is the usual context when software people talk about reuse. There is no reason that prevents us having it on the code level, but it is not the only interesting type of reuse in software engineering. What can give even higher productivity is reuse in other development phases. Other parts of the construction phase may benefit when reusing entire designs in several systems. Additionally, reuse should also be viewed as natural during analysis and testing.

When developing an engineered product it is desirable to be able to choose between existing units (application modules and components) and develop the system from a set of reusable parts. In the previous chapter we considered how such reuse is exploited in the building construction industry. We would like to develop software in a similar manner.

Reuse should thus occur on several different levels of granularity. A system is assembled from a set of application modules. A module, in turn, is composed of other modules or of components. The application modules at the lowest level consist of components only. In other words, system developers must have access to a set of components in order to build application modules.

The components are thus the finest level of granularity for reuse. It is here that reuse must start. However, to increase productivity further, we also need to reuse larger modules. This can be accomplished by reuse in earlier phases when the system is being structured.

Problems with reuse include the finding, understanding and appropiateness of the thing to be reused. Object-orientation gives a completely new technique that strongly supports these issues. Reusing previously-developed parts in a product is a significant way of decreasing the product's life-cycle cost. As we will see later, OOSE focuses largely on this when structuring the system.

## 2.3.1   Components

First of all we need a technique for building really good components. By **components** we mean already implemented units that we use to enhance the programming language constructs. These are used during programming, and correspond to the components in the building industry (that is, windows, doors and so on). They must be powerful, have simple well-defined interfaces, be simple to find, understand and use, and have a wide area of application. Moreover, it should be possible to build new components with the aid of existing components.

Traditionally, software components have been available in the form of procedures and functions for numerical and statistical applications. These should be complemented by software components providing, amongst other functions, the buffers, queues, lists and trees that are often needed in the coding of algorithms. They may also provide windows, icons or scroll bars for human user interfaces. These components often form a good base to start with. It is not the number of components, but the usefulness of them that determines the success of reuse.

Components are listed in catalogues. For catalogues stored in computer files there are special tools (browsers) which make it possible to consider the components more carefully. Catalogues of electronics components or for building construction provide useful analogies. Let us therefore compare the situation of the programmer and the electronics designer. The electronics designer's shelves contain catalogues of electronic components from different firms, whereas the programmer has computer science and software engineering textbooks on his shelves. On the whole, the programmer must carry his knowledge of standard solutions around in his head while the electronics designer can find standard solutions in handbooks. It may be possible to reuse entire programs, but opportunities to reuse parts of standard programs are few with today's design techniques. On the other hand, it is often difficult to design entire programs that are reusable. Therefore a programmer often finds it easier to write a new program than to find and learn an old one and then change it. However, handbooks offering standard solutions are beginning to appear on the market.

There are, of course, a number of macro libraries, subroutine libraries, procedure libraries and so on available for general use. However, with the exception of the libraries for numerical and statistical computations identified above, they have not proved very successful. As a rule, programmers with such an environment do not look for ready-made routines that can be referred to via a detailed interface. They prefer to build their own routines by using part of an earlier program as a model and then making the necessary additions and changes. In such situations, the well-defined subroutine library is less suitable. It is only in recent years that component libraries have begun to be found on the market. These are still quite simple, supporting mainly data structures and window management systems, although they are often very good as a starting point.

## 2.3.2   Changeable applications

An application must be designed so that it permits frequent alteration. The most rational manner of building an application is to join together changeable application modules, each of which is built using components. Consider once again the analogy with prefabricated walls in the building construction industry.

The application modules must be framed so that requirements for changes, in all probability, occur only in one module and only rarely in two or more modules. Further, modules should be chosen so that they can be combined in different configurations for different customers or in different installed systems. By partitioning the system in this way, modules can be reused for different configurations in one or several systems.

Moreover, the modules should be alterable in a straightforward manner without incurring a greater cost than is justified by the size of the change. Today, a seemingly small change often results in a disproportionately expensive alteration. It must become possible to bring intuitive costs into line with real costs.

### 2.3.3  Reuse of other descriptions

As described in the introductory chapter, a system consists of the program code and a significant number of other related documents forming steps on the way from the requirement specification to the finished system. Apart from these documents, there are various forms of user-related documentation such as handbooks and educational material. It should also be possible to reuse these documents. Document reuse early in the development chain may have considerably greater effects than the reuse of application modules at the source code level.

## 2.4  System development and methodology

When developing large systems, it is important to know how the different steps of the method interact and how they fit into the development **process** as a whole. This section broadens the discussion to encompass both the development process and the basic ideas behind the **method,** as well as what it is that determines the selection of an **architecture** from a universe of potential architectures. Finally, we add a few comments about how CASE tools should be designed to support development, starting from the more fundamental properties of the architecture, method and process (see Jacobson (1991)).

Consider the pyramid in Figure 2.5, first introduced in Chapter 1, where it is made clear that a method should be developed from an architecture. From the method, a process, and the appropriate tools, can be designed.

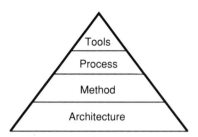

**Figure 2.5**  The foundation of a method is an architecture. The method may then be scaled up into a process which, when defined, can be supported by different kinds of tools.

### 2.4.1    Architecture

A key property of a software system is its internal structure. A good structure makes the system easy to understand, change, test and maintain. Thus properties of the system's architecture determine how the system must be treated during its lifetime. Using our previous building construction analogy, we observe that software systems can be compared to houses. A stone house and a log house have different properties; they are built and maintained differently. Unlike a house made of cards, however, they are both sound structures. Similar differences are found in software systems. For example, function/data methods that separate data from functions have proved, in the long run, to be a house of cards. Small changes in such a system, for instance a change in the format of a date, can have significant consequences. Object-oriented systems, on the other hand, are composed of a number of communicating and well-delimited objects. Such systems are easier to develop and understand, as well as being simpler to maintain and modify. Thus we can assert that object-oriented systems have important and desirable architectural properties. These architectural properties are extremely important and form the basis of the method. The architecture thus defines the types of model that can be built and the characteristics each model will have. For instance, the following types of model may form an architecture: an analysis model, a design model and an implementation model.

### 2.4.2    Method

As discussed earlier, a method is a planned procedure by which a specified goal is approached step by step, not to be confused with methodology, which is the science of methods. Most work descriptions for program development are method descriptions. They describe, often in a very abstract manner, how one should think and reason in developing a software system. Most methods also indicate the sequence of steps to be followed. The different steps of a method can be divided into still more detailed elements, all describing how the work is to be carried out assuming a certain underlying basic architecture. A method is based on a preconceived notion of the architecture of the working system. This means that the description of the method is formulated in terms of the concepts of the architecture to be realized.

A basic requirement of a good method is that it simplifies the development of systems of a particular architecture. Thus a good method for object-oriented system development should help us to identify the appropriate objects. This may seem obvious, but many methods for object-oriented development actually treat this requirement quite superficially. They imply that the objects can easily be found directly from the activity being modeled. It is true that many objects of a system should have real-life counterparts, but they must also be justified by the architecture of the system. The objects that are needed, and how detailed they must be, depends to a large extent on how the system will be used. It is, for instance, hardly appropriate to include the entire spare parts information system in the system that supports the sales department, whereas it is most important to include it in the support system for the service department.

It is usually not difficult to find suitable information-carrying objects in an enterprise. However, it is the dynamics describing how the system is used that are difficult to define correctly. Many people assert that the dynamics need no particular modeling: they simply constitute operations on information-carrying objects and therefore can be included in them. However, systems often exhibit behavior that cannot naturally be assigned to any particular information-carrying object. For this reason it is better to model separate dynamic objects.

### 2.4.3   Process

A **process** is the natural scaling up of a method. We described the relationship of method and process for our building construction analogy. To emphasize this essential difference, let us consider one further analogy, originating from Dave Bulman. Producing a new chemical substance in the laboratory differs greatly from producing the same chemical on an industrial scale in a factory. In the laboratory, the goal is to find a method to produce the chemical. To make this method appropriate for large-scale industrial use, a process must be defined. This usually means changing the working method. Nobody would dream of industrializing the laboratory method by simply building a larger laboratory with gigantic test tubes and Bunsen burners. Yet this is often the way system development methods are scaled up for large projects.

The solution lies in changing the working method so that it can be scaled up and carried out with great parallelism – as a process. If the method is developed for use on a large scale from the start, the growing pains will not be so intense when the work has been scaled up. It is therefore advantageous to adopt a development technique for designing large systems from the start.

Let us clarify the difference between method descriptions and process descriptions. Methods are typically described in a waterfall model – a step-by-step procedure (with various degrees of granularity in the steps). This is similar to saying that a method is described as a system development project for one product version. It is often described as the first development project because a method is normally presented as starting from nothing and resulting in a first system version (see Figure 2.6). Note that maintenance is often an activity of its own in a waterfall model. However, maintenance also includes analysis of the requirements, design, testing and so on, and thus can be described by these other activities.

A development organization not only has projects for developing the first version, but also several other kinds of projects with properties similar to those of maintenance projects. These other projects include changing an existing system, tendering projects, error handling projects and others. All these different types of project include activities for analysis, design, testing and so on. Thus the activity descriptions should be reusable in different kinds of projects in an organization ready to develop systems in an industrial manner. A development process defines these activities and can thus offer more than one project type. Different activities are combined for different project types and the process should offer all the project types required by the organization using it (for example, new development, further development, prototyping, change, error handling and so on) (see Figure 2.7). These different types can all be regarded as different **development cases** offered by the same

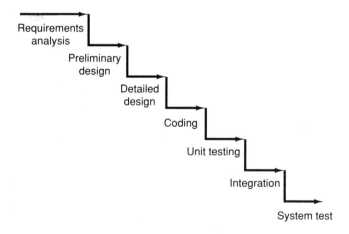

**Figure 2.6** A method is described as a project developing the first product version. The figure illustrates a typical waterfall model.

The system development process

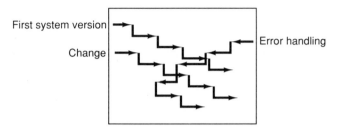

First system version

Change

Error handling

**Figure 2.7**   A development process should describe the activities required to manage a product over its lifetime. These activities are combined to describe different types of project.

process. The process should thus focus on a specific system and describe how a product is handled during its lifetime.

The process will continue to exist so long as the developed system is in operation, whereas a project only exists for a limited period of time. To summarize, a method is described as the (ideal) development of a first version of the system, whereas a process is described as the ideal principle of the organization managing the system during its entire lifetime.

Just as a method can be split up into a number of phases with underlying steps, so a process is composed of a number of interacting subprocesses (see Figure 2.8). These subprocesses define the different activities of the development and must be defined in such a way that they are clearly delimited, thus enabling each activity to be performed as independently of other subprocesses as possible. Each developer is responsible for the work carried out in one or more subprocesses and thus makes use of the information sent to those processes. Moreover, the developer should also design the objects that other processes need as the basis of their work. The term 'software factory' has been coined to describe this division into processes and subprocesses.   Each of the subprocesses must be

System development

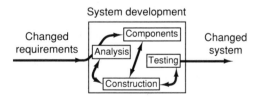

Changed requirements

Changed system

**Figure 2.8**   System development can be described as a set of interacting subprocesses, such as analysis, construction, testing and components.

described in the process descriptions in terms of how it works, the input it requires and the output it produces.

Taking this point of view, the development process itself can be regarded as a set of communicating objects. Processes are thus a kind of object. This will be further examined in Appendix A. A process is thus an application or, if you like, the industrialization, of a method. In summary, a process presupposes a method which, in turn, presupposes a basic architecture.

### 2.4.4   The process expresses more than the method

The transition from principles to practice requires attention to a number of new aspects. A process must be able to express much more than what is covered within the underlying method.

The process description defines how different subprocesses should cooperate and to what extent they should be carried out in parallel, that is, how the people involved in the project should cooperate. Each subprocess is independent of the location of other subprocesses. Development work can therefore be split up and carried out at several locations. Another way of expressing this is to say that a process description is an enterprise model for the system development organization (see Appendix A).

When system development is industrialized, the activity becomes less dependent on individuals. A handicraft is extremely dependent on the craftsmanship of an individual artisan. An industrial process has fewer key persons. Most work tasks are well defined and can therefore be moved between different individuals. The whole process is more resistant to disruption caused by the promotion of developers or other personnel changes.

If system development is viewed as a process, it becomes natural to see development as a process of change. All work is developed relative to the existing system. This is true both when maintaining one version of a system and when developing a new version. A well-organized process provides version control as well.

It is possible to replace a subprocess with a new subprocess performing an equivalent task. This is one way of adapting the development process to a completely new kind of application, or of making a change in the development environment, such as employing a new programming language. Some subprocesses may be of such a type that they cannot be designed in exactly the same way in all types of project. They will have to be replaced by a process adapted to each specific project. Yet this special subprocess must retain the same interfaces to other subprocesses. This requirement is especially true for the subprocess responsible for implementing the modeled objects of the design. For example, it will be customized for each specific database management system and programming language.

To be able to describe the **specialization** consistently, we allow process classes to **inherit** other process classes. In a similar way to specialization in object-oriented programming languages, we say that a process can be a specialization of another process class (see Figure 2.9). We can start from a general process containing the principal behavior and make a number of specializations to describe separate properties. This technique of specializing the process is important since it permits adaptation of the development process to the needs of different organizations and their specific requirements as will be discussed in Section 2.4.7.

### 2.4.5   Computer-aided systems engineering

In the sections above, we have argued that the development of large systems requires that the development method be broadened into an industrial process. To be fully efficient, the development work also needs computer-based tools, namely a Computer-Aided Systems Engineering (CASE) environment. Introducing tools need not change the actual form of the process, though it often does.

When large systems are developed, all documentation must be consistent. This means, among other consequences, that an object

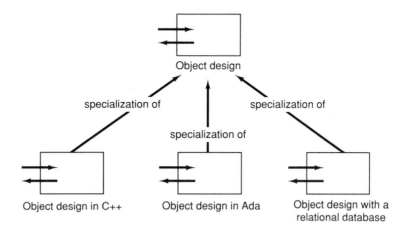

**Figure 2.9**   Process classes can be specialized.

must be given the same name everywhere in the documentation; this is not necessarily a simple task. However, a tool that supports hypertext links or, even better, object-oriented text (see Bergner (1990)), simplifies this task. When developers refer to an object in a document, they add a reference to the desired object instead of writing its name. The tool then presents the reference as, for example, the object's name, composed from the same information.

Tools can be used to automate a large number of tasks, especially trivial but cumbersome ones. If the tasks in the underlying process are seamlessly connected, a great deal of the work can be automated, as the output of one subprocess can easily become the input of another.

When documenting a complex system, it is desirable to present the same information in several ways so that different people can gain a better understanding of the system that is being modeled (see Figure 2.10). Developers typically want to view associations

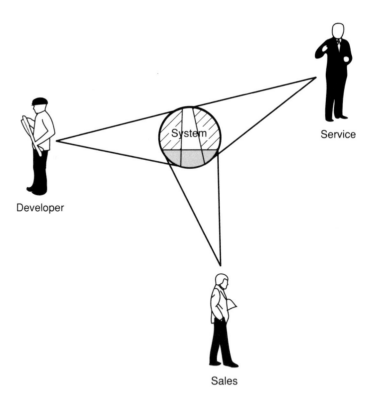

Developer

Service

Sales

**Figure 2.10**   Different persons need different views of the system. These views may be composed from the same information.

between objects as purely textual descriptions in a document, arrows in diagrams and compilations in cross-reference editors (browsers). A more sophisticated development environment may adapt this support to different categories of developers. Each developer can then receive precisely and only the information that he or she needs. A project leader, for instance, may only be interested in overall object descriptions, whereas a designer needs to see all the details. Working documents as well as finalized documentation are also desirable.

A tool to be used on a large scale must support the process it is based on. The process can be integrated into the tool as an extension, for example, by supporting modeling decisions or handling change proposals.

Computer-aided tools can lead to massive productivity improvements, but they are only part of a greater whole. The choice of a development technique has its roots in the basic philosophy chosen to govern the overall system structure of the designed systems, namely the architecture. To this base is then added a method, a process and, finally, computer-aided tools.

## 2.4.6   Small-scale projects

It seems reasonable that we need a method, a process and tools for very large projects, but can a simple method, which is not developed into a process, together with good computer support be sufficient for small projects run by small teams? In our opinion it cannot. Coordination around the maintenance activity is necessary even for quite small projects. Yet projects are often mistakenly deemed to be so small that they can be handled without very detailed instructions. In this case, the project members are left to solve problems as they arise. However, *ad hoc* solutions arrived at beside the coffee vending machine lead to bad work routines, inferior systems and project delays. Even so, projects both large and small are sometimes carried out without a clear idea of how future maintenance work is to be carried out.

The conclusion is evident. What is needed is a system development process that can be packaged and placed into operation in an arbitrary enterprise. The development process naturally precedes the product development. Once it has been decided that program products are to be developed, it becomes natural to choose a reliable development process which suits software products. Only then should the details of the product itself be considered. In this book we will primarily describe a method intended for complex system development. It is, however, important to realize that, like other methods, this method is not sufficient for successful system development. It needs to be adapted to the specific needs of the organization and extended with other techniques, such as configuration management, into a complete process.

### 2.4.7    Adapting the process to the needs of the organization

All system development projects differ more or less from one another. Some projects are, for instance, undertaken by small homogenous teams close to their customer. Other projects involve several teams with varying background and responsibilities, who are very much accustomed to working in an organization with lots of coordination needs, possibly between different sites. It is therefore impossible to define *the* system development process which is streamlined to meet all the needs for development support for an arbitrary organization.

We think of a system development process as consisting of several configurable building blocks (subprocesses). Each such building block offers more architectural concepts, documents and method steps than the developers will probably need. This means that the developers, acting as a whole team, can *deselect* the support they will not need. It is even possible to decide that certain subprocesses should be left out. Such process adaptations for a specific organization could be specified in a **development case description**. Such a description specifies one way of using the complete process, primarily by specifying which simplifications can be done by deselecting certain features. The intention is that the developer teams are much better than the process developer at pinpointing the details of the development process, given the proper support – we here mention two ways of giving this support. First of all the process adaptors should have access to a complete default development case description such that it will suit most of the needs of the organization. Secondly it is necessary to describe the pros and cons of each feature that can be deselected. It should be possible to use the default development case description right away, but small deviations may be necessary.

## 2.5    Objectory

We have now described some important properties that can be expected of a modern development technique:

- It must support the iterative development of a system over the entire life cycle.

- It should view each iteration as a change to an existing system.
- It must support the entire chain from changed requirements to the functioning system.

Objectory (the Object Factory for Software Development) is such a development technique. The framework of Objectory is a design technique, hereafter called **design with building blocks**, derived from the Swedish telephone exchange company Ericsson and now spread throughout the whole field of telecommunications. This technique is the essential idea behind the Commité Consultatif International Télégraphique et Téléphonique (CCITT) recommendation of the Specification and Description Language (SDL) (see CCITT (1988)).

With the building block technique, a system is viewed as a number of connected blocks, each block representing a system service. When all the required system services have been completely specified, building blocks are designed using a top-down approach keeping in mind the criteria of insuring that the system being developed can support changes to its functionality and can be adapted to new technology. This latter property is particularly important if systems are to have a long lifetime.

The building block technique has been employed for about twenty years in the development of large commercial systems. It has been employed in projects involving hundreds of designers, and today more than four thousand designers all over the world are using it. The telecommunications technique has yielded positive results when used in large systems, be they centralized or decentralized. The experience of using this technique for a large project is further elaborated in Jacobson (1992).

In combination with two other techniques, conceptual modeling (see Bubenko and Lindencrona (1984)) and object-oriented programming (described in the coming chapters), the building block technique has been significantly improved. This combination has been developed further in Objectory in a number of ways:

- The technique has been generalized from telecommunications; it is now being used in various systems such as information systems, real-time systems, process control systems, CASE tools and graphic presentation systems. Furthermore, the technique has been adapted to different programming languages (for example Ada, C++, Smalltalk or COBOL), database management systems and operating systems, to name just a few. It has, moreover, been extended from being object-based to being object-oriented (see Wegner (1987)), as it now supports inheritance between classes.

- The technique has been simplified and scaled down for application to small projects as well as to the large ones for which it was originally intended.

- The three techniques of design with building blocks, conceptual modeling and object-oriented programming have been formalized and tied together, made unambiguous and interrelated.

- Conceptual modeling has been extended with object-oriented concepts and the ability to describe dynamic behavior.

It is worth noting that the Objectory product itself has been viewed and described as a system, which made it possible to develop a new version of Objectory from an earlier one. Thus we can conclude, as described in the introductory chapter, that the technique can be employed with equal potential during the enterprise or business modeling phase that often precedes system development. Through the development case concept, every organization can adapt Objectory to its specific needs. This is further described in Appendix A.

## 2.6   Summary

All larger systems will have changes made during their life cycles. This fact must be considered in an industrial process approach to software engineering. System development is a process of progressive change as new and changed requirements will continue to be imposed on any product.

Incremental development offers a way to handle such changing requirements during development of a specific version. It also provides a way to speed up the feedback of a development. The complement to incremental development is to do prototyping early. A prototype normally aims at investigating and highlighting uncertain properties at an early stage of the system development. The aim of the prototype must be decided at the beginning – particularly whether it should be incorporated in the product (with maintainability requirements as a consequence) or not.

Reusability has failed in software engineering. Awareness of this has been commonplace for quite some time. Still, reuse is kept at a minimum level because of its associated difficulties. To increase productivity in software development significantly, reuse must be a natural ingredient. Object-orientation gives us new techniques that are far better for supporting reuse than traditional techniques. Reuse must occur at several different levels. During the coding phase is the most obvious, but it is also important to reuse previous work during other phases.

One of the most, if not *the* most, essential properties of a system is that it must have a stable structure during its lifetime. Therefore, when defining a system development process, it is important to have concepts and models that strongly support the development of such a structure. We call this foundation an architecture. A **method** describes how to work with these concepts and models in an ideal development. The method should also support the goal of getting a stable system structure. However, a method is not sufficient when scaling up for industrial development of a product, covering its entire life cycle and often involving several different types of projects. We call the activities to support this a process. The process will express more than the method, since it describes the complete management of a product over its entire life cycle. To manage such an industrial development process, tools must be developed to support the work. The support often consists of different kinds of documentation, although other tools may also be appropriate. In general, as many activities as can be automated should be automated.

We have argued that we must change the way that we currently develop systems. This change has already begun. Important ingredients of this work are object-oriented technology, a process approach to development work and a well-developed tool box. In a few decades, system development will have advanced just as the building construction industry has. A large number of components will be available for reuse at all levels of detail, from small, general components to large, application-oriented modules. To a large extent, the development work will correspond to the process model that we have been describing. The basic architecture and foundations of the method, such as object-oriented technology, will have been developed and enriched.

We have briefly introduced a technique that yields object-oriented systems and that is itself object-oriented. The rest of the book will cover the fundamental ideas of this technique. Object-orientation provides the basis. In the following chapters, the reader will gain a deeper understanding of what object-orientation is, our view of Object-Oriented Software Engineering (OOSE) and how they can be applied throughout development. The reader will also find case studies describing various application areas.

# 3 What is object-orientation?

## 3.1 Introduction

This chapter introduces some of the basic concepts of object-oriented technology. The aim is to introduce the actual idea, not to give strict and precise definitions. An introduction to object-orientation in use both for system development and for programming is found in the two following chapters.

Object-orientation is a technique for system modeling. It offers a number of concepts which are well suited for this purpose. The word 'system' is used here with a wide meaning and can be either a dedicated software system or a system in a wider context (for example an integrated software and hardware system or an organization).

Using object-orientation as a base, we model the system as a number of objects that interact. Hence, irrespective of the type of system being modeled, we regard its contents as a number of objects which in one way or another are related. Our surroundings, for instance, consist of objects, such as people, trees, cars, towns and houses which are in some way related to each other. Thus what the objects model depends on what we wish to represent with our object model. Another model of our surroundings would, perhaps, consist of taxation, government and politics as objects. The objects which we include within our model are, therefore, dependent on what the object model is to represent.

People regard their environment in terms of objects. Therefore it is simple to think in the same way when it comes to designing a model. A model which is designed using an object-oriented technology is often easy to understand, as it can be directly related to reality. Thus, with such a design method, only a small **semantic gap** will exist between reality and the model (see Figure 3.1).

Interest in the object-oriented method has grown rapidly over the last few years. This is mainly due to the fact that it has shown

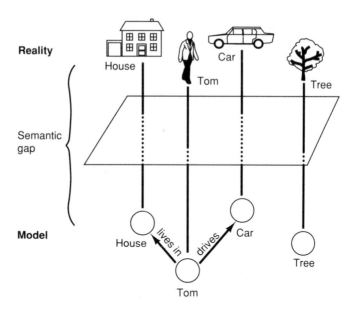

**Figure 3.1**  Since objects from reality are directly mapped into objects in the model, the semantic gap is minimized

many good qualities. Amongst the most prominent qualities of a system designed with an object-oriented method are the following:

- **Understanding** of the system is easier as the semantic gap between the system and reality is small.

- **Modifications** to the model tend to be local as they often result from an individual item, which is represented by a single object.

In the following sections, we shall introduce the basic concepts of object-orientation. This introduction is only an overview and is independent of both the programming language and the development method used. We shall not give any precise and formal concept definitions, but hope to provide you with a good understanding of these concepts. We shall use the concepts and meanings most commonly used within the object-oriented environment (see Wegner (1987)).

We will introduce the concepts by simulating a familiar example. We have chosen an example easy to understand for a person unfamiliar with the fundamental concepts of system development. As mentioned earlier, object-orientation is ideally suited to creating models of real systems, and especially for simulating the system. The example will help explain and demonstrate the fundamental concepts discussed. The example will be expanded and used again in the chapter on object-oriented programming.

## 3.2  Object

The reality we will describe involves a number of people who perform certain activities. Our task is to try to model this system. We shall see that it is very natural to construct a model which simulates this reality.

The reality consists of a number of people including, amongst others, John, Mary and Tom. We shall now consider each of these people as an object (see Figure 3.2). (We use 'person' and 'object' in this description to mean the same thing; we actually mean the object that represents the person. As always, one should be careful to separate the reality from the model.)

The first and most important concept that we describe is, of course, the concept of **object**. What is an object? The word 'object' is misused and is used in nearly all contexts. What we mean by an object is an entity able to save a state (information) and which offers a number of operations (behavior) to either examine or affect this state.

> An object is characterized by a number of operations and a state which remembers the effect of these operations.

An object-oriented model consists of a number of objects; these are clearly delimited parts of the modeled system. Objects usually correspond to real-life entity objects, such as an invoice, a car or a mobile telephone. Each object contains individual information (for example, a car has its registration number).

John          Mary          Tom

**Figure 3.2**  John, Mary and Tom are regarded as objects.

To each of the objects in the example, we thus attach the behavior and information that we wish to associate with the corresponding person. An example of the information which we might wish to save for each object is age, address, male/female and so on. To access or be able to affect this information, we must, for each object, define a set of operations which can affect or read the saved information. We can also define operations which perhaps need not affect any internal information, but only perform a behavior (for example, walk, jump, dance). The only part of the object we can see is its operations; the inside is hidden to us (see Figure 3.3). Note that, from outside, we see only those operations that exist for each behavior and not how they work. We can only see how the different objects perform their behavior if we look inside them.

Within the information, any associations to other objects are also specified; for example an invoice knows which customer to invoice. The model's objects therefore have relations with one another. For instance, we wish to model that the people will recognize each other. These relations can be of two sorts: firstly, **static** relations, namely relations existing over a longer period, which mean that two objects know about each other's existence; secondly, **dynamic** relations, namely relations by which two objects actually communicate with each other. There is an abundance of different static relations in connection with semantic modeling (see Peckham and Maryanski (1988)). We shall not describe these relations in any more detail, but content ourselves with calling them static relations. An object can thus be composed from other objects and this is described using these relations; for example, Tom can be composed of his head, his arms, his legs and his body (see Figure 3.4).

By means of this **composition**, we can structure the object Tom in parts. The reason for structuring may depend on many factors. It often depends on a combination of wishing to describe the object in detail, increase understanding and obtain reusable parts.

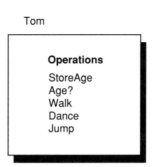

**Figure 3.3**   The object Tom and its operations

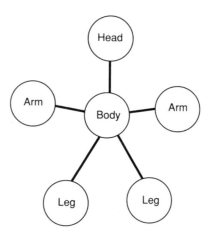

**Figure 3.4** A model of a person can be composed with the objects head, legs, arms and body.

A similar method of joining different parts together is through use of **partition** hierarchies. This means that an object can be constructed from other objects; these relations are therefore often called **consist of** relations. The word 'partition' originates from the Latin *partitos* and means divide. Figure 3.5 illustrates an example of a partition hierarchy.

A similar possibility for showing how something is interrelated is through the use of an **aggregate**. Partition hierarchy and aggregate are used as synonyms, but there is a difference. The word 'aggregate' comes from the Latin verb *aggregare*, meaning 'to join together', which is the opposite of 'to partition'. As it is difficult to express this grouping in a single way, a new object and a partition hierarchy can be used to express the aggregate. In a family relationship, the grouping of Man, Woman and Child establishes the aggregate Family. Since we cannot represent this triangular

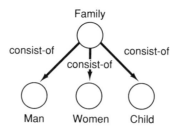

**Figure 3.5** Example of a partition hierarchy. The object Family exists only to link together the other objects. When one turns to the whole family, one turns, therefore, to the object Family.

relationship, an object Family is added to express the joining of several objects. This object thus *represents* the aggregate, but it is not the aggregate itself. An aggregate is a union of several objects, and the union as such is often represented by an object of its own.

If we look at the inside of the object, we shall see both its information structure and how its operations work (see Figure 3.6). We can see the **attributes** that the object needs to store, the parts the object consists of and how the behavior for the operations is defined.

The dynamics in an object-oriented model are created through the dynamic relations, by means of objects sending **stimuli** to other objects. Here 'stimulus' means the event of one object communicating with another. In a programming context, the word 'message' is often used instead but, in order to avoid the message semantics, we use the stimulus concept. Additionally, the word 'stimulus' indicates that it stimulates some behavior to take action and does not necessarily include any message information. A stimulus, which is received by an object, causes an operation to be performed in the receiving object. This operation can in turn cause new stimuli to be sent. Hence, if we wish an object to perform a behavior, we send a stimulus to this object. For example, if we wish Tom to jump, then we send the 'Jump' stimulus to him. When Tom receives the stimulus, he interprets it and performs the actions which have been defined for him to do when this stimulus is received. Tom uses his legs and arms and therefore sends stimuli to his legs and arms (see Figure 3.7).

Tom

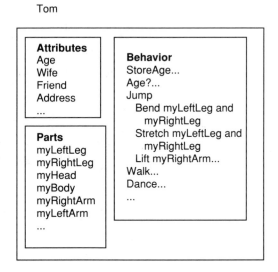

**Figure 3.6** The inside of object Tom. Only the behavior for Jump is shown.

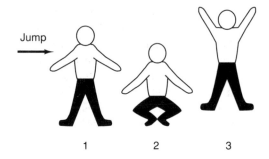

**Figure 3.7**    Tom jumps as a result of receiving the stimulus Jump.

We can also consider more complicated cases. If we want the object Mary to dance, we send a stimulus 'Dance' to the object Mary. When she receives this, she performs the behavior associated with dancing. She, perhaps, will only dance with her friend. She will therefore send a stimulus to this friend to start dancing (see Figure 3.8).

All information in an object-oriented system is stored within its objects and can only be manipulated when the objects are ordered to perform operations. The behavior and information are **encapsulated** in the object. The only way to affect the object is to

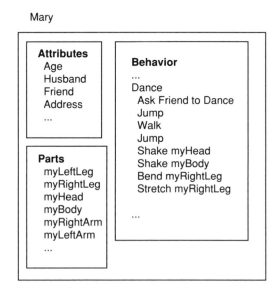

**Figure 3.8**    When Mary dances, she wants to have someone else to dance with.

perform operations on it. Objects thus support the concept of **information hiding**, that is, they hide their internal structure from their surroundings (see Parnas (1972)). Every one of the object's operations performs part of the object's behavior, and can modify information in the object. In order to use an object, we do not need to know how the object's behavior or information is represented or implemented internally. We only need to know which operations it offers.

Note that we describe the problem in terms of items or objects taken from real life and what we wish these objects to perform. We do not know how John, Tom and Mary perform their tasks or how they look inside. We have used the concepts object, operation and encapsulation to understand the problem. Encapsulation means that all that is seen of an object is its interface, namely the operations we can perform on the object.

These important concepts have their roots in abstract data types (see Aho *et al.* (1983)). An **abstract data type** is a model (structure), with a number of operations which affect this model. It is similar to our definition of an object and, in fact, they are closely related. Both are abstractions and are defined in terms of what they perform, not how they perform it. They are both generalizations of something specific, where encapsulation is the central concept. One of the advantages of abstract data types is that they should be able to be used independently of their implementation (information hiding), which means that even if the implementation is modified, we should not need to modify how we use the abstract data types. Another advantage is, quite simply, the reduced complexity since it is impossible to become involved in their internal structure; you can use them only according to their specifications.

So far, we have only introduced the object concept. Many people using the term 'object-orientation' mean only this, but, as we have seen, we have actually not come much further than abstract data types. To be truly object-oriented, we need some further properties and concepts.

## 3.3  Class and instance

In the system we model, there will be a number of communicating objects. Some of these objects will have common characteristics and we can group the objects according to these characteristics. When we look at the objects in the example, we notice that all three people have similar behavior and information structures. These objects have the same mold or template. Such a group represents a **class**. In order to describe all objects that have similar behavior and information structures, we can therefore identify and describe a class to represent these objects.

A class is a definition, a template or a mold to enable the creation of new objects and is, therefore, a description of the common characteristics of several objects. The objects comprising a certain class have this template in common. As an example we can view this book. The book you are holding in your hand is an instance of the book. The book description at the publishers represents the class from where instances can be created.

> A **class** represents a template for several objects and describes how these objects are structured internally. Objects of the same class have the same definition both for their operations and for their information structures.

A class is sometimes called the object's **type**. However, a type and a class are not the same thing. As we mentioned above, an abstract data type is defined by a set of operations. A type is defined by the manipulations you can do with the type. A class is more than that. You can also look inside a class, for example to see its information structure. We would therefore rather view the class as one (of possibly many) specific *implementation* of a type.

Using the class concept, we can associate certain characteristics with a whole group of objects (see Figure 3.9). We can consider the class as being an abstraction that *describes* all the common characteristics of the objects forming part of the class.

In object-oriented systems, each object belongs to a class. An object that belongs to a certain class is called an **instance** of that class. We therefore often use object and instance as synonyms.

> An **instance** is an object created from a class. The class describes the (behavior and information) structure of the instance, while the current state of the instance is defined by the operations performed on the instance.

We can thus define a class Person, and each object that represents a person becomes an instance of this class. In our example, we can describe a class Person, where Tom, John and Mary are instances of this class (see Figure 3.10).

The behavior of the instance and its information structure are thus defined by its class. Each instance also has a unique identity. Several different instances can be created from a certain class, where each instance is manipulated by the operations defined by the class. Different instances can be manipulated by different sequences of

**Figure 3.9**   The class Person describes what is common to all persons.

operations and, as a result, have different internal states. If these instances had been manipulated in exactly the same way, their state would also have been the same.

Now, we do not need to describe how each person will appear, as this description is made in one place only, namely in the class. The class will therefore contain the information structure for age, for example, and operations to examine or modify this age. When we have created an instance (for example, John), we need to store John's age in this instance. This is achieved by using the operation for storing age.

In the same way, we can make all the people's arms, legs and heads into classes. Thus we can define an individual class for head, arm, body and leg. The class for person can now use these classes to construct a person's body (see Figure 3.11).

As all people are instances of the same class, they will have similar behavior. If we wish to describe the fact that men and women have different behavior, for example when they dance, we will need to create two classes, one for Male and one for Female. John and Tom are created as instances of the class Male, and Mary as an instance of the class Female (see Figure 3.12). We must now, for both these classes, describe their behavior and information structures.

Class Person

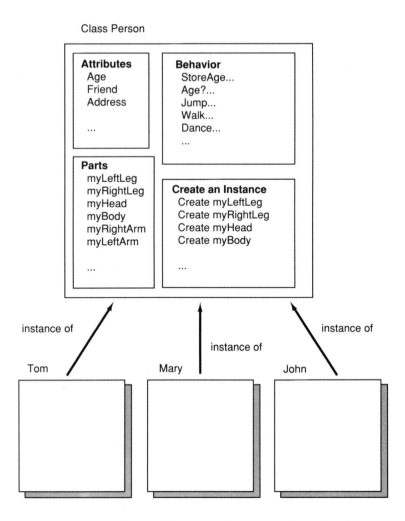

**Figure 3.10**    Tom, John and Mary are all instances of the class Person.

Why didn't we make John, Mary and Tom into separate classes instead? This is surely feasible and, if they had different behavior and/or information structures, we would have had no choice but to do so. We have simplified things by saying that all men appear in one way and all women in another. Both these classes have certain parts in common. At the moment, we must repeat these similarities, but later we shall describe how inheritance can be used to avoid this duplication of descriptions.

What is contained inside the classes Male and Female? In Figure 3.13, we can see both the information structure and the

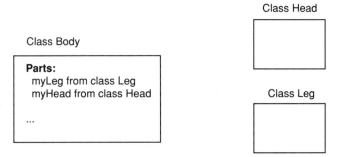

**Figure 3.11** Instances of one class can recognize instances of another. The relevant classes are defined in the original class.

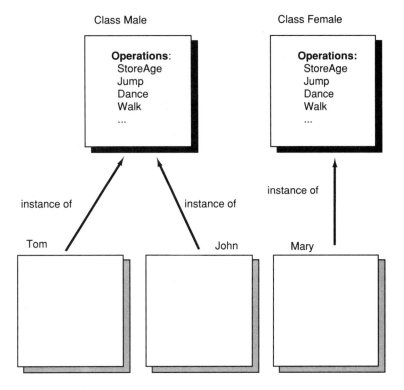

**Figure 3.12** Male and Female are separate classes.

operations in each class, and we can see that they have a lot in common. The operation to create a new instance of a class (that is, create a new person) creates also legs, arms, head and body for the new person.

Class Female

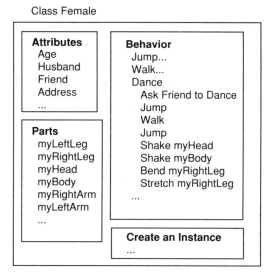

Class Male

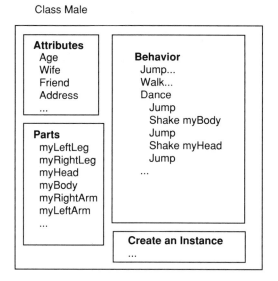

**Figure 3.13**   The inside of classes Male and Female.

We also see how we have defined the operation to dance. It differs only slightly, in this example, between the two sexes. Both men and women move their bodies, but in slightly different ways. Moreover, women will only dance if they have a friend to dance with.

To summarize, we can consider the class as being the definition of operations and information structure for objects, and the instance as defining an individual object's state.

## 3.4  Polymorphism

Instances, created from classes, will together provide us with the dynamic behavior that we wish to model. It is when these instances start to communicate with each other that the system's behavior is performed. An instance may know of other instances to which stimuli can be sent. If an instance sends a stimulus to another instance, but does not have to be aware of which class the receiving instance belongs to, we say that we have **polymorphism**. Polymorphism means, at least in object-oriented contexts, that the sending instance does not need to know the receiving instance's class and that this class can be any class.

> **Polymorphism** means that the sender of a stimulus does not need to know the receiving instance's class. The receiving instance can belong to an arbitrary class.

All people have a best friend. We can see this in the information structure of the classes Male and Female; both have information on a friend. We have not specified any special conditions for this friend, but we can assume that it is another person. A person's friend must, therefore, be either of the class Male or Female. We therefore have polymorphism in this model, as friend can refer to an instance of one of two classes. Mary's friend is either Tom or John and as these are both associated with the same class, Male, we have no use for the polymorphism characteristic. However, Tom's friend is either Mary or John and, as they are from different classes, class Male will not know with which class the friend will be associated. Here, the reference friend must be polymorphic. Polymorphism means that different *instances* can be associated, *and* that these instances can belong to different classes. It is in the latter case, as with Tom, that we have use of the polymorphic characteristic.

A stimulus can be interpreted in different ways, depending on the receiver's class. It is, therefore, the instance which receives the stimulus that determines its interpretation, and not the transmitting instance. Often polymorphism is said to mean that one operation can be implemented in different ways in different classes. This is actually only a consequence of what is said above and not polymorphism in itself. (Polymorphism and dynamic binding are also often confused. Dynamic binding means that the stimulus is not bound to a certain operation in the receiving instance's class until it is sent. We shall discuss dynamic binding in more detail in the chapter on object-oriented programming.)

As we have not specified any conditions on the class, we should, in theory, be able to associate an instance of any class to friend. It is therefore possible to associate an arm with friend. To avoid errors of this kind, it is often necessary to restrict the receivers of a stimulus. If we know, in advance, the receiver's class, then we don't need polymorphism, but if we allow the receiver to be of varying class, within limits, we must specify this restriction in the polymorphism characteristic. Thus, we need to restrict the instances which can be associated. This is often called **limited polymorphism**. We require only instances of the classes Male and Female to be friends. This restriction can be made in different ways. Normally, inheritance hierarchy is used. We shall soon return to this problem.

Polymorphism is a very important characteristic for our models. It is the receiver of a stimulus that determines how a stimulus will be interpreted, not the transmitter. The transmitter need only know that another instance *can* perform a certain behavior, not which class the instance belongs to and thus not which operation actually performs the behavior. This is an extremely strong tool for allowing us to develop flexible systems. We have, in this way, only specified *what* shall occur and not *how* it shall occur. Through delegating what shall occur in this way, a flexible and modification-resistant system is obtained. If we wish to add an object of a new class, this modification will affect only the new object, and not those sending stimuli to it.

## 3.5  Inheritance

When we describe our classes, it is soon noticed that many classes have common characteristics (behavior and information structure). For instance, when we compare the classes Male and Female, we see that they are very similar to each other. The similarities can be shared between the classes by extracting them and placing them in a separate class Person. In Person, we describe everything that is common to Male and Female. In this way common characteristics can be shared by several classes. We collect the common characteristics into one specific class and let the original classes **inherit** this class; then we need only describe the characteristics that are specific to the original classes. We therefore allow both Male and Female to inherit Person and, in this way, obtain access to all the characteristics defined there (see Figure 3.14). Male and Female now

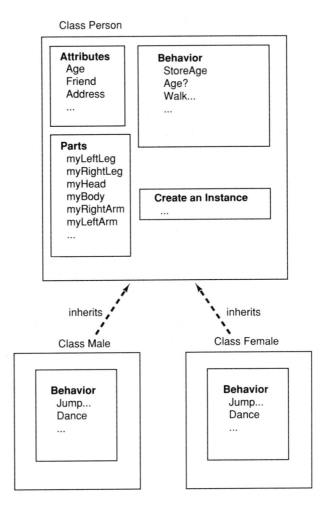

**Figure 3.14**   Classes with inheritance.

contain the same things as before, but their description has been simplified by means of inheriting Person.

> If class B **inherits** class A, then both the operations and the information structure described in class A will become part of class B.

By means of inheritance, we can show similarities between classes and describe these similarities in a class which other classes can inherit. Hence we can reuse common descriptions. Inheritance is therefore often promoted as a core idea for reuse in the software industry. However, although inheritance, properly used, is a very useful mechanism in many contexts including reuse, it is not a prerequisite for reuse. We shall come back to this issue in Chapter 11.

Through inheritance, we have also obtained another advantage. If we want to modify some characteristic in Person (for example, how a person walks), it is sufficient to perform this modification in one place. Thus, if such a modification is made, both Male and Female will inherit this new definition of walk. Hence inheritance is very useful for easy modification of models.

We also see from the examples that the descriptions of Male and Female have been greatly reduced. The only information remaining is that which *differs* between them. Inheritance is thus also useful for avoiding redundancy, leading to smaller models that are easier to understand.

The ease of modification does not only occur inside class descriptions. Adding new classes can be easily done by just describing changes to existing classes. However, adding new classes may sometimes involve restructuring the inheritance hierarchy. We shall come back to this issue later.

By means of extracting and sharing common characteristics, we can **generalize** classes and place them higher up in an inheritance hierarchy. In the same way, if we wish to add a new class, we can find a class that already offers some of the operations and information structure required for the new class. We can then let the new class inherit this class and only add anything which is unique for the new class. We then **specialize** the class.

Classes lying below a class in the inheritance hierarchy are called **descendants** of the class. Classes lying above are called **ancestors**. Sometimes the concepts of subclasses and superclasses are used instead, but we prefer descendant and ancestor. The reason for this is discussed in the box on super- and subclasses. Hence, if class B inherits from class A, then class A becomes class B's ancestor (see Figure 3.15). Class B is then a descendant of class A. Since

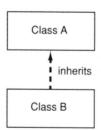

**Figure 3.15**   Class B is a descendant of class A and class A is an ancestor of class B.

inheritance hierarchies may include several classes, we may want to emphasize the relation between two classes. If a class directly inherits from another class, we call it a **direct descendant**. The first class is then the **direct ancestor** of the second class. A direct ancestor is sometimes called the **parent** and a direct descendant is sometimes called the **child.**

In this book, inheritance relations are indicated by a dashed arrow drawn *from* the descendant *towards* the ancestor class. We will also write 'inherits' (or shorter, 'ihs') on the arrow to avoid any misunderstandings. Note that the direction of the arrow is *from* the descendant towards the ancestor. In some other notations the direction is the opposite. The reason that we use this convention is that the descendant should know about its ancestor, but the ancestor should not know about its descendant.

The inherit association is a **class association**, that is, an association between classes. Class associations are drawn with dashed arrows here. Associations between instances are drawn with a full arrow.

Ancestors developed with the main purpose of being inherited by others are often called **abstract classes**. Usually, instances are not created from abstract classes, although it is possible. A class developed with the main purpose of creating instances of it is called a **concrete class**. Also, concrete classes may of course be ancestors of other classes.

**The concepts superclass and subclass**

The concepts of superclass and subclass have varying definitions. For instance, superclass is sometimes defined as the class directly above another class and sometimes as all classes above a certain class. Subclass is, in the same way, sometimes defined as the class level existing directly under a given class in an inheritance hierarchy and sometimes as all classes lying under a given class. When the concepts are used in the right connection, it is usually understood what is meant, but concept confusion is not uncommon – at least for beginners in object-orientation. To realize the confusion, those familiar with Smalltalk can ask the following questions. Is the class Object a superclass to all other classes? Which superclass has the class Array? How many subclasses has the class Object?

Another problem with the concepts is that the prefixes super and sub have a meaning which does not really agree with how they are understood. The concept super is often understood as something that is more capable than anything else. In this context, it may mean quite the opposite. The inheriting class has often been expanded with some characteristics and is therefore often more capable than its superclass; but a descendant may also involve a restriction or specialization of its ancestor, that is, a subset. It is actually from here that the concept sub originated, the subclass instances representing a subset of the superclass instances.

Bertrand Meyer (1988) has also observed this problem. He proposes that inheritance can be regarded as both an extension and a specialization (restriction). If we consider the class to be a definition of operations with an information structure, then inheritance is an extension. If we consider the class to be an implementation of a type, then inheritance can be used to specialize the type, as the instances of descendants represent a subcollection of all instances of the ancestor.

## 3.5.1   Using inheritance

An inheritance hierarchy can consist of many levels; that is, classes can be inherited from other classes which, in turn, can be inherited from new classes, and so on. How then should you use inheritance to get a good and robust inheritance hierarchy? We will discuss here some topics from our experience to explain how to get a good inheritance structure.

Class structuring occurs with the help of inheritance hierarchies. This structuring of classes in an inheritance hierarchy enables us to work with classes and to define new classes by specifying the differences between the new ones and the already existing ones. If this expansion becomes extensive, then the inheritance hierarchy may become less suitable and a restructuring may be necessary.

For instance, what happens if we add two further individuals to the example, James and Lawrence? They are both men and can therefore be instances of Male. Such an addition is trivial, but what if we want to describe them as old men having a few characteristics differing from those of their younger colleagues? For instance, they cannot dance in the same way as the younger men. Their dance style is a little more rigid. To describe the older men, we can add a new class: Old Male. How will this new class be related to the existing ones? It is clear that the class Old Male has all the characteristics of the class Person. It also has a lot in common with Male. Basically we have three relevant possibilities (see Figure 3.16):

(1) Old Male is a descendant of Person and we define the differences between Old Male and Person.

(2) Old Male inherits Male and we define the differences; that is we redefine dance.

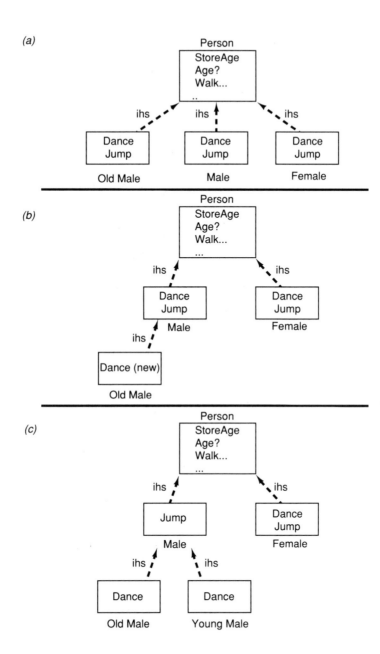

**Figure 3.16**   Three possibilities to add a new class Old Male in the inheritance hierarchy.

(3) We create a further class, Young Male, and define dance there as well. In this way, both Old Male and Young Male can inherit Male.

Which of these three alternatives should be selected? This will depend on how the classes are to be used. How will further modifications be handled? What do we really want to model? How important is a clear understanding? How difficult is it to restructure the classes? What is the price of restructuring? The best alternative will depend on how you answer these questions.

Ideally, for the purposes of understanding, we would select the third alternative: to create a further class, Young Male, extract the similarities and place these in class Male. With this, we now have no redefinition, and we keep a clear and understandable structure that can be further developed. The cost has been the work involved in restructuring the existing class structure and creating the new class.

When a new class is to be added, we try to find a suitable candidate to be the direct ancestor. As we have seen, some operations may need to be modified for the inheritance. Normally we have four possibilities for adding a new class:

(1) We can go upwards in the inheritance hierarchy to see whether an ancestor is more suited for inheritance (the characteristics that we wish to avoid may not exist in the ancestor).

(2) We can describe the class from the beginning, independent of any other class (that is, without inheritance).

(3) We can restructure the inheritance hierarchy, so that we obtain a class that suits the inheritance required; see Figure 3.17 for an example. However, this is not always possible.

(4) We can redefine the characteristics that we wish to change.

The first two solutions are trivial and we shall not discuss them any further. The third solution is the most acceptable, as it maintains a clean class hierarchy. To restructure in this way, though, often requires a lot of work, partly owing to the work involved in finding a better structure and partly owing to the consequences that the modification will have on a system designed on the basis of an already existing class hierarchy. This solution is usually not as easy as shown in the figure and thus compromises may need to be made in order to find where the operations can be defined most suitably.

The fourth solution is often called **overriding**. It means that we redefine some behavior and/or some information structure from an ancestor. Whether overriding should be used is widely discussed in the object-oriented community. Overriding is both easy and

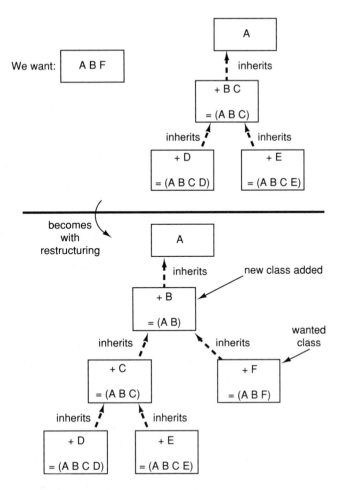

**Figure 3.17**   By restructuring an inheritance hierarchy, one can, in most cases, obtain the required classes. The letters in the boxes mean that the classes have the characteristics represented by these letters which can either relate to behavior or information structure. (ABC) means that the class has these properties.

flexible to use for modifying existing classes, but it can damage understanding of a class hierarchy, as operations with the same name can have different semantic meanings in different classes. An inheritance chain must then be followed upwards to the place where the operation is defined to find its definition. After the inheritance has passed from one class to another, the inherited characteristics can be modified. With override, therefore, inheritance is not transitive. Thus the descendant has not inherited all the ancestor's characteristics; only some of them have been inherited, while others have been redefined.

To understand better how we should use inheritance in a proper way we shall review the main purposes of inheritance.

**Reuse**. The most common reason for using inheritance is that it simplifies the reuse of code. Reuse can, in principle, occur in two different ways in combination with inheritance. The first is that two classes are found to have similar parts; these parts are extracted and placed in an abstract class, which both the original classes inherit. This abstract class represents the common parts of both classes and need not always be meaningful in itself. The other way to reuse is to start from a class library. Find a class which has the operations that you need, inherit this class and make the required modifications.

**Subtyping**. A class can be regarded as an implementation of a type. A class A defines a certain behavior. If it is possible to use one of A's descendants in all the places where class A is used, then we say that the classes are **behaviorally compatible**. The descendant represents a subtype to class A. In practice this often means that the descendant should at least have the same interface as its ancestors. We can say that the ancestor here represents a subset of the behavior common to all the descendants. Subtyping normally occurs if the inheritance performs only an extension, rather than overriding something already defined in the ancestor. The additions must be disjunct with the existing classes, and therefore must not create any restrictions on them. This use of inheritance is tightly coupled to describing the role played by an object; the role is defined by the operations of the object. To think in terms of roles or responsibilities is often appropriate for modeling object-oriented systems and provides a good tool.

**Specialization**. If the descendant is modified in such a way that it is no longer behaviorally compatible with its parent (that is, if the parent class can no longer be exchanged with the descendant), the class is said to be specialized. Normally, the operations and/or information structure have been redefined or deleted. A parent class that has been specialized cannot always be replaced by its descendant. An example of specialization is if a class Adult inherits from another class Person (see Figure 3.18). The class Adult has a more restricted age interval than class Person. We cannot, therefore, arbitrarily replace the class Adult with the class Person. Consider the case when one wishes to enter a person's age as 5. This is not possible for instances of the class Adult, but is possible for instances of the class Person.

**Conceptual**. This use of inheritance corresponds closely to the intuitive semantic, 'a dog is a mammal' (that is, in all places where

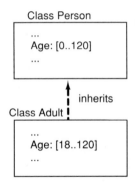

Figure 3.18  Inheritance as specialization. The class Person has defined age to be in the range 0 to 120 years. The class Adult restricts this to the range 18 to 120 years. The class Person is now no longer exchangeable with the class Adult, as one cannot specify an age of, for instance, 5 years for the class Adult.

we use mammal, we can also use dog, as dog maintains all the characteristics of mammal).

These different ways of using inheritance are not exclusive or disjunct in any way. For example, reuse can be a reason for subtyping. In order to optimize the use of inheritance and be able to recognize both good and bad solutions, more experience must be gained and more research done on the use of inheritance. However, from our experience, focusing on an object's protocol normally leads to appropriate inheritance structures. This means that focusing on the subtyping issue at all times will lead to proper inheritance hierachies that are maintainable and robust. This usage is also natural from a logical perspective. What should be avoided is the use of inheritance for reuse of single operations; that is, even if you can only reuse a single operation, you inherit the class anyway. Although this may be proper and efficient for prototyping purposes, such use of inheritance often leads to code that is not maintainable or robust in the long run. We may talk about this type of use as *spaghetti inheritance.*

The use of inheritance is discussed by, for example, LaLonde and Pugh (1991b), Wegner and Zdonik (1988) and LaLonde, Thomas and Pugh (1986).

### 3.5.2  Multiple inheritance

When describing a new class, if we wish to use characteristics from two or more existing classes, we can inherit both these classes. We call this **multiple inheritance.** This means that one class can have more than one direct ancestor. The use of multiple inheritance is, as with overriding, controversial in the OO community.

Multiple inheritance can however be justified if we regard inheritance as a way to model roles played by an object. If we regard inheritance as a way of structuring roles, we can, for example, construct a houseboat by inheriting both a house and a boat since a houseboat can play both roles, being a house and a boat. Critics of multiple inheritance say that we could just as easily have obtained a boathouse with this use of inheritance, but here we can see the use of roles in this context: a boathouse cannot play the role of a boat.

Multiple inheritance is also often justified as a way of providing reusable descriptions. If a description of a class includes behavior which partly exists in two other classes, then this behavior can be extracted so that we can inherit the common behavior from two classes (see Figure 3.19). We wish to create a new class containing the behaviors A and E. The behaviors A and E are integrated with other behaviors in separate classes. By extracting A and E and creating individual classes for them, we can inherit these classes and, in this way, share their descriptions.

This use of multiple inheritance is often the main target for the critics of multiple inheritance. As was said above, this usage, if not

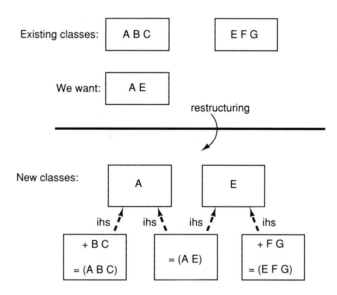

**Figure 3.19** Multiple inheritance. The middle class inherits the descriptions from two other classes.

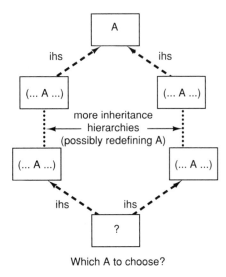

**Figure 3.20** Repeated inheritance. The same characteristic exists in two parents. How is this detected and which should be chosen?

carried out properly, may very well lead to spaghetti inheritance. If it is hard to understand such inheritance in single inheritance contexts, it is far harder in multiple inheritance contexts. The above example could be correct, but then the roles described by the classes should be viewed instead. Using the subtyping rule will not always result in proper use of multiple inheritance. In the example the descendants seem to be acceptable subtypes of the ancestors. It all depends on whether the roles are conflicting. Hence we see here that the use of roles provides great support for the development of the inheritance hierarchy.

The main disadvantage with multiple inheritance is that it often reduces understanding of a class hierarchy. The problem arises especially if both ancestors have an operation with the same name, but with different definitions. We must then either define a new operation or explicitly select one of the existing definitions. In the majority of programming languages that support multiple inheritance, the user is forced to redefine the name so that it becomes unique. This is the most acceptable solution, as only the user has sufficient knowledge to solve this conflict. A special case is that where the same operation exists in both parent classes, since these classes may have a common ancestor (see Figure 3.20). This is called **repeated inheritance** and must be solved. In the case of the same operation appearing in two places, the problem is actually solved once this is realized (that is, the selection of which to use doesn't matter). If, though, it was originally the same operation, but has been overridden, then the problem is to know which one to select.

## 3.6  Summary

Object-orientation is a technique for developing models. It maps very well the way people think about reality. Therefore object-oriented models are often easy to understand. Additionally, modifications are often local since changes frequently evolve from some individual item that is modeled.

An object is a representation of some entity with both behavior and information tied to it. Only the operations that can be performed on the object are seen from the outside of the object. Objects are related and the overall dynamics of the model arise when the objects start to interact by sending stimuli to each other. However, supporting objects is not in itself object-orientation.

Many objects may be similar. A class describes the similarities of objects. Every object is then an instance of the class and the behavior and information structure of the instance are defined by its class. To make the description of classes more flexible, polymorphism is used. This means that, when defining relations between objects, one object does not need to know the exact class of the other object. In this way, new classes can be introduced without needing to change other classes.

Classes can be described as changes to existing classes with inheritance. This makes the definition of new classes easy as only differences need to be described. However, although inheritance is a very strong tool when properly used, when improperly used it can lead to models that are hard to understand and maintain. Multiple inheritance is a much stronger tool than single inheritance. Improperly used, though, multiple inheritance can be very much worse than single inheritance.

# 4 Object-oriented system development

## 4.1 Introduction

In order to design large systems, a systematic approach should be adopted. There is an abundance of such approaches and all of them are aimed at producing a good system. But what is a good system? This question can be answered partly from an external viewpoint and partly from an internal viewpoint of the system. The external viewpoint is that of all those who in some way use the system. They want the system to give correct results quickly, to be reliable, easy to learn and use, effective and so on. The internal viewpoint is that of the system developers and those who have to maintain the system. They want the system to be easy to modify and extend, easy to understand, to contain reusable parts, to be easy to test, compatible with other systems, portable, powerful and easy to manufacture.

The definition of a good system varies in certain respects between different applications. In some, it is performance that is important and in others perhaps user-friendliness. It can, in fact, depend on the structure of the system, for instance, whether it is distributed or centralized. What is common to all (larger) systems is that they will need to be modified.

**A system's entropy**

The second law of thermodynamics, in principle, states that a closed system's disorder cannot be reduced, it can only increase or possibly remain unchanged. A measure of this disorder is **entropy**. This law also seems plausible for software systems and we can assume that this law is plausible for the systems discussed here; a system's disorder, or entropy, always increases. We can call this **software entropy**.

Within software development, there are similar theories; see Lehman (1985), who suggested a number of laws, of which two were, basically, as follows:

(1)     A program that is used will be modified.

69

(2)        When a program is modified, its complexity will increase, provided that one does not actively work against this.

Assume that a system initially has a certain software entropy. Experience shows that it is reasonable to assume that the increase in software entropy is proportional to the entropy of the software when the modification started. This means that it is easier to change an ordered system than a disordered one, something that all experience shows. This would mathematically be expressed as

$$\Delta E \sim E$$

or, with differential calculus

$$\frac{\mathrm{d}E}{\mathrm{d}t} = kE$$

which is a simple differential equation having solutions as shown in Figure 4.1. We can see from the figure that a system's life span is dependent on how well structured the system was initially. When a certain software entropy is reached, it is no longer economically justifiable to continue with this system, as it has become unreasonably expensive to modify. One possibility is that, at such a stage, we apply re-engineering to reduce this software entropy, so that we can continue to maintain the system at a reasonable cost.

When we design a system with the intention of it being maintainable, we try to give it the lowest software entropy possible from the beginning. This is one of the aims of a system development

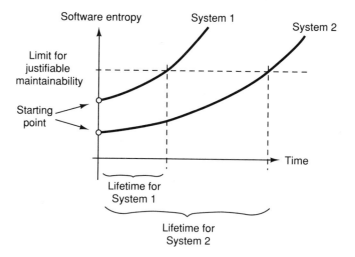

**Figure 4.1**  A system's entropy and how it increases at different speeds depending on the starting entropy.

method. By this means, we hope to increase the life span of the system. We know, though, that sooner or later we shall, nevertheless, reach a limit beyond which it is too expensive to maintain the system.

There is much to learn from these kinds of analogies, but analogies should only be used as idea generators. Even if there are similarities to system development, we are not yet experts in software entropy. The main difficulty with this kind of 'law' is, of course, that people are involved.

In order to design a good system, different system development methods have been proposed to describe either a project for development of a first product version or a global view of the entire system life cycle. Traditionally, the work is structured and described using different types of **waterfall model** (see Figure 4.2). These waterfalls describe the flow of the development process. The work begins by creating a requirement specification for the system. This is normally performed by the person who ordered the system or those developing it in cooperation with the orderers. From this requirement specification, an analysis and logical description of the system is made. Alternatively, this can be produced together with the requirement specification. The design of the system is then completed and followed by implementation in smaller modules. These modules are first tested individually and then together. When the last integration test has been completed, the entire system can be tested and delivered and the maintenance phase begins. Initially, the

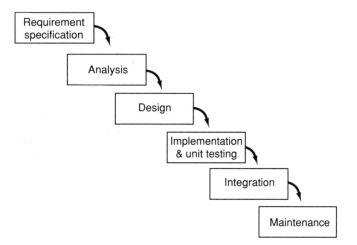

**Figure 4.2**   A typical waterfall model.

idea was that one should complete one phase before the next one is started. This principle, though, was abolished relatively quickly and thus a phase was allowed to be started before the previous one was totally complete. The waterfall model has had a tremendous effect on software engineering methods, although it was never intended to be taken so literally when first introduced.

Not long after, it was discovered that water must fall upwards, so to speak, in order to fully describe the development cycle. The major problem, though, in more and more cases, was the maintenance phase, which in reality contained a new requirement specification, analysis, design and so on. Various other models were developed in order to describe these new facts; one of the more popular is the **spiral model** (see Boehm (1986)), shown in Figure 4.3. The spiral model can describe how a product develops to form new versions, and how a version can be incrementally developed from prototype to completed product.

System development usually contains all of these phases (even if they are given different names in different methods), and development always occurs incrementally over them. This development scenario is true irrespective of the method used. We can characterize system development as being initially rather turbulent, but stabilizing subsequently. The development method used should therefore help to make the development process stable as soon as possible. The idea is that we should work on analysis long enough to understand the system totally, but not so long as to consider details which will be modified during design. This often means that a relatively large part of the work performed is carried out during the analysis phase. A typical time division for the projects

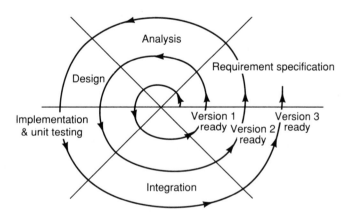

Figure 4.3    A spiral model.

Project
work

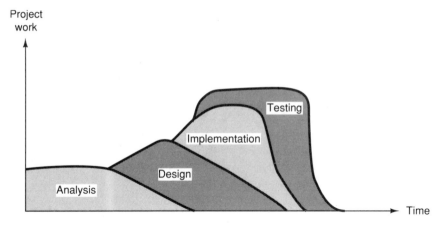

**Figure 4.4** Total division of efforts over time between different activities.

we have been involved in is shown in Figure 4.4. Initially, a small group of people performs analysis and subsequently design. These activities are worked on iteratively. As the system structure stabilizes, more people are involved in implementation and testing. However, analysis and design activities may also be done even when testing is started. At this stage it is mainly changes in the analysis or design models that are incorporated.

## 4.2 Function/data methods

The existing methods for system development can basically be divided into **function/data** methods and object-oriented methods. By function/data methods we mean those methods that treat functions and/or data as being more or less separate. Object-oriented methods view functions and data as highly integrated. These paradigms are shown schematically in Figure 4.5. Most traditional software engineering methods are function/data methods, for example, SADT (Structured Analysis and Design Technique), see Ross (1985), RDD (Requirement Driven Design based on SREM), see Alford (1985), and SA/SD (Structured Analysis and Structured Design), see Yourdon and Constantine (1979) and Yourdon (1989).

Function/data methods thus distinguish between functions and data, where functions, in principle, are active and have behavior, and data is a passive holder of information which is affected by functions. The system is typically broken down into functions, whereas data is sent between those functions. The functions are

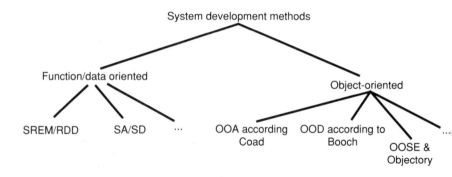

**Figure 4.5**   Software development methods in different paradigms.

broken down further and eventually converted into source code. This function/data division originates from von Neumann's hardware architecture, where the separation of program and data is greatly emphasized. The first machine language also had this division in its instruction set-up and it was thereafter logical to give high-level languages a similar structure. This approach has been difficult to escape from, but there have been several different attempts to do so. One such attempt is object-oriented programming, another is functional programming (see Backus (1977) or Bird and Wadler (1988)).

A system developed using a function/data method often becomes difficult to maintain. A major problem with function/data methods is that, in principle, all functions must know how the data is stored, that is, its data structure. It is often the case that different types of data have slightly different data formats, which means that we often need condition clauses to verify the data type. The programs, therefore, often need to have either IF-THEN or CASE structures, which really do not have anything to do with the functionality, but relate only to the different data formats. The programs thus become difficult to read, as we are often not interested in data format, but only in the functionality. Furthermore, to change a data structure, we must modify all the functions relating to the structure. Systems developed using such methods often become quite unstable; a slight modification will generate major consequences. In the same way, the instability of the development process, which we discussed earlier in this chapter, will become unnecessarily lasting, as any modifications made will create consequences in other areas.

Another problem with function/data methods is that people do not naturally think in the terms they structure in. The requirement specification is normally formulated in normal human language. It often describes in 'What-terms' what the system will do, what functionality the system will support and what items should exist in the system. This is often reformulated into 'How-terms' for the functional breakdown when the focus changes. In this way we create a large semantic gap between the external and internal views of the system. Note that nothing in the methods explicitly tells you to change focus to the implementation. We shall see that, with an object-oriented method, the system will even be internally structured from the model taken from the requirement specification.

This is yet another reason that function/data systems become more difficult to modify. Owing to the fact that they are designed around how a certain behavior will be carried out (this being a common area of modification), modifications often generate major consequences. Object-oriented methods structure the system from the items which exist in the problem domain. This is often a more natural way to describe the system. These items are normally very stable and change very little. The changes which do occur normally affect only one or a few such items, which means that the changes made are usually local in the system. If we wish to have a stable system, we should consider what has a tendency to change, and then design according to this knowledge. Peter Coad and Ed Yourdon (1991) inspired us to propose the following table:

**Table 4.1**   Tendency for change in various items

| Item | Probability for change |
| --- | --- |
| Object from application | Low |
| Long-lived information structures | Low |
| Passive object's attribute | Medium |
| Sequences of behavior | Medium |
| Interface with outside world | High |
| Functionality | High |

However, this topic has not been investigated scientifically. Most object-oriented methods base their structure on the items that have a low probability of change. This can, though, lead to troublesome consequences, as, for example, Constantine (1990) has observed. We have also noted this and the approach we describe later in the book is designed to handle this. The aim of our approach is to manage *all* changes in a controlled and preferably local way.

This especially means that the items with a high probability for change must be managed by the method as well.

It has been claimed that it is possible to use a function/data method initially and later, usually in the design or programming phase, change to an object-oriented point of view. However, this becomes unnatural as the division of function and data is a central idea all the way down to the programming level. To start joining program and data, at any stage, in order to design your objects and classes becomes awkward, as the method is based on separating them. Thus, before programming commences, a paradigm shift will occur, making it difficult to use all the object-oriented programming qualities in full. Object-oriented programming requires a different approach from that of the function/data development methods.

The shift in approach means that the decision on which object is fundamental for the system structure is made too late in the development process. A central opinion in connection with object-oriented programming is that important items from the application domain will be represented as objects. If one uses a strict functional analysis method in combination with an object-oriented programming language, the object will not be identified until the design stage, and will be identified by people who have not had contact with either the orderer or the final user. This in turn suggests that the objects will probably not represent all the important items from the application domain. We have to reformulate the items the system will work with into How-terms in order to once again reformulate these 'Hows' as objects.

We shall now discuss, from an object-oriented point of view, the different system development phases. We assume that there is an existing requirement specification in some form. This is analyzed with the aim of finding which objects will exist in the system. The object models obtained are designed when we perform design and implementation. Finally, we will briefly discuss how testing is carried out.

## 4.3  Object-oriented analysis

The purpose of object-oriented analysis, as with all other analysis, is to obtain an understanding of the application: an understanding depending only on the system's functional requirements.

The difference between object-oriented analysis and function/data analysis is, as previously mentioned, the means of expression. While function/data analysis methods commence by considering the system's behavior and/or data separately, object-oriented analysis combines them and regards them as integrated objects. Object-oriented analysis can be characterized as an iteration between analyzing the behavior and information of the system. Moreover, object-oriented analysis uses the object-oriented techniques introduced in the previous chapter.

Object-oriented analysis contains, in some order, the following activities:

- Finding the objects
- Organizing the objects
- Describing how the objects interact
- Defining the operations of the objects
- Defining the objects internally

## 4.3.1   Finding the objects

The objects can be found as naturally occurring entities in the application domain. An object becomes typically a noun which exists in the domain and, because of this, it is often a good start to learn the terminology for the problem domain. By means of learning what is relevant in the application domain, the objects will be found. It is often the case that there is no problem in finding objects; the difficulty is usually in selecting those objects relevant to the system. The aim is to find the essential objects, which are to remain essential throughout the system's life cycle. As they are essential, they will probably always exist and, in this way, we hope to obtain a stable system. Stability also depends on the fact that modifications often begin from some of these items and therefore are local. For example, in an application for controlling a water tank, typical objects would include Contained Water, Regulator, Valve and Tank; for a banking application typical objects would include Customer, Account, Bank and Clerk.

The majority of object-oriented methods today have only one type of object. In this way, one obtains a simple and general model. Yet there are reasons for having several different object types: with only one object type, it can be quite difficult to see the difference between different objects. By having different object types, one can more quickly obtain an overview of the system. One can also obtain more support in improving the system's structure by having different rules for different objects. An example of this is that a passive object containing persistent information should not be dependent on objects which deal with the interface, as modifications in the interface are very common.

Different object types can be organized according to different criteria. Some examples are to group them by characteristics, such as active/passive, physical/conceptual, temporary/permanent/persistent, part/whole, generic/specific, private/public, shared/ non-shared.

### 4.3.2    Organizing the objects

There are a number of criteria to use for the classification and organization of objects and classes of objects. One classification starts by considering how similar classes of objects are to each other. This is normally the basis of inheritance hierarchy; a class can inherit another class. Another classification can be made by considering which objects work with which other objects, or how an object is a part of another; for example a house can be built of doors and windows. A similar classification is to see which objects are in some way dependent on another and thus have modification as a basis of grouping into subsystems.

### 4.3.3    Object interaction

In order to obtain a picture of how the object fits into the system, we can describe different scenarios or use cases in which the object takes part and communicates with other objects. In this way, we can fully describe the object's surroundings and what the other objects expect from our object. The object's interface can be decided from these scenarios. We then also consider how certain objects are part of other objects.

### 4.3.4    Operations on objects

The object's operations come naturally when we consider an object's interface. The operations can also be identified directly from the application, when we consider what can be done with the items we model. They can be primitive (for example, create, add, delete) or more complex such as putting together some report of information from several objects. If one obtains very complex operations, new objects can be identified from them. Generally, it is better to avoid objects that are too complex.

### 4.3.5 Object implementation

Finally, the object should be defined internally, which includes defining the information that each object must hold. Even the number of instances that can be created of each object is interesting; one may wish to have alternative ways of storing information. Some of the attributes can be inherited.

To summarize the above points, we can note that all of these steps are dependent on other steps and that, during development, these steps are typically worked with iteratively. It is important in an analysis phase to concentrate on understanding the problem domain, as the result here will affect the whole of the remaining work. Experience has shown that objects identified from the application domain are very stable and, after some work has been performed, both work and documentation will revolve around these objects.

We mentioned earlier that one of the advantages with object-oriented analysis is that it reduces the semantic distance between the domain and the model. This is due to the fact that object-oriented analysis bases the system structure on the human way of looking at reality, namely the objects, classification and hierarchical understanding used when people understand their surroundings. Thus the result of the object-oriented analysis is easier to understand and thus easier to maintain than the result of a function/data analysis.

Another advantage of object-oriented analysis is that items with a low modification probability are naturally identified and it is possible to isolate at an early stage items with a high probability of modification.

We shall see later how OOSE contains all of the above mentioned parts, in a slightly different order. Several of the issues discussed here are treated in OOSE in different ways. We shall postpone the discussion of OOSE analysis until a later chapter.

## 4.4 Object-oriented construction

Object-oriented construction means that the analysis model is designed and implemented in source code. This source code is executed in the target environment, which often means that the ideal model produced by the analysis model must be molded to fit into the implementation environment.

As with all design activities, it is difficult to achieve a good balance between structure and efficiency. The analysis model has provided us with an ideal structure which we shall try to keep as long as possible. It is, as you know, modification resistant. During the design, though, one must take care to follow all restrictive demands on the system, (for example, demands of the target environment, maximum memory usage, reliability and response times). All this can affect the structure.

The goal is that the objects identified during the analysis should also be found within the design. We call this **traceability.** We must therefore have straightforward rules for transforming the analysis model into a design model and the programming language.

The objects may be implemented using previously developed source code. We call such parts **components.** Such components are often simpler to create in an object-oriented environment, owing to the integration of functions and data.

Previously, we mentioned that object-oriented programming demands object-oriented system development as, otherwise, a difficult paradigm shift will occur. The opposite procedure, to go from object-oriented analysis to traditional programming, also incurs a paradigm shift. However, this causes less of a problem as, even for non-object-oriented languages, we can structure the system to be object-oriented. Additionally, we can program in an object-oriented style, even for other languages (see Jacky and Kalet (1987) or Linowes (1988)). Hence object-orientation is also a style of programming and not only the name of a programming language family having language constructs such as inheritance, encapsulation and polymorphism. A paradigm shift will occur, but it can be made relatively smooth. We shall later see that if we have, for example, a relational database, which is typically function/data oriented, we can incorporate this inside the objects and perform the paradigm shift locally.

Of course, many good techniques have been developed in function/data methods, which can also be used in object-oriented methods. Just because we shift paradigm, we should not forget all that we have learned. An example of a technique usable within object-orientation is state diagrams. In the chapter on construction, we shall see how these can be used to describe an object.

## 4.5   Object-oriented testing

The testing of a system which has been developed with an object-oriented method does not differ considerably from the testing of a system developed by any other method. In both cases, we verify the system, namely check that we have correctly designed the system in accordance with a specification. This verification should start as early as possible. The program testing begins at the lowest level, with unit testing, and progresses to integration testing, where the units are tested together to see that they interact correctly. Finally, testing of the entire system is done.

Traditionally, integration testing is usually a 'big bang' event and is very critical during system development. It is at this stage that the developed parts are put together and we then see whether they actually work together. Such a 'big bang' event is not as dramatic in an object-oriented system.

An object-oriented system consists of a number of objects which communicate with each other. These objects contain both data and behavior, which makes them larger units than the individual routines that one works with in a traditional system development method. An object's operations are developed around specific data and the same designers normally develop all operations for an object (see, nevertheless, the later discussion on inheritance). This leads to unit testing (that is, testing on the lowest level) becoming a test of a larger unit than in a traditionally developed system. Integration testing is carried out at an early stage, since communication is essential to the system development. All objects have predefined interfaces which also contribute to a less dramatic integration testing. The integration testing continues on higher levels and more and more objects are put together incrementally.

However, inheritance between classes can create new difficulties with testing. Inheritance means, as you know, that the operations defined in one class are inherited by another class and can also be executed there. Therefore, there may be abstract classes of which there will never be instances, as they only contain common parts from other classes. Is it worth testing these abstract classes? Normally it is worthwhile, since you have then tested an operation once instead of testing it several times in all descendants. However, one must be aware of how the classes are to be used in order to be able to test them properly. An operation in an abstract class may use properties that are changed in the descendants, so, when the context of an operation is changed, the operation normally needs to be retested in the new context.

Testing of inheritance hierarchies thus requires a more exhaustive testing method; you must be aware of how the system will appear in operation. For instance, as we have pointed out, it is not always true that if you test an operation higher up in an inheritance hierarchy a test is not required lower down. An operation can find itself in another (new) environment and may not have been tested in that environment. This means that if we modify an operation in an ancestor, we may need to test this operation in the descendants. In the same way, if we add a new descendant, we may need to test all the operations inherited by this descendant, as they will find themselves in a new environment. Regression and automated testing therefore often play a larger role in the testing of systems developed using an object-oriented technique. Here one must, though, be careful about which test data is used. If you override operations in a descendant, the test data developed earlier may not be adequate for the new operation. As test data often starts by testing possible ways to use an operation, it is not certain that the old test data can test the new operation. In extreme cases we may therefore need to develop special test data for each level in the inheritance hierarchy. Other problems in testing object-oriented software include polymorphism. We shall discuss OO testing in greater detail later.

Another problem arises if the object sends stimuli to itself. Such stimuli, perhaps, are only relevant in a descendant and it is therefore not worthwhile testing the abstract class in this situation. It requires a lot of work to go up and down in a class hierarchy in order to understand the consequences of a message which is sent to the object itself. This problem is called the Yoyo problem (see Taenzer *et al.* (1989)).

With an object-oriented approach, we can more or less consider a test to be an object. The test thus has a class (the test specification) and one or more instances (when we carry out the test). The test is encapsulated, since we are only concerned with the test result and not with how it runs internally. We can even inherit

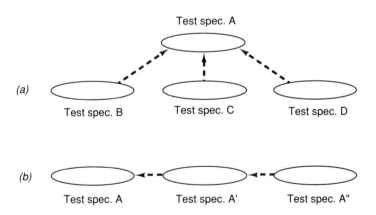

**Figure 4.6** Different ways to use inheritance between test specifications. In *(a)*, inheritance is used to describe similarities between different test specifications. In *(b)*, inheritance is used to describe the incremental development of a test specification.

common parts of the test specification when we either write the test specification or further develop a test (see Figure 4.6). In the first case, similar parts of test specifications, such as start-up sequences, can be reused. In the latter case, a test specification can evolve in different versions for different versions of the system.

## 4.6  Summary

The development of qualitative software systems should be carried out using a development method. Different methods focus on different quality properties. Additionally, different models have been proposed to describe the development, the most common by far being the waterfall model. Most developments, however, have an iterative nature.

Traditional methods treat functions and data as separate. Such an approach often leads to problems during maintenance since a function/data structure is quite sensitive to changes. Object-oriented methods do not separate functions and data, but view them as an integrated whole.

Object-oriented analysis aims at understanding the system to be developed and building a logical model of the system. This model is based on natural objects found in the problem domain. The objects hold data and have behavior in terms of which the entire system behavior can be expressed. Since objects in the problem domain will be stable, the overall structure of the system will normally be quite stable. Changes will of course occur but, since changes often come from the domain, it is hoped that these changes should be local and affect as few objects as possible.

The design and implementation of the analysis model is straightforward. The aim is to keep the logical structure of the analysis model in the final system. Thus an important characteristic of object-oriented development is to have built-in traceability. An object identified during analysis must be found again in the code so that the system is durable to easy modifications.

Testing of object-oriented systems does not substantially differ from testing other kinds of systems. The main differences are that the integration testing does not come as a 'big bang' event, but is done throughout the development. Although inheritance often leads to less code, it must not also lead to less testing – quite the opposite. Inheritance hierarchies may lead to more exhaustive testing whereby each inherited operation must be tested in each descendant class.

# 5 Object-oriented programming

## 5.1 Introduction

Object-oriented programming essentially means programming using objects and the other concepts introduced in Chapter 3. In this chapter, we describe how the concepts are used in a programming language and how they can be implemented. This style of programming has been used, until recently, only on a small scale. The major strengths of object-oriented programming are that it encourages the reuse of code and that it is usually easier to understand and maintain than other types of programming.

Defining what is and what is not object-oriented programming is a difficult task. Is it a style of programming or is it language dependent (one can write pure C programs in C++)? We believe it to be, essentially, a style of programming; but to optimize the use of this style of programming, a thorough understanding of the core concepts is required. One also requires a lot of knowledge to be able to use these techniques efficiently. The question of what a good object-oriented programming style is has been discussed in the literature. We shall not enter into this discussion here, but refer to other sources, such as Rochat (1986), Johnson and Foote (1988) and Lieberherr and Holland (1989).

We have previously introduced the essential concepts in object-orientation. An object-oriented language should, at least, support these concepts, so that the programmer can utilize them to the full. Hence an object-oriented language must support the following:

- Encapsulated objects
- The class and instance concepts
- Inheritance between classes
- Polymorphism

We shall describe how an object-oriented language operates by means of lifting its lid and studying its main machinery. The aim is to provide an understanding of the different parts of an object-oriented language. We will not present an exact picture, but will content ourselves with providing an outline of the principles. A more precise description of the details can be found in any book that describes a language, for example Goldberg and Robson (1983). We shall not dedicate ourselves to any specific programming language, but will mostly refer to an abstract syntax in our examples and only sometimes to an existing language, usually C++, Eiffel or Smalltalk. Different programming languages have sometimes chosen different solutions; we will discuss some of these when they are of extra interest. Further reading about the languages that we discuss here can be obtained as follows: for Smalltalk, see Goldberg and Robson (1983) or LaLonde and Pugh (1990, 1991a); for Eiffel, see Meyer (1988); for C++, see Lippman (1991) or Ellis and Stroustrup (1990); for Ada, see Barnes (1982, 1984) or Booch (1987b); for Simula, see Birtwistle *et al.* (1979) or Eriksson and Holm (1984); and for Objective-C, see Cox (1986). Peter Wegner (1987) has made a generally accepted classification of different programming languages in the object-based world. He states in this classification that Ada is object-based because it supports the object concept, although not the class concept. Simula, Eiffel, C++, Smalltalk and Objective-C are examples of object-oriented languages according to his classification since they also support the class and inheritance concepts.

To enable us to understand how the object appears, we shall use environments and algorithms to understand how these environments should be interpreted. Environments are used a lot within the LISP world. An environment describes an object's state and behavior. Environments can be illustrated in several ways, such as by a Weizenbaum diagram (Weizenbaum (1968)), or with frames (Abelson and Sussman (1985)). We shall illustrate the environments with diagrams similar to the Weizenbaum diagram. Such diagrams are a description technique in which the majority of programming language computation can be explained. An example is shown in Figure 5.1. By studying these diagrams, we shall examine how the programming language's machinery works.

This chapter's contents follow roughly the contents of the chapter on object-orientation. We begin by discussing the object concept, and see how this can be solved in a programming language. We then go on to discuss the class and instance concepts. Inheritance is discussed before polymorphism, as inheritance is often used to structure polymorphism in object-oriented languages. Polymorphism and the connection to dynamic binding are then discussed, along

| Variable | Value |
|:--------:|:-----:|
| A | 3 |
| B | 'atext' |
| C | nil |

**Figure 5.1**   Example of a Weizenbaum diagram.

with their mutual relationship. We shall use the same example that was used in the chapter on object-orientation to help us in our discussion and, because of this, we shall formalize it.

## 5.2  Objects

The most important concept that an object-oriented language must support is the object concept. Thus the language must support the definition of a set of operations for the object, namely the object's interface, and an implementation part for the object (which a user of the object should not know about). The object implementation is thus encapsulated and hidden from the user.

Each object has a well-defined interface which specifies which stimuli the object can receive, that is, which operations can be performed on the object. Each stimulus received causes an operation to be performed, where the stimulus is interpreted by the receiving object. If one tries to send a stimulus to an object which has no corresponding operation (that is, the stimulus is not represented in the object's interface), an error occurs.

An object is implemented internally as a number of variables which store information and a number of operations, or routines, for the object (see Figure 5.2). In Smalltalk, the only way to affect the internal variables is to perform an operation on the object. In C++ or Eiffel, for instance, it is possible to define whether the user should be able to directly access these variables.

Each object is able to receive a specified number of stimuli. The object interprets a stimulus and performs an operation or, perhaps, directly accesses a variable. In Smalltalk, this stimulus is called a message and the operation executed as a result of receiving a message is called a method. To be able to match stimulus and operation, they must have the same name. In Eiffel, the stimulus is not made explicit; instead the terminology is that an object performs an operation on another object. If we wanted to send a stimulus (for example, jump) to an object Tom, it may look as follows:

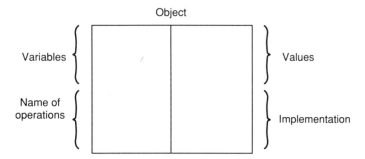

**Figure 5.2**   A Weizenbaum diagram for an object.

In Smalltalk:      tom jump
In C++:            tom−>jump();
In Eiffel:         tom.jump;
In Ada:            jump(tom);

We can see from the above example that the syntax in the different languages reflects the approach adopted by the program language designer. In Smalltalk, C++ and Eiffel, the object Tom is central and the operation is performed on tom. However, in Ada it is the operation which is central and operates on the object. We shall not describe how the object is internally structured in this section, but shall discuss this when we discuss class and instance, in the next section.

## 5.3   Classes and instances

In object-oriented languages, each object is described by a class. This class is both a module for source code and a type for the class instances. The programming language Ada comes close to this approach with the package concept, but the package in Ada is not a type. Inside a package, however, types can be defined with associated operations. These types can in turn be used to create objects, where the package's interface may specify the operations that can be performed on the object.

A class defines the operations that can be performed on an instance. It also defines the variables of the instance. A variable associated with a specific instance is often called an **instance variable**. These instance variables store the instance's state. All object-oriented languages have instance variables, even though they may have a different name. In Eiffel, the variable is called a field and the declaration of it is called an attribute, in accordance with Eiffel's main source of inspiration, Simula. The reason for calling them instance variables, and not just variables, is that some languages, such as Smalltalk and, in some senses, C++, have other variables which are only associated with the class. These are called **class variables**. Additionally, variables could also be local to a specific operation. These are called **temporary variables.**

Instances are created from the classes which declare the instance variables. The current values of these variables, though, are stored in the instances. The operations are thus defined in the class. An alternative is that, as with instance variables, they should exist in the instances as well. However, this would create much duplication, as the operations are identical for all instances of a specific class. Normally, therefore, each instance has a reference, instanceOf, to the class which contains all the operations (see Figure 5.3). By means of this reference, each instance is linked to its associated class. In such a way, the instances only store information unique to the individual instance, namely the instance variables, while information common to all instances, namely operations and (possibly) class variables, is stored in the class.

When an instance is to perform an operation, its associated class selects the required operation and performs it using the instance's variables. This means that when an operation reads or

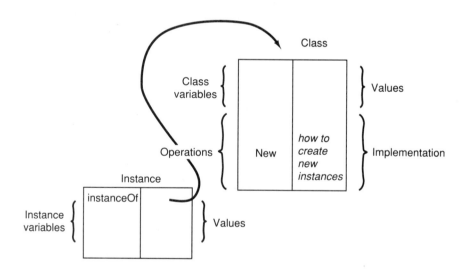

**Figure 5.3**   Class and instance environment. The class contains the names of operations and their implementation. The instance contains the variables and the values unique to the instance.

writes an instance variable, the current instance's variables are used. The operation is selected by finding an operation that has the same name as the stimulus (and, possibly, even the correct parameter set-up). The machinery which interprets a stimulus sent to an instance therefore operates according to Algorithm 5.1.

---

**Algorithim 5.1**   Operation of the machinery to interpret a stimulus

---

Given an instance and a stimulus to the instance:
1. In the environment referred to by instanceOf, that is, the associated class, the operation corresponding to the stimulus' name is searched for.
2. Interpret the selected operation using both the stimulus' parameters and the instance's environment.
3. Return any values from the execution of the operation.

---

The algorithm uses the stimulus name to access the required operation from within a table in the class. When a stimulus is sent to an object, an operation is performed by applying the algorithm that uses both the stimulus and a specified environment.

As the instance's environment only consists of information unique to itself, and all operations are stored in the instance's class, one must be able to perform the same operations on all instances. The difference is in the environments in which they are executed. Normally, all operations can access all instance variables. The operation environment is thus the current instance's environment (see Figure 5.4).

For an instance to be able to send a stimulus to another instance, a variable will have to exist to reference the other instance. Figure 5.5 illustrates an example of how a variable, aPerson, in the instance Mary, refers to another instance, Tom. Thus, in order to send a stimulus Jump to Tom, the instance Mary would need to execute the following:

aPerson.Jump

When the instance referred to by aPerson receives this stimulus, the algorithm outlined above is performed. Thus Tom interprets Jump and performs the behavior associated with this operation.

Encapsulation, and the approach from abstract data types, mean that there is only one way to affect an object's state, and that is through its operations. Thus variables can only be directly accessed by defining an appropriate operation. This approach is chosen in Smalltalk, for instance. It is recommended, though, that if an

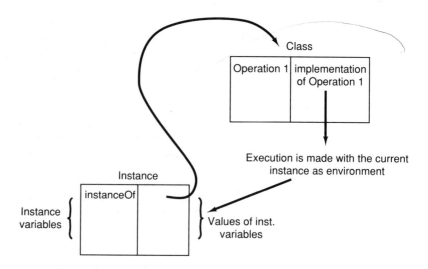

**Figure 5.4** Different instances execute the same operation, but in different environments. This means that it is the instance's variables which are used by the operation.

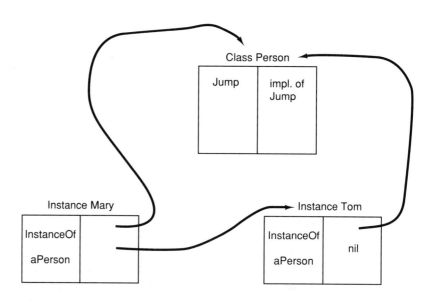

**Figure 5.5** The instance variable aPerson refers to the instance Tom (nil means that nothing is referenced).

operation is to read a variable, then the operation should have the same name as the variable. In Simula, which is an old language, all instance variables are accessible even from outside the object, unless the variable has been explicitly declared as *protected*. In Eiffel, a compromise between the above two methods has been made: all instance variables are inaccessible, unless the opposite is explicitly stated. This means that if we execute the expression:

Age := Aperson.myAge;

in, for example, Eiffel or Simula, we do not really know if the operation myAge is performed or if we only read the variable myAge. This is an elegant solution since we could change the implementation without changing an object's clients.

Some languages also support the notion of class variables and class operations. An example of the information class variables may contain is how many instances are created from this class. Several programming languages do not allow the programmer to declare and use class variables. This is the case in Eiffel, for example, where the distinction between the class and the instance is carefully made. The class is viewed as a description, or the program text, while instances are viewed as executions of the program text. Thus instances are the only things that execute during run-time, and not classes. In Smalltalk, and to a certain extent in Objective-C, classes are regarded as instances of a metaclass (see the box on classes as objects). In C++, the programmer hasn't really the capability to declare class variables, but can declare an instance variable as 'static', which gives all instances the same value for this variable. In such a way, it can be used as a class variable.

**Classes as objects**

Some object-oriented programming languages also view classes as objects, that is, as instances of another class. This is the case in Smalltalk and Objective-C. An advantage of this is that it is possible to send a stimulus to a class and thus affect all its (existing and not yet created) instances. If, for example, we want all cars manufactured from now on to be blue, it is easy to express this using class variables and operations. By regarding classes as objects, a more flexible system is obtained, allowing classes to be modified during execution (which makes it more difficult to understand the classes).

As classes are now referred to as instances, they must be instances of some class. This class is often called a **metaclass.** Each class has therefore been supplied with a reference, instanceOf, which refers to this metaclass. Figure 5.6 illustrates the use of a metaclass. A metaclass contains operations which all classes can understand. Thus

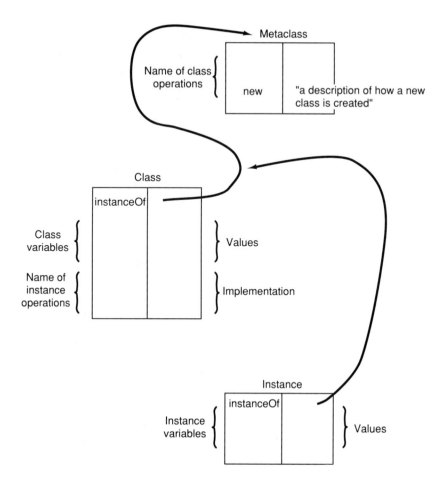

**Figure 5.6**   Classes and metaclasses.

all classes have, at least, the protocol defined by the metaclass. For example, the operation 'new' is often defined in the metaclass. In Smalltalk-78, there is only one metaclass common for all classes, but in Smalltalk-80, each class has an individual metaclass. In this way, a whole shadow hierarchy is found behind the 'real' class hierarchy.

Which class is the metaclass an instance of? In Smalltalk-78, the problem of this potential limitless chain has been solved by naming the root class Object as the metaclass' instanceOf. In Smalltalk-80, the solution is more complicated.

Metaclasses are really only a method for implementing the class concept and the underlying system. Even if it is possible, the average programmer should not use metaclasses. The more advanced user can, by means of modifying the metaclasses, modify the language's syntax and semantics; but, as mentioned, this is not recommended for the average programmer.

Languages such as Eiffel, C++ and Simula have chosen not to consider classes as objects. In Eiffel, this is a very deliberate choice, as the class is regarded as implementing a type, while the object is regarded as an instance of this type. The class is static and described in the program text, while the instance is dynamic and exists only during execution. Thus, in Eiffel, the distinction between description and corresponding execution is made fundamental. The aim with this approach is to avoid any misunderstanding and obtain a clear distinction between class and instance.

Normally, operations are only performed on instances, but some languages allow operations to be performed directly on the class. In the same way as with instance and class variables, we can also have instance operations and class operations. Class operations are normally used to operate on class variables or to create new instances. In Smalltalk, class operations are common, while in Eiffel, they have been avoided so as to separate clearly the description from the execution.

However, every programming language has operations for creating new instances. This can be seen as a class operation as it operates on the class. In Smalltalk, this is not significant, but in Eiffel, it is considered to be an exception. The stimulus is often named new (Smalltalk, C++, Simula and Objective-C) or Create (Eiffel). The stimulus is sent directly to the class, as there will be no instance, as yet, that can receive it. Each class has, therefore, an operation (corresponding to) new or Create, and when the class receives the stimulus, a new instance is created by allocating storage area for the instance and initiating instance variables (set to default values). The operation also makes sure that one of the instance variables, instanceOf, refers to the instance's class. Figure 5.7 shows, using Smalltalk/V, Eiffel and a Weizenbaum diagram, how classes are declared with instance variables, how an instance Tom is created, how aPerson is specified to reference Tom and how Tom is made to Jump.

## 5.4 Inheritance

Inheritance means that we can develop a new class merely by stating how it differs from another, already existing class. The new class

| Smalltalk/V | Eiffel |
|---|---|
| (1)  Object subclass:  #Person | (1)  **class** Person |
| (2)  inst.variable: 'aPerson' | (2)  APerson : Person; |
| (3)  jump ... | (3)  Jump **is** ... |
| (4)  aperson := Person new: 'Tom'. | (4)  aPerson := Person.Create("Tom"); |
| (5)  aPerson jump. | (5)  aperson.Jump; |

**Weizenbaum diagram**

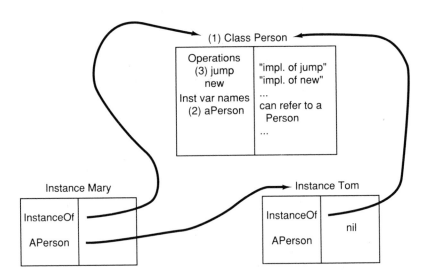

**Figure 5.7**  (1) Declaration of a class. (2) Declaration of an instance variable. (3) Declaration of an operation. (4) Creation of a new instance (Tom). (5) Jump is sent to Tom. The example shows Smalltalk/V, Eiffel and a Weizenbaum diagram. The code is not complete.

then inherits the existing class. The main advantage with this approach is that existing classes can be reused to a great extent. The more general classes are placed higher up in the inheritance hierarchy, whereas the more specialized ones are placed lower down. It is not only classes which have been designed for the current system that can be reused, but also those designed earlier, maybe in earlier projects. In Smalltalk, this is one of the major ideas. Smalltalk is delivered with an extensive class library and, as such, the programming is based to a large extent on reusing these classes. Even other object-oriented languages, such as C++, Eiffel and Objective-C, have class libraries.

The inheritance mechanism thus simplifies the process of reuse. In traditional programming languages, procedures are the reuse 'level', but in an object-oriented programming language, the reuse levels are classes. A class contains several operations (procedures) and a data structure. This makes the reuse of classes a much more powerful feature than the reuse of procedures. The inheritance mechanism enables the reuse of whole classes and class hierarchies. However, inheritance is not a prerequisite for reuse, as will be discussed in Chapter 11.

Inheritance enables modifications to be performed in a simple way, as a property common to several classes is implemented in a class inherited by these classes. If we wish to modify this property, we need only modify the corresponding ancestor to update the characteristic in all descendants.

As a result of an operation being possibly defined in a class higher up in the inheritance hierarchy, the previously outlined algorithm for operation searching will need to be slightly modified. If we cannot find the operation in the instance's class, we must proceed to the class' parent, and so on. Thus the class must have a reference, parent, to its parent class. Figure 5.8 illustrates this.

If the operation does not exist in the environment referred to by parent, then the search is continued upwards in the hierarchy until, if necessary, the root class is accessed. (The root class is the class at the top, that is, the root, of the inheritance hierarchy.) If the operation is still not found in the root class, then there is no interpretation for the received stimulus and an error occurs. Algorithm 5.2 for binding a stimulus to an operation will, therefore, now look as follows:

---

**Algorithm 5.2**   Binding a stimulus to an operation with inheritance

---

Given an instance environment and a stimulus to the instance:

1. In the environment referred to by instanceOf the operation corresponding to the stimulus' name is searched for.

2. If the operation is not found, perform Step 1 in the environment referred to by parent. Continue until the operation is found. If parent does not refer fo another class, the stimulus is unknown. In this case perform error handling.

3. Interpret the corresponding operation using both the stimulus' parameters and the instance's environment.

4. Return any values from the execution of the operation.

---

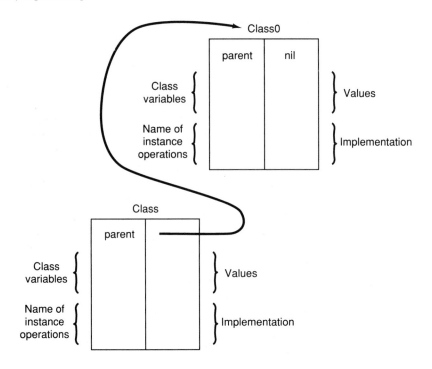

**Figure 5.8**   Environment for inheriting classes.

Inheritance can be used in different ways, as discussed in Chapter 3. Abstract classes can be used to define a common protocol for several classes. The protocol then only provides the operation's signature, that is, which stimuli can be received, while the actual implementation may exist in the descendants. Thus the implementation can be different for different descendants (see also below on polymorphism).

Inheritance can, as previously mentioned, be used to reuse an implementation. This type of reuse can sometimes contradict the intuitive picture one has of inheritance. A typical example is how the relation between a stack and a double-ended queue (deque) should be shown. Which class should inherit which? If we regard inheritance as a way of expressing conceptual relations then neither of the solutions will be appropriate. A double-ended queue is not a stack, nor is a stack a double-ended queue. The reason for wishing to inherit in this situation is to reuse code. The implementation existing for one can be used for the other. As, in this case, it is only the implementation that is required, it is possible to declare, in a class stack, an instance variable to reference the deque. The operations push and pop can then use suitable operations on the local deque for its implementation (see Figure 5.9).

```
class DEQUE[T] export
   add _ at _ front, add _at _ back,
   get _at _ front, get _at _ back, ...

feature

   ...
   add _ at _front (x: T) is
      -- add x at front of deque
   do
      ...
   end -- add_at_front

   get _at _ front : T is
      -- get element at front of deque
   do
         ...
   end -- get _at _front

   ...



class STACK[T] export
   push, pop, ...

feature
   store: DEQUE[T];
   max _size : INTEGER;

   Create (n : INTEGER) is
         – Create a stack with depth n
   do
      store.Create(l,n);
      max _size:=n;
   end – Create

   push(x: T) is
         – Add x on top of stack
   do
      store.add _at _first(x)
   end – push

   pop: T is
         – get top of stack
   do
      Result:=store.get _at _front
   end – pop

   ...
```

**Figure 5.9**   How an implementation can be reused without using inheritance. Eiffel-like syntax is used.

It seems wrong to use inheritance in the above example, as it contradicts what was discussed as proper use of inheritance in Chapter 3. As an alternative to inheritance for reusing code, composition can be used (see Taenzer *et al.* (1989)). This means that we can use classes when we develop new classes, not by inheriting them, but by creating instances of them and using these instances, as in the example above. Thus designing a class with the help of instances from other classes is another way to reuse code: when we implemented the stack, in the above example, we reused the deque by creating instances of it. It is thus possible to reuse code by using two totally different strategies, with inheritance or through composition, even though they have completely different characteristics. Both these methods are very powerful and should be used in programming. Lieberman (1986) discusses delegation of common behavior between objects as a complete alternative to inheritance.

Partition hierarchies, as discussed in Chapter 3, are very useful for showing how the system is constructed, and should be used together with an inheritance hierarchy. These hierarchies enable classes to be structured in a different way to the inheritance hierarchy. Partition hierarchies provide a hierarchy between classes, where class instances can delegate behavior to other instances.

When should we use inheritance hierarchy and when should we use other hierarchies, such as partition hierarchy? The use of inheritance was discussed extensively in Chapter 3. We will here only highlight one simple rule for this decision. We can often view inheritance as 'is-A' and partition as 'has-A'. A dog *is* a mammal and a house *has* a door. This simple rule though, is not always sufficient. In languages which allow us to control which operations, including inherited operations, are accessible to individual users, such as C++ and Eiffel, we can specify which operations a user has access to. In C++, we do this by specifying them as public and, in Eiffel, by placing them in the export clause. However, in Smalltalk, a user has access to all inherited operations and it is not possible to specify the protocol used by an object, as this is controlled by the inheritance hierarchy. We can see that both strategies have advantages and disadvantages, and so the one selected will depend on a number of factors, some of which were discussed in Chapter 3. Efficiency and how the hierarchy is to be used are two other factors affecting this choice.

The number of inheritance hierarchies in a system varies between different languages. In Smalltalk, there is only one inheritance hierarchy, and thus one root class. Behavior, which is common to all system classes, is collected and stored in a root class which in Smalltalk is called Object. All classes inherit Object, either directly or indirectly. Examples of behavior which may be common to instances of all classes are: the test for determining which class an instance is associated with; comparison between instances; copying of instances; and so on. As Object does not have any parent class, it is also used for error handling in Smalltalk.

In Eiffel, C++ and Simula, several parallel inheritance hierarchies can exist. You can therefore create different hierarchies for different structures in the system. It is thus possible to create new classes without using the existing ones. Both approaches have their advantages and disadvantages. Smalltalk is often used for training in object-oriented programming, as it forces the programmer to work with the inheritance hierarchy. When a new class is to be created, the class *has* to be placed somewhere in the inheritance tree. In this way the programmer is forced to think according to the inheritance hierarchy and also to consider which class is to be used as a basis for the new class to be developed. Programmers who have previously worked in C and begin using C++ may have difficulties both in building inheritance hierarchies and in identifying abstract classes. Therefore C-programmers may initially be trained in Smalltalk and later continue in C++, so that they are forced to learn the use of an inheritance hierarchy and thus learn to use the inheritance mechanism in C++ to a greater extent.

Encapsulation and inheritance are both essential within object-oriented programming. Irrespective of this, though, they are somewhat incompatible with each other. Encapsulation means that the user of a class should not see its internal representation; but, if we regard a descendant of a class as a user of the class, then the user has complete access to the internal parts of the class. This contradiction is due to the fact that we have three types of user: those who use the class via its interface, those who use the class through inheritance, and those who actually implement the class. In C++, therefore, three possibilities for encapsulation of operations and data structures are used: 'public' means that all three user types can access the class operations, 'protected' means that only the class itself or descendants of the class can access the parts of the class, and 'private' means that only the class itself can access the parts. Of course, these three types are combined when a class is developed. The problem with inheritance and encapsulation has been discussed by, for example, Snyder (1986) and Meyer (1988).

## 5.5 Polymorphism

The algorithm discussed in the previous section shows clearly that the receiving instance is responsible for searching for and finding the appropriate operation to be executed. Polymorphism means that the transmitter of a stimulus does not need to know the class of the receiving instance. The transmitter provides only a request for a specified event, while the receiver knows how to perform this event. In this section, we discuss both how polymorphism can be implemented and how it behaves in relation to dynamic binding. The consequences for both typed and non-typed languages are also briefly discussed.

The linking of the received stimulus to the appropriate operation to be executed is performed by binding the stimulus to this operation. If this binding occurs during compilation, it is said to be a **static binding**. The polymorphic characteristic sometimes makes it impossible to determine at compile time which class an instance belongs to and thus to decide which operation to perform. This information will not be available until execution time, when it must of course be known. If this binding occurs when the stimulus is actually sent, that is during run-time, it is said to be **dynamic binding**. Other names for this are late, delayed and virtual binding. Dynamic binding is flexible, but reduces performance; in principle, the operation look-up algorithm is now carried out during execution. This means that each time a stimulus is sent, the algorithm mentioned in the previous section must be executed. However, in most language implement-ations, sophisticated caching strategies or special function tables are used to minimize this overhead. The advantage with dynamic binding is the flexible system obtained. This flexibility is of most use to systems which are regularly modified. By not binding before execution, many of the modifications made will not affect the transmitting object.

Static binding, however, is more secure and efficient. It is more secure, if we have a typed language, owing to errors being noticed at the time of compilation and not left to cause failures during run-time. It is more efficient due to the operation look-up algorithm being performed only once during the compilation.

Polymorphism often conveys the message that the receiver of a stimulus cannot bind the stimulus to an operation before the stimulus is actually sent during run-time (as the class is unknown until then). If we do not know beforehand (during compilation) which operation is to be executed on the receipt of a certain stimulus, then we must use some kind of dynamic binding. Dynamic binding is therefore a way of implementing the polymorphism characteristic.

The word 'polymorphism' originates from Greek and means 'many forms' or 'many types'. This means that the referenced item can be of different types. How does this relate to non-typed languages such as Smalltalk? Is polymorphism useful for non-typed languages?

Yes, it is. The confusion occurs because Smalltalk is often referred to as being a non-typed language. In reality, though, it is the *variables* in Smalltalk that lack type, whereas each instance has a very clear type, namely its class. It is this type that is referred to when discussing polymorphism in Smalltalk. In Smalltalk, polymorphism is normally not restricted through the use of an inheritance hierarchy (see below), as is often the case with strongly typed languages. In Smalltalk, the referenced instance can be associated with any class in the system.

In strongly typed languages, however, such as Eiffel, Simula and C++, each reference to an instance has a type that specifies the classes to which the reference can refer. When the program text is written, the variables are declared and the stimuli to be sent are specified. Both the instance's class and the stimuli to be sent must be known at that time. Consequently, it should be known at the time of compilation which operations are to be executed and we should be able to bind the operation and stimulus statically. Is polymorphism then useful for strongly typed languages? Yes, but the reason is that we need not specify *exactly* with which class the receiving instance is associated. Typically we only specify that the instance shall be associated with class A or some of class A's descendants. The operation can be defined in a descendant and we thus cannot bind before execution, as it is only then known *exactly* with which class the instance is associated.

Polymorphism can, in fact, be used without having dynamic binding. This is the case if we have declared a variable containing a pointer to an instance, and the type of the variable is a parent of the instance's class, and the operation to be performed is declared in this parent class and is not overridden in any descendant. Irrespective of the descendant class with which the instance is associated, the exact operation will be known during compile time. We can then statically bind the operation to the stimulus. Note that we have still used polymorphism, as we do not know *exactly* to which class the actual instance belonged.

An uncertainty arises though, if the operation, in the above mentioned case, is redefined in a descendant. Can we still statically bind the operation? No, since we do not know the actual class associated with the instance and thus we do not know the correct operation. In Eiffel, dynamic binding will occur in all situations. In C++ and Simula, however, the language designer has in this case chosen to statically bind the stimulus to the operation known during compilation, namely that which applies in the parent class. This is then regarded as a deliberate choice by the programmer. If you want to delay operation binding until execution, you can declare an operation as 'virtual', which means that it can be redeclared in a

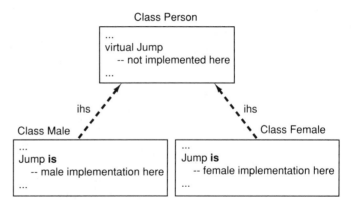

**Figure 5.10**   Example of use of virtual operations.

descendant. Then we force the compiler to postpone the binding until run-time. In Eiffel, you can only declare an operation in a parent and force descendants to implement it (this is called a deferred routine in Eiffel). This is used when there is no implementation in the parent class to force the descendants to implement the operation. Figure 5.10 illustrates an example of the use of virtual operations.

Dynamic binding can also be used without using poly-morphism, as in Prolog for example, where a variable can be bound to an arbitrary term that has no type. Dynamic binding and polymorphism can thus be used independently of each other, and it is unfortunate that the two concepts are often confused in the object-oriented community.

## 5.6   An example

We shall here consider how we can use the classes from Chapter 3 to construct a whole game, where people interact with each other. The people involved are a father with his two sons, a woman and an anonymous person. We shall begin by looking at the class Game:

```
Class Game
             parent    GeneralGame
    instance Variables    first_son : Male
                          second_son : Male
                          woman : Female
                          father : Male
                          aPerson : Person

               new    "how to create a new game instance"
```

```
startGame   first_son := youngMale new("John")
            second_son := youngMale new("Tom")
            woman := Female.new("Mary")
            father := oldMale.new("Donald")

            .  .  .

            woman.storeAge(27)
            woman.friend(father)
            second_son.jump
            first_son.walk

            .  .  .

            woman.dance
            aPerson := first_son
            aPersonjump

            .  .  .

            aPerson := father
            aPerson.jump
```

The class is created as a direct descendant of the existing class GeneralGame. The instance variables of the game are declared. Game has two operations: new, which creates and initiates a new game instance, and startGame, which starts a game. To create an instance of the class Game, the following expression is executed:

```
currentGame : = Game.new
```

The operation new, in the class Game, is now executed and an instance of Game is created. The instance's environment will be as follows:

```
Instance currentGame
        instanceOf   Class Game

        first_son    nil
      second_son     nil
          woman      nil
          father     nil
         aPerson     nil
```

We can see that the instance contains the instance variables declared in the class. The instance variables have not yet received any values and therefore have a value of nil (no reference). In order to create new people which the instance variables can reference, we require classes for them. We therefore use the class structure developed in Chapter 3, with a class Person, two classes Male and Female which inherit Person, and two classes oldMale and youngMale which inherit Male. The class Person is created as a descendant to the class Object, and is as follows:

Class Person

| | |
|---|---|
| *parent* | Object |
| *instance Variables* | name : String<br>age : Integer<br>myHead : Head<br>myLegs : Legs<br>myBody : Body |
| new | myHead := Head.new<br>myLegs := Legs.new<br>age := 0 |
| StoreAge(Age) | age := Age |
| Age? | **return** age |
| walk | myLegs.walk |

Note that the operation new creates new instances of Head and Legs, but not of Body. This is due to males and females having different bodies and this difference is specified in classes Male and Female. These two classes are direct descendants of Person and implement individually their differences from Person. When new is performed on a class, it thus must execute in both the actual class and all its parent classes.

Class Male

| | |
|---|---|
| *parent* | Person |
| *instance Variables* | – – |
| new | myBody := MaleBody. new |
| jump | myLegs.bend<br>myLegs.stretch<br>myBody.jump |

Class Female

| | |
|---|---|
| *parent* | Person |
| *instance Variables* | friend : Person |
| new 1 | myBody := FemaleBody.new |
| Friend(name) | friend :=name |
| jump | myLegs.bend<br>myLegs.stretch<br>myBody.jump |
| dance | friend.dance<br>myBody.shake<br>myLegs.bend<br>myHead.shake<br>myLegs stretch |

Note that myBody is a polymorphic reference as it can refer to instances of both classes MaleBody and FemaleBody. These classes are not shown, and their creation is an exercise for the reader. The classes oldMale and youngMale contain two variations of the operation dance and their declaration may also be exercises for the reader.

In order to start the game, we perform the operation startGame on the instance currentGame. Thus we execute the following statement:

currentGame.startGame;

When this is executed, instances will be created as specified in the operation startGame. We show here only the instance woman after execution of this operation:

Instance
woman *instanceOf*   Class Female

| | |
|---|---|
| name | 'Mary' |
| age | 27 |
| friend | [reference to "father" instance] |
| myHead | [reference to woman's Head] |
| myLegs | [reference to woman's Legs] |
| myBody | [reference to woman's Body (Female)] |

## 5.7   Summary

Object-oriented programming is a style of programming where the core concepts of object-orientation are used. In this chapter we have looked at mechanisms for these concepts.

The things to program in an object-oriented programming language are the classes. In the class, the programmer defines the variables and the operations associated with the class and instances of the class. From these classes, instances are dynamically created during execution of the program.

Inheritance provides a mechanism for creating new classes as modifications to existing classes. However, since an operation can be implemented in an ancestor class, an operation look-up alghorithm must be executed to find the correct operation. Inheritance is not a prerequisite for reuse. The construction of a new class can very well benefit from existing classes without inheriting them.

Polymorphism can be implemented using dynamic binding. This means that the actual binding of a stimulus to a specific operation is not done until the stimulus is actually sent during run-time. This often means that the operation look-up must be done dynamically during run-time. However, many language implementations have solved this efficiently so that the look-up overhead cost is minimized.

# Part II
# Concepts

# 6 Architecture

## 6.1 Introduction

This chapter discusses the architecture of the pyramid (see Figure 6.1). Here, we wish to provide a reason and motivation for the models created and the concepts used when working with Object-Oriented Software Engineering, OOSE. The chapter is relatively abstract, and thus may be skipped on the first reading. It is intended for readers who wish to obtain a deeper understanding of the architecture layer.

### 6.1.1 System development

In an organization, work is continually modified. One of the means we use to carry out these modifications is to develop new systems. Here, we use the concept 'system development' to describe the work that occurs when we develop computer support to aid an organization. We wish to emphasize the importance of regarding system development as a means for supporting parts of an organization. Thus the system should be seen from the organization's and user's perspective.

When a requirement for a system is identified, system development begins. The requirement and picture of the system

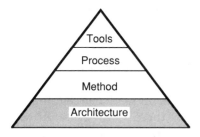

**Figure 6.1** This chapter discusses the architecture layer of OOSE.

become firmly identified. Eventually, we decide to develop the system and write a requirement specification in some form, describing what we wish to obtain from the system. If the system is to be developed by someone outside the organization, this specification is used as the basis for obtaining quotations and ordering the system; if the system is to be developed internally, the specification is used to plan and control the development process. (Often all of this is actually enterprise modeling, which produces a requirement specification (in one form or another), but since we do not discuss enterprise modeling in this book, this naive view of it will be sufficient.)

From this requirement specification, we develop the system. Our wish is to deliver a system with the required functionality and quality, and make it as effective as possible. When delivery has been made, the most important period for the system begins, namely its operation. This will comprise a large amount of maintenance and further system development, and may span some decades. This is often the most expensive part of system development, that is, of the system's life-cycle cost.

One can, of course, debate whether all these activities belong to the same system development or are actually several different ones, but this is not of interest to our discussion here. What is of interest is that this process goes on for a long time and that maintenance and further development form a major part of this process. This is not unique to the development of software systems, but is true for all manufacturing industries. What is unique, though, is that development of software systems is extremely complex, and that we handle this complexity poorly (see Brooks (1987)).

OOSE may be used from the time that the requirement specification exists in some form, and all through the system's lifetime until it is replaced by another system; that is, we include new development, further development and maintenance of the system in the period of OOSE use. We have even gone so far as to say that the main case is further development of a system and that new development is only a special case of this, even though it is a very important case.

## 6.1.2    Object-orientation, conceptual modeling and block design

As mentioned in Chapter 2, the basis of our approach originates from three totally different techniques which have all been used for a long time. These are object-oriented programming, conceptual modeling and block design.

**Object-oriented programming** started with Simula, which was developed at the Norwegian Computing Center during the 1960s. It was developed initially as an extension of ALGOL to handle simulation applicatons (see Dahl and Nygaard (1966)), but it was soon discovered by a few groups that it was usable for many other application areas too. However, it was not until the 1980s that object-oriented programming established itself widely. The real breakthrough was due to object-oriented programming being very suitable for developing Graphical User Interfaces (GUIs). Such systems are difficult to describe with traditional programming languages. It is actually only during recent years that it has been widely noticed that object-orientation is usable in most application areas. So object-oriented programming has had quite a difficult childhood, often being rejected. The concepts we have borrowed from object-oriented programming are mainly those of encapsulation, inheritance and the relationship between classes and instances.

**Conceptual modeling** has been used in several different contexts since it appeared in the 1970s; examples are analysis of information management systems and organization theory. The aim is to create models of the system or organization to be analyzed. Depending on which system and which aspects one wishes to model, different conceptual models are created. As one normally models a system where information handling is central, the concept of conceptual modeling is often used as a synonym for data modeling and is often discussed with structuring and the use of databases. For more information on conceptual modeling, see Hull and King (1987), Tsichritzis and Lochovsky (1982) or Brodie *et al.* (1984). In OOSE, we have expanded the technique with object-oriented concepts and the ability to express dynamic behavior. The models we develop are used mainly to understand the system and to obtain a good system architecture. These models form the basis for the actual system design.

The method of **block design** originates from Ericsson, a Swedish telecommunications company, and was developed from the 1960s onwards. It is now in widespread use over the whole telecommunications area, but has also been used in totally different application areas. The ideas were developed from considering how hardware was designed. A number of modules, each providing a specific functionality, were connected together with well-defined interfaces. One should be able to do the same thing with software: collect together programs and data into modules (blocks) and describe their mutual communication through interfaces. A new software approach was required in an attempt to avoid the problems that a program error could create; an error could shut down the whole system. By encapsulating program and data, these program errors would have less effect. By working with blocks, it was easier to change and introduce new functionality during operation; a new block is loaded and only one pointer is changed to point to the new block. Additionally, whether certain parts of a system would be developed in software or hardware was not clear. It was thus desirable to be able to change the implementation easily. Now the technique has been generalized and simplified to be usable in several different application areas. It is mainly used during construction. Most of the fundamental concepts were already present in the late 1960s and early 1970s. Furthermore, the early modeling concepts were proposed as contributions to the development of the CCITT standard, the Specification and Description Language (SDL). Concepts like blocks with encapsulation of data and behavior, signals between these blocks, and what we now call service packages were present, as well as the interaction diagram technique, in those early days.

These three techniques, which have all been used for a long time, have thus been background technologies for OOSE as described in this book. Note that this approach was developed long before many of the widespread methods used today in object-oriented development; see Coad and Yourdon (1991) or Booch (1991). Thus these methods could not have been background technologies for OOSE. The ideas and working methods have been put together and the concepts made unambiguous and related to each other. The result has shown itself to be a powerful and flexible development method. The technique should not be seen as being fully developed, as further development occurs continuously. We have also started to generalize the method, so that it can be used in even more areas. The latest domain in which we have started to work is enterprise modeling. Just for interest, we can mention here that we use the method, to a large extent, to develop the method itself (see further details in Appendix A). We thus regard Objectory as a system to be developed further in new versions.

We shall discuss first in this chapter what we wish to obtain from an architecture for a system development method, process and tools, and what problems we really want to solve. Common characteristics within all the models are then discussed. Each model is thereafter covered in an individual section, where the model's object types are briefly presented. The discussion in these sections is informal and aims to give an intuitive understanding of the architecture.

# 6.2   System development is model building

### 6.2.1   Models

System development is a complex task. Several different aspects must be taken into consideration. What we wish to achieve is a reliable computer program that performs its tasks properly. But typically system development is such a complex task that we cannot cope very well with handling so many requirements simultaneously. It may be the case that for very small programs we can take the requirements and write the program directly, but this is utterly implausible for the systems discussed here. What we need to do is to handle the complexity in an organized way. We do this by working with different models, each focusing on a certain aspect of the system. By introducing the complexity gradually in a specific order in successive models, we are able to manage the system complexity.

We work with five different models:

- The **requirements model** aims to capture the functional requirements.
- The **analysis model** aims to give the system a robust and changeable object structure.
- The **design model** aims to adopt and refine the object structure to the current implementation environment.
- The **implementation model** aims to implement the system.
- The **test model** aims to verify the system.

Each model tries to capture some part or aspect of the system to be built. These models are the output of the activities shown in Figure 6.2 which are discussed in the forthcoming chapters. We will discuss in more detail later how the models relate to the different activities.

Actually, other types of model may be appropriate and thus also be used (for example, specific hardware models) and some of the

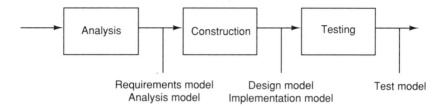

**Figure 6.2**   The models developed associated with the processes that produce them.

models can be merged or only used as working models and not saved. However, we have found these models appropriate to several different kinds of applications of varying size. When discussing the different activities in subsequent chapters we will also give some comments on how this model structure can be modified for certain reasons.

The basic idea with these models is to capture right from the start all the functional requirements of the system from a user perspective. This is accomplished in the **requirements model**. Here we describe how a potential user will use the system. This model is often developed in close participation with end users and orderers. When this model becomes stable, the system is structured from a logical perspective into a form that is robust and, above all, maintainable during the system life cycle. This is done in the **analysis model**. Here, we assume an ideal implementation environment; that is, we do not take into consideration which DBMS to use, hardware, the current implementation language, whether the system should be distributed or not, real-time requirements and so on. We have two main reasons for this. The first is that it is much easier to work with ideal circumstances: it allows us to reduce complexity and thus focus efforts on giving the application a stable, robust and logical structure. Secondly, the implementation environment will change during the life cycle – think what has happened with hardware technology in the past ten years – and we do not want the current circumstances to affect the system structure. However, the world is not ideal. When we have developed an ideal structure, we adopt this maintainable structure with as little violation as possible in the **design model**. The reason for this is that we want the design model to be maintainable as well. In this model we decide, for instance, how to integrate a relational DBMS into the application or how to handle a distributed environment. Whereas the analysis model mostly cannot be implemented straightforwardly, the design model should be. When all of these decisions are made and the application further refined and formalized, the **implementation model** is gradually developed. This is the actual code to be composed and/or written. Finally the **test model** is developed to support the verification of the developed system. This mainly involves documentation of test specifications and test results.

The system is gradually refined using these models. The models should not be viewed as sacred or 'the final answer' or anything like that. Every organization must decide which models are appropriate to use. We have found that these models form a sound base on which to develop many kinds of systems, and that it is possible to manage the complexity as it is introduced step by step in the models. By focusing on the more important aspects early, a base which enables the system structure to be modifiable is laid.

The relations between these models are of course important. The transitions between the models are **seamless**. By seamless we mean that we are able to tell, in a foreseeable way, how to get from objects in one model to objects in another model. This is absolutely crucial for an industrial development process since the result must be repeatable. The method layer will define these transformation rules. To be able to maintain the system it is also necessary to have **traceability** between the models. By this we mean that we are able to trace objects in one model to objects in another model. Traceability will in our case actually come as a side-effect of the seamless nature of model transformations.

The models are tightly coupled to the architecture, and our aim is to find concepts which:

- are simple to learn and use;
- simplify our understanding of the system;
- provide us with a changeable model of the system;
- are sufficiently powerful to express the information which is required to model the system;
- are sufficiently defined that different people can discuss the system in terms of these concepts without being misunderstood.

We will discuss these topics in this chapter. In the box on expressable information spaces we give a theoretical perspective to the problems associated with these issues.

**Expressible information spaces**

This discussion is aimed at giving an intuitive understanding of the problems of system development. We draw an analogy with different areas in mathematics and computer science. It should nevertheless only be read as a presentation of ideas, since the basics are not fully expanded. Neither have we handled the terminology very strictly and we make no attempt to be detailed. However, we believe that the analogy can help to improve your understanding.

An **information space** is a space where information can be expressed. It consists of a certain number of dimensions and, in order to create models in this space, it uses concepts that have meaning within this information space. These concepts allow us to express models in this space. The concepts are thus the tools with which to express oneself, and the success of any software engineering technique depends on the appropriateness of the concepts chosen.

We can consider the systems we construct as systems to solve problems; for example, a telephone exchange will connect together a number of subscribers, a banking system will control the accounts of the customers, a process control system will control a critical process. If a problem can be solved within a finite time, it is called deterministic. The problems we shall solve may therefore be placed in the information space for deterministic problems (otherwise it is not even worth trying). (This information space is often called the set of NP-complete problems. NP is an abreviation for non-deterministic polynomial and means that one can at least determine whether the problem is solvable in polynomial time.) Amongst these deterministic problems exist the most difficult problems that we can hope to solve within a predetermined time. There are problems that lie outside this space, which are thus not certain of a solution within a predetermined time. An example is 'Guess which number I'm thinking of. You have one try.'

This can feel safe so long as we confine our attention to deterministic problems, and this relates to (nearly) all of the systems we develop. Now, it has been proved that all deterministic problems can be solved with a Turing machine. A computer has the same power of expression as a Turing machine, with the exception of not having infinite memory, but that is seldom the critical problem. So, the question is: why do we have such difficulty in building a system to solve a problem, when the problem has been proved to be solvable? The answer is that we do not fully master the complexity. Our understanding is too limited. What we want from the concepts is, as you now may realize, to manage the complexity of the information space. We can unquestionably do this with the concepts a Turing machine offers (an infinitely long tape where we can read and write symbols accompanied with a state transition graph). Even if these concepts can express our space, they are so primitive to work with that they can hardly help us. We can compare this with unit vectors in a space or with symbols to count with. If we have only one symbol to count with, we would have to print the symbol 1000 times to express the number 1000; if we have two symbols we can combine these symbols and thus have a length of only 10 symbols ($2^{10} = 1024$). It is therefore insufficient to have concepts theoretically able to express the information space; they must also be powerful to work with. Another computational tool is lambda calculus. This is just as powerful as a Turing machine, but in order to work out, for instance, $4 \times 5$, a whole page of calculations would be required. Owing to this problem, certain reduction rules have been added to the lambda calculus, but it is still too complex to work with for larger problems.

The development of programming languages also aims to solve these problems. Initially, computers were programmed with very primitive languages using ones and zeros to represent the state of some switches. This was at a very low level and the number of errors made increased exponentially with the size of the programs. Assembly languages developed to represent these ones and zeros in a more human way. Although this was of great help, it was still too low a level for larger programs. Still higher-level languages, more readable for humans, were developed to cope with this increase of complexity in the larger programs that were being developed. Compilers were invented to translate automatically from the high-level language to a lower-level machine language. One of the goals for programming language developers is to develop a suffienciently expressive programming language, often for some family of applications, and at the same time keep this language as small and simple as possible. Preferably the language concepts should be close to the way people think of a problem.

The family of object-oriented programming languages is no exception to this; quite the opposite, as they try to follow the way people think and directly map this onto an executable program. Although this is a tremendous improvement for software developers, it is still too low-level to manage the complexity and understanding of large systems, the development of which we are discussing in this book.

Actually, much of the development of programming languages has been to increase linearly the level of abstraction of the computers. Starting with the von Neumann architecture for the first computers (von Neumann (1945)), the basic principle was to build the computer out of five parts: *memory, central control, arithmetical unit, input* and *output*. Computers have since then in most cases been built in basically this way (often called the von Neumann architecture). The first programming languages were naturally designed to cope with this architecture and this forced programmers to think the way computers do, that is, to use control statements that manipulated data in the memory. In the early days it was necessary, for reasons of efficiency, to think in the same way as computers, but higher-level languages have also kept this division of data and programs. However, with the benefit of hindsight it is even more galling to accept that we have also kept this division at the higher levels of analysis and design, as in the function/data methods of software development. In object-oriented languages and methods this tradition is finally broken to incorporate data and programs, and to encapsulate the data into the programs. We should not blame John von Neumann for us being on the wrong track for so many years, quite the opposite; he is one of the greatest mathematicians of our century and has contributed a lot to the evolution of our field. It is the rest of us who lacked the creativity to realize that programming paradigms should not be developed in the same way as computer hardware paradigms, but rather as people think.

## 6.2.2   Architecture

System development thus includes the development of different models of a software system. Our goal is to find a powerful modeling language, notation, or as we will call it, a modeling technique, for each of these models. Such a set of modeling techniques (one for each model) defines the **architecture** upon which the system development method is based. Another, more formal way to express this is: *the architecture of a method is the denotation of its set of modeling techniques*. Here we use the term 'denotation' in the way it is traditionally used in the area of formal semantics for programming languages; the denotation of a language construct is what the construct stands for, or the semantics of the construct. Intuitively, you may also think of architecture as the set of all (good) models you can build using the method-defined modeling technique. We may thus view the architecture as the class of models that can be built with a certain modeling notation.

A modeling technique is normally described by means of **syntax**, **semantics** and **pragmatics**. By syntax we mean how it looks, semantics is what it means, and by pragmatics we mean heuristics and other rules of thumb for using the modeling technique.

The modeling techniques are used to develop models. These models should be powerful enough to build the systems we are interested in developing. The techniques should be easy to use and contain a few, but powerful, modeling objects to enable easy learning. They should, most of all, help us to handle the complexity that characterizes the systems we build.

To build these models, we require a **method** to show us how to work with the modeling techniques in order to develop systems. The method describes how we, with the aid of the modeling techniques, can create models of different systems. The specific system architecture we then obtain is formulated in terms of the modeling objects used. A specific system's architecture is therefore the result obtained after applying a method to a system.

**An object-oriented view of architecture**

In order to make a comparison with object-orientation, we can regard the architecture as a class. For each system we design, we create an instance of this class. The specific system architecture is thus an instance of the architecture that the method is based on. All system architectures have the same characteristics (modifiable, understandable, and so on), but they can all look different. One specific new system development can be seen as sending a Create stimulus to the architecture class which then applies the development method to the architecture for a given problem (see Figure 6.3), and thus creates a new instance (system architecture). The development method can thus be seen as an operation (in Smalltalk: method!) on this architecture, where parameters can be, for example, requirement specification, implementation environment and so on.

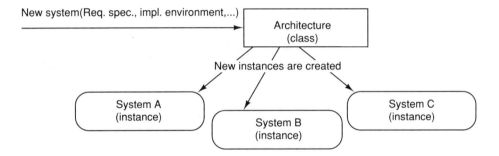

**Figure 6.3**   The architecture forms the basis (the class) on which new specific system architectures (instances) are created. The actual instantiation is described by the method.

> To make this development method usable in larger contexts, we need to define a process and tools. To continue the analogy with object-orientation, we can regard this process as being the union of all operations one can perform on the instances.

### 6.2.3   Development processes

We mentioned previously that we assume that the requirement specification exists in some form. From this specification the system is developed into a first version. Almost all systems will then be further developed continuously, including maintenance of the system. Maintenance will of course also include analysis of new requirements. In Chapter 2 we discussed the problems of describing a development process using a waterfall model. A waterfall model only describes an ideal new development. In reality, a system development process is a number of different waterfalls, as discussed in Chapter 2.

Instead of focusing on how a specific project should be driven, the focus of the process is on how a certain **product** (deliverable application) should be developed and maintained during its entire life cycle. This means that instead of describing a **project** in a waterfall description, we have to divide the development work for a specific product into processes, where each of these processes describes one activity of the management of a product. The processes work highly interactively. Each process handles a specific activity of the system development (see Figure 6.4). For instance, most types of project will involve some construction activities. This is described in

**The system development process**

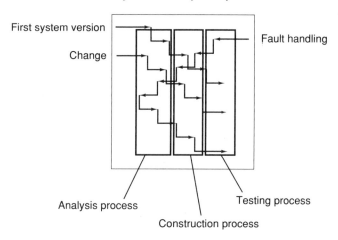

First system version

Change

Fault handling

Analysis process

Testing process

Construction process

**Figure 6.4**    Processes intersect several waterfalls.

the construction process. In this manner, the product will be managed by a number of processes. The development work thus extends over all these processes and the processes exist during the whole system development, namely during the whole system life cycle. All development work is managed by these processes. Each process can in its turn consist of a number of communicating subprocesses.

The main processes are the analysis, construction and testing processes (see Figure 6.5). Linked mainly to the construction process, there is also a component development process.

In the **analysis process**, we create a conceptual picture of the system we want to build. Here the requirements model and the analysis model are developed in order to understand the system and to communicate it to its orderer and to the construction process. In the **construction process**, we develop the system from the models created within the analysis process. This process develops two models: the

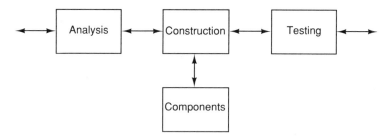

**Figure 6.5**    Main processes and their relations.

design model and the implementation model. This process thus includes the implementation and results in a complete system. The **testing process** integrates the system, verifies it and decides whether it should be passed on for delivery.

Apart from these main processes there is the **component development** process, which mainly communicates with the construction process. This process develops and maintains components to be used during construction. The components are implemented code, which can be used in several different applications. The component process is thus not tied to a specific product, but is a multi-product process.

In Chapters 1 and 2, we discussed the concepts of architecture, method, process and tools. In this chapter, we discuss the architecture forming the basis of the method and process, that is, the concepts of each model. In the following chapters, we shall discuss the method layer of each main process in more detail. Each process has its own chapter. The discussion within these chapters will be confined to the method base from which each process is built. We will also discuss some parts of the processes that are of special interest although most aspects of the process and tool layer are omitted in this book.

Each process can be supported by tools. These tools are essential, especially when the process is used on a large scale. With the help of the tools, we can automate many work steps and also obtain an invaluable aid in keeping documentation consistent.

So, we regard a development as a set of communicating processes. This suggests that they are not some set of fixed and complete procedures able to replace each other mechanically, but quite to the contrary, they communicate intensively with each other and each of them depends heavily on the work done in the other processes. The system development thus iterates over these processes. This is one of several essential differences between method and process.

### 6.2.4   Processes and models

During a development, we create models of the system we are to design. To design these models, we work from a process description that describes the process with which we develop the system. Each such process works with models of the system. These models are expressed, or placed, in a certain information space. Each process takes one or several models and transforms it into other models (see Figure 6.6). The final model should be a complete and tested

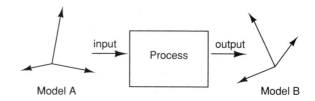

**Figure 6.6**    Processes transform one model to another model.

description of the system. This description normally consists of source code and documentation.

To develop software by transforming models from a requirement specification to source code has founded its own paradigms within software engineering (see Agresti (1986)). Depending on the level at which the transformations are made, they can be divided into either operational or transformational paradigms. The **operational paradigm** first converts the requirement specification into a totally problem-oriented operational specification which the users can test (see Zave (1984)). Once this is complete and accepted, one can proceed to the implementation factors affecting development. Now, the design and implementation of the system can take place. In the **transformational paradigm**, the transformations are performed on a much lower level (see Partsch and Steinbruggen (1983)). Each transformation should be proved correct, to guarantee that the final result is also correct. All transformations are saved for administration of the system. Today, one can only develop very small systems (programs) using the basic ideas of this paradigm since it is extremely hard to define correct transformations.

The transformations in OOSE cannot entirely be associated with either one of these schools. It is, in fact, closely related to the operational approach. In comparison with the transformational approach, it is not as formal, but the design and implementation require a lot of intellectual and creative work. Certain parts can be performed mechanically and thus can be supported by CASE tools.

We can regard the system's requirement specification (and what it really means) as a model, placed in an information space. This information space normally has quite unspecific concepts, that is, they are often not very precise, resulting in the need to clarify what is really meant by the requirement specification. The requirement specification is one-dimensional in the sense that it is often only a textual description, where the references are forwards or backwards in the text. It is also quite usual that one 'forgets' requirements in the requirement specification. Irrespective of all this though, it represents the initial model within our chain of transformations.

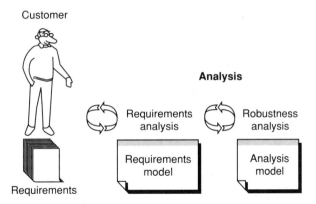

Customer

Requirements

**Analysis**

Requirements analysis

Robustness analysis

Requirements model

Analysis model

**Figure 6.7**  The analysis process and subprocesses and the models they produce. Note that the arrows between processes are bidirectional to illustrate that information may flow in both directions.

The analysis process produces two models (see Figure 6.7). From the requirement specification, a **requirements model** is created in which we specify all the functionality of the system. This is mainly done by **use cases** in the **use case model** which is a part of the requirement model. The use case model will also form the basis of both the construction and testing processes, and it controls a large part of the system development. We see here a typical example of reuse on a higher level, on a model level, where one model will be used as input to several processes. The requirements model also forms the basis of another model created by the analysis process, namely the **analysis model**. The analysis model is the basis of the system's structure. In this model, we specify all the logical objects to be included in the system and how these are related and grouped. These two models are the result of the analysis process. They will provide input data for the construction process.

In the construction process, we design and implement the system (see Figure 6.8). We shall see that the requirements model and the analysis model provide much support for this process. First a design is made that results in a **design model** where each object will be fully specified. The implementation subprocess will then implement these objects and result in the **implementation model** which consists of the source code.

This implementation model provides, along with the design and requirements models, input data for the testing process (see Figure 6.9). The testing process tests the implementation model, partly from the requirements model and the design model, and produces a **test model**. This test model is really the result of testing the implementation model.

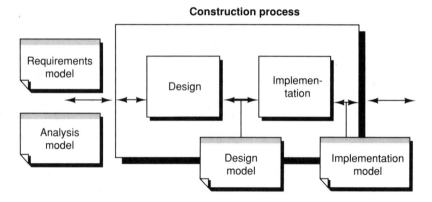

**Figure 6.8**  The construction process with its major subprocesses and the models produced.

These transformations of models are not as mechanical as has been indicated, quite the opposite: the development of these models is an iterative and incremental activity requiring much effort from talented developers. The development work flows over these processes which interact with each other. The processes follow a product and exist as long as the product exists. For a specific project, the issue is to man all or part of these processes. We will come back to this issue in Chapter 15.

As has been discussed, an extremely important characteristic that all our models must support is traceability. We must, from one model, be able to trace an object to an object in another model, and

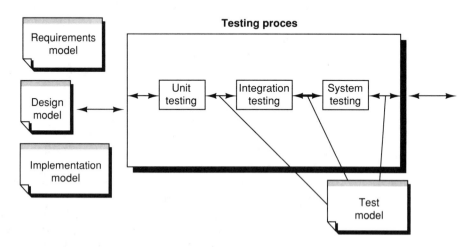

**Figure 6.9**  The testing process with its major subprocess.

from this new object, be able to return to the same object in the first model. For example, we wish to be able to trace something from the test model when a failure is detected, and find the reason for this failure within the implementation model. We may wish to trace the fault further back to the design and analysis models and also to the requirements model and, perhaps, even to the requirements specification. When we modify a model, we wish to see directly its effect on the other models. This traceability between models can be difficult to maintain manually during the iterative development work. A CASE tool to maintain this traceability is therefore essential for a large development project.

   Before we review each model in depth, we shall first discuss several common characteristics for the objects which we use in the models. In the following chapters we shall look at how we work with these models and how they are transformed to new models.

## 6.3   Model architecture

We have seen that system development is basically concerned with developing models of the system. The work is concerned with both identifying and describing **objects** in a certain information space, and with building models using these objects. Before we look closer at these models, we discuss the object concept common to all models.

   The object concept was introduced in Chapter 3. All the models built during development in OOSE are built using objects. With the help of objects, we will build **object models**. The objects that we work with in the models all have the properties discussed in Chapter 3.

   For each model we develop, there exist different types of object. By modeling with objects in all models, we gain all the benefits of object-orientation, namely locality of changes, encapsulation, reuse and so on.

   What, then, is a good object? Much of the work within object-oriented analysis and design consists of trying to find a good object. There are several such criteria in various object-oriented methods. Usually, we say that the object should have an interpretation in reality. We also say that the objects should be obvious, tangible things, things that we can focus on. Others say that the objects are just there for the picking.

   The methods available today to find objects are based closely on learning and analyzing the terminology in the problem area: see Shlaer and Mellor (1988), Wirfs-Brock *et al.* (1990), Coad and Yourdon (1991a,b), Booch (1991) or Rumbaugh *et al.* (1991). (Object-oriented methods are discussed in Chapter 16.) By analyzing the terminology, we can extract what seem to be candidates for objects in the system. When we evaluate how the system needs to handle these objects, we can decide whether an object should be included or left out of the model being created.

However, a good object does not exist on its own. We believe that the criteria should reflect good object models instead. An object can be perfectly right for one model, but totally wrong in another. This means that an object must be placed in a context to see whether it is an appropriate object. Therefore, what is really of interest is how an object works with other objects and under what conditions.

What, then, is a good object model? The most important criterion is that it should be robust against modification and help the understanding of the system. As we know for certain that all systems we build will be modified, we must create a robust model structure. Therefore we must analyze how modifications will affect the system. Our structure should be affected by this analysis. After we have worked with a model for a while, a stable structure will evolve for the system.

By working a long time with the early models, we will obtain a good understanding of the system. The development process must therefore be designed so that it results in a sound and robust structure as quickly as possible. This reduces the risk of having to change the system structure at a later stage and it should also force us to use a sound and understandable structure. We will see that the first model designed in OOSE is determined totally by the orderer's functional requirements, often resulting in modifications being local (owing to simple traceability), as they often depend on how an orderer's perspective gets modified. We obtain, in such a way, an orderer-governed structure.

## 6.4  Requirements model

### 6.4.1  Actors and use cases

The first transformation made is from the requirement specification to the requirements model. The requirements model consists of:

- A use case model
- Interface descriptions
- A problem domain model

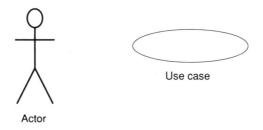

**Figure 6.10**   The use case model consists of actors and use cases.

The **use case model** uses **actors** and **use cases** (see Figure 6.10). These concepts are simply an aid to defining what exists outside the system (actors) and what should be performed by the system (use cases).

The actors represent what interacts with the system. They represent everything that needs to exchange information with the system. Since the actors represent what is outside the system, we do not describe them in detail. Actors are not like other objects in the respect that their actions are non-deterministic. We differentiate between actors and **users**. The user is the actual person who uses the system, whereas an actor represents a certain role that a user can play. We regard an actor as a class and users as instances of this class. These instances exist only when the user does something to the system. The same person can thus appear as instances of several different actors. For instance, for a system we may have the actors pilot and clerk. Jim Smith is a user who sometimes acts as a pilot and sometimes acts as a clerk; but he performs different use cases dependent on the roles he plays.

An instance of an actor carries out a number of different operations on the system. When a user uses the system, she or he will perform a behaviorally related sequence of transactions in a dialogue with the system. We call such a special sequence a **use case**. An example of a use case could be to Acknowledge a flight to be performed by a Pilot. Each use case is a specific way of using the system and every execution of the use case may be viewed as an instance of the use case. When a user inputs a stimulus, the use case instance executes and starts a transaction belonging to the use case. This transaction consists of different actions to be performed. A transaction is finished when the use case instance again awaits an input stimulus from an actor instance. The use case instance exists as long as the use case is operating.

These use case instances follow, as do all instances in an object-oriented system, a specific class. When a use case is performed, we therefore view this as we instantiate the use case's class. A use case class is a description. This description specifies the transactions of the use case. The set of all use case descriptions specifies the complete functionality of the system. See Figure 6.11 for an illustration of a use case model.

To view use cases as objects, classes and instances is often unnatural to people used to OOP; but let us refer to the definitions in Chapter 3. There we stated that an object should have behavior and a state. A use case is a complete flow in the system. Apparently such a flow does have a state (how far it has reached, what the state of the system is). It also has behavior. We may view every interaction between an actor and the system as the actor invoking new operations on a specific use case (for example, 'start use case'). Thus a use case may be viewed as an object. Let us investigate the class and instance concepts. We see that many flows invoked by an actor have similar behavior (the same use case). In this way we can describe this use case and view this description as the use case's class. Likewise, when we start a use case we may view this as we create instances of this class. We see that use cases fit into all these definitions. The purpose of this is that we can use all the benefits of object-orientation when working with these concepts. Another possible way of looking at the use case is to view the system as an object and the use cases as operations that are invoked in the system, but this is not the way we have chosen. If the reader has a hard time viewing use cases as objects, it is actually not very crucial when reading this book. However, the reason we do it is to make it easier to work with architecture matters. We may thus view use cases as transactions with internal states, having something that represents the course which we can manipulate.

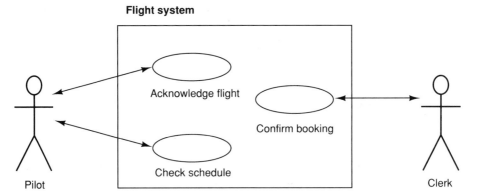

**Figure 6.11** Example of a use case model. The system is bounded by a box. Each actor is represented by a person outside the box, while the use cases are represented as ellipses inside the box.

Hence the use case model is described by a number of actors and use cases. For the use cases, we make detailed **descriptions.** When the system is in operation, instances are created from the descriptions in this model. We will later see that these descriptions are crucial to the identification of the actual objects in the system.

### 6.4.2   Use case driven design

As we design in this way, the system model will be **use case driven**. When we wish to change the system behavior, we remodel the appropriate actor and use case. The whole system architecture will be controlled by what the users wish to do with the system. As we have traceability through all models, we will be able to modify the system from new requirements. We ask the users what they want to change (which use case) and see directly where these changes should be made in the other models.

Another important characteristic of the requirements model is that we can discuss it with the users and find out their requirements and preferences. This model is easy to understand and formulate from the user perspective, so we can easily talk to the users and see if we are building the correct system according to their requirements. Since this is the first model to be developed, we can evaluate whether the users are pleased with what we are about to design, before we start to build the actual system (see the operational paradigm of Agresti (1986)).

To support the use case model it is often appropriate to develop the **interfaces** of the use cases as well. Here a prototype of the user interface is a perfect tool. In this way we can simulate the use cases for the users by showing the user the views that she or he will see when executing the use case in the system to be built. Additionally, to communicate with the potential users, it is often appropriate to sketch a logical and surveyable **domain object model** of the system. Such an object model should consist of problem domain objects, that is, objects that have a direct counterpart in the problem domain under consideration, and serve to support for the development of the requirements model. This approach will be further discussed in Chapter 7.

The requirements model can thus be regarded as formulating the functional requirement specification based on the needs of the system users. In reality, a requirements model would be acceptable as a part of the requirement specification, and we may perhaps use this for system tendering.

The use case model will control the formation of all other models (see Figure 6.12). It is developed in cooperation with the

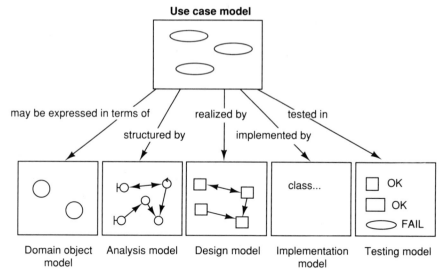

**Figure 6.12**    The use case model is used when developing all other models.

domain object model and it may, in cases where the domain object model is worked into a detailed object model, be expressed in terms of domain objects. The functionality specified by the use cases is then structured into a logical, robust but implementation-environment-independent model – the analysis model – that is stable to changes. This model is adapted to the actual implementation environment and further refined in the design model, using the use cases to describe how the use cases flow over the design objects. The use cases will then be implemented by the source code in the implementation model. Finally the use cases will give us a tool when testing the system, mainly during integration testing. The use case model will also give us support when writing manuals and other operational instructions.

## 6.5  Analysis model

### 6.5.1  The objects of the analysis model

We have seen that the requirements model aims to define the limitations of the system and to specify its behavior. When the requirements model has been developed and approved by the system users or orderers, we can start to develop the actual system.

This starts with development of the **analysis model**. This model aims to structure the system independently of the actual implementation environment. This means that we focus on the logical structure of the system. It is here that we define the stable, robust and maintainable structure that is also extensible.

It would have been possible to use the object model developed in the requirements model as a base for the actual construction of the system. In fact, many other object-oriented methods use such a model as the only input for construction. However, this does not result in the structure most robust to future changes. We will come back to the reasons for this. The analysis model represents, in our experience, a more stable and maintainable system structure that will be robust for the entire system life cycle. We will come back to this issue in more detail later.

Since many future changes will come from changes in the implementation environment, these changes will not affect this logical structuring. We shall see when discussing how to adapt to the actual implementation environment that we want as few changes as possible to this ideal, logical and stable structure.

In the information space for this model, our aim is to capture **information, behavior** and **presentation** (see Figure 6.13). The information dimension specifies the information held in the system, both short term and long term. Along this dimension, we describe the system's internal state. In the behavior dimension, we specify the behavior which the system will adopt. Here, we specify when and how the system will change state. The presentation dimension provides the details for presenting the system to the outside world.

The analysis model is built by specifying objects in this information space. One possibility is that of having objects which only express one dimension. This is the case with function/data

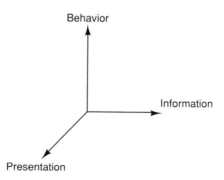

**Figure 6.13**   The dimensions of the analysis model.

Entity object   Interface object   Control object

**Figure 6.14**   The object types used to structure the system in the analysis model.

methods, where functions are placed along the behavioral axis and data is placed along the information axis. If we design in this way, we will obtain a system which is sensitive to modification, as we must often modify some behavior when we modify the information structure. We do not want this situation to arise, so our objects should be able to contain both information and behavior, and even the presentation of this if required.

Many object-oriented analysis methods choose to have only one object type, which can be placed anywhere within this space. We have chosen to use three object types. The simple reason for this is to help us get a structure that will be more adaptable to changes. The object types used in the analysis model are **entity objects, interface objects** and **control objects** (see Figure 6.14). We will soon come back to the purposes of these object types. Each of these object types captures at least two of the three dimensions discussed above. However, each of them has a certain inclination towards one of the dimensions (see Figure 6.15).

Hence we have different purposes for the three object types. The entity object models information in the system that should be held for a longer time, and should typically survive a use case. All behavior naturally coupled to this information should also be placed in the entity object. An example of an entity object is a person with his or her associated data and behavior. The interface object models

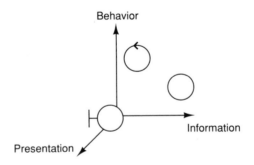

**Figure 6.15**   The dimensions and object types of the analysis model.

behavior and information that is dependent on the interface to the system. Thus everything concerning any interface to the system is placed in an interface object. An example of an interface object is the user interface functionality for requesting information about a person. The control objects model functionality that is not naturally tied to any other object, for example, behavior that consists of operating on several different entity objects, doing some computations and then returning the result to an interface object. A typical example of a control object is calculating taxes using several different factors. This behavior could be placed on any of the other types of object (since they are also able to model behavior), but the actual behavior does not in fact belong to any specific entity object or interface object.

Why do these three object types give us a stable system? The basic assumption is that all systems will change. Therefore stability will occur in the sense that all changes will be local, that is, affect (preferably) only one object in the system. Let us first consider what kinds of changes are common to a system. As we mentioned in Chapter 4, the most common changes to a system are to its functionality and its interface. Changes to the interface should typically affect only interface objects. Changes to functionality are more difficult. Functionality may be placed over all object types: so how do we achieve localization of these changes? If it is functionality that is coupled to information held by the system, for instance, how to calculate a person's age, such changes affect the entity object representing that information. Changes of functionality of an interface, for instance, how to receive and collect information about a person, should affect the corresponding interface object. Changes of interobject functionality, for instance, how to calculate taxes from several different criteria, should be local to a control object. Typically, functionality unique to one or a few use cases is placed in a control object.

We do not believe that the best (most stable) systems are built by *only* using objects that correspond to real-life entities, something that many other object-oriented analysis and design techniques claim. When comparing a model developed with one of these techniques and an analysis model using OOSE, great similarities will be found between the entity objects in the analysis model and the objects yielded in other methods. Thus entity objects often represent a problem domain object, although this is not always necessarily so, as we shall see further on. However, behavior that we place in control objects will, in other methods, be distributed over several other objects, making it harder to change this behavior.

The reason that we model with these three object types is thus to have localization in changes to the system. Then how do we know that these are the 'right' object types? This is something you cannot draw any conclusions about until a system has been changed a number of times. Our experience comes from the block design technique mentioned earlier. That was an object-based technique where objects (there called blocks) typically had counterparts in the problem domain. The techniques were used in developing telephone exchanges and the experience was quite good; it was very modular and quite easy to introduce most kinds of modifications. However, certain modifications are unreasonably expensive to introduce. For example, in the system there was a block called Trunk representing data and behavior that should be tied to a trunk (a telephone line between exchanges). When the system had been in operation for more than ten years, and had undergone several changes, we investigated what had happened to this block. Of course, many changes had been made to it to adapt to the new requirements and these changes were local to the block. This also included many new operations that had been introduced to the block. What we found, however, was that 23 (!) operations had been added that were unique to only one specific use case. The operations were thus not generally reusable and when a new use case needed to be added, typically operations for that specific use case also needed to be added. Some operations could be reused in several use cases; these were typically designed with not just one use case in mind.

Thus the actual problem here was that too much specific functionality had been incorporated in the block (entity object in OOSE). Instead we should model this specific functionality in the control object so that, firstly, the (operations of the) entity object will be more reusable in several different use cases and, secondly, the specific functionality should be local and not distributed so that it is easier to introduce changes in this functionality.

Similar observations of object-oriented structured systems are not very common since very few of these systems have undergone changes over several versions. Even so, the experience so far with an object-oriented structure is that, in general, it is more maintainable than a function/data structure. However, there are similar observations on system changes. One example is given by Scharenberg and Dunsmore (1991), where a system for inventory control was developed with a 'problem domain object' analysis method. The first observations were that these initial classes were only used as more complex data types and with a not-so-stable structure. The system was refined and further developed, leading to another class structure that was more stable. An 'artificial object domain' was reached which did not directly reflect the problem domain, but instead was more stable to changes and more robust. The 'artificial object domain' consisted of the three object types we use.

Another approach which may look similar to this approach is the Model, View, Control (MVC) paradigm used in Smalltalk. However, the MVC distinguishes the output presentation from the inputs whereas that is not the intention here. Another approach, which is more similar to ours, is the PAC model by Coutaz (1989). The PAC model distinguishes between Presentation, Abstraction (Application) and Control. These relate very well to the interface object, the entity objects and the control objects.

A similar distinguishing of these three different categories can be found in Davis and Morgan (1993). Here these three different categories have split the system architecture into three layers, each of them implementing one of these three categories. The highest layer implements only interface functionality (interface objects), the middle layer implements the processes (control objects) and the lowest layer implements the business objects (entity objects).

**Robust structures**

> Object-orientation is often claimed to give more changeable and extensible software than traditional methods. Inheritance and encapsulation are then often claimed to be important parts of the solution. In Chapter 4 we discussed the problems with function/data methods and showed the object-oriented solutions. However, object-orientation by itself does not guarantee robust and extensible software. We will here look at an example of this. The example is an extension to previous examples discussed by the authors of the forewords to this book: Dave Thomas (1989) introduced the OO solution to the example, and Larry Constantine (1990) introduced the functional solution.
>
> The example system must deal with a number of different types of account. Three account types are included in the example: passbook savings, checking and bonus savings. A number of different transactions are valid for each account type; for simplicity, only three are shown, but in a real application there may be many more. Figure 6.16 shows a structure chart based on a conventional function-structured decomposition (for example, structured analysis/design). Each transaction processing module must deal with distinct variations for each of the account types. There will, however, be portions in the modules that will be reused over several modules, such as database access, and portions that are unique, such as the processing of the bonus savings. In a good structured design, functions are decomposed so that common processing is located in subordinate modules that can be reused wherever needed without duplication of design and coding.
>
> A typical object-oriented solution to the same problem is shown in Figure 6.17. The various account types will now be modelled as descendants of the abstract class Account. The operations (Open,

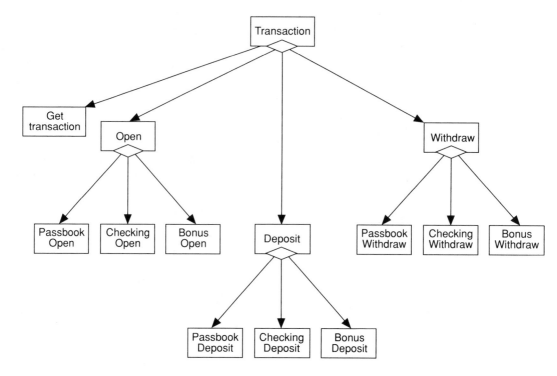

Figure 6.16    A function/data solution to the banking application.

Deposit and Withdraw) are inherited. Possibly they need different implementations, but at least they have the same interface. The 'other objects' represent those objects that manipulate these objects in the various transactions. Most of these objects can be described as operating on Account using polymorphism since the object interfaces are common. However, the creation of objects at least must differ between the various account types.

Now, which of these solutions is easier to change? Let us consider some typical changes. What if we want to add a new account type, such as a money market account? Adding a new account type to the function/data solution requires us to add a new module for each of the valid transactions on this account type as shown in Figure 6.18. These modules may of course use existing lower-level modules such as database access and so on. Additionally, we need to modify the modules that decide upon the account types, that is, all transaction modules. Typically in these modules the body is a CASE-statement deciding upon the specific type for the application. We thus need to add a new case for all applicable transactions. Hence, in this case the

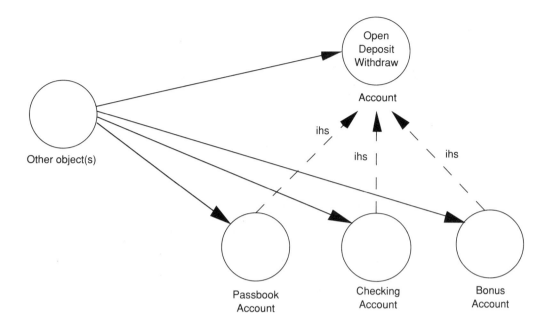

**Figure 6.17**   An object-oriented solution to the banking application.

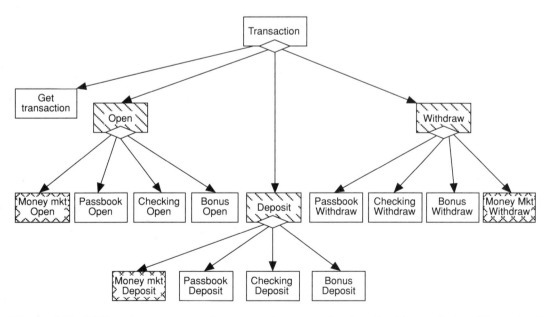

**Figure 6.18**. Adding the money market account type to the function/data solution. The striped modules need to be changed, and the double cross-hatched modules need to be added as new.

change for adding a new account will not be local, but spread all over the transactions in the application.

Adding a new account type to the object-oriented solution requires only the adding of one new descendant of the Account class. The interface will be the same, but probably we need to implement the variations in the operations. Additionally, we need to modify the objects that distinguish the various accounts, at least the creation of the money market account. This modification is shown in Figure 6.19. We can see that in the object-oriented solution the modification is much more local than in the function-oriented solution.

The conclusion is that we would favor the object-oriented solution; one object added and one modified versus three modules added and three modified in the functional solution. However, the amount of new and changed code is probably around the same for both solutions. The difference is that of locality.

Let us consider another enhancement to the application. The above example introduced a new account type. What if we introduce a new transacation type? Consider the transaction of producing a special report, for example a report for bank auditors to inspect any account.

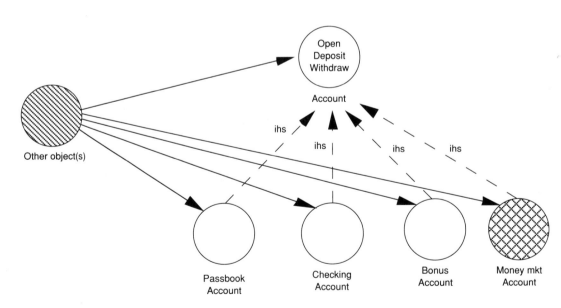

**Figure 6.19**   Adding a new account type to the object-oriented solution of the banking application.

The changes needed in the function/data design are shown in Figure 6.20. The added modules are now localized under the Report module. We also need to modify the Transaction module to cope with this new transaction type. This change was thus quite easy to incorporate into the structured design.

What about the object-oriented solution? Following the traditional object-oriented approaches, which base the solutions only on domain objects (we sometimes call this naive object modelling), we would add a new operation for this report on every object type (see Figure 6.21). We see that this change will have a dramatic effect on the design. We would need to modify all existing account type objects as well as the initiation of the new report somewhere else.

These two additions illustrate two typical kinds of changes, that is, adding a new data structure item and adding a new transaction type. An object-oriented structure is built around these data items, while a function-oriented structure is built around the transaction types. Of course, the ease of adding a new feature is very dependent on whether the system is structured around that type of feature. But usually changes comes in both of these 'dimensions'. In some extensions or modifications, one solution will have clear advantages

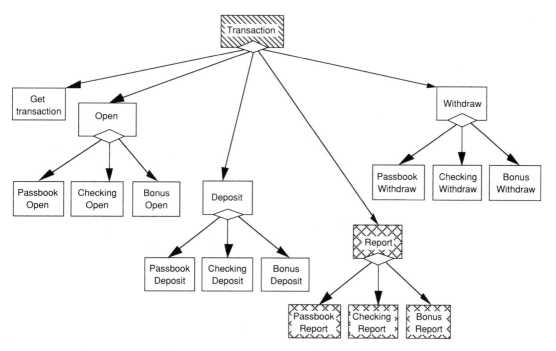

**Figure 6.20** Adding a new transaction type to the function/data solution.

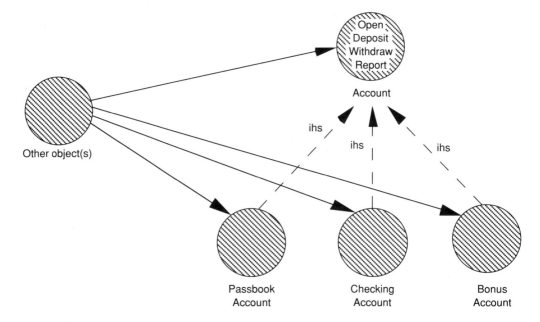

**Figure 6.21**    Adding a new transaction type in the object-oriented solution.

and in others the other solution will fare better. Over a balanced suite of modifications including adding data structures and functions, neither solution will emerge with an overall advantage. No published empirical studies of the frequencies of these modification categories exist to our knowledge. A typical application will be exposed to both types of modification.

This is the problem we are trying to address with our categorization into three different object types. The entity objects should capture the data structure changes, the control objects should capture the functional changes and the interface objects should capture the interface-related changes.

Let us review the example to see what the solution would look like in OOSE. Surely the transaction types would map quite clearly to use cases. The analysis model would be as in Figure 6.22. The addition of the money market account would be done by adding a new descendant to the Account class. The descendant would basically support the Open, Withdraw and Deposit transactions (with the appropriate interface object) since these may be viewed as basic operations on the entity objects. Each of these transactions would also have an interface object supporting the specific use case. However, a specific control object would not be needed. The report use case, on

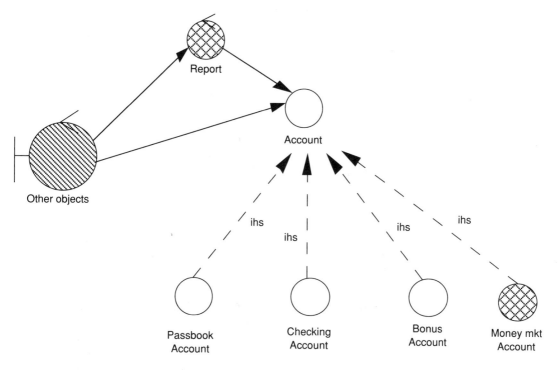

**Figure 6.22**   The banking application in OOSE using the various object types.

the other hand, would not be spread out over the entity objects. Instead we would add a new control object to support this use case. This control object would reuse the basic operations on the account objects, such as balance enquiries and so on. The report-specific issues would then be local to the control object Report. We see here the importance of arriving at the correct, reusable operations on the entity object. This is a critical factor of success for the changeability of the application.

### 6.5.2   The requirements model is structured in the analysis model

The analysis model is formed from the use case model. Each use case will be entirely divided into objects of the three types described in the previous section. In the requirements model we specify the entire functionality of the system. This functionality should now be structured to obtain a robust and extensible structure. In this way the use cases will be partitioned into analysis objects (see Figure 6.23). In

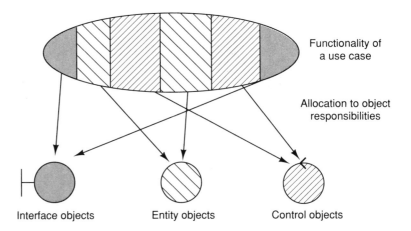

**Figure 6.23** The functionality of the use case should be partitioned and allocated to the objects, thus yielding that the analysis model will offer the use cases of the system.

practice this means that the functionality specified in the use cases should be allocated to different objects. In this way, each use case will be offered by objects in the analysis model. An object can of course be common to several use cases. This is actually desirable since it gives objects that are reusable in several different use cases, which suggests that they will also be reusable in future changes of the system. This transformation from use cases into objects forms one of the most important parts of OOSE. It is now that we form the basis of the system architecture. We here only touch upon the principles of this transformation, which will be discussed in more detail in Chapter 7.

Basically, we partition the use case according to the following principles:

- Those use case functionalities which are directly dependent on the system's environment are placed in interface objects.
- Those functionalities dealing with the storage and handling of information which are not naturally placed in any interface object are placed in the entity object.
- Functionalities specific to one or a few use cases and not naturally placed in any of the other objects are placed in control objects.

By performing this division, we obtain a structure which helps us to understand the system from a logical view and also one which gives high localization of changes and thus less sensitivity to modifications. For instance, changes to an interface, a quite common modification as we have seen, affect only one object, the interface object that handles this interface. Changes of data format would affect only the entity object (structure and behavior) where the change should be introduced.

The allocation is quite difficult in practice, and we shall discuss it much more in the analysis and construction chapters. It is when doing this partition of functionality that we decide upon the robustness and maintainability of the system. The basic underlying principle is to get localization of changes.

Since it is often hard to draw clear borders between functionalities in a system, in practice the developers are forced to make many judgements about where to split functionality between objects. We have seen from real projects that the best developers often reason in terms of the potential changes to this system. How will these potential changes affect this structure? From this they develop a structure that is stable for the most likely changes. We have also seen that this 'speculation of potential changes' rapidly becomes a skill for an experienced developer. Giving developers the architecture of OOSE allows them to use their creativity to develop stable and robust systems.

As the objects are identified and specified, we also describe how these objects are related through different types of association. We shall come back to this issue in Chapter 7.

The analysis model is now designed directly from the user's requirements, that is, the requirements model. This analysis model will form the basis of the specific system's architecture, and we see that no consideration has been made of the actual implementation factors. This provides an ideal and sound system architecture, as it is the problem which controls the architecture and not the factors of the actual implementation environment. During the design work, we shall take into consideration these points, but it will then only be a matter of adapting to these circumstances; the basic system structure, as far as possible, remains untouched.

## 6.6 The design model

### 6.6.1 The design model's object

In the construction process, we construct the system using both the analysis model and the requirements model. First, we create a design model that is a refinement and formalization of the analysis model.

The initial work when developing the design model is to adapt to the actual implementation environment. The analysis model was developed assuming ideal conditions. We must now adapt it to reality. As mentioned previously, we have two main reasons for not introducing the implementation environment earlier. The first is that we do not want it to affect the basic structuring of the system, since the current circumstances probably will be changed in one way or another during the system life cycle. The second reason is that we do not want the problem to be blurred by the complexity typically introduced when looking at the implementation environment. In this way we can focus on the essentials when developing the most important aspect of the system, namely, the basic structure of it.

We can thus regard this design model as a formalization of the analysis space, where we adapt the analysis model so that it fits into our implementation environment. The design space has, relative to the analysis space, been expanded to include a dimension for the implementation environment (see Figure 6.24). This dimension means that further concepts are introduced, which the analysis model must be adapted to suit.

This means that we want to keep and massage the analysis model to fit the actual implementation environment at the same time as we refine it. Our goal is to refine it until it is easy to write the source code from it. Since the analysis model has all the properties we want for the system, we want this structure to form the basis of the design model. However, there will be changes to this model when introducing, for instance, a relational DBMS, a distributed environment, performance requirements, a specific programming language, concurrent processes and so on. This is the reason that we develop a new model.

How much should we work with the analysis model and when should we start the design model? This is the classical question.

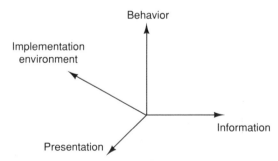

**Figure 6.24**    In the design space, yet another dimension has been added to the analysis space to include the implementation environment.

'When is analysis ready?'. There is no uniformly applicable answer to this question. On the one hand we want to do as much work in the analysis model as possible, where we can focus on the essentials, but on the other hand we do not want to do so much that we need to change it when adapting to the implementation environment. What we really want is a continuum of refinement in the models where the switch of models will occur where we start to see the consequences of the implementation environment (see Figure 6.25).

Hence, when the transition from analysis to design should be made must be decided for each specific application. If there will be no adaptation problems with the DBMS, distributed environment, real-time requirements, concurrent processes, hardware adaptations and so on, it is fine to be quite formal in the analysis model. However, if these circumstances will strongly affect the system structure, the transition should be made quite early. The goal is not to redo any work in a later phase that has been done in an earlier phase. In one project using Objectory, the development team saw that the implementation environment would have very little con-sequence in one part of the application since it would be entirely within one process at one site and would be affected only slightly by the database technology used. Here the analysis model was refined significantly to include operations on the objects and the parameters of these operations. In another part of the application the consequences were much greater. Here they foresaw consequences from distributed hardware involving different operating systems, a changeable protocol between the different nodes (not yet standardized), hard real-time requirements and so on. This part of the analysis model was developed in a much more shallow way, postponing important decisions until the design model stage.

One possibility is to continue working on the analysis model, and to continue on that model even when incorporating the implementation environment into it. However, this is not recommended from a product-oriented view. When further developing

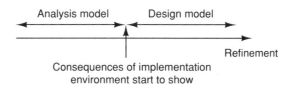

**Figure 6.25** The transition from the analysis model to the design model should be made when the consequences of the implementation environment start to show.

the product, the analysis model is needed to reason about when to incorporate the changes, since it has far less complexity than the design model. Therefore, it is desirable to keep the ideal analysis model of the system during the entire system life cycle. Likewise, many changes of a system come from changes in the implementation environment. Such changes are then easily incorporated, since it is the same analysis model that will form the basis of the new and modified design model. In this way we may view the design model as a specialization of the analysis model for a specific implementation environment. However, the cost of keeping the analysis model must be judged for each product.

This also prompts the question of when changes in the analysis model should be made when working with the design model. If a change of the design model comes from a logical change in the system, such as that two objects should be logically related, then such changes should also be made in the analysis model. However, if the change is a consequence of the implementation environment, for instance that two objects should not communicate directly owing to the process structure chosen, then such changes should not be incorporated in the analysis model.

The structures which we mainly work with are thus basically the same as for the analysis model. However, now the view has changed since this is a step towards implementation. We therefore use the concept of a **block** to describe the intention of how the code should be produced. The blocks are the design objects and they are drawn as rectangles, as shown in Figure 6.26. One block normally aims to implement one analysis object. Here it could be possible to use different types of block, if preferable, for instance interface blocks, entity blocks and control blocks, to highlight the traceability.

It is important to understand, though, that the blocks are *not* the same objects as the analysis objects. We have briefly touched on this before as we mentioned that it is desirable to keep the ideal analysis model. Changes will be introduced in the design model, for example to split one block into two owing to the need to handle, for instance, loosely coupled process communication. Such a split should not affect the analysis model since we do not want changes due to design decisions to be illustrated in the analysis model. To highlight the difference we use the term 'block' instead of 'object'.

Another difference between the analysis and design models is that the analysis model should be viewed as a conceptual and logical model of the system, whereas the design model should take us closer to the actual source code. We can view it as a drawing or map of the code to be developed. This means that we change the view of the design model into an abstraction of the source code to be written later

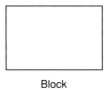

Block

**Figure 6.26**   The object type used in design is the block, and it is the design object of the functionality in the analysis model.

on. Hence the design model should be a drawing of how the source code should be structured, managed and written. Since we want a strong and easy-to-maintain traceability from the analysis model through the design model to the implementation model (source code), we will try to map the design objects (blocks) to the module concept used in the programming language we are implementing in. We will discuss this topic in greater depth later.

We view the blocks as an abstraction of the actual implementation of the system. The blocks will group the source code. To know how to implement the blocks, we need to refine the design model further. We do this by describing how the blocks will communicate during execution. To describe the communication between the blocks we use **stimuli.** The concept of stimuli was introduced in Chapter 3. A stimulus is sent from one block to another to trigger an execution in that block. This execution may send new stimuli to other blocks.

To describe a sequence of stimuli, we use **interaction diagrams**. In these, we can describe how several blocks communicate by sending stimuli to each other. As a base for these interaction diagrams we use the use case model again. Thus we describe in detail, for each use case, how and which stimuli will be sent and in what order. We thus describe the use case as a sequence of stimuli sent between the blocks. An interaction diagram is shown schematically in Figure 6.27.

When we have described all sequences, that is, all use cases, including any alternative flows and error flows, we have described all external communications between the blocks. From this we have also gained a complete interface description of each block. The notation to describe stimuli should therefore be the one used in the chosen programming language. The design model thus consists of a complete description of the blocks with their interfaces.

We mentioned that the blocks should be viewed as abstractions of the code to be written and that it is desirable that traceability between blocks and the code is easy. In, for instance, C++, a typical block will be mapped to one file (actually two: .h and .c files)

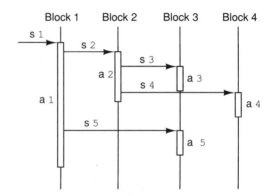

**Figure 6.27**    An example of an interaction diagram. The diagram shows how stimuli, $s_n$, are sent between the blocks and invoke activities, $a_n$, in these blocks.

including one or several classes. In Ada it is natural to map a block to a package. We denote this module concept by the generic term **object module**; that is, in C++ an object module is the class, in Ada it is a package. The interfaces of the blocks will be mapped onto the object module of the particular language, so serving as the interfaces of these modules (the .h file in C++ and the specification part of the Ada package).

One problem in the construction process is that complexity increases enormously. To master the system development, it is essential to be able to manage this complexity. Therefore it is important to have concepts in the information space which allow us to manage the complex systems that we build.

To manage the system more abstractly, we use the concept of the **subsystem.** A subsystem groups several objects. Subsystems may be used in both the analysis model and the design model. Subsystems may also include other subsystems; the concept is recursive. In this way we may have a hierarchical structuring of the system to manage its complexity. The highest level we use is the **system** level. The system is the actual application we are working with. The system also defines the borders of the application. We will discuss the subsystem concept in more depth later and we shall also see that subsystems may be used as an aid to managing product development.

## 6.6.2    Working with the design model

During the construction work, we proceed from the analysis model. For each object in the analysis model, we assign a block in the design model. This transformation occurs totally mechanically and can be performed by a tool. The transformation is seamless. Depending on, most importantly, the implementation environment, we may need to make a deviation so that this one-to-one relationship may be modified. In the design model we thus formalize the analysis model and adapt it so that it fits into the required implementation environment.

When we have created the block structure, we draw interaction diagrams to show how these blocks communicate. Normally, we draw an interaction diagram for every use case. In reality, the use case model will also henceforth form the basis of the construction process, and we thereby guarantee that the system we construct is exactly what the users want.

In the first part of the construction process we work mainly with the blocks. This is often an appropriately detailed level to work with. However, when maintaining and developing new versions of the product, it is often appropriate to extract the interfaces to a subsystem level; in this way, we only specify the interfaces between subsystems early on whereas, inside each subsystem, the development team can work with the blocks. So, it is unnecessary for all the teams to know the internal structure of each subsystem. In Chapter 8 we discuss different techniques to manage this.

## 6.7   The implementation model

The implementation model consists of the annotated source code. The information space is the one that the programming language uses. Note that we do not require an object-oriented programming language; the technique may be used with any programming language to obtain an object-oriented structure of the system. However, an object-oriented programming language is desirable since all fundamental concepts can easily be mapped onto language constructs.

The base for the implementation is the design model. Here we have specified the interface of each block and also have described the behavior of what is expected behind this interface. How this description may look will be discussed in the construction chapter.

We stated earlier that it is strongly desirable to have an easy match between a block and the actual object module (that is, class, package, module or whatever the concept is in the programming language). In many cases we can do a very easy match from one block to one class in the implementation language. When we have a very smooth implementation environment this is typically the case. However, in more complex environments this is not always the case.

In one project where Objectory was used, an entity block ended up using 17 (!) classes in C++ for the implementation. However, it was a very complex implementation because a relational DBMS was used. The implementation included things like type conversion, keying, error handling, versioning and suchlike. This is not a normal case. Typically, one block will map onto about 1–5 classes. In the example chapters later on, we will illustrate some more complex blocks.

The ability to use components is a very powerful implementation tool. Components are fully implemented parts which enable us to build a system with more powerful concepts (higher abstraction) than the programming language can offer us. Components can be regarded as completed building elements which are already placed in the implementation space and that can be used directly in our system. Components and how to use them will be discussed in more detail in Chapter 11.

## 6.8  Test model

The test model is the last model developed in the system development. It describes, simply stated, the result of the testing. The fundamental concepts in testing are mainly the **test specification** and the **test result.**

Initially, the lower levels, such as object modules and blocks, are tested. These are tested by the designers. Lower subsystem levels are then tested. The integration test does not come as a 'big bang', but rather these tests are introduced on varying levels when integrating larger and larger parts. One tool for integration testing involves using the use case model to integrate one use case at a time. This is normally performed by an independent testing group. The test is thus performed by starting to test the lower levels, in order later to test the use cases and finally the whole system. The requirements model again forms a powerful tool here; as we test each use case, we check that the objects communicate correctly in that particular use case. Similarly, we check the user interfaces described in the requirements model. We thus see that the requirements model is **verified** by the testing process.

We may also view a test as an object just as we view use cases as objects. By doing this we can view the test specification as the test's class, and thus we can also inherit common parts or compose them from several test specifications, which is valuable when writing and thus reusing the specifications. In this way, we view a test execution as an instance of this class. The instance thus, quite clearly, has behavior and also a state. The outcome of such an execution is a test result. We have test results for all different types of test. The testing model will be discussed in more detail in Chapter 12.

# 6.9   Summary

This chapter discussed the underlying architecture of the OOSE method. Here we have defined the concepts and the models that are developed when using OOSE.

System development includes many activities during the system life cycle. When developing a product, it is essential to focus on all these activities. When taking a life-cycle view, one of the most important properties of a system is that it is maintainable, that is, changes can be made to the system at a reasonable cost.

System development is a complex task and by building models at different levels of granularity this complexity can be managed. Five different models are developed for a product in OOSE. The transitions between these models are seamless, which means that the model transformation is repeatable by different developers. Another important property we should have is traceability between the models, that is, we should be able to trace changes from one object in one model to objects in another model. The transitions between these models are handled by processes. These processes manage a product over its life cycle. Four processes are used: analysis, construction, testing and components. In all models, objects are handled.

The first model, the requirements model, consists of actors and use cases supported by an intuitive domain object model and interface descriptions. The actors model something that will interact with the system and a use case specifies a flow that a specific actor invokes in the system. The object model gives a conceptual, easy-to-understand picture of the system and the interface descriptions describe the system interfaces in detail. The requirements model will thus completely define the functional requirements of the system from a user's perspective. Since the model has a user perspective, it is easy to communicate with potential users in terms of this model.

The analysis model is developed from the requirements model. The aim is to get a logical and robust structure that will be maintainable during the system life cycle. Three object types are used. Interface objects are used to model functionality that is directly dependent on the system interfaces. The entity objects model information that the system should manage for a longer time, and behavior tied to this information. Entity objects typically survive a specific use case. The control objects should model functionality that is transaction-oriented for a specific use case and that should be kept together for maintainability purposes. Typically, they do not survive a use case. The reason for having these three object types is that a change should preferably be local to one object only.

The design model refines the analysis models further and takes into consideration the current implementation environment. The blocks describe how the system will be implemented. The ideal analysis model must often be changed owing to a complex implementation environment, even if this is not desirable. However, the basic system structuring should be kept as far as possible as defined in the analysis model. In the design model, the blocks are further specified using the use case model to explicitly specify the interfaces and the communication between the blocks.

The implementation model consists mainly of the source code written to implement the blocks. Here common and sound implementation techniques should be used. OOSE does not require an object-oriented language for implementation, although this is preferable since all the essential concepts exist in these languages.

The testing model is developed when testing the system. Testing is done on several different levels of granularity. The lower-level objects are tested initially when performing unit testing. The use case model is used as the primary tool when doing integration testing.

# 7 Analysis

## 7.1 Introduction

### 7.1.1 Why an analysis process?

The aim of the analysis phase is to analyze, specify and define the system to be built. The models developed will describe *what* the system is to do. The basis of this modeling is basically the requirements (expressed in some form) of the system. It is important to carry on a dialogue with the prospective orderers and users, so that the system that is built is really what is wanted. In the analysis phase, it will then be possible to build models that will make it easier for us to understand the system.

The models that are developed during analysis are fully application-oriented, and no consideration is paid to the real implementation environment where the system is to be realized, for instance the programming language, DBMS, distribution or hardware configuration that should be used. This will be our definition of analysis: modeling the system with no regard to the actual implementation environment (see McMenamin and Palmer (1984)). The purpose is to formulate the problem and to build models able to solve the problem under ideal conditions. As the models are entirely problem-oriented, and no attention is paid to the real implementation environment, they are fairly straightforward to develop from a functionality viewpoint. The models can be discussed from the application's perspective, with application-oriented concepts. Thus it will be possible to discuss the models with the users of the system without using implementation terms.

Sooner or later the system will have to be adapted to the prevailing conditions, of course. This is done in construction, when all those considerations that have been neglected in analysis are taken into account. The fact that little heed is paid to the implementation environment will guarantee that the ensuing system architecture will be based on the problem and not on the conditions prevailing during the implementation. It will, of course, be impossible to develop the models entirely without consideration of their realization; the models and their architecture must be built so that everything in them can be realized. Another great advantage with this procedure is that our analysis models will remain intact, if and when the implementation conditions change. Hence we can use the same models without changing them even if the implementation environment changes.

## 7.1.2    What is done in analysis?

Two different models are developed in analysis, the requirements model and the analysis model. The real base is the requirements specification and discussions with the prospective users (see Figure 7.1). The first model, the requirements model, should above all make it possible to delimit the system and to define its functionality. For this purpose we develop a conceptual picture of the system using problem domain objects and also specific interface descriptions of the system if they are meaningful for this system. We also describe the system as a number of use cases that are performed by a number of actors. The actors constitute the environment of the system, and the use cases are what takes place within the system. The use case concept is one of the unique concepts of OOSE.

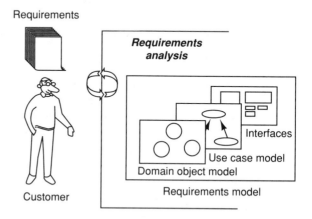

**Figure 7.1**    On the basis of the requirements specification, both the requirements model and the analysis model are developed in the analysis process.

The analysis model gives a conceptual configuration of the system, consisting of control objects, entity objects and interface objects. The purpose of this model is to develop a robust and extensible structure as a base for construction. Each of the object types has its own special contribution to make to this robustness, and together they will offer the total functionality that was specified in the requirements model. The analysis model does not have any counterpart in other methods, but is unique to OOSE, although, since the techniques that we use are orthogonal to the rest of the development, it is possible to add this model to other approaches as well. To manage the development, the analysis model may group objects in subsystems.

The analysis model comprises a total functional specification of the system we wish to develop, without any reference to the implementation environment. In the construction process we will construct the system from the analysis model. This is when adaptations are made to cater for the implementation language, the database management system, the architecture of the computer system and so on. Thus the design model and the analysis model are both models of the system we wish to build, but with different purposes. An object in one model can be directly traced an object in the other model, and vice versa. We call this **traceability.**

## 7.1.3   An example system

Throughout the discussion of the analysis and the construction activities, we will show how the different concepts are used in practice, by developing a system. The system controls a recycling machine for returnable bottles, cans and crates (used in Europe to hold several bottles). The machine can be used by several customers at the same time and each customer can return all three types of item on the same occasion (see Figure 7.2).

Since there may be different types and sizes of bottle and can, the system has to check, for each item, what type has been returned. The system will register how many items each customer returns and, when the customer asks for a receipt, the system will print out what he or she deposited, the value of the returned items and the total return sum that will be paid to the customer.

The system is also used by an operator. The operator wants to know how many items of each type have been returned during the day. At the end of the day, the operator asks for a printout of the total number of items that have been deposited in the machine on that particular day. The operator should also be able to change

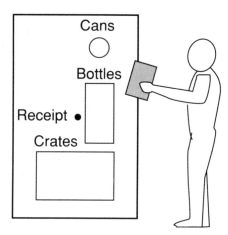

**Figure 7.2**  The recycling machine can receive several different types of returnable item from several customers at the same time.

information in the system, such as the deposit values of the items. If there is something amiss, for instance if a can gets stuck or if the receipt roll is finished, the operator will be called by a special alarm signal.

This example system is chosen as a case study that is easy to describe and to understand; it is not intended as an example of a good recycling machine. The system should be viewed as a toy example and should not be used as a basis for real system modeling. The descriptions that we give are too simple to be used in system design; nor should they be used as templates. The system is small, so the models will be small; consequently, all the properties of OOSE will not be fully obvious in this example. Later chapters of the book contain examples of OOSE used in larger systems, and they will give a clearer picture of how OOSE is used in larger developments.

## 7.2  The requirements model

### 7.2.1  System development based on user requirements

The requirements model aims to delimit the system and define the functionality that the system should offer. This model could function as a contract between the developer and the orderer of the system and thus forms the developer's view of what the customer wants. Therefore it is essential that non-OOSE practitioners should also be able to read this model.

The requirements model will govern the development of all the other models, so this model is central throughout the whole system development. The requirements model will be structured by the analysis model, realized by the design model, implemented by the implementation model and tested by the testing model. Not only will the other models be verified against the requirements model, but the other models will actually be developed directly from it. The requirements model will also function as a basis for the development of operational instructions and manuals, since anything that the system should do is described here from a user's perspective. The requirements model, and especially the use cases, will be the unifying thread running through the whole of OOSE.

Since the whole system development starts from what the users wish to be able to do with the system, we build the system from the users' point of view. In this way, it will be easy to discuss the requirements model with the users, and changes to the model will be simple to make.

The requirements model consists of three parts: the use case model, the problem domain object model and user interface descriptions. The use case model specifies the functionality the system has to offer from a user's perspective and we define what should take place inside the system. This model uses **actors** to represent roles the users can play, and **use cases** to represent what the users should be able to do with the system. Each use case is a complete course of events in the system, seen from a user's perspective. If appropriate, interface descriptions may also be developed. These will specify in detail what the user interface will look like when the use cases are performed. To give a conceptual picture and a better understanding of the system, we use objects that represent occurrences in the problem domain. This model will serve as a common foundation for all the people involved in the requirements analysis, developers as well as orderers.

## 7.2.2   Actors

In order to identify the use cases to be performed in the system, we will identify the users of the system. This is done by means of **actors.** Actors model the prospective users; the actor is a user type or category, and when a user does something he or she acts as an occurrence of this type. One person can instantiate (play the roles of) several different actors. Actors thus define roles that users can play.

The actors model anything that needs to exchange information with the system. Actors can model human users, but they can also model other systems communicating with our system. The essential thing is that actors constitute anything that is external to the system we are to develop.

Thus we will have to make a **system delimitation** to define where the boundary is between actors and use cases.

In our example of the recycling machine we can see from the problem description that we have two actors, namely *Customer* and *Operator*. These are the only ones who should interact with the system. They interact with the system in different ways: the *Customer* puts in bottles and suchlike and receives a receipt from the machine, while the *Operator* maintains the machine and gets daily reports (see Figure 7.3).

To stress the difference between actor and user, we think of an actor as a class, that is, a description of a behavior. A user, on the other hand, can play several roles, that is, serve as many actors. For instance, think of Brian. He is the operator of the machine, so he normally acts as an instance of the *Operator* actor. However, sometimes he deposits his own bottles and cans, and then he acts as an instance of *Customer*.

Finding actors can entail some work, and all the actors are seldom found at once. A good starting point is often to check why the system is to be designed. Who are the actors that the system is supposed to help? The actors who are going to use the system directly (maybe in their daily work) we call **primary** actors. Each one of these actors will perform one or some of the main tasks of the system. In our example, *Customer* is a primary actor, as it is for the customers that the system is built.

As all the important functions of the system are investigated, more and more primary actors are identified. Besides these primary actors there are actors supervising and maintaining the system. We call them **secondary** actors. The secondary actors exist only so that

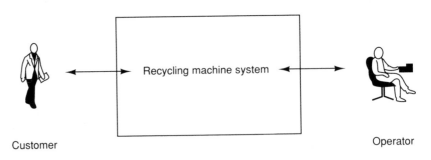

Customer                                                                    Operator

**Figure 7.3**   The recycling machine has two actors: the *Customer* and the *Operator*.

the primary actors can use the system. In our example, *Operator* is a secondary actor, for we would not need an operator if there were no customers.

We make the division into primary and secondary actors because we want the system structure to be decided in terms of the main functionality. The primary actors will govern the system structure. Thus, when identifying use cases, we will start with the primary actors. In this way, we can guarantee that the architecture of the system will be adapted to the most important users. Changes to the system will mainly come from these actors.

It is often simple to find actors that model people. It is more difficult to identify those which are machines, but as the use cases are specified, it will become clearer that they are necessary. These actors can of course be both primary and secondary actors.

Normally, we do not view the functionality of the underlying system (for example, the operating system) as an actor. For instance, a system clock is not normally modeled as an actor. However, nothing stops us from modeling it as an actor. In some cases, for instance where the underlying system has an active role with respect to the application, it is very meaningful to model it as an actor.

### 7.2.3   Use cases

After we have defined what is outside our system we can define the functionality inside it. We do this by specifying **use cases**. A use case is a specific way of using the system by performing some part of the functionality. Each use case constitutes a complete course of events initiated by an actor and it specifies the interaction that takes place between an actor and the system. A use case is thus a special sequence of related transactions performed by an actor and the system in a dialogue. The collected use cases specify all the existing ways of using the system.

To understand use cases we can view their descriptions as state transition graphs. Each stimulus sent between an actor and the system performs a state change in this graph. We can thus view a use case as existing in different states. The related transactions mentioned above are thus the transitions in this graph.

The reason that we have identified actors initially is that they will be the major tool for finding the use cases. Each actor will perform a number of use cases in the system. By going through all the actors and defining everything they will be able to do with the system, we will define the complete functionality of the system.

Like actors, use cases can be instantiated and this is done every time a user performs a use case in the system. Thus there is also a relationship between class and instance. This topic was discussed in greater depth in Chapter 6.

As several use cases can begin in a similar way, it is not always possible to decide what use case has been instantiated until it is completed. Consider for instance a telephone exchange system. One actor here is a subscriber, and a typical use case is to make a local telephone call. This use case starts when the subscriber lifts his telephone. Another use case is to order a wake-up call. Both use cases start when the subscriber lifts his telephone. But when a subscriber lifts his telephone we do not know which use case he wants to perform. Thus use cases may begin in a similar manner and we may not know which use case was carried out until it is over. In other words, the actor does not demand that a use case should be performed; he only initiates a course of events that will finally result in a complete use case.

The use cases are identified through the actors. For every complete course of events initiated by an actor we identify one use case. By considering each actor, we decide which use cases this actor is supposed to perform. To identify the use cases, we can read the requirements specification from an actor's perspective and carry on discussions with those who will act as actors. It will help to ask a number of questions, such as:

- What are the main tasks of each actor?
- Will the actor have to read/write/change any of the system information?
- Will the actor have to inform the system about outside changes?
- Does the actor wish to be informed about unexpected changes?

In the recycling system we can identify a number of use cases. Let us use the actors as a starting point. The *Customer* is the primary actor so let us start with her. She should of course be able to return deposit items. This forms one use case, *Returning Item*. This use case should include everything until a receipt is received, if it is to be complete. Are there any more use cases for *Customer*? The situation where an item is stuck is an alternative for this use case and we will discuss later how to handle alternatives. Otherwise, any more use cases are not obvious at the moment, so let us continue to the *Operator*. The *Operator* is a secondary actor. He should be able to get a

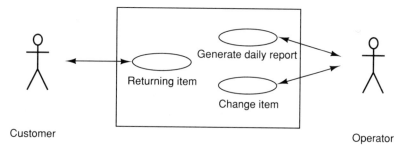

**Figure 7.4**   The first attempt at the use case for the recycling machine.

daily report of what items have been deposited today. This will be one use case, *Generate Daily Report*. He should also be able to modify information in the system, such as each item's deposit value. Let us call this use case *Change Item*. A use case is drawn as an ellipse with its name beneath the ellipse (see also the box on notation). We now have the use case model as illustrated in Figure 7.4.

The use cases can be summarized as follows:

*Returning Item* is started by *Customer* when she wants to return cans, bottles or crates. With each item that *Customer* places in the recycling machine, the system will increase the received number of items from *Customer* as well as the daily total of this particular type. When *Customer* has deposited all her items, she will press the receipt button to get a receipt on which the returned items have been printed as well as the total return sum.

*Generate Daily Report* is started by *Operator* when he wants to print out information about the deposit items returned during the day. The system will print out how many of each deposit item type have been received, as well as the overall total for the day. The total number will be reset to zero to start a new daily report.

*Change Item* is used by *Operator* to change information in the system. The return value as well as the size of each returnable item can be changed, and new types of item can be added.

**On the notation convention**

The notation used in figures has the convention of one standard-sized symbol for each object type and the name of the object beneath the symbol. Additionally, relations are expressed in the figure. However, no other information is normally introduced. Some other methods introduce much more information in a figure, such as having information inside the symbols.

We have chosen this notation in order to have a changeable and surveyable picture. If we had information inside the symbols, these they would need to be extended in size when we add more information. This extension affects the picture and may force us to move the other objects as well. Hence the picture then depends on how far the details of the model have evolved. Additionally, as we add more and more information it is very easy to lose the surveyability of the model.

Instead we think of the figure as a graphic view of information concerning the model in some information bank (database). We therefore assume a CASE tool will be used to handle this information bank. To add information to the model, we would just like to point at a specific object and retrieve some information aspect of this object, such as a use case's detailed description or operations on an object. In this way there is no need to have different sizes of object, but rather we can preserve a view that does not change when we change some information from another view and that information is also shown in the first view.

It is not always obvious what functionality should be placed in separate use cases, and what is only a variant of one and the same use case. The complexity of the use cases is important in this context. We have a number of different ways of expressing variants. If the differences are small, they can be described as variants of the same use case, either as just a selection within a use case or as separate variants of a use case. If the differences are large they should be described as separate use cases. For instance, remember the telephone call use case. If the person being called does not answer, is that a different use case from the one where he answers? It will surely be different behavior. However, we would regard them as variations of the same use case since they are logically highly correlated.

We have as yet only discussed the identification of use cases. This is often a very iterative process where several attempts are made. When the picture stabilizes, each use case should be described in more detail. First we describe the **basic course**, which is the most important course of events giving the best understanding of the use case. Variants of the basic course of events, and errors that can occur are described in **alternative courses**. Normally a use case has only one basic course, but several alternative courses. The descriptions could be made earlier, but since the requirements model will undergo several changes initially, too much work should not be done early on, as it will be thrown away.

Thus we describe each use case in more detail. Below is the flow description of the use case *Returning Item*:

When the customer returns a deposit item, it is measured by the system. The measurements are used to determine what kind of can, bottle or crate has been deposited. If accepted, the cusomter total is incremented, as is the daily total for that specific item type. If the item is not accepted, 'NOT VALID' is highlighted on the panel.

When the customer presses the receipt button, the printer prints the date. The customer total is calculated and the following information printed on the receipt for each item type:

name
number returned
deposit value
total for this type

Finally, the sum that the customer should receive is printed on the receipt.

When analyzing and describing the use cases in detail, the system is studied very closely. It is not surprising then that points which are unclear in the requirements specification are revealed during this process. Vagueness in the requirements specification thus becomes obvious at a very early stage.

Since the use cases often focus on a particular functionality of the system, it is possible to analyze the total functionality of the system in an incremental way. In this manner we can develop use cases for different functionality areas independently and later join these use cases together to form the complete requirements model. We can thus focus on one problem at a time. This ability to take one part at a time also opens the way to parallel development.

**Extension**

A powerful concept that is used to structure and relate use case descriptions is the **extension** association. Extension specifies how one use case description may be inserted into, and thus extend, another use case description. Extensions to use cases can be described in a very simple way and, in particular, changes and additions to functionality are more easily made.

The use case where the new functionality is to be inserted must be a complete course in itself. Hence this description is entirely independent of the inserted course. In this way, the description pays no attention to any courses that might be inserted, and this additional degree of complexity is thus avoided. So, we describe the first basic use cases totally independently of any extended functionality. Similarly, we can add new extensions without changing the original descriptions.

In our example we can see one use of the extension concept. When an item is stuck the system should issue an alarm. We can describe this alarm as a use case description that extends the *Returning Item* use case description. This new use case we call *Item Stuck* (see Figure 7.5). The extension association is drawn with a dashed arrow since it is a class association (concerns the descriptions). Instance associations, as mentioned, are drawn with full lines. We have actually already seen such associations in the use case model, namely in the figure where actors communicated with use cases. This is an instance association since it is always an instance of an actor that will communicate with an instance of a use case.

Thus *Returning Item* is described entirely independently of this new flow, which makes the description simple. The use case *Item Stuck* can be described as follows.

> When an item gets stuck the alarm is activated to call the operator.
> When the *Operator* has removed the stuck item he resets the alarm and the *Customer* can continue to return items. The *Customer*'s total so far is still valid. The *Customer* does not get credit for the stuck item.

What we see here is another use case property: they can communicate with several different actors. *Customer* will start the use case, but *Operator* will also communicate with it.

By means of the extension association the system will be given a good and modifiable structure, as we shall see later. As it is possible to describe several use cases independently of each other, their descriptions will be simple. To understand extension better we can view a typical situation where we have a simple use case *Login/Logout*, and describe all use cases that may be done when a user is logged in by means of extensions to the use case *Login/Logout*. It will then be simple to add new options without having to make changes in the old use cases; new use cases are simply defined and used as extensions to *Login/Logout* (see Figure 7.6). (This situation is so common that models often assume this functionality without specifying it.)

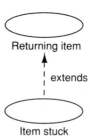

Returning item

extends

Item stuck

**Figure 7.5**  *Item Stuck* is inserted into *Returning Item* when a deposit item gets stuck.

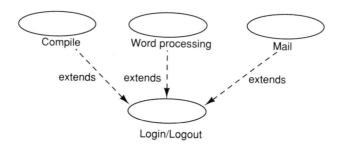

**Figure 7.6**   A common situation is having a use case *Login/Logout* into which several other use cases can be inserted.

Another example of use of the extension association is when you want to collect statistics in a specific use case. Say, for instance, that you have a use case that controls an industrial process. Every time you execute this use case, you also want to measure and collect some statistics in this process. You can describe this by having a use case *Collect Statistics* as an extension use case to the control use case.

Extension is thus used to model extensions of other, complete use cases. Here are some examples of when to use extend:

- To model optional parts of use cases.
- To model complex and alternative courses which seldom occur, for instance *Item Stuck* in our example.
- To model separate sub-courses which are executed only in certain cases.
- To model the situation where several different use cases can be inserted into a special use case, such as *Login/Logout* mentioned above or a menu system with options.

We might view the extension association as an interrupt in the original use case which occurs when the new use case is to be inserted. The original use case does not know whether an interrupt will happen or not.

For each use case that is to be inserted into another use case, we state the position in the original use case where the extension use case is to be inserted. This position is stated as exactly as possible, and is described in the extension use case (not in the original use case). The position is expressed as a reference to a place in the original use case's description.

What happens when a course is inserted in this way is as follows. The original use case runs as usual up to the point where the new use case is to be inserted. At this point, the new course is inserted. After the extension has finished, the original course continues as if nothing had happened. When we described *Item Stuck* we were somewhat inaccurate: the use case is not inserted only when an item gets stuck, but instead always takes place. Actually, whether an item has got stuck is always checked. If it has, the whole course is initiated; otherwise the original course *Returning Item* continues directly.

## 7.2.4    Interface descriptions

When describing the use cases and communicating them to potential users, it is often appropriate to describe the interfaces in more detail. If it is a Man–Machine Interface (MMI ) we can use sketches of what the user will see on the screen when performing the use case or provide more sophisticated simulations using a User Interface Management System (UIMS). In this way we can simulate the use cases as they will appear to the users before even thinking about how to realize them. We can thus liven up the use case descriptions with real computer interaction by the potential users. Such a technique will eliminate several possibilities for misunderstandings. If the interfaces are hardware protocols, we can refer to the various standards. These interface descriptions are thus an essential part of the use case descriptions and should accompany them.

When designing user interfaces, it is essential to have the users involved. By doing a user interface design at this early stage, this can be guaranteed. It is also essential that the interface reflects the user's logical view of the system. The problem domain model (discussed next) is exactly such a perspective. By using this model as a conceptual base to define the concepts and semantics of the system, we can guarantee that the user interface will be consistent with the user's logical system perspective. This is actually one of the most fundamental principles of human–interface design: the consistency between the user's conceptual picture of the system and the system's actual behavior.

It is not only user interfaces that are interesting to specify in detail at this early stage. Since the requirements model may be used as a functional requirements specification, it may at this stage also be interesting to define other system interfaces such as communication protocols that should be standardized. These interface descriptions may also take the form of protocols to other systems.

The recycling machine has different kinds of interface. There is the customer panel which we mentioned earlier, including buttons, holes and alarm devices. There is also the receipt layout. These interfaces are for the customer. The operator also needs an interface for changing information, resetting alarms, requesting day summaries and so on.

### 7.2.5  Problem domain objects

When working with the requirements model it can sometimes be difficult to define the task of the system and especially the system boundaries. This is typically the case when the requirements specification exists only in a very vague form. Then, a very good tool is to start to develop a logical view of the system using problem domain objects, that is, objects that have a direct counterpart in the application environment and that the system must know about.

Such a problem domain model will help us develop a noun list which will be a strong support when we specify the use cases. From this model it is possible to define the concepts that the system should be working with. In this way we will have a glossary that can be used to formulate the functionality of the use cases. In the recycling system we see that we have used the words 'returnable item', 'can', 'bottle' and 'crate' quite extensively without really defining them. When several people are involved in the specification of use cases, such a noun list derived from a problem domain model can be of great value.

The major benefit of such a model, though, is that it is a very good tool with which to communicate about the system. Since the users and orderers will recognize all the concepts, the model can be used when defining what the system will do. A technique we have used when working with such a model is to give the customer a pen and paper and ask him to draw a picture of his view of the system. By discussing it with him, a quite extensive problem domain model will evolve. In this way we can also develop, as described above, a common terminology when reasoning about the use cases, and so lessen the probability of misunderstandings between the developer and the potential user.

Many other object-oriented methods, such as those of Coad and Yourdon (1991) and Booch (1991), focus entirely on such models, and the heuristics in these methods can very well be used for the identification of these objects. In these methods, this model will also form a base for the actual implementation, that is, the objects are directly mapped onto classes during implementation. However, this is not the case in OOSE, as discussed in the previous chapter. Our experience with such an approach tells us differently. Instead we develop an analysis model that is more robust and maintainable in the face of future changes, rather than using a problem domain model to serve as the base for design and implementation.

How extensive should a problem domain model actually be? In Figure 7.7 we have illustrated different possible degrees of refinement.

Since the main purpose is to form a common base of understanding for developing the requirements model, and not to define the system entirely, we believe that the object name and possibly also the logical attributes and the static instance associations (that is, the static references between these objects) are an appropriate level to stay at. However, it is of course possible to further refine these objects if it helps understanding and thus specify the functionality of the system completely using these objects. It is fully possible to express the entire functionality as behavior associated with these objects, but this will not yield the most robust and extensible structure for the system. Keep in mind that too much work here may result in it being hard to free yourself from this structure when developing the more stable and maintainable analysis model. Experience shows that many (if not all) of these domain objects will

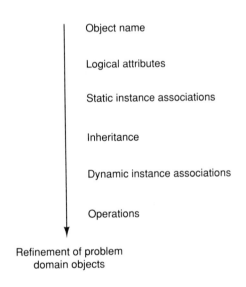

Refinement of problem
domain objects

**Figure 7.7**  Suggested possibilities to refine the problem domain objects. By static instance associations we mean associations that are used when an object should statically know of another object, namely a static reference to an object. Dynamic instance associations indicate such associations where one object can send stimuli to another object, which implies a dependence on the other object's protocol.

show up as entity objects in the analysis model. However, it is dangerous to do this mapping mechanically, since there may very well be changes (for example, if it is obvious that information on an object is not actually needed in the system). Additionally, often there will be even more entity objects in the analysis model than objects in the problem domain model.

In the recycling system, a problem domain model would be quite small since it is such a trivial system. The main concepts used are *Can*, *Bottle* and *Crate*. These will all be handled in the same manner and we can thus identify an abstract class *Deposit Item*. Since the customer will have a receipt printed when all items have been returned, we may also need to be able to manage the objects *Receipt* and *Customer*. We will now have the domain model shown in Figure 7.8.

In larger systems the use of the domain model becomes more obvious. In the example chapters later, we illustrate the use of a problem domain model as a support for understanding a system in more detail.

The problem domain model can be used for several different purposes. We have discussed above its supporting role in the formulation of use case descriptions and also in MMI design. We can also elaborate this model to gain a better understanding of the system. In this way we can focus more on the problem domain objects. We can then specify the functionality of the system fully by using such a model and including formal operations on objects, in which case we can also use it as a requirements model expressed without use cases. However, when continuing the development with the method presented here, the use cases will be of much more help in the forthcoming work, and therefore we recommend elaborating these instead.

A problem domain model can also be used when doing enterprise modeling. Then it is essential to capture all the important

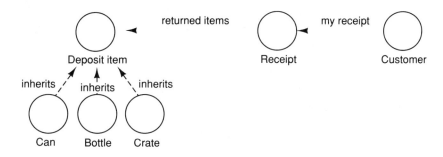

**Figure 7.8**  A problem domain model of the recycling machine.

and fundamental concepts in one model. Actually, the extension of OOSE to include enterprise modeling will deliver just such a problem domain model as output, that is, to be used as input to the system development process. Accompanying this will be a first version of a requirements model of the systems required in the enterprise. In such a way the transition between enterprise modeling and system development can be achieved in a seamless way.

This means that a problem domain model, developed with some kind of technique, will serve as a very solid input to system development. In some projects we have been involved in, such a problem domain model already existed. Then the idea of the system to be developed was quite mature, and the development of the requirements model and the analysis model could be done in a quite straightforward manner without too many iterations.

### 7.2.6    Further refinement of the requirements model

The requirements model as described thus far will be sufficient to specify the functionality of the system. However, we can elaborate this model further not only to enhance reuse, but also to prepare for the transition to the analysis model. This work is not really very interesting to the orderer of the system since it is moving into areas which do not concern him.

This refinement is mainly done by identifying similar parts of the use cases and extracting these similar parts. In this way we only have to describe the similar part once instead of in all use cases showing this behavior. Any changes to this part will thus automatically affect all use cases that share this part. We call the use cases that we extract **abstract** use cases since they will not be instantiated on their own, but are only meaningful to describe parts which are common to other use cases. We call the use cases that really will be instantiated **concrete** use cases.

The descriptions of the abstract use cases are thus used in the descriptions of the concrete use cases. This means that, when an instance of a use case follows the description of a concrete use case, at a certain point it continues by following the description of the abstract use case instead. This relationship is thus some kind of inheritance. However, it does not have exactly the same semantics as inheritance has in an object-oriented programming language. Therefore we give it a different name. We call this relation a **uses** relation. Intuitively, this is also easier to understand than inheritance as used in an OO language, since it is not discrete operations that are used, but rather sequences. Therefore these sequences may have to be explicitly interleaved in the concrete use cases. Since it is a class association it is drawn as a dashed arrow from the concrete towards the abstract use case that is to be used.

Normally, similar behavior between use cases is identified *after* the use cases have been described. However, in some cases it is possible to identify them earlier. In the recycling example we see that the two use cases *Returning Item* and *Generate Daily Report* will both print out a receipt. We can thus identify an abstract use case *Print* that performs this printing (see Figure 7.9).

Reuse between use cases is not limited to one abstract use case. Several parts that are common to other use cases may be extracted from a use case. One specific use case can then use all these abstract use cases.

In use case decomposition, the entire course is always used. The course need not be an atomic sequence, although this is often the case. However, we may have a situation where the abstract use cases can be used through interleaving them into the concrete use case (see Figure 7.10). In the left-hand side abstract use case we have a sequence that consists of the subsequences A and B. These sequences should be integrated with subsequences C and D as illustrated in Figure 7.10.

Abstract use cases can also be used by other abstract use cases. It is difficult to state exactly when there is no point in extracting more abstract use cases. A good rule of thumb is that when the level of separate operations on objects has been reached, you ought to stop. The effort to find common sequences has then been carried too far. With some experience, it will soon become easy to discern where the limit should be drawn.

A technique to extract abstract use cases is to identify abstract actors. An abstract actor typically describes a **role** that should be

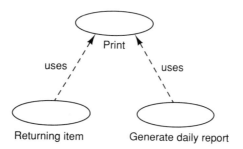

**Figure 7.9**   An abstract use case *Print* has been identified to describe common parts between two other use cases.

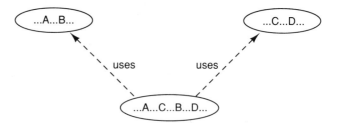

**Figure 7.10**   A concrete uses case uses the two abstract use cases and decides explicitly how the interleaving is to take place.

played against the system. When different actors play similar roles they may inherit a common abstract actor. The advantage of abstract actor modeling is that it expresses similarities in use cases. If the same (part of a) use case may be performed by several different actors, the use cases need be specified only with respect to one actor instead of to several.

In the recycling system the actors actually have one common behavior: they can receive a receipt. It is therefore possible to identify one abstract actor, *Receipt Receiver*, which both *Customer* and *Operator* inherit (see Figure 7.11). Now both our concrete actors can receive a receipt and this needs to be specified only once.

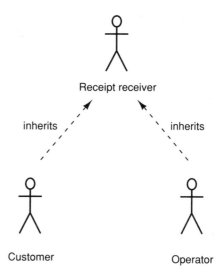

**Figure 7.11**   *Receipt Receiver* is an abstract actor which is inherited by both *Customer* and *Operator*.

Abstract actors can also be used to specify different privileges in a system. An example of this will be shown in Chapter 13.

The uses association is thus used when two or more use cases have common behavior. Normally, there is no reason to create abstract use cases that are used only by one use case. However, in fact, we had this situation with the extension association. An extension use case may be viewed as an abstract use case since it is seldom meaningful on its own.

Since the extension and uses associations between use cases are both class associations, you may ask when should uses be chosen rather than extensions and vice versa? In fact, in most cases the choice is quite obvious, and causes no problems. An important criterion is how strongly functionally coupled the use cases are. If the course to be extended is meaningful in its own right, the addition could be described using extension. The extension then only needs access to the flow of control of the use case being extended. If the courses are strongly functionally coupled, and the insertion must take place in order to obtain a complete course, uses should be chosen. There is also a difference in how they are found; uses are found through extraction of common sequences from several different use cases, whereas extensions are found when new courses are introduced, or when there are extensions to an existing use case that the user wishes to perform in some specific cases. You can be deceived by this rule, since extension use cases can also be common to several use cases.

## 7.2.7   Discussion

As has been pointed out several times, the use case is the core running through all OOSE activities when developing all models. Our experience with use cases is that they help us to focus on the problem, as they constitute a strong tool for defining the system functionality. Additionally, since they are logical and straightforward to find, they force the development forward as the use cases are identified and specified. They will also be a strong support when developing the subsequent models, since these models are based upon the use cases. So, a disciplined way of working is natural as you control the work through the use cases. It is also possible to estimate the amount of work in subsequent models since you know how many use cases you have and you can predict the time needed to handle one use case. This topic is discussed further in Chapter 15.

When working with use cases, a common question concerns how complete the use cases should be. For instance, in the recycling example, we could have viewed the sequence when the customer pushes the start button and inserts the items as one use case and the sequence when he or she pushes the receipt button as another use case. But we chose to have them as one complete use case instead. Generally, it is better to have longer and more extensive use cases than several smaller ones. We want complete and real courses and not several sub-courses. Otherwise there will be very many use cases that are hard to keep track of and it will be harder to see how they are related, in time, for instance. The arguments in favor of having the sequence as one complete use case are:

- When specifying the use case, we may follow a complete flow through the entire system.
- From the orderer's point of view it is a logical cohesive flow of events in the system.
- It may be more effective when testing the use case since it covers more logical cohesive events in the system and failures can be found more easily.
- It is easier to synchronize the use case since it is one sequence that starts different events in chronological order.

The arguments in favor of separating the use case into several different use cases are:

- It may be troublesome to find the right instance of a use case that is of large extent since the use case may very well last for several days.
- From a potential actor's view it is more logical to have use cases that the actor starts.
- It may be easier to test the use case since every use case starts from external events and not from internal system events.

## 7.3 The analysis model

When the requirements model has been developed, and often also signed off by the orderers, we can focus on the structuring of the system. This is done initially by developing the analysis model. In the analysis model we describe the system using three different types of object: **interface objects**, **entity objects** and **control objects** (see Figure 7.12). Each of these objects has its own purpose and will model one specific aspect of the system. We also use subsystems to group these objects into manageable units.

In the requirements model we have specified what is to take place within the system. The analysis model aims at creating a good

Entity object   Interface object   Control object

**Figure 7.12** The object types used to structure the system in the analysis model.

platform for the system design and will also form the basis of the design. The requirements model is thus structured by the analysis model.

The work in developing the analysis model really entails distributing the behavior specified in the use case descriptions among the objects in the analysis model (see Figure 7.13). An object can be common to several different use cases. Thus we should state explicitly which object is responsible for which behavior in the use case. This does not mean that the behavior must be broken down into operations at this stage, although this is possible. A more natural procedure is to write a verbal description of the responsibilities of or roles played by each object.

We will now study the different object types more closely and discuss how it is possible to find them from the use cases.

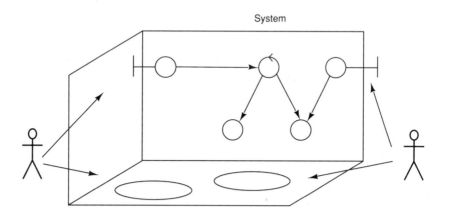

**Figure 7.13** Use cases and objects are different views of the same system. An object can therefore typically participate in several use cases.

## 7.3.1    Interface objects

All functionality specified in the use case descriptions that is directly dependent on the system environment is placed in interface objects. It is through these objects that the actors communicate with the system. The task of an interface object is to translate the actor's input to the system into events in the system, and to translate those events in the system that the actor is interested in into something which is presented to the actor. Interface objects can, in other words, describe bidirectional communication between the system and its users.

Interface objects are quite simple to identify. We have at least three strategies. Either they are clearly identified from the system interface descriptions accompanying the requirements model, or we can start from the actors, or we can read the use case descriptions and extract the functionality that is interface-specific. Let us initially use the second alternative, namely to start from the actors.

Each concrete actor needs its own interface for its communication with the system. In many cases an actor may need several interface objects. In the example of the recycling machine, each of the concrete actors, *Customer* and *Operator,* needs its own interface object to the system. The *Customer* needs the panel with the push-buttons and the slots in which to insert the items and the *Operator* needs his interface to be able to change information in the system and to generate daily reports. Furthermore, we need an interface object to call the *Operator* when an alarm is issued, as well as one to print out a receipt. We thus have the interface objects shown in Figure 7.14. Finding an interface object for an abstract actor does not always occur, as in this case.

Let us now look at the third strategy, namely to identify interface objects from the use case descriptions. We have marked the places in the use case description below where interface functionality is involved. Note that the use case description has been taken directly from the requirements model.

> When the customer *returns a deposit item, it is measured* by the system. The measurements are used to determine what kind of can, bottle or crate has been deposited. If accepted, the customer total is incremented, as is the daily total for that specific item type. If the item is not accepted, the *light for 'NOT VALID' is highlighted on the panel.*
>
> When the customer *presses the receipt button, the printer prints the date.* The customer total is calculated and the following information *printed on the receipt* for each item type:
>
> name
> number returned

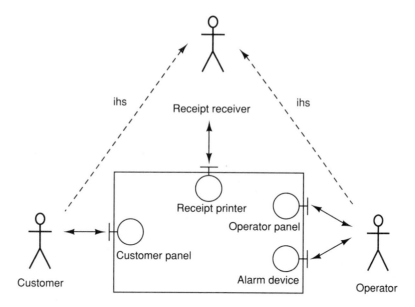

**Figure 7.14**   We have four interface objects in the recycling machine: *Customer Panel, Operator Panel, Receipt Printer* and *Alarm Device.*

deposit value
total for this type

Finally the sum that the customer should receive is *printed on the receipt.*

We see that this technique yields the same interface objects, namely *Customer Panel* and *Receipt Printer* for this use case.

The following is a short description of the interface objects identified:

Customer panel

The functionality that manages the sensors in the deposit slots, start button and receipt button.

Operator panel

Interface for changing information in the system and for generating daily reports.

Alarm device

Controls a signal device and also has a reset button for that device.

Receipt printer

Writes text on a paper roll. After printout the paper is cut off. When the paper roll is almost finished the operator should be called through the alarm device.

It is evident that the interface objects are not entirely independent of each other, but that they must know of each other to be able to solve certain tasks. For instance, the *Receipt Printer* must know which *Alarm Device* to sound when the paper roll is finished. This is solved by the introduction of **acquaintance associations** between the objects. An acquaintance association is a static association between instances and means that an instance knows of the existence of another instance. It does not give the object the right to exchange information with the other object; for that purpose a dynamic association is needed as will be discussed below. Instance associations are, as mentioned, drawn with solid, directed lines.

An object may associate several other instances of the same class. Therefore we should also describe how many instances can be associated with the acquaintance association. This is done by assigning a **cardinality** to each association. This cardinality says how many instances can be associated. We also give the acquaintance association a name clarifying what the relationship entails. The properties of these associations and naming conventions are discussed in the box on naming associations. A complete view of the interface objects in the example is shown in Figure 7.15. The cardinalities in this example are all [1] since the different interface objects can only know of one object each. Another example of cardinality is [0..N], which means that we might associate any number between 0 and N. An acquaintance association is thus a static instance association that is drawn with a solid, directed line having a

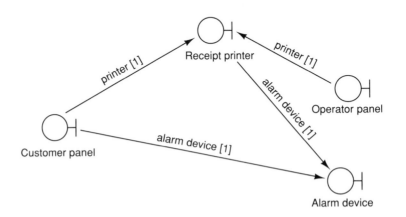

**Figure 7.15** The interface objects and acquaintance associations of the recycling machine.

name and a cardinality. Note that the associations are only unidirectional.

**On naming associations**

Models including relations often represent a model of the real world. It is common to name associations so that the sequence object–relation–object naturally forms a sentence. Consider for instance the relation shown in Figure 7.16. Here a verb phrase is used and we can read 'A *Car is driven by a Person'*. This is very convenient.

However, another way of expressing the same relation is to express what **role** another object plays in relation to the first object. Then a noun phrase should be used as shown in Figure 7.17. Here it is harder to read directly a complete sentence, but instead we can use the role played to express the relation 'The object *person* plays the role of a *driver* to *Car*.'

We see that both of these strategies will be appropriate in this example. In the literature, the verb phrase strategy is often chosen, and it is also often used as an argument to show how useful object orientation is; you can directly read sentences from the model. Actually, this is not unique to object orientation. The same technique is very often used in data modeling (see Barker (1989)).

However, we would like to promote the second solution instead: the noun phrase. The reasons for this are as follows:

(1)   There is a large and fundamental difference between data modeling and object orientation. In data modeling you think of the model as a flat structure viewed from above. In this way it is natural to see the relationship as a binding between two objects. The relationship here is often bidirectional. In object orientation however, the view is instead taken from an object. When you look at this model, you place yourself at an object and then see what references you have to other objects. That is, you want to see what roles exist around you. Here the relationship is unidirectional. This fundamental difference is often hard to get used to for people used to data modeling. But object orientation often models reality, so think about how the world around you looks. One Objectory user, experienced in data modeling, stated: 'If I'm married to my wife, I want my wife to be married to me.

Car                                    Person

**Figure 7.16**   An example of how an association could be named using a verb phrase.

**Figure 7.17**   An example of how an association could be named using a noun phrase.

So why aren't the relations bidirectional?' True, but what if you know about the king of Sweden? Does that mean that he knows about you? Normally not. Relations in the real world may be both bidirectional and unidirectional. However, the relations always start from the objects. In the married example, the wife knows about her husband and the husband knows about his wife. To treat the associations as unidirectional is thus the more general case.

(2) Data modeling is often used in combination with relational databases. Here the relationship between objects will not be explicit, but rather it will be implicitly expressed as foreign keys and JOINs between tables. In an object-oriented implementation, however, the relationship will be made much more explicit. Here the relationship will exist in some way, normally as an instance variable implemented in a class.

If the name of such a variable were driven-by, or even worse, has-a, it would be almost impossible to understand the implementation. It is better to have names like driver or engine instead. In this way we increase the traceability between the models and the actual code. (This argument is strongly related to the first, being actually a special case of it.)

(3) This naming principle will normally give better names, avoiding names like has-a, consists-of or operated-by. Instead, the roles an object plays are expressed explicitly. These role definitions may sometimes give rise to subtypes of referred objects. Refer to the example above; the driver may need some additional information in addition to being a person. The driver will then naturally form a subtype of person, since we need to add attributes and operations to those of person in order to cope with its new role of being a driver as well. This technique will thus help us to formulate proper inheritance relations as discussed in Chapter 3.

As a consequence of the noun-phrase strategy we will sometimes end up having the same name for the association as for the referred object. This should not be viewed as something wrong, but quite the opposite; it is good. This is because you have made a proper use of the object, using it as a role for what it was intended for in the first place. We thus name the association as a **role** of the object associated.

To avoid confusion between objects and relationships, we normally write object names with a capital first letter and relationships with a lower-case first letter.

A special type of acquaintance association is the **consists-of** association, which is used to state that an object is composed of other objects. Such a structure, where a uniting object has associations with participating parts, is sometimes called an **aggregate,** as discussed in Chapter 3. This is common with interface objects. In a window system, for instance, we want to state that a window can consist of buttons, menus and scroll bars. Each such unit can then be modeled by an interface object of its own. The result will be an interface structure forming a tree. In *Customer Panel* the buttons and the sensors can become interface objects in their own right, depending on how we wish to model the customer panel. This is illustrated in Figure 7.18. We call the interface object *Customer Panel* the **central** interface object. This is also often called a **containment hierarchy** or a partition hierarchy as discussed in Chapter 3.

Having identified the interface objects, it will be easy to modify an interface in the system. If, for instance, we wish to exchange the receipt printer in the recycling machine system for another one, the changes will concern only this interface object. By having everything that concerns a specific interface in one object, every change to that interface will be local to this object. Since changes to interfaces are very common, it is vital that these be manageable.

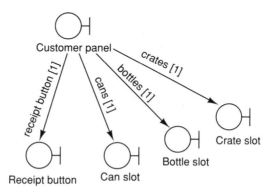

**Figure 7.18**   An example of an interface structure using a containment hierarchy.

It soon becomes obvious that there are two different types of interface to model. There are those that are interfaces to other systems and those that are interfaces to a human user.

For interface objects which communicate with other systems the communication is usually described in terms of communication protocols. These interface objects can be of a type that translates to a standardized protocol, or may be of a type that just sends out stimuli that are produced internally without any complex conversions. This constitutes another advantage: if the protocol is changed, these changes will be local to this interface object. Actually, in one project where we knew that the protocol was to be changed, we modularized the interface object so that changes (in this case climbing the OSI layers) would be very easy to incorporate. A significant problem arises when there are continuous signals from the outside world, such as in measurement and/or control systems. Then our interface object must either sample the input signal or trigger when certain values are passed, since internally in the system there is only discrete communication via stimuli. The interface objects must then translate from continous information to discrete information. Quantification problems may then arise and should be resolved.

The other kind of interface object communicates with human users. Today, we often request Graphical User Interfaces (GUIs) between the system and the user. Such interface objects can be complex to model; but they can be modeled as whole structures of the interface objects as previously shown. Several different techniques exist for good interface design. It is fundamental that the user has a logical and coherent picture of the system. This can be accomplished by using the problem domain objects as discussed earlier. By doing interface design at that early stage and having the prospective users take an active part, we also guarantee that the interfaces will satisfy the user needs. In interface-intensive applications it is not abnormal for the user interface to be the major part (up to 80%) of the entire application. When developing interface- intensive applications supporting tools should be used. Such tools include different kinds of User Interface Management Systems (UIMSs) (see Hix (1990)), as well as different kinds of windowing systems, frameworks and development environments with predefined parts (such as X Windows, NeWS, MacApp, NewWave, Smalltalk, NeXTStep's Interface Builder, Windows and Presentation Manager). Additionally there are several different kinds of class library, for example, C++ that also support the development of GUIs like InterView or CommonView. Note, however, that the use of class libraries is often redundant when UIMS systems are used.

The purpose of each separate object was discussed in Chapter 6. It became evident that interface objects are suited for presentation, but that they can also handle information and have behavior. How much information and behavior should be tied to an interface object must be decided from case to case. At one extreme, the interface object just passes on the stimuli it receives from the actor to other objects in the system, without actively participating itself in the course of events. At the other extreme, the behavior of the interface object is very complex; complex information is tied to the interface object and it can function almost independently of other objects.

How is it possible to decide what behavior in the use case should be tied to a particular interface object? Generally, the potential for change should decide this. Any change of functionality directly coupled to the interface should be local to the interface object. Other changes should not affect the interface object. Experienced users are very ingenious when inventing potential changes. This is a skill that should be learned and applied in all modeling activities. Every approach to a model should be viewed in the light of possible changes to the system.

Thus, to identify which part of the flow in a use case should be allocated to interface objects, we focus on the interactions between the actors and the use cases. This means that we should look for units displaying one or more of the following characteristics:

- They present information to the actor or request information from him.
- Their functionality is changed if the actor's behavior is changed.
- Their course is dependent on a particular interface type.

We can differentiate between several different strategies for allocating the functionality (see Hartson and Hix (1989)):

(1) **Computation dominant control** or **embedded control** is where we place the controlling functionality inside the system, that is, in the control objects and the entity objects. Here the interface objects do not have very much functionality. This structuring can be efficient in execution but hard to prototype from, since not much functionality is introduced in the interface object. As we will see later, we can place the overall system sequencing locally anyway, in the control objects, for ease of modification.

(2) **Dialogue dominant control** is where we place much control functionality in the interface objects and these objects model much of the functionality of the system. In this case we do not

have many control objects in the model. This strategy is easy to prototype from, but increases the complexity of the interfaces since different abstraction levels are mixed, for example, mixing of event detection and global control.

(3) **Mixed control** places the control on both sides allowing invocation of dialogue from the computational side and vice versa. This offers more flexibility, but requires programmers to be more disciplined in order to maintain dialogue independence.

(4) **Balanced control** is where we separate the control from both the dialogue and the computation. The global control component, which typically is a control object, governs sequencing among invocations of dialogue and computational functions.

Which type of control to choose must be decided on from application to application. OOSE allows modeling of all four types, and actually highlights which strategy was chosen since the analysis models will look different for each strategy. In most cases, however, OOSE promotes alternative (4): the separation of control from other types of functionality. The reason for this is to have high localization in future changes to the functionality.

## 7.3.2    Entity objects

To model the information that the system will handle over a longer period of time we use entity objects. Typically such information survives use cases, so the information should be kept even if the use case has been completed. Besides the information to be handled, we also allocate the behavior that naturally belongs to this information to the entity object.

The entity objects are identified from the use cases, just as the interface objects are. Most entity objects are found early and are obvious. These 'obvious' entity objects are often identified in the problem domain object model. Others can be harder to find. Entities usually correspond to some concept in real life, outside the system, although this is not always the case. It is very easy to model too many entity objects, in the belief that more information is necessary than is really called for. The hard thing is to model only the entity objects actually needed. It is therefore essential to work in a structured way when modeling the entity objects. The needs of the use cases should be the guidelines and only such entity objects as can be justified from the use case descriptions should be included.

In the example of the recycling machine, we look at the information that must be kept for a longer time. Below is the use case description, with italics to show where we mention some information functionality:

> When the customer returns a deposit item, it is measured by the system. *The measurements are used to determine what kind of can, bottle or crate has been deposited.* If accepted, *the customer total is incremented, as is the daily total for that specific item type.* If the item is not accepted, the light for 'NOT VALID' is highlighted on the panel.
>
> When the customer presses the receipt button, the printer prints the date. The *customer total is calculated and the following information printed on the receipt for each item type*:
>
> *name*
> *number returned*
> *deposit value*
> *total for this type*
>
> *Finally the sum that the customer should receive* is printed on the receipt.

From this text we can reason as follows. Since we must remember how many cans, bottles and crates of each type have been deposited during the day, we need something that handles this information. We thus identify the entity objects *Can*, *Bottle* and *Crate*. These entity objects can also handle their size, deposit values and other information that can be tied to these objects. These entities have common properties and thus could actually be modeled as instances of the same class. However, we want to handle the sizes of the objects a little differently. Cans have a width and a height, bottles have a neck width and a bottom width and crates have height, length and width. Nevertheless, some properties can be extracted (for example, deposit value, day total) and placed in an abstract entity object. We place these common properties which the other entity objects will inherit in *Deposit Item* (see Figure 7.19).

To store information, objects use **attributes.** To each entity object we can thus tie several attributes. Each attribute has a **type,** which can be either a primitive data type, such as integer or string, or a composite data type which is more complex and which is specially defined. An attribute is described as an association with a name and cardinality indicating the attribute's type (see Figure 7.20). Note the similarities between this and the acquaintance association. Actually, attributes and entity objects have many properties in common and it can sometimes be hard to know when to use an entity object and when to use an attribute. This will be discussed further soon. Attributes can be used in all object types to describe the information to be stored.

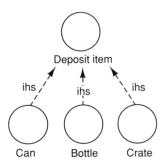

**Figure 7.19**  *Can, Bottle* and *Crate* have common properties inherited from *Deposit Item.*

**Figure 7.20**   An attribute of an object.

The attributes of an entity object develop as the use cases are analyzed. We have already mentioned some of the attributes of the entity object in the recycling example. These are shown in Figure 7.21.

Let us continue analyzing the recycling system. We now have the means to handle the information about the items and also their daily number. To be able to print out the receipt for a specific customer when she has finished depositing items, we will need something to keep track of all the items which should be printed on the receipt. This is not actually information that will survive the use case, but since it is very essential information for the system, we model it with an entity object anyway. We therefore identify an entity object *Receipt Basis*. Since a specific customer may insert several different kinds of item, we must keep the information on how many of each type she has deposited. We have here two alternatives. The first is that *Receipt Basis* handles only one specific type of item and, when several different types are deposited, we create new instances of *Receipt Basis*. The second alternative is to have only one instance of *Receipt Basis* handling all items, and if several different types of item are inserted this will be handled internally to *Receipt Basis*. Since we want to encapsulate as much as possible, to decrease dependency between the objects, we choose the second alternative, namely to have only one *Receipt Basis* for each customer. *Receipt Basis* thus keeps track

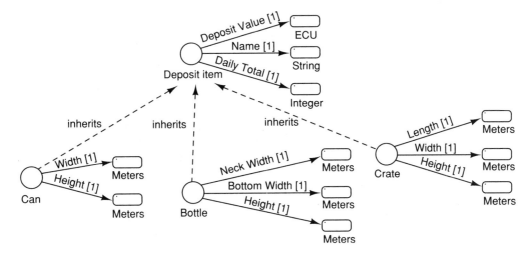

**Figure 7.21**   Attributes of some of the recycling machine entity objects.

of all items the customer deposits. Since we need to know which type of item we are counting we will need an aquaintance association between *Receipt Basis* and *Deposit Item*. Note that we will actually never count instances of *Deposit Item*, but here we use the polymorphic property that is fundamental to all object-oriented systems. We thus do not need to know exactly to which class the instances we are counting belong. By the association we have limited the polymorphism to being a descendant of *Deposit Item*. We will set the cardinality to [0..N] since we may count several different instances with *Receipt Basis*. We thus have the picture shown in Figure 7.22.

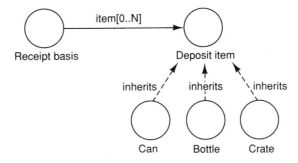

**Figure 7.22**   The entity objects that are necessary to deposit items in the recycling machine.

*Receipt Basis* keeps track of how much a specific customer returns and of which type. In the entity object will be an attribute storing the number received for each type. The number information that the *Operator* wants at the end of the day will be placed in the entity object for the items. We must therefore create an instance of each type of item that the system is able to receive at system start-up. In them we will store information about the deposit value, the size of the items and the number of items that have been returned that day. *Receipt Basis* will have acquaintance associations with these instances, and in an instance of *Receipt Basis* we will store information about the number of each particular item type that the customer has returned. Hence, for each specific association, we assign a number. This can be done by just noting this attribute of the relation or by adding a new entity object to hold this information.

It is not always easy to decide whether a certain piece of information should be modeled as an entity object or as an attribute. To be able to decide, we must see how the information will be used. Information that is handled separately should be modeled as an entity object, whereas information that is strongly coupled to some other information and never used by itself should be made into an attribute of an entity object. In other words, what is decisive is how the use cases handle the information. Certain information can become an entity object in one system, while it may very well become an attribute in another system. If it is used from two different directions and for different reasons, it should form a separate entity object.

Let us look at an example. Say we need to model a car and its owner. Will this be two entity objects? Well, we don't know. In one system we could very well end up with two entity objects, if both are needed for performing the use cases. In another system we could very well have just one entity object Car with an attribute Owner. In yet another system we could end up with an entity object Person with an attribute Car. Hence, there is no need to model the reality as such, but only to model it as needed by the use cases. In the first case, two use cases could use Owner and Car independently of each other, in the second case we always use the Owner in combination with its owned car and in the third case we only use Car in association with a specific owner or Person.

It is usually easy to find the necessary entity objects, but it is much more difficult to identify what operations and which attributes these entity objects are to offer. The only way to manipulate an entity object is via the operations. Therefore the identified operations must be sufficient for all those who wish to use the entity object. The detailed description of the use cases is an extremely valuable means of finding the desired operations. By following them, we will naturally come up with the necessary operations. The whole course of events is described in the use cases, and by extracting those parts that concern our entity object, the operations will appear. In Chapter 8 we will describe the technique used in OOSE for doing this in a structured way. The technique mainly uses interaction diagrams. Although these are described in the construction chapter, they may very well be used here to identify operations. We will later discuss the pitfalls and benefits of identifying operations in the analysis model relative to the design model. The normal case is *not* to identify operations in the analysis model, since these often change in the design. The normal case is therefore to postpone the identification until construction, but we will discuss some aspects of operations here anyway.

Operations can be more or less complex. One extreme case is where an entity object comprises only reading and writing operations; the other extreme is having whole courses of events included in the operations. As always, the right thing is a middle course between these extremes. The same basic rules apply to entity objects as to other objects, that is, everything (behavior and information) that is naturally connected with the entity object should be placed in it. In the same way it is important to see what consequences any changes will have. The aim is that any type of change should be as local as possible. Beginners sometimes only use entity objects as data carriers and place all dynamic behavior in control objects (as will be discussed later). This should, however, be avoided. Using this extreme, we will end up with a function/data structure: we have earlier discussed the problems with such a structure. Instead, quite a lot of behavior should be placed in the entity objects. Often an appropriate way of realizing how behavior should be placed is to model initially without using control objects at all, that is, just using interface objects and entity objects. In fact, we can build any system with just these two object types. However, when such a model has been developed, you will notice that there are certain behaviors that are not naturally placed, from a maintainability view, in either entity objects or interface objects; or even worse, they are spread over several objects. These behaviors should be placed in the control objects. When continuing with the recycling example and allocating behavior in more detail, as we will do in the construction chapter, please feel free to eliminate the control objects from the model and think of how you would place behavior without them.

The following is a list of typical operations that must be offered by an entity object:

- Storing and fetching information
- Behavior that must be changed if the entity object is changed
- Creating and removing the entity object

Receipt basis                    Deposit item

**Figure 7.23**  *Receipt Basis* increments *Deposit Item* number when a new item has been received.

An operation on an entity object may mean that the entity object contacts another entity object and asks for information about something (see Figure 7.23). This communication takes place through **communication associations**. A communication association models communication between two objects. Through these associations, an object sends and receives stimuli. The association starts from the object that is to perform the manipulation (that is, sends the initiating stimuli), and is directed to the object where the manipulation is to take place. Since it is an instance association, it is solid; and since it is dynamic, we will not name the association.

As the entity objects are modeled, it will be found that similar entity objects occur in several use cases. It must then be decided whether there should be separate entity objects. Even if the use cases do not make exactly the same demands on them, the entity object may offer operations so that the use cases may use them in the way that they wish. The basic rule to follow when deciding if two entity objects are actually are one and the same is to see what occurrences they represent. If it is the same occurrence, there should be only one entity object; otherwise the two objects should remain separate. When it is decided that entity objects should be merged, operations, associations and attributes should also be integrated into the new entity object. The same functionality that existed in the separate entity objects should be found in the new entity object. Though it is possible to create operations on entity objects, this possibility should not be overused. The operations are, after all, going to be designed and implemented later.

### 7.3.3  Control objects

We have now partitioned the flow of the use case into interface objects and entity objects. In some cases everything in a use case has been placed in objects of these two types, in which case no control objects are needed for that use case. However, in more complex use cases, there often remains behavior that is not naturally placed in either of these two object types. Such behavior is placed in **control objects**. The reason that such behavior is hard to place in either of the other object types is that it is behavior that does not really belong to the interface of the system or to how the information is handled. One possibility is to spread the behavior over these object types anyway, as suggested by some methods, but that solution is not ideal from a changeability perspective. A change in such behavior (often functionality) could then affect several objects and thus be hard (expensive) to incorporate; see the discussion on control objects in Chapter 6.

The control objects typically act as glue which unites the other objects so that they form one use case. They are typically the most ephemeral of all the object types and usually last only as long as the performance of one use case lasts. It is, however, difficult to strike a balance between what is placed in entity objects, control objects and interface objects. We will here give some heuristics as to how to find and specify them.

Control objects are normally found directly from the use cases. In a preliminary draft we will assign one control object for each concrete and abstract use case. Each use case normally involves interface objects and entity objects. Thus behavior that remains after the interface objects and entity objects have been assigned their behavior will be placed in the control objects.

Deviations from this initial approach can be made for several reasons. The first is the extreme case where there is no behavior in the use case left to model. A control object is not, of course, needed then. If, on the other hand, there remains behavior of a very complicated type (after the distribution of relevant behavior among interfaces and entity objects), the functionality may be divided into several control objects. They should then have limited tasks and will thus be simpler to understand and describe. If a control object is coupled to several different actors this might indicate that the behavior is different for the different actors and that it should therefore be split across several control objects. The aim should be to tie only one actor to each control object. The reason for this is that system changes often originate from actors and, if each control object is dependent on only one actor, then changes in the system can be isolated.

Typical types of functionality placed in the control objects are transaction-related behavior, or control sequences specific to one or a few use cases, or functionality thats separates the entity objects from the interface objects. The control objects tie together courses of events and thus carry on communication with other objects.

Let us again look at the use case description from the recycling model to see if we have any functionality typical of control objects. We have marked those parts of the use description case in italic.

When the customer returns a deposit item, it is measured by the system. *The measurements are used to determine* what kind of can, bottle or crate has been deposited. *If accepted, the customer total* is incremented, as is the daily total for that specific item type. *If the item is not accepted*, the light for 'NOT VALID' is highlighted on the panel.

When the customer presses the *receipt button, the printer prints* the date. The *customer total is calculated* and the following information *printed* on the receipt for each item type:

name
number returned
deposit value
total for this type

*Finally the sum that the customer should receive* is printed on the receipt.

This is a concrete use case that inherits an abstract use case *Print*. The first option, namely one control object for each (abstract and concrete) use case, would have given us two control objects here. *Returning Item* is a use case that involves coupling the interface objects and the entity objects together. This behavior is a good candidate for a control object. The *Print* use case, however, involves the behavior of printing on the line printer, but this behavior should be tied to the interface object *Receipt Printer*. We thus do not assign a control object for this abstract use case. We have not described the other use cases in detail here yet, so it is harder to tell whether or not a control object is needed for them. However, as a first approach, we could assign control objects for these use cases as well. Whether this is correct or not will be seen at the latest during construction, when explicitly defining the courses and the stimuli sent between the objects. The control objects will thus be as shown in Figure 7.24.

The description of a control object is found indirectly from the use cases by checking how the use case runs over the other object types. In those places where a control object needs to be involved, the role the control object will take and what that role involves are stated.

Uses between use cases are often mapped to communication associations between the corresponding objects. If use cases have an extension association, this association can normally be transferred directly into an extension association between objects.

To model the extensions in the recycling example we choose to use extensions between the control objects. The reason for this is that we do not want to blur the specification of the *Deposit Item Receiver* object. Instead we describe the *Alarmist* as something that will be injected when an alarm occurs. We thus have the picture shown in

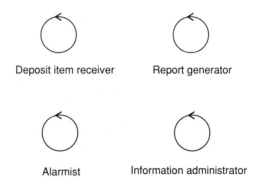

**Figure 7.24**   Controllers in the recyling machine.

Figure 7.25. Note that in this example there are no communication associations between the control objects.

### 7.3.4   Working with the analysis objects

When working on the development of the analysis model, normally we are working with one use case at a time. Thus, for one specific use case, we identify interface objects, entity objects and control objects before continuing with the next use case. However, since the analysis objects are orthogonal to the use cases, in the sense that one object may participate in several use cases, this process is iterative. This

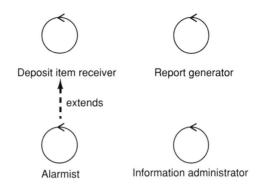

**Figure 7.25**   The complete view of the control objects in the recycling example.

means that when a set of objects already exists, these may be modified to fit also the new use case. The goal is to form as stable a structure as possible, reusing as many objects as possible.

The specification of the objects should be written in a text form. The simplest way of doing this is just to copy the text from the use cases and paste it into the object descriptions. However, this is not recommended as the text will then be out of context and thus can be hard to comprehend. It is better to describe each object's **role** and **responsibilities** bearing in mind those of the other objects.

We have mentioned the use of operations to specify the objects. This is possible, but it introduces a formalism that the model may not be sufficiently stable to handle yet. Changes would then have serious consequences. Even if operations are used, a formal syntax should definitely be avoided. When specifying an operation, it is tempting to use almost pseudo-code to do the specification, but this should be avoided. Any changes (and there will be changes!) will be very hard to introduce when the specifications are rewritten. When describing behavior, concentrate on what will happen, not how it will happen. Generally, in system development the formalism should come creeping in when the structures grow stable and it should be introduced incrementally.

A technique for finding operations on the objects from the use cases will be described in the next chapter. This technique could very well be used, as previously mentioned, in the analysis model. In our experience, however, it is too much work to use it in both analysis and design. If it is used in the analysis model, then the operations should as far as possible be kept the same in the design model to reduce the amount of redundant work. Thus, if you realize that the implementation environment will have very little effect on your analysis model, you can define operations during analysis; otherwise we recommend doing it during design.

When the objects have been identified and described, though, we may describe how the objects offer the use case; not as formally as specifying what stimuli will be sent between the objects, but in a more prose-like form. Initially, then, we often create a **use case view** of the objects showing how they will be used in the use case. Let us look at the use case *Returning Item*. Its view is shown in Figure 7.26.

We may also describe the use case in terms of these objects to show how they will provide the use case. This description will help you to understand the use case and how it has been distributed over the objects. Here is such a description for the use case *Returning Item*.

When the customer returns a deposit item the *Customer Panel*'s sensors measure its dimensions. These measurements are sent to the control object *Deposit Item Receiver* which checks via *Deposit Item*

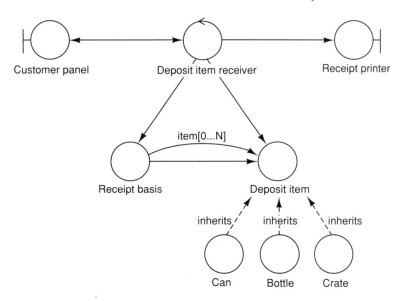

**Figure 7.26**   The objects supporting the use case *Returning Item*.

whether it is acceptable. If so, *Receipt Basis* increments the customer total and the daily total is also incremented. If it is not accepted, *Deposit Item Receiver* signals this back to *Customer Panel* which signals NOT VALID.

When the customer presses the receipt button, *Customer Panel* detects this and sends this message to *Deposit Item Receiver*. *Deposit Item Receiver* first prints the date via *Receipt Printer* and then asks *Receipt Basis* to go through the customer's returned items and sum them. This information is 'sent back to *Deposit Item Receiver* which asks *Receipt Printer* to print it.

We have seen here that the analysis model will not be a reflection of what the problem domain looks like. This is important to understand. The reason is simply to get a more maintainable structure where changes will be local and thus manageable. We thus do *not* model reality as it is, as object orientation is often said to do, but we model the reality as we want to see it and to highlight what is important in our application.

## 7.3.5   Subsystems

When the analysis objects have been identified, the system will contain a large number of objects. For a medium-sized project, typically between 30 and 100 objects will be specified. It is seldom possible to get a clear overview of this number of objects, so the objects need to be placed in groups. This can be done at one or several levels depending on the size of the system. Such groups of objects are called **subsystems.** The system thus consists of a number of subsystems which can themselves contain subsystems. At the bottom of such a hierarchy are the analysis objects. Subsystems are thus a way of structuring the system for further development and maintenance.

The task of the subsystems is to package the objects so that complexity is reduced. The subsystems also work as handling units in the organization, for example for development, marketing, sales and delivery. A subsystem can be a compulsory system unit, but it can also be an optional unit.

The lowest level of subsystem is to be viewed as a change unit. We call these units **service packages**. These should be viewed as atomic; if the customer wants it, he will have the whole of it, otherwise he will get nothing. When the system is to undergo a minor change, this change should concern no more than one such subsystem, or rather the objects contained in this subsystem. This means that the most important criterion for this subsystem division is predicting what the system changes will look like and then making the division on the basis of this assumption. One subsystem should therefore preferably be coupled to only one actor, since changes are usually caused by actors.

The division into subsystems should also be based on the functionality of the system. All objects which have a strong mutual functional coupling will be placed in the same subsystem (see Embley and Woodfield (1988) or Yourdon and Constantine (1979)). To identify objects with a strong mutual coupling, we can start with one object and study its environment. Another criterion for the division is that there should be as little communication between different subsystems as possible.

What is most convenient is to start looking for optional subsystems. Optional subsystems are not only those that are optional for a specific delivery; anything that *could* be optional should be considered.

In the recycling example we can view all objects handling the alarm as optional (the machine would work without an alarm) and also functionally related. We thus may have one subsystem *Alarm* that includes the control object *Alarmist* and the interface object *Alarm Device*.

After the optional subsystems have been identified, what remains is often those objects that are central to the system and therefore always have to be delivered. To distribute these among different subsystems, we will need to look at the functionality of the system. All the objects involved in a particular part of the functionality will be placed in the same subsystem. To identify functionality parts, we can look at each object. What will happen if we remove this object? Objects that then become superfluous in one way or another, and are connected to the removed object, should therefore be part of the same subsystem. There are several similar criteria which can be used to decide whether two objects are strongly functionally related. There follows a list of a few of them:

- Will changes in one object lead to changes in the other object?
- Do they communicate with the same actor?
- Are both of them dependent on a third object, such as an interface object or an entity object?
- Does one object perform several operations on the other?

The aim is to have strong functional coupling within a subsystem and a weak coupling between subsystems. A good start is to place the control object in a subsystem and then place strongly coupled entity objects and interface objects in the same subsystem.

If it seems very difficult to place a particular object in a subsystem, it can be placed outside all subsystems. This may be because it is completely separate from other subsystems, or because it has the same functional coupling to two or more subsystems so that it is difficult to choose which one to place it in.

Let us apply these criteria to the recycling example. We have already identified the *Alarm* subsystem. The functionality to handle all depositing is functionally strongly coupled and thus could be placed in one subsystem, *Deposit*. All objects involved in the management of the system could be placed in one subsystem, *Administration*. The interface object *Receipt Printer* could be placed in either of these two subsystems since it is used in both places, so we choose to place it outside the subsystems. We thus have the picture in Figure 7.27. Further levels of subsystem are not needed here; the next level would be the system itself.

We can test some criteria on this division, for instance, the number of actors dependent on a certain subsystem. *Deposit* is only dependent on *Customer*; *Administration* is only dependent on *Operator*. *Alarm* is not related directly to one actor, but is used indirectly by both actors. The reason why it was placed as a separate subsystem was that it constituted a certain part of the functionality of the system.

When the division into subsystems is made, in some cases it may also be desirable to modify the analysis objects. This may be the case, for instance, when an entity object has separate behavior that is

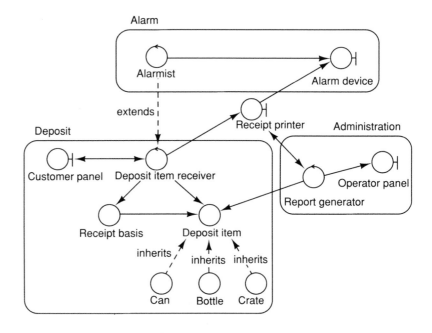

**Figure 7.27**  Subsystems in the recycling machine.

functionally related to more than one subsystem. If this behavior is extracted, it may be easier to place the entity object in a subsystem.

To express how subsystems are related we can assign a **dependsOn** relation between subsystems. This relation means that objects in one subsystem will use, in some way, objects in another subsystem. In the example above we see that the *Administration* subsystem depends on the *Deposit* subsystem since *Report Generator* uses *Deposit Item*. Hence, if we deliver one subsystem, we must also deliver any subsystem that this subsystem depends on.

The subsystem division in small projects is normally made at the end of the analysis, when the architecture is clear. In larger projects, however, it often must be done much earlier (in many cases, even before the analysis model has been developed). For large projects there may thus be other criteria for subsystem division, for example:

- Different development groups have different competence or resources and it may be desirable to distribute the development work accordingly (the groups may also be geographically separated).

- In a distributed environment, a subsystem may be required at each logical node.

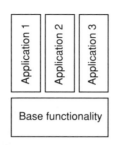

**Figure 7.28**   An example of structuring the system into one subsystem for base functionality which is used by all application programmers and separate subsystems for each application.

- If an existing product can be used in this system, this product may be regarded as a subsystem.

In large systems it is often essential to develop the system in layers. In that case a subsystem for base functionality is developed on which applications are built; the applications then use this base functionality. Figure 7.28 illustrates an example of such an architecture.

# 7.4   Summary

The analysis process aims to define and specify the system to be built. Two models are developed, the requirements model and the analysis model. Both of these models are logical in the sense that they do not incorporate any requirements from the actual implementation environment.

    The requirements model uses actors and use cases to describe in detail each and every way of using the system from a user's perspective. Actors model external factors such as people or machines that interact with the system. Use cases are the flows that these actors will perform on the system. Use cases can be understood intuitively by non-technical personnel and thus can form a basis for communication and definition of the functional requirements of the system, in collaboration with the potential users. As a support for defining the requirements model, a problem domain object model is a strong tool, as it will form a common platform determining what the system will handle. To attain a high degree of maintainability, these problem domain objects will not form a base for the realization of the system. As a complement to the use cases and the problem domain objects, it is also appropriate that the requirements model be accompanied by descriptions of the system interfaces.

The use case model will form a thread running through all development work in OOSE, from structuring the system to defining operations on the objects, and, not least, as a tool for doing integration testing. We thus have a high degree of reusability for this model.

The analysis model is the second model developed in the analysis process. This model aims to form a logical and maintainable structure in the system. It is logical in the sense that the actual implementation environment is not taken into account. The reason for this is mainly to focus on the essential system functionality. Three object types are used to structure the system: interface objects, entity objects and control objects. The interface objects model all functionality that concerns the system interfaces, the entity objects model all functionality that handles the actual information kept in the system for longer periods and the control objects model such functionality as is not naturally tied to any of the other objects (often mainly behavior). These object types are identified when the use cases are analyzed and broken down. The objects should provide the complete functionality of the use cases. Subsystems are used to structure the system in larger units. Subsystems group the objects in the analysis model.

The development of these models forms an iterative process, as they will undergo many changes before they become stable. Therefore not too much detail should be put into these models before they have reached a mature state. However, even if it is often wise to sketch subsequent models when developing the earlier ones, the early models must be stable before work starts on the subsequent models.

# 8 Construction

## 8.1 Introduction

### 8.1.1 Why do we have a construction process?

We build our system in the construction phase, based on the analysis model and the requirements model created during analysis. The construction process lasts until the coding is completed and the code units have been tested. Construction consists of **design** and **implementation**.

Following the construction process we have the testing process in which the use cases and the entire system are tested and certified. This does not mean that you must wait until all parts have been constructed before starting the verification of the system; instead we try to do as much as possible in parallel. Also, verification involves a lot more than just testing code. If possible we also try to start construction before analysis has been completed.

What, then, is the purpose of the construction phase? Could we not write the source code directly from the analysis model? There we described the 'objects' in the system and how they are related.

There are three main reasons for having a construction phase:

(1) The analysis model is not sufficiently formal. In order to move seamlessly to the source code we must refine the objects; which operations should be offered, exactly what should the communication between the different objects look like, which stimuli are sent, and so on?

(2) The actual system must be adapted to the implementation environment. In analysis we assumed an ideal world for our system. Alas, there is no ideal world, so in reality we must make adaptations to the environment in which the system is to be implemented. This means that we must initially

transform the analysis model from the analysis space to a space with still more dimensions (see Figure 8.1). We must for example consider performance requirements, real-time requirements and concurrency, system software, the properties of the programming language, the database management system to be used, and so on.

(3) We want to validate the analysis results. As our system grows and becomes more formalized, we will see how well the analysis model and the requirements model describe the system. During construction, we can see at an early stage whether the result of the analysis will be appropriate for construction. If we discover points which are unclear in the analysis model or the requirements model, we must clarify them, perhaps by returning to the analysis process.

These three reasons may look as though there are deficiencies in the result of the analysis phase that we must clarify here. This is an incorrect view since the purpose of analysis is to understand the system and to give it a good structure. It is consequently important to understand that the considerations taken into account during construction should influence our system structure as little as possible; we want to keep the good properties in the system that the analysis model focused on. It is the application itself that mainly controls the structure, not the circumstances when implementing it. We therefore made an informal and comprehension-oriented analysis where these considerations did not disturb the work.

Changes in the system architecture to improve **performance** should as a rule be postponed until the system is being (partly) built. Experience shows that one frequently makes the wrong guesses, at least in large and complex systems, when it comes to the location of

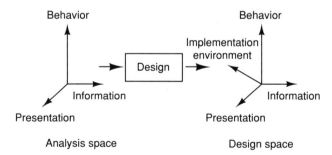

**Figure 8.1** Construction initially transforms a model in the analysis space into a model in the design space. This is mainly done in the design part of construction.

the bottlenecks critical to performance. To make correct assessments regarding necessary performance optimization, in most cases, we need something to measure. Otherwise we will only make guesses which may or may not be appropriate. Since we have nothing to measure until the system has been built, we cannot make these optimizations at an early stage. One way of avoiding this dilemma is to simulate the critical parts of the system. Another way is to perform prototyping to get an early opinion of what the system will look like, but this is a risky method since you can easily make unrealistic simplifications. A prototype always aims to highlight particular issues. General conclusions on other issues    therefore cannot be drawn from a prototype that does not highlight these issues. However, if you know for sure where the performance-critical parts are, for instance because you have a very good knowledge of the application, optimizations could be done at an early stage. For a similar discussion, see Barry (1989).

## 8.1.2    What is done in the construction phase?

Construction activity produces two models, the design model and the implementation model. Construction is thus divided into two phases, design and implementation, each of which develops a model (see Figure 8.2). The design model is a further refinement and formalization of the analysis model where consequences of the implementation environment are taken into account. The implementation model is the actual implementation (code) of the system.

To develop the design model we perform three main steps:

(1) *Identify the implementation environment.* This step includes identifying and investigating the consequences that the implementation environment will have on the design. Here all

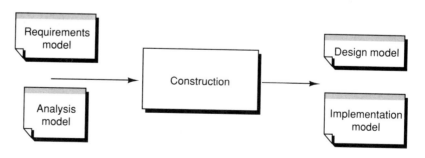

**Figure 8.2**    The input and output models of construction.

strategic implementation decisions should be made. How will the DBMS be incorporated into the system? What component libraries will be used and how? How should processes and process communication be handled? What about error handling and garbage collection? The list goes on. This work aims at drawing conclusions about how these circumstances should be handled in the system. This step can (and should) be done in parallel with the analysis work so that it is ready when the actual design starts.

(2) Incorporate these conclusions and develop a *first approach to a design model*. Here we use the analysis model as a base and translate the analysis objects into design objects in the design model that fit the current implementation environment. From a project perspective this could be directly incorporated in the analysis model, but for maintenance purposes and understandability this is not recommended. When doing further development, the analysis model forms a logical basis for understanding the system and thus is an essential model to keep during the entire system life cycle.

(3) Describe how the *objects interact* in each specific use case. Here the design model is formalized to describe all stimuli sent between the objects and also to define what each operation will do to each object. The use case model will be of great help during this work as it will help us to specify each specific flow in the system in detail. This step gives us the object interfaces.

The implementation activity then implements each specific object. From the design model we get very detailed specifications of all objects, including their operations and attributes. Various techniques may be used here and we will discuss some of them later. The programming language and the component library used will of course be fundamental tools for implementation.

We will now discuss these steps in more detail and make some comments on the various techniques used. The recycling example analyzed in the previous chapter will be used and design and implementation models will be made for it.

## 8.2  The design model

### 8.2.1  Traceability

The design model will further refine the analysis model in the light of the actual implementation environment. Here we will explicitly define the interfaces of the objects and also the semantics of the operations. Additionally, we will decide how different issues such as DBMSs, programming language features and distribution will be handled.

The design model will be composed of **blocks** which are the design objects. These will make up the actual structure of the design model and show how the system is designed. These blocks will later be implemented as source code.

The blocks will abstract the actual implementation. The implementation of the blocks may be one specific class in the source code, that is, one block is implemented by one class. However, often a block is implemented by several different classes. The blocks are therefore a way of abstracting the source code.

The module level of the programming language we denote by the generic term **object module** (see Constantine (1990)). In an object–oriented language these modules (that the programmer actually writes) will be the actual classes. When we use a specific language we have a direct correspondence to a language concept and this concept should of course be used, for example *class* in an OO language or *package* in Ada. Here we will use the terms 'object module' and 'class'.

The first attempt at a design model can be made mechanically, based on the analysis model. Initially each analysis object becomes a block. This transformation rule means that we obtain a clear **traceability** in the models. We started by modeling the system in the analysis model in a manner which provides a robust structure for the system. As each analysis object is traceable to a block, changes introduced in the analysis model will be local to the corresponding block in the design model and thus also in the source code. Note that the traceability is bidirectional, that is, it also goes the other way – we can trace a class in the source code back to the analysis and see what gave rise to it.

Traceability is a tremendously important property in system development. Each major system will be altered during its lifetime. Whether the changes emanate from changed requirements or responses to troubleshooting, we will always need to know where the changes need to be made in the source code.

Here we have the great advantage of traceability; you can easily find your way in the system even if it has been subjected to major changes. It is also important to have a high functional localization (that is, high cohesion) (see Yourdon and Constantine (1979)) in order to know that changes will not influence large parts of the system.

In this chapter we will construct the example described in the previous chapter. This description will be in overview form and simplified, but the mode of work should appear clearly enough to permit a complete construction to be done fairly easily. As we go along we will introduce new terms and concepts that are used in the example.

Our analysis model is as shown in Figure 8.3. We will from now on concentrate on the use cases *Returning Item* and *Item Stuck*, and consequently we will focus on the objects that participate in these use cases.

Based on this analysis model we can now mechanically, and seamlessly, find the first attempt at a design model. The first attempt is simply to assign the same model as the analysis model. To differentiate between the two models, we use another notation and draw these blocks as rectangles instead of circles (see Figure 8.4).

The semantics of the design model is somewhat different from that of the analysis model. The analysis model is developed in logical terms and is only a conceptual picture of the system to be built. Therefore it is essential to keep and freeze the analysis model for future maintenance even after the design is finished. The design model, however, is an abstraction of how the actual system really is built. The first attempt at this model is a direct mapping from the analysis model. Its final structure, however, will reflect how the implementation environment has affected construction. The goal is to keep the structure found in the analysis model and not violate it

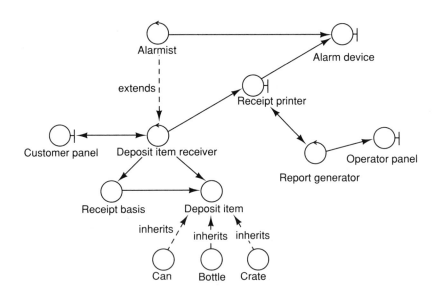

**Figure 8.3**  Analysis model of the recycling machine.

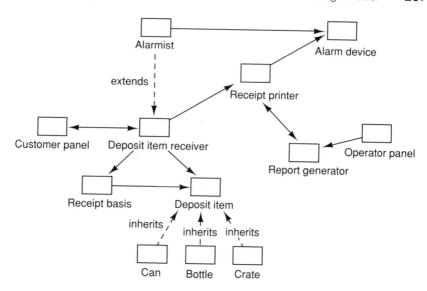

**Figure 8.4** First attempt to design the structure of the recycling machine.

unnecessarily in the design. We also want the design to have a logical and robust structure.

The semantics of the blocks should thus reflect the semantics of the objects existing in the actual system and, likewise, the associations between the objects should also reflect how the objects in the system are really related. For example, most programming languages do not have any way of implementing the extension association. During design we must decide how this association should be implemented and change the design model to reflect this. Similarly, if the programming language does not offer any technique to support inheritance, we must reflect on how the inheritance in the analysis model is really implemented. We will discuss these topics in more detail later.

This is consequently the first idea for a system architecture. We emphasize that this is the first idea because it may be changed, since we must consider the implementation environment. We may have to break up or divide blocks because we want to distribute them on different nodes in our computer system, or we may even need completely new blocks to encapsulate an existing DBMS. We will discuss how to consider the implementation environment shortly.

The design model enables us to reduce the complexity of the system. The blocks are actually an abstraction mechanism for the source code. By speaking in terms of blocks we can discuss the system on an overview level and understand the architecture of the system.

Through this abstraction mechanism we reduce the complexity radically, which means that it is easier to build a correct system that will avoid errors caused by complexity. It has been noted, (see Levendel (1990)) that it is qualitatively better to avoid construction errors by reducing complexity at an early stage than to search the system for faults when it is completed and to correct each error. The latter variant is (unfortunately) often typical of today's traditional system development.

### 8.2.2    The implementation environment

To adapt the design model to the actual implementation environment, we must first identify the actual technical constraints under which the system should be built. This identification may (indeed should) be done early, ideally before the analysis model is developed, since it affects how far the analysis model should be refined.

What do we include in the implementation environment? The most obvious things are perhaps the target environment (where the system should execute during operation), programming language and existing products that should be used (for example, DBMSs), but in fact everything that affects the realization of the system must be included in this concept. We will here discuss some of these aspects in more detail, but let us first discuss the overall strategy for handling the implementation environment.

Since one of the more common changes to a system is a change in the implementation environment, it is preferable to handle this in the same 'changeable' way used for the rest of the system. This implies that as few objects as possible should be aware of the constraints of the actual implementation environment. Therefore, the overall strategy for handling it should be to have such commitments *locally* and to *encapsulate* them as much as possible. In this way any change of environment should be local and not have an effect on several objects. (This is not unique to object-oriented software engineering, but rather a traditional style of good programming. However, in the light of the design model this will be apparent here, and thus we will have a controlled way of handling it.)

So, what is included in the implementation environment? We will here discuss some topics.

If we want to be able to change parts in the **target environment**, these parts should be encapsulated in a new block. You will thus create new blocks that represent occurrences in the target environment. For example, if your application will handle files in the operating system, you should create a block that interfaces the application's file handling and the operating system's file handling as shown in Figure 8.5.

In Figure 8.5, the *File Manager* block should offer operations such as *Create file* to the application objects. This block may then have different implementations for different configurations of the system. There are different realizations for this. Either an abstract class that specifies the interface can be defined, which is implemented in environment–specific descendants that are instantiated as required by the chosen platform; or the object can check at run-time which platform it is running on and execute the correct statements for this environment. A third way is to decide this when the system is delivered for different configurations. In C++ (or C) you would then have several .c files (one for each platform) implementing the same .h file which specifies the interface to the application. When producing the software it would be decided which module should be linked into the final product. Which way is chosen is dependent above all on the programming environment. The first is natural for object-oriented programmers, while the second would typically yield CASE statements in languages where polymorphism is not present. The third, which may very well be combined with the first, is more a choice of how the production and delivery of the software should take place.

Likewise it is important to investigate whether the target environment will execute in a distributed way on different processors or in different processes. We will discuss this in more detail in Chapter 9 where we discuss operating systems processes.

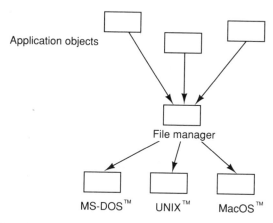

**Figure 8.5** A special block should be included to encapsulate the special properties of the target environment.

Which **programming language** is used will affect the design. We will later discuss how the concepts we use will be translated into the programming language, but the more basic properties of the language and its environment are also fundamental for the design. The existence of inheritance, multiple inheritance, typing, standards and portability are examples of such properties. Furthermore, strategies for handling errors during run-time must be decided early. Ada has its exception mechanism and Eiffel its assertions. C++ does not have any such mechanisms (in Version 2 of the language). It is essential to decide early on how this strategy should be incorporated in the design. Likewise the memory management strategy must be chosen early. Some object-oriented languages have automatic garbage collection, but in other languages it is up to the programmer to clear away instances that are not used any more. In that case the programmer must keep track of all references to these instances.

Closely related to the programming language is the use of **components** for programming. The use of component libraries may also affect the design. One example is the design of the interface objects. There are components (or tools) for building interfaces, and this will affect how the design is made. The use of components implies several new questions, whose discussion we will postpone until Chapter 11.

Often **existing products** are used when developing new systems. Examples of such products are DBMSs, User Interface Management Systems (UIMSs), network facilities and other internally or externally developed applications that should be incorporated in this new system. The normal strategy for handling these products is to introduce new blocks to encapsulate them in the same manner as was described for the target environment. In Chapter 10 we will discuss in more detail blocks that encapsulate a relational database.

Products that are used only during development (mostly development environments) may also affect the design. Such products include compilers, debuggers, preprocessors and other tools. These may affect how the code is written and configured. Other such implications may come from standards and coding rules.

During construction we must also take into consideration any **requirements for performance** or **limitations of memory**. Such requirements may also affect the design. One common example is when databases are used and frequently used transactions are too slow. Then a redesign (or modification) of the database design may be necessary. Access paths to the database may then be changed or we may have to introduce new index tables in the database, or change existing ones, to speed up operations on the database. However, the principal strategy on these topics should be, as previously mentioned, to postpone such optimizations until they are needed or you are absolutely sure that they will be needed. It is far too common that a good design is ruined for performance optimizations that are only sub-optimizations. Often the real bottlenecks are missed and then new optimizations are necessary.

To investigate potential optimization problems early, simulation or prototyping may be used before the actual design is done. Then the designers have much a better basis for determining where the real optimizations should be made. Of course, extensive experience in the application area may also help you to judge at an early stage where optimizations should be made. The message here is that if you are not sure of the correctness of a performance optimization, you should not make it until you are sure of how it should be done.

The **people** and **organization** involved in the development could also affect the design. For instance, if the design has to be done at different sites, a division of the design work is necessary. The different competence areas of the development staff may imply that the design should be done in a specific way. We will not discuss these issues in this book, but the principal strategy should be that such factors should not affect the system structure. The reason for this is that the circumstances (organizations, staffing, competence areas) that are in effect today will probably change during the system's life cycle. To build these circumstances into the system will have a bad effect on future maintenance of the system.

To achieve maximum robustness these issues should affect the design as little as possible. The overall principle is that changes can and should occur, but all changes should be justified and documented (also for robustness reasons). We may have to change the ideal design model in various ways:

- To introduce new blocks in the design model which do not have any representation in the analysis model.
- To delete blocks from the design model.
- To change blocks in the design model (splitting and joining existing blocks).
- To change the associations between the blocks in the design model.

Normally, adding blocks to handle the environment is a good change. Adding blocks for other functionality should not normally be done, since they should be introduced through the analysis model.

Deleting blocks is more suspicious. Why are you deleting the block? If you have good reasons for it (often implementation reasons), it is fine, but if you are actually changing the logical structure of the system, such a change should be made in the analysis model first. If it is not, you should view such a change with great reservation.

Splitting and joining blocks are also suspicious changes. Any such change will often decrease the robustness of the system and should be done with great care. For implementation or performance reasons it may be justified, but the designer should devote a great deal of thought to such changes.

Changes of associations are perhaps the most common change in the design model. These changes often come from the implementation environment. Synchronization and communication between processes is one example of where the communication between objects may be changed. Another example is the actual implementation of associations. Additionally, we must decide how to implement the associations. For instance, the extension association has no direct implementation technique in the common programming languages. We must therefore decide how this association should be implemented.

What extension actually means is that a behavior, b1, will be inserted into another behavior, b2 (see Figure 8.6). We want the (description of) behavior b2 to be completely independent and have no knowledge of behavior b1. Ideally we would like b1 itself to take the initiative and insert itself into b2. However, there is no mechanism in some ordinary programming languages by which this can be expressed. One solution to this is to have b2 take the initiative by sending a stimulus to b1. How we do this in the source code will be described when we implement the blocks. We will therefore have a communication association from b2 to b1 where this stimulus could be sent.

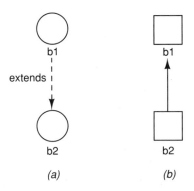

Figure 8.6 Behavior b1 extends behavior b2. This will normally be implemented with a stimulus being sent from b2 to b1.

In the example of the recycling machine we have one extension association. We choose to implement this in the manner described above. The other associations in the model, however, will not be changed since they are straightforward to implement.

In the analysis model we have a conceptual picture of the functionality. The extension association has come from the *Alarm* use case. When an alarm is detected during insertion of items, the *Alarm* use case should be inserted. The detection is done by *Customer Panel* which sends the error stimuli to the system. The receiver is now *Deposit Item Receiver* extended with *Alarmist*. It is thus *Alarmist* that will take part in this use case. The communication association should thus be between *Deposit Item Receiver* and *Alarmist* since this is the way the stimuli will be sent in the design. We now have the design model shown in Figure 8.7.

Any inheritance associations must also be reviewed if we cannot implement them in the programming language. Such associations can often be designed with a communication association between the blocks. This should then reflect that a stimulus is sent upwards through the 'inheritance hierarchy', so it is called **'call-through'**. Another possibility is to delete the abstract block and implement this functionality in the concrete block instead. In the example we will use C++, which supports inheritance. We will come back to implementation of inheritance in languages that do not support it directly.

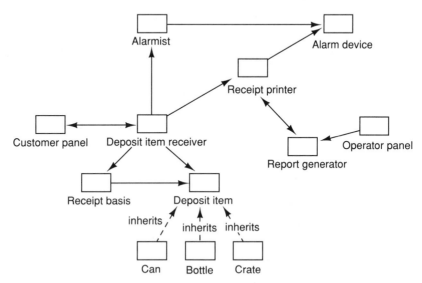

**Figure 8.7** The refined design model for the recycling machine. Note the communication association between *Deposit Item Receiver* and *Alarmist*.

The implementation environment for the recycling machine is made very simple. We will run the application in one process only. (In Chapter 9 we will discuss an implementation using several processes.) Also, we will not have a database for persistent data. (In Chapter 10 we will discuss an implementation using a relational DBMS.) The programming language will be C++, and this will not normally introduce any seams from this refined design model.

What should be reviewed, however, is how the hardware interface of the recycling machine should be incorporated in the application system. This interface can be viewed as an existing product introduced into the system. Normally these products would yield new blocks to encapsulate the product as discussed previously, but we could also use the block implementing interface objects as this encapsulating object. We will assume that a primitive software interface to the hardware panel does exist, and we will develop C++ classes that encapsulate this interface.

We should also mention something about the use of components. At an early stage it is essential to decide upon which component libraries to use. This is to encourage the use of components before the actual implementation work is done. When a component library exists, investigations should begin early to find out what functionality it will offer. To use a component library effectively, it is essential to be familiar with the library; this will require some time to be spent studying the classes and their operations. The use of, and especially finding where to use, components will be discussed more in Chapter 11. We will assume here that we have a class library in C++ for commmon data structures, for instance the NIH library (see Gorlen *et al.* (1990)). In Chapter 11 we will give some rules of thumb for finding places where components could be used. One of these rules is to look for acquaintance associations with cardinality [0..N]. This will typically yield a list or array to hold several references. We have this situation in our example, namely between *Receipt Basis* and *Deposit Item*. *Deposit Item Receiver* creates one instance of *Receipt Basis* for every new customer. *Receipt Basis* then holds references to the different *Deposit Items* that the customer has deposited and also to how many of each type. *Receipt Basis* will thus be implemented using such a component. We now have the first sketch of the implementation of the block *Receipt Basis*, shown in Figure 8.8. We will come back to the details of this issue when we consider the implementation of this block.

The blocks that we have now identified will correspond to the modules in which the source code is included. We will later show the files for the block *Receipt Basis*. In this way the blocks become a way

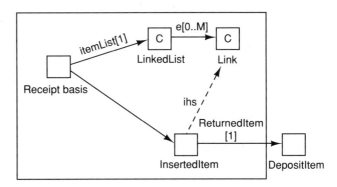

**Figure 8.8** The first proposal of the classes that implements the *Receipt Basis* block. Classes with a C are ready-made components (from the NIH library).

of grouping the source code. These blocks will contain our source code and our object modules (classes). Since different customers may want different configurations, different blocks may be delivered to different customers.

Before we can implement the blocks we must describe in detail how they are to communicate with one another. This is done by defining the stimuli to be sent between them. When we have described the block interfaces completely, we can implement them seamlessly using the rules that describe how the different terms are implemented in the relevant programming language, as described later.

### 8.2.3 Interaction diagram

When we have identified the system architecture we describe how the blocks are to communicate. This is done by **designing the use cases** which were described in the analysis phase. As mentioned before, the use cases constitute the key to OOSE. They control the analysis phase and structure the analysis model; they are designed in the construction phase and define the external requirements on the blocks; they will be tested in the testing phase to make sure the system is correctly built; and finally, they will be the basis for preparation of the system manual(s).

For each concrete use case we will draw an **interaction diagram**. The interaction diagram describes how each use case is offered by communicating objects. The diagram shows how the participating objects realize the use case through their interaction.

The interaction takes place as the blocks send stimuli between one another. As we draw the interaction diagrams, we will also define all the stimuli, including their parameters. The main purpose of the use case design is thus to define the protocols of the blocks.

With the use case model we have described what takes place in each use case. The analysis model describes which objects offer this behavior. Now, in the design model we refine the description of the use cases by showing in the interaction diagram how the objects behave in every specific use case.

The work on identifying the blocks in the design model is performed rather quickly; at best it is done automatically by means of a tool. On the other hand, the design of use cases implies a great amount of work. Here we must define exactly how the participating objects will communicate. The descriptions made in analysis, which are the basis of this work, may now have to be changed, which in turn may cause a change in the system structure. This may then give rise to proposals for changes in the analysis model or the requirements model.

Since the work on designing the use cases is done early in construction, we will discover whether the system architecture is good or whether it should be modified at an early stage, when the inherent resistance against changes is low. This means that the architecture has a chance to stabilize to a good architecture. Note that this is actually a consequence of the work done in the analysis phase.

When we design a use case we start by identifying the blocks participating in the use case. This is easily done by looking at which blocks offer the use case in the analysis model; the corresponding objects will be included in the design. This identification is therefore also a completely mechanical process. Furthermore, there may be new blocks introduced during construction (for example, for the implementation environment) that should also participate in the use case.

The interaction diagram is a type of diagram used for a long time in the world of telecommunications. There it has the same function as we are striving for, namely to describe the communication between different blocks.

Each participating block is represented by a bar. These bars are drawn as vertical lines in the diagram. The order between the bars is insignificant and should be selected to give the greatest clarity. The aim is to obtain a good overview. The skeleton of an interaction diagram is shown in Figure 8.9.

If there will be several instances of a block's classes, we can draw the instances either as different bars or as one and the same bar depending on which is most legible. All behavior of an object will be attached to the bar representing the actual block.

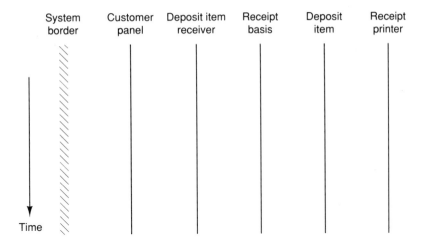

**Figure 8.9**  The skeleton for the interaction diagram for the use case *Returning Item* consists of bars for each block that participates, and a bar for the system border.

In the interaction diagram we have drawn a bar for the *Deposit Item*. When the use case is carried out, this object will actually be *Can, Bottle* or *Crate*. We have therefore also used polymorphism in the interaction diagram; this is a very useful technique.

In almost all the interaction diagrams we also have a bar for the surrounding world, namely for what is outside that which we want to describe. We usually call this bar the **system border**. This bar represents the interface with everything outside the blocks in the diagram, such as external actors, and consequently it can correspond to different interfaces outside the system. There may be several such border bars.

The time axis in the interaction diagram is viewed as going downwards. The use case thus starts with the behavior described at the beginning of the interaction diagram. The time axis of the interaction diagram is not linear, but should be regarded as event controlled. The distance between two events in the diagram has no relation to the real time between these events.

At the left edge of the interaction diagram, to the left of the system border, we describe the sequences. This description is textual and consists of structured text or pseudo-code. If we use pseudo-code, constructs that exists in the chosen programming language could be used. This is to ease our later migration to the current implementation. However, it makes us dependent on the specific language. The text describes what is happening in this part of the use

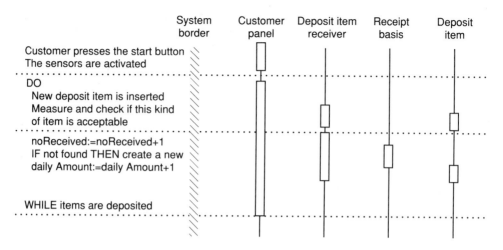

**Figure 8.10** Interaction diagram of the recycling machine with operations in the participating blocks. The item axis points straight down. Only part of the use case has been included.

case. Such a part we call an **operation.** We also mark the bar to which the operation belongs with a rectangle representing the operation. The textual description consequently belongs to the block where the operation takes place and where it will later be implemented; its bar is therefore marked at the place of the operation. Between operations we may draw horizontal grid lines for clarification purposes. This technique could also be used for any other partitioning of the use case. This is shown in Figure 8.10.

Parallel sequences, such as when several processes participate in a use case, can also be described in the interaction diagram. This will be further discussed in Chapter 9.

### 8.2.4    Definition of stimuli

The interaction diagrams are controlled by events. A new event gives rise to a new operation. These events are **stimuli** that are sent from one object to another and initiate an operation.

A stimulus is drawn in the interaction diagram as a horizontal arrow that starts in the bar corresponding to the sending block and ends in the bar corresponding to the receiving block. Most interaction diagrams (and thus use cases) start with a stimulus from the outside: it is drawn from the system border. From the use case description we can do a use case design. Here is the decription of the use case *Returning Item*:

When the customer retuns a deposit item, it is measured by the system. The measurements are used to determine what kind of can, bottle or crate has been deposited. If accepted, the customer total is incremented, as is the daily total for that specific item type. If the item is not accepted, the light for 'NOT VALID' is highlighted on the panel.

When the customer presses the receipt button, the printer prints the date. The customer total is calculated and the following information printed on the receipt for each item type:

name
number returned
deposit value
total for this type

Finally the sum that the customer should receive is printed on the receipt.

From this description we can develop an interaction diagram. In this example the interaction diagram will look as shown in Figure 8.11.

The use case starts as the customer inserts a bottle, can or crate into the system. The block *Customer Panel* is activated by the sensors that are external to our system. The customer can then continue feeding in the return bottles, empty cans and crates. This is solved by a DO...WHILE statement that is ended when the customer requests a receipt. In this loop we measure the item and check if it is acceptable. If so, we increment the attribute that knows how many objects the customer has fed in of each type, and how many have been fed in in total today. Note that the incrementation of the daily number is delegated to the block *Receipt Basis.*

When the customer is ready he or she presses the button for receipt. *Deposit Item Receiver* receives a stimulus for printing the receipt and starts by printing the logo and today's date. Then it hands over a stream to *Receipt Basis* which puts together the information to be printed and prints it on the stream. (A stream is a buffer to store characters to be printed.) Finally, the total sum in favor of the customer is printed. The stream is sent to *Receipt Printer* for printing. *Receipt Basis* is then deleted and the *Customer Panel* is ready for use again.

The interaction diagram for *Returning Items* is only drawn for the basic course. Naturally, you must consider faults that may occur, for example you may press the receipt button without previously submitting any returnable items but, for overview purposes, this is not considered here.

When working on the design of the use cases you will define the stimuli that each object should be able to receive. The definition

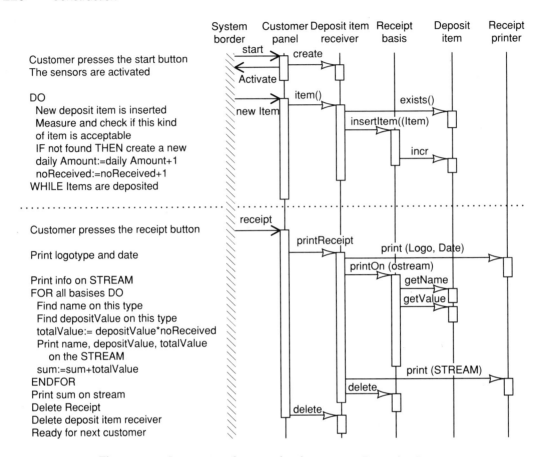

**Figure 8.11**  Interaction diagram for the use case *Returning Item*.

comprises the name and parameters of each stimulus. Defining stimuli is one of the more critical parts of a development. Since several persons are normally involved in the design of the use cases, the stimuli to one and the same block will be designed by different people. The aim should be to reuse existing stimuli as much as possible. Then it becomes much easier to design the objects, since the stimuli define the external requirements on each object. When you define the stimuli you should keep the following in mind:

- Reusability increases if we have only a few parameters. Having only a few parameters will make the stimulus easier to understand and also increases the probability that stimuli are similar to one another and therefore resuable. A stimulus with many parameters should be redefined and possibly divided into several stimuli. This point has also been noticed by Johnson and Foote (1988) who also discuss other rules for obtaining a reusable design.

- Stimuli that invoke similar behavior should have the same name regardless of the parameters they contain or which objects they are sent to. Hence there is no conflict between duplicate names. If stimuli have the same names it is easier to see clearly the similarity between two stimuli.

- The naming of stimuli should reflect the distribution of responsibilities between blocks. To make each object as independent as possible is one of the basic principles in all software engineering contexts.

- Each stimulus should clearly show the exchange of information, that is, the name must be selected carefully. Naming is one of the most difficult skills in programming and therefore rules for this purpose often exist. The names indicate an intuitive semantics; consequently the name is an extremely important aid to understanding and finding stimuli that can be reused.

- Handling and creation of new instances or initiation of new processes are performed in the same manner as ordinary stimulus handling.

The description of a use case is normally divided into **basic courses** and **alternative courses**. The basic course is the most common (important) sequence in the use case. It is always designed first. The alternative courses constitute all other sequences that the use case can follow, typically fault-handling sequences. When the basic course has been designed, you continue with the alternative courses. The aim is to describe as many alternative sequences as possible. The more alternative sequences we describe, the more sequences have been anticipated and hence the more we have increased the robustness of the designed system.

A stimulus can have different semantics, for example be either interprocess or intra-process communication. An intra-process stimulus is a normal call inside one process. We normally call this kind of stimulus a **message**. A message corresponds to a message in Smalltalk or invoking an operation in Eiffel or C++. That is, it is the normal mode of communication in object-oriented languages. An interprocess stimulus is a stimulus sent between two processes. We usually call such a stimulus a **signal**. Signals may be either synchronous or asynchronous (the execution of the sender continues directly after the signal is sent). In Ada, the rendezvous mechanism

Message            Signal

**Figure 8.12**  Different kinds of stimuli may be used in OOSE. Messages are intra-process and signals are interprocess communication.

for communication between tasks is synchronous; one task must wait for the other task to finish. In, for instance, CHILL (see CCITT (1984)), a programming language used in the world of telecommunications, signals are asynchronous; when a signal is sent the sender continues its execution immediately and does not wait for the receiver. The receiver may be active when the signal arrives and therefore the signal must be queued at the receiver until processed.

Generally, the concepts used in OOSE are generic terms. When we specialize OOSE for a specific implementation environment we should use the concepts of the implementation environment. For instance, when working with Ada, we should talk about rendezvous mechanisms instead of signals.

Messages and signals will be used in this book and will be drawn differently in the interaction diagram, as shown in Figure 8.12. Messages are drawn with a closed arrow and signals with an open arrow.

If necessary, the exact semantics of the stimuli should be specified from project to project. For instance, different kinds of synchronization or time-out should be specified when necessary. Then again, the chosen operating system or the programming language's properties should normally be used. We will discuss the use of signals further in Chapter 9. In this chapter we will assume that all stimuli are messages.

### 8.2.5  Structure of interaction diagrams

Interaction diagrams give the designer a unique ability to see the entire sequence in a use case at an overview level. The designer can therefore quickly get a picture of how the sequence progresses over the objects participating in the use case. We can also quickly see what the structure of the use case looks like. This structure often tells us a lot about the realization characteristics of the use case. Here we can, in principle, validate the structure of the use case that was defined in the analysis model. We will now look at a use case that is designed in two fundamentally different ways.

The use case is based on a real application and is built to handle a warehouse with automatic trucks that move pallets. A technician gives an order specifying only where the pallet is located and where it should be moved to. All loads are placed on pallets that can be moved around automatically in the warehouse. Since the pallets are moved automatically, the loads must be checked at intervals, say every tenth move, to make sure that the loads are still stable on the pallet. We must therefore keep in mind how many times a specific pallet has been moved. We will now design the use case to move a pallet. This is done by drawing an interaction diagram for it. We will look at two different variants for implementing this.

Figure 8.13 shows the first case. The use case starts as the technician sends a stimulus to *Transporter*. *Transporter* then asks *Pallet* how many times it has been moved. If it has been moved the maximum number of permitted times we must check whether the move is to be made in the warehouse or whether it is to be made to a checking station. If it is to a checking station we can make the move, otherwise we must not move the pallet.

In this interaction diagram we can see that everything is handled and controlled by *Transporter*. This object controls the flow and operates on the other objects, and then it decides what to do. This object must therefore contain rules for moving a load. We have a **centralized** structure.

In the second design, shown in Figure 8.14, we have delegated the decision as to whether the *Pallet* can be moved or not to *Pallet* itself. *Transporter* now only asks whether the load can be moved or

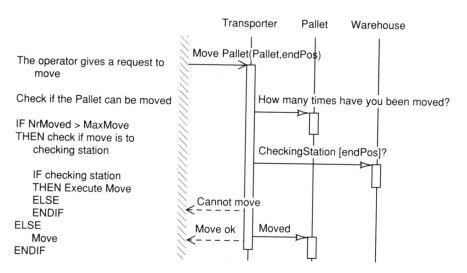

**Figure 8.13** Transport with the *Transporter* controlling the detailed flow.

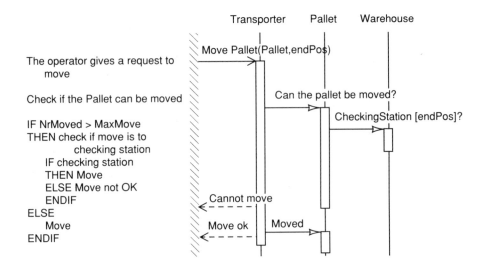

The operator gives a request to
move

Check if the Pallet can be moved

IF NrMoved > MaxMove
THEN check if move is to
checking station
IF checking station
THEN Move
ELSE Move not OK
ENDIF
ELSE
Move
ENDIF

**Figure 8.14**    A use case design where the pallet itself knows if it can be moved.

not. *Pallet* now checks whether it is permitted to move the load and
whether it will be moved to a checking station or not. It only replies
yes or no to *Transporter,* and then *Transporter* moves the load if this is
possible.

Here we can see that the decisions are decentralized and are
made by the unit knowing the conditions, in our case *Pallet.*
*Transporter* is only interested in whether the pallet can be moved or
not, and has now been freed of knowing under which conditions the
load can be moved. We have a **decentralized** structure.

The difference between these use cases is actually fundamental
and it has already come about in the analysis phase where we have
allocated the use cases to the analysis objects. Which of the use case
designs is actually more sensitive to changes? Let us assume that we
want to move painted bicycles in the warehouse. The bikes must not
be moved until they have dried, perhaps for six hours. Therefore, we
must add a check of attributes that keep track of whether there is a
painted bike on the pallet and how long ago it was painted. These
attributes belong to the bike, but must be checked by *Pallet.* In the
first use case design we must make changes in both *Transporter*
(which must ask *Pallet* what it contains) and *Pallet* (where we must
add new attributes). In the second design we only have to make
changes in *Pallet* (where we add the attributes and the checking
required).

In the interaction diagram, we can see the structure of the use cases very clearly. The interaction diagram helps us to assess how decentralized the system is. We can distinguish two extreme types of structure for interaction diagrams (see Figure 8.15).

The first extreme we call a **fork diagram**. This type is characterized by the fact that it is an object acting like a spider in a web and so controls the other objects. Much of the behavior is placed in the controlling object which knows all other objects and often uses them for direct questions or commands.

A fork diagram indicates a centralized structure. Typically the control sequence is placed in one object, often a control object. The other objects are typically used as information carriers or as an interface to a user. A fork structure often places great responsibility on the designer of the controlling object, since this often becomes much more complex than other objects.

The other extreme we call a **stair diagram**. This type is characterized by delegated responsibility. Each object only knows a few of the other objects and knows which objects can help with a specific behavior. Here we have no 'central' object.

Stair diagrams often indicate a decentralized structure. Each object has a separate task and it only knows the surrounding objects it needs in order to get help in carrying out this task.

Which of these two types should be chosen? Which is better? Often it is claimed that the stair structure is more object-oriented and thus better. The more the responsibilities have been spread out, the better. However, this is not always true. What we want is to be able to introduce changes easily and also to design reusable objects and stimuli. Different kinds of change can of course occur.

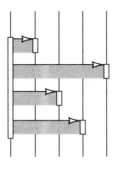 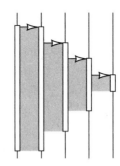

Fork — centralized          Stair — decentralized

**Figure 8.15**  The interaction diagrams show clearly what the structure of the use case looks like. The extreme points are the fork structure and the stair structure.

To handle changes in how a sequence is actually performed you should encapsulate the actual sequence and thus obtain decentralized structure. If you want to change the actual order of the operations, it is better to have a centralized structure, since then such changes will be local to one object. We thus see that both structure have their benefits. What is crucial is whether the operations have strong connection to each other. A *strong connection* exists if the objects:

- Form a 'consists-of' hierarchy, such as country–state–city;
- Form an information hierarchy, such as document chapter–section–paragraph–character;
- Represent a fixed temporal relationship, such a advertisement–order–invoice–delivery–payment;
- Form a (conceptual) inheritance hierarchy, such a animal–mammal–cat.

We have found the following principal rules:

- A decentralized (stair) control structure is appropriate when:
  - the operations have a strong connection (see above);
  - the operations will always be performed in the same order.
- A centralized (fork) control structure is appropriate when:
  - the operations can change order;
  - new operations could be inserted.

This also leads to the conclusion that these two structures very well may be, and indeed should be, combined to yield a stable and robust structure.

We see here that the *ordering* of operations is also a potential source of changes. We cannot regard behavior or data from robustness viewpoint alone, but also need to consider ordering. The natural solution for robustness is normally to encapsulate things that can be changed. Hence we should also be able to encapsulate ordering of operations. That is exactly what is done in the centralized approach where we have the ordering of operations defined in only one object.

## 8.2.6    Use cases with extensions

The possibility of using one use case to extend amother use case i described by means of an extension association between the two use cases. In the interaction diagram this is described by a probe position A probe position indicates a position in the use case to be extended and is often accompanied by a condition which indicates under what circumstances the extension should take place. The probe position is described in the interaction diagram of the extension use case and it indicates a position in the interaction diagram of the use case to be extended. The probe thus belongs to the extending use case and not to the one to be extended; this is to avoid changing the original use case when new extensions are added. The position indicated by the probe is some point in the description of an operation in a block (see Figure 8.16).

The semantics of a probe is as follows. The original use case runs, obeying its description. When the use case reaches the probe position, it checks whether the extension condition is true. If it is, the use case now starts to follow the extension use case's description. When it reaches the end of that description, it returns to its original description and continues where it left off

The description of the *Item Stuck* use case thus extends the description of *Returning Item*. The probe position therefore refers to a place in the description for *Returning Item*. During execution, the probe gives the place where the *Item Stuck* behavior is inserted.

The use case *Item Stuck* will extend *Returning Item* when an item is stuck. From the description in the interaction diagram we shall be able to find exactly where the probe is to be inserted. We describe *Item Stuck* in just the same way as other use cases. The description of *Returning Item* has not been affected and hence can be described independently of *Item Stuck*.

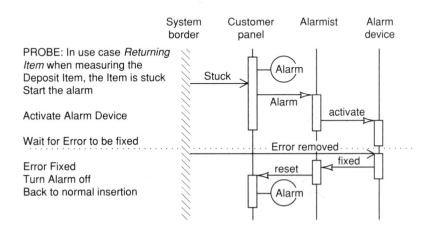

**Figure 8.16** The use case *Item Stuck* has a probe position *Alarm*. The new behavior is inserted at the probe position.

### 8.2.7  Homogenization

The use cases are normally designed in parallel and by several designers who can work more or less independently of one another. This means that stimuli are defined by several different designers. Normally you should agree on the definition rules for stimuli, at least in the project or for the product, but preferably in the entire organization. We have discussed earlier how stimuli can be handled uniformly, but despite this there will still be stimuli with the same meaning or purpose but with different definitions. We therefore have to **homogenize** all stimuli when the use cases have been designed. Homogenization can of course also be done as the work on the design of use cases proceeds.

Homogenization means that we try to get as few stimuli as possible, all of which should be maximally reusable and easy to work with. What we should strive for is a set of powerful stimuli that can be reused. Sometimes it may be sufficient to change the name of a stimulus or to change the parameters, but we may also have to divide some stimuli or create a completely new set of stimuli. This new set of stimuli must (of course) have the same power of expression as the old set, but should consist of as few stimuli as possible.

For instance, imagine you have the following set of stimuli defined on an object Person by different developers:

```
What_is_your_phone_number?
Where_do_you_live
Get_address
Get_address_and_phone_number
```

These could be homogenized to:

```
Get_address
Get_phone_number
```

We have reduced the number of stimuli, but we can get everything that we got with the first set of stimuli. It must be decided from time to time on which level the stimuli should be defined. It is very hard to give any strict rules, but reusability and robustness should be the main criteria.

You can compare homogenization with orthogonalization in mathematics, but you should normally not be as strict as to require all stimuli to be orthogonal in an information space. The reason is that we also set the requirement that our stimuli must be efficient. To send a stimulus is perhaps very expensive (in some sense). So it may be preferable to keep a more complex stimulus than to divide it into more homogenized stimuli which will always be used together. An important criterion in homogenization is consequently how the stimuli are to be used. The purpose of homogenization is to prepare for a not-too-complex block design – all operations that the stimuli should trigger must be implemented later.

In the same manner as we homogenize stimuli, we should review all the use cases to see whether we can find common behaviors that we missed earlier. Subsequences can perhaps be taken out, and maybe we will find common parts of use cases not discovered during the analysis phase (typical examples are fault handling in different situations).

## 8.3 Block design

### 8.3.1 The block interface

When we have designed all the use cases, or at least all the use cases for a specific block, we can design the block(s). Through the design of the use cases we now have a complete description of all external requirements of the block. Of course we also have requirements from our analysis model that specifies what each block will implement. From these requirements we can now design the block.

The actual implementation of the blocks in the source code can start when the block interfaces start to stabilize and are frozen. Often we refer to the source code as the implementation model since it too is a model with a finer granularity than the design model.

When the implementation of blocks starts, normally ancestor blocks should be implemented prior to descendant blocks. Hence, in the recycling machine example, the block *Deposit Item* should be designed prior to *Can, Crate* and *Bottle*.

Through the use case design, we have implicitly specified the protocol of each block. By taking all interaction diagrams where a block participates and extracting all the operations defined for that block, we will have a complete picture of the interfaces of the block. These interfaces have appeared during the design of use cases where normally several people are involved and the interfaces are usually not collected in one document. The interfaces exist explicitly, though, and they are connected to the appropriate block. It is therefore simple to extract these interfaces mechanically; this can be done by means of a CASE tool.

Let us see how this looks for a block in the example. We go through all interaction diagrams and extract all the operations defined on a block. Figure 8.17 repeats the interaction diagram for the use case *Returning Items*.

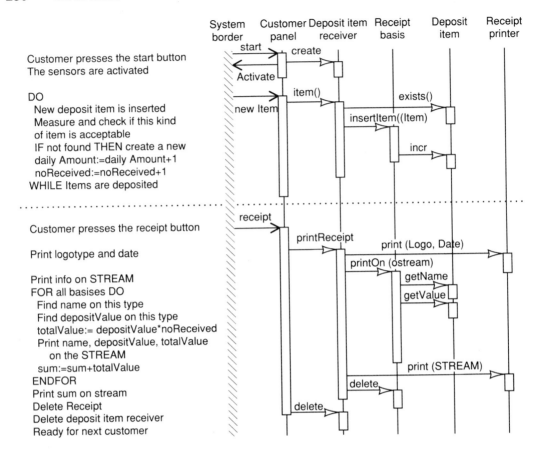

Customer presses the start button
The sensors are activated

DO
  New deposit item is inserted
  Measure and check if this kind
  of item is acceptable
  IF not found THEN create a new
  daily Amount:=daily Amount+1
  noReceived:=noReceived+1
WHILE Items are deposited

Customer presses the receipt button

Print logotype and date

Print info on STREAM
FOR all basises DO
  Find name on this type
  Find depositValue on this type
  totalValue:= depositValue*noReceived
  Print name, depositValue, totalValue
    on the STREAM
  sum:=sum+totalValue
ENDFOR
Print sum on stream
Delete Receipt
Delete deposit item receiver
Ready for next customer

**Figure 8.17**   The interaction diagram for the use case *Returning Item.*

From this interaction diagram we can extract the following
interface for *Deposit Item*:

exists()
incr
getName
getValue

and the following for *Receipt Basis*:

insertItem(item)
printOn(ostream)
delete

Hence, from the interaction idagrams we can extract the first
interfaces of the blocks. Let us focus on the *Receipt Basis* block. We

now have the following information about the public object module, or class since in this case we will implement it in C++:

**Class** ReceiptBasis;
**Operations**:
   create;
   insertItem(DepositItem);
   printOn(stream);
   delete;
**Attributes**:
   itemList: **listOf** ReturnedItem;
   sum: ECU;
**endClass**

This can now be expressed in the programming language. Below is the header file in C++ for the block *Receipt Basis*. We have used the block design previously discussed, also shown in Figure 8.18. We have two component classes that are only visible through the "#include "linkedlist.h"" statement. Additionally, we have a supporting class for the implementation which is private to the block, that is, the class *InsertedItem*

```
// File ReceiptBasis.h

#include "linkedlist.h"
#include "stream.h"

// private classes (encapsulated to the block)

class InsertedItem : public Link {
    private:
        DepositItem *returnedItem;
        int             totalNumber;
    public:
        insertedItem(DepositItem *di);
        DepositItem *getItem();
        void        incr();
        int         getTotal();
        ~InsertedItem();
};
```

// **public classes**

```
class ReceiptBasis {
```

// **Attributes**
```
    private:
        LinkedList *itemList;
        float       sum;
```

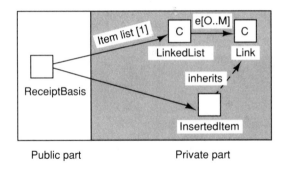

Figure 8.18    The block *Receipt Basis* with its public and private classes.

```
//Operations
public:
    ReceiptBasis();                          // Create in C++
    void insertItem(DepositItem*);
    void printOn(ostream&);
    ~ReceiptBasis();                         // Delete in C++
}.
```

By going through all interaction diagrams, we will get th
complete interface to a block. We will also have the first descriptio
of the operations from the text in the left margin.

Hence, at this stage it is possible to *freeze* the interface of th
blocks. By freezing the interface of the blocks we can start bloc
design activities in parallel.

In addition to the requirements set by the use case desigr
there are also other requirements on the block. These requirement
can also be identified from the analysis model where we find, fo
example, which attributes and attribute types the block should have
Other requirements may come from the requirements specificatio
for example, real-time requirements or memory space requirements.

In many cases a block will correspond to exactly one class an
its instances. Then it is easy to map the interface of an object in th
design model to a specific class interface in the source code. Othe
times, as we have seen, many classes must be used to implement on
block. In most cases, the reason is to handle the implementatio
environment, but other common cases include the implementation c
attributes, use of components and the extraction of commo
functionality into abstract classes.

To handle the interface of a block we can use concepts from th
programming language as shown above. However, the blocks are als
an abstraction and an encapsulation mechanism. Thus we want t

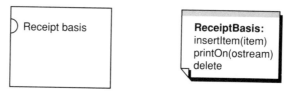

**Figure 8.19** The block *Receipt Basis* and its exported type. The type's specification is documented in some way clarifying the role to be played by it.

express the interface of a block more explicitly and also be able to encapsulate its actual implementation. We do this by defining **public** and **private** object modules. The public object modules can be accessed from the outside of a block and are thus exported from the block, but the private object modules cannot be accessed from the outside. In the example above we will only make the *Receipt Basis* class public, and encapsulate the details of the block's internal structure. This is illustrated in Figure 8.18.

Hiding internal implementation details is a way of handling the complexity of the source code. However, in this technique we must determine early which classes should be public, and thus take early decisions concerning the internals of the block. What is actually needed is just to be able to specify an interface to a role that the block should export. For other block implementors who need to program using our block, we need to define the **types** we offer and the operations we offer on these types. One or several such types could then map to a class in the block. Using this technique we could define these types as **responsibilities** and **contracts** as discussed by Wirfs-Brock *et al.* (1990). This is illustrated in Figure 8.19.

## 8.3.2 Object behavior

As an intermediate level for the internals of the object, before looking at the actual implementation, we may use state transition graphs. Their purpose is to provide a simplified description that increases understanding of the block without having to go down to source code level, and to provide a description that is less dependent on the selected programming language. In these graphs we describe which stimuli can be received and what will happen when a stimulus is received. For a discussion on state transition graphs, refer to the box.

**On states and**
**state machines**

States are actually dependent on what you want to describe and are in that sense relative. For our recycling machine we can have states indicating that it is full of bottles, that it is busy or idle, that the standard height of cans is set to 20 cm and so on. We see here that there is not just one state in the machine, but many. To be absolutely correct and complete, a state is the union of all values describing the present situation. With a state we must be able to fully recreate the present situation. We can quickly see that it is impossible to describe each state since this would mean that we would have to define an almost infinite number of values. If we want to describe a state in a computer, we must define what each memory cell contains, and this is impossible in practice in a development.

When we describe how our blocks will work internally, it is suitable in our case to use state machines, especially to implement objects that emanate from control objects.

In order to continue and to discuss states we differentiate between internal states and computational states. The **internal state** is what characterizes all the values of our variables that are important for our description, as well as variables relating to the application and variables that are included because of the implementation environment. The **computational state** describes how far we have come in the execution, as well as the potential future execution. In principle we only want to describe an object behavior in terms of computational states. It is essential to understand the fact that underlying the computational states we have internal states that contain the information we use to move between the computational states. The internal states are also used to describe the state of the object.

A computational state transition graph thus describes the class. When a class is instantiated, an instance is created that follows a path in this graph throughout its lifetime. For a class that can be traced to a control object, we normally have several states in this graph, whereas for a class that emanates from an entity object, we usually have only one computational state. The state indicates to some extent the potential that this object has at that moment. We can clearly see which stimuli the object can receive, and we can also see what will happen in these cases. When the object receives a stimulus, it will follow a path in the graph and enter another state (that may be the same from which it started). The path selected is consequently dependent on the received stimulus, but also on the internal, underlying state.

States and state transitions can be described in many ways. We will here show some different notations that can be used. For the example we will use a stack. A stack is a linear structure on which to store elements. All insertions and deletions take place at one end. A insertion is performed by a push operation and a deletion is done by a pop operation. Another name for a stack is a LIFO (last-in-first-out) list, since the last inserted element is the first to be deleted. The most obvious way is to use ordinary state transition diagrams (see Sudkamp (1988)), often called Mealy machines. In a Mealy machine each transition must be well defined by the stimulus received. However, this is not plausible in our graphs since it also depends on the internal state. To make it practical we need to express conditions at the transition edges. This technique is illustrated in Figure 8.20.

A transition is dependent on the stimuli received and on the underlying internal state expressed with some conditions. This can be described so as to place the conditions on the edges between the nodes, as in Figure 8.21. Not until a certain computation has been made can we see which path to take. Mealy machines do not have this facility to describe a path selection during a state transition, and we have therefore modified the semantics.

This description could also be made in textual form as shown in Figures 8.22. Here each state is represented by a textual construct as all computation. A similar notation has been described by Berzins and Luqi (1990).

Other techniques can be used to describe the computation of an object, for instance state transition graphs as used in structured methods (see Ward and Mellor (1985)) or the notation used in JSD,

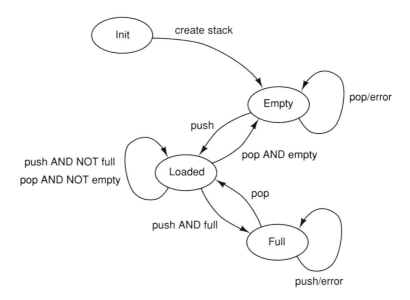

**Figure 8.20**   A state transition graph for describing a stack.

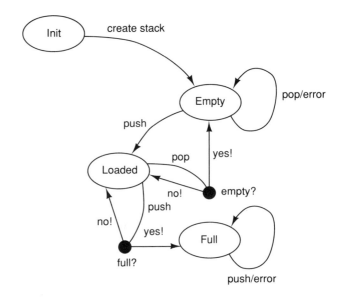

**Figure 8.21**   State transition graph with conditions on the edge.

(see Jackson (1983)). SDL, the Specification and Description Languag
a CCITT (1988) standard used for a long time, is still another techniqu
for this notation. To describe a specific operation, further techniqu
such as data flow diagrams can be used. Which technique is chosen f
this description is actually not very important; the important thing
that it helps you to abstract the actual coding. For our examples he
we will use a notation extending SDL, but in principle any notatic
could be used. Our notation is described in Figure 8.23.

These symbols are connected to describe the computation of a
object. The **start** symbol indicates where the creation of an obje
starts. A **state** symbol shows a stable state of the object betwe
different operations. **Send message** performs an operation on anoth
object and corresponds to a **receive message** in the object to b
operated on. To describe the return from such an operation, a **retu**
symbol is used. **Sending** and **Receiving** signals are denoted by th
corresponding symbols. The actual computation, not includi
explicit communication, is denoted by a **Perform task** box. Th
**Decision** symbol is used to describe alternatives in the execution a
the **Destroy** object describes where an instance is deleted. The **Lab**
symbol is used to make the diagrams easier to read and is often use
to describe loops and the like.

Every operation must start beneath a state, or the start symb
and end in a state (possibly the same state). This means that after ea

**machine**  Stack
  **state**  init
    **input**  createInstance
      **nextState**  empty
    **otherwise**  error;

  **state**  empty
    **input**  push(e)
      **do**  store[e] on top
        **nextState**  loaded
    **input**  (e)pop
      print "Stack is empty."
    **otherwise**  error;

  **state**  loaded
    **input**  push(e)
      **do**  store[e] on top
      **if**  isFull **then**
        **nextState**  full
    **input**  (e)pop
      **do**  return top,
        delete top
      **if**  isEmpty **then**
        **nextState**  empty
  **otherwise**  error;

  **state**  full
    **input**  push(e)
      print "Stack is full"
    **input**  (e) pop
      **do**  return top,
        delete top
      **nextState** loaded
    **otherwise**  error;

**endmachine**;

**Figure 8.22**   The description of the stack using a textual notation.

state we must have a receive symbol, either a receive message or a receive signal. The return symbol is only used if we have a return value. If no return value is explicit, the default condition is that a receive message is ended just before the next state. Let us look at an example. In Figure 8.24 we have used this notation to describe the same computation as we have previously done to describe the stack. The '--' in the state symbol refers to the immediately previous state.

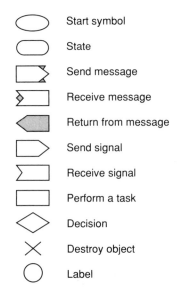

**Figure 8.23**    The notation used in the state transition graphs in this book.

This notation maps directly onto the interaction diagram presented earlier (see Figure 8.25). In (*a*) we have extracted a operation from the interaction diagram. This operation will b described by the state transition in (*b*). This sequence could b generated automatically from the interaction diagram. However, i the general case the exact semantics could not be generated. Also, th interaction diagram describes one specific path through the graph but the graph must describe all paths. Therefore only path skeleton can be generated and the developer must relate the paths and state to each other.

In this manner we can describe the classes of all objects in th system. The complete state transition graph for *Deposit Item* extracte from this interaction diagram is shown in Figure 8.26.

An object that will perform the same operation independent c state when a certain stimulus is received is called a **stimulus controlled** object. The order in which the stimuli are received in th object is of no significance; it performs the same task every time receives the same stimulus. This is the way objects normally act i object-oriented contexts; the operations can (in principle) be execute in an optional order. This is sometimes called 'the shopping lis approach' (Meyer 1988) since it reminds us of a shopping list; th order in which you pick out the items is uninteresting, what i

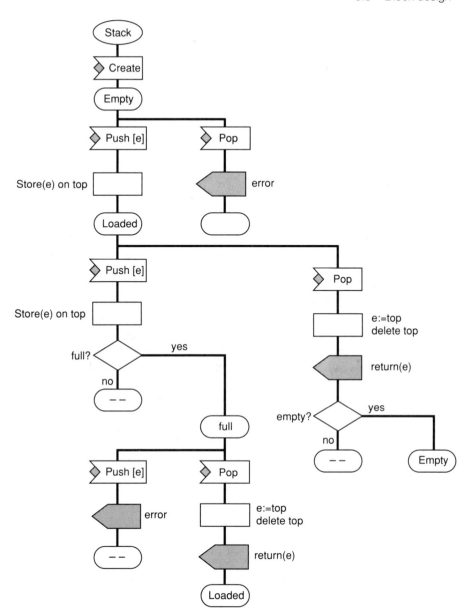

**Figure 8.24**   The stack described with the notation for a state transition graph used in this book.

important is that all the items can be picked out. Objects that implement entity objects are usually stimulus-controlled.

Objects that select operations not only from the stimulus received, but also from the current state, are called **state-controlled**

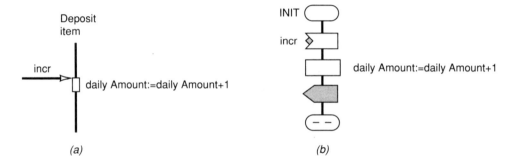

**Figure 8.25**    The operation in (*a*) will yield the state transition described in (*b*).

objects. These show a strong temporal relation between the current state of the object and the stimuli it can receive; for example, an operation may only be executed in specific states. The Stack, for example, is state controlled. We cannot do push when it is empty – will result in an error. Objects that implement control objects often have a tendency to be state-controlled. This, of course, does not mean that a state-controlled object is independent of the stimulus received, but there is a high correlation between the stimuli it can receive and the stimuli the object as previously received and in which order they were received. In the recycling example, the *Deposit Item Receive* block is a stimulus-controlled object. Its state transition graph shown in Figure 8.27. When a stimulus is sent, we have used the common object-oriented notation for the receiver, for instance RB.create means that create is sent to the block RB *(Receipt Basis).*

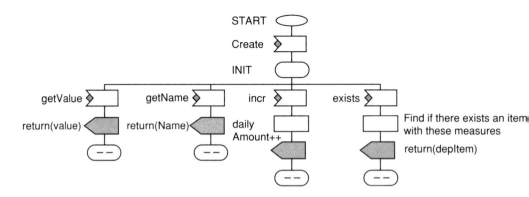

**Figure 8.26**    State transition graph for *Deposit Item*.

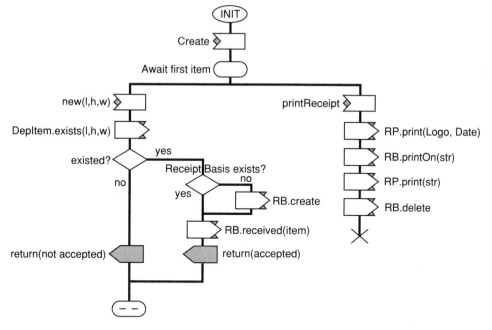

**Figure 8.27**   The state transition graph of *Deposit Item Receiver*.

We see that this graph is more complicated. For stimulus-controlled objects and for simple state-controlled objects it is not necessary to draw a state transition graph since this would be of little value owing to their simplicity. The benefits of these graphs increase the more complicated the behavior is. Especially in behavior where the states are important, these graphs will be of great help. In Chapter 14 we will see the benefits of these graphs for complicated sequences.

We should also describe the state transition graph of *Receipt Basis* (see Figure 8.28). Here we have several task boxes. These boxes represent the computation that is encapsulated in the object.

### 8.3.3   Internal block structure

When we have identified these properties of the block, we can outline the internal block structure. The internal structure of the block will consist of object modules as previously discussed. If our implementation language is object-oriented, these object modules will in reality become classes in the language; if we do not have classes naturally in the language, then they will be module units in the

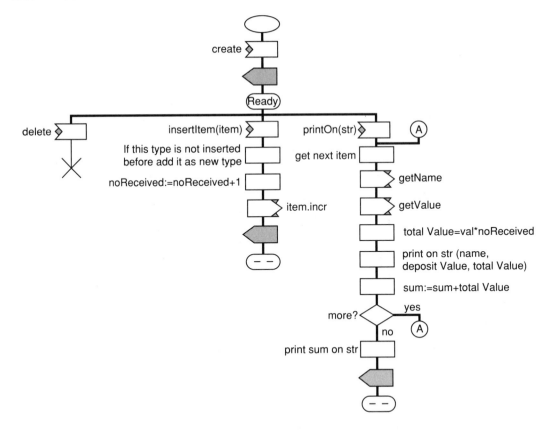

**Figure 8.28**   The state transition graph of *Receipt Basis*.

source code. We have already discussed the internal structure of block.

The blocks used in the design model are actually an abstraction mechanism for these object modules. Often the block can be implemented as only one class; otherwise we may need a handful of classes for each object. Generally, there will be more classes than objects. Often, these will be components, but, for instance, attribute types that you have defined may also be new classes. Other reasons for introducing new classes can be seen in the internal structure of *Receipt Basis*. There we used components, but we also introduced new class to handle the reference to the inserted item.

When the structuring of a block is done, we define the classes in the system. Here it is of course of interest to design reusable and high-quality classes. In the same manner as we talked about homogenization between stimuli, we also want the classes to be homogenized. This means that we do not want two classes offering similar functionality, unless they are related through inheritance. Additionally we want classes to offer functionality that is internally strongly coupled. For instance, if half of the operations of a class access half of the instance variables and the other operations operate on the other variables, we should consider splitting it into two classes. Other heuristics of good class design include judgement of the potential reusability value of the class. Will a change make the class more reusable to others? However, it takes time to design a good class, and it is not always efficient to develop every class in the system to be as general as possible. A common estimation is that it takes something like 5–10 times longer to design a component class than an ordinary class.

The most straightforward way to implement a block's interface is to have one class implementing the entire interface. This is often an appropriate solution. However, there may be times when it is better to split the block interface so that it is implemented by two or more classes. An example of this is when the block plays several roles. There may be reason to separate these roles to be implemented by different classes, although this should not be taken as a rule. Another typical example is when you encounter a situation in which the actual handling of instances is placed in the same block as the block that represents the instances themselves. In the recycling example we have such a case. Think of *Deposit Item*. This block can receive the stimulus exists, which invokes an operation to look among all items to find if there exists an item that fits the appropriate parameters. On the other hand, the block can also receive a stimulus like incr, which is sent to one specific instance. We thus have encapsulated the handling of instances and the actual instances in the same block. In some object-oriented languages, like C++ or Smalltalk, you can implement behavior as class operations. Another solution is to have one class that represents the actual instances and one class that implements the management of these instances. Which solution to use is a matter of programming techniques and philosophy, and also depends on the actual environment.

Sometimes a block's functionality will not need to be implemented as a class and instances of this class. The reason in this case is that there is no need for any instance variables. A collection of free operations may then be sufficient. This is possible in C++, but in some other object-oriented languages it is not. In that case they could be placed as class operations.

It is important to use components in structuring the internals of a block. Sometimes components must be adapted before they can be used and therefore they may give rise to new classes that act as a shell for the component. However, we shall have more to say about components in a subsequent chapter.

### 8.3.4    Implementation

Now that we have described the blocks using state transition graphs we can seamlessly implement them in the programming language. There are already systems that automatically translate from SDL descriptions into source code, but this requires of course that the SDL graphs are extended with programming language-like formalisms. Normally, however, we will still need human beings to make this final transition to source code.

The adaptation to the programming language will be made according to a specialization of the construction process to the selected language. The adaptation to programming languages is not just left to this late phase; we have seen that during the entire design process we are forced to consider how to solve problems that arise because of the implementation environment in question.

Note that we have maintained traceability from our analysis model all the way down to the source code. When we read the source code we can directly trace what gave rise to it in the analysis model. This property in a system is very valuable; when a system is changed during its life cycle, this property is invaluable for the engin-eers who work on the maintenance and development of the system.

The specialization to the programming language describes how we translate the terms used in the design into the terms and properties in the implementation language. Although the methods described here are general and largely independent of the actual language, all languages will have their specialities during the implementation. In this discussion we will consider programming languages that are object-oriented. We will also discuss differences relative to languages that are not object-oriented. The ideas described in this book can be used for various languages. The techniques are a a higher system structuring level and thus not dependent on particular constructs in any specific language.

Many projects and organizations have **coding rules** concerning how the source code should be written. The purpose of these rules is to obtain a uniform source code that not only facilitates understanding and reading, but also achieves portability between different environments. The specialization described here should no need to influence these rules, but the coding rules should be applied regardless of this specialization.

**Object-oriented languages**  Let us start by looking at languages that offer classes and inheritance. Here we include among others C++, Smalltalk, Simula, Eiffel and Objective-C. These languages have classes, and these classes will correspond to the object modules that we have designed.

It would be desirable to group these classes in the same manner as they were grouped earlier, in blocks and subsystems, for example. The programming languages usually have no further terms for this grouping (except for Simula), and here you will have to use local standards. Usually you use different files and file directories for this purpose. One block could then correspond to a file and a subsystem to a directory. We have previously seen how one block could be specified in a C++ file. However, in modern environments there is support for this partitioning.

Inheritance between object modules is straightforwardly mapped onto inheritance between classes in the programming language. Inheritance between blocks can be more complicated. Here we want all the functionality in one object also to be accessible from another. This problem can often be solved by direct inheritance between the main classes in the objects.

Attributes that have been identified during the analysis phase or that appeared during the design work are usually implemented as a variable of a specific type. If the type has a complex data structure, we often have to make a new class of the attribute type; otherwise it could be made of a more primitive type (in C++, for example, a struct). We saw an example of this in the header files where we wanted InsertedItem to have one attribute totalNumber storing how many of this type the customer had returned:

```
class Inserteditem : public Link. {
    private:
        DepositItem *returnedItem;
        int totalNumber;      // here is the attribute of type int
        ...
```

Acquaintance associations are normally implemented in the same way as attributes, namely as ordinary instance references or pointer variables to instances. The same could apply for communication associations, but these could also be represented by ordinary local variables in an operation or by nothing at all if a return value is used as an object reference. For these associations we also want to handle stimuli. Stimuli normally become messages or ordinary routine calls. This is how the incr stimulus looks in the code:

```
    ...
    ii–>incr();      // ii is a pointer fo the inserted item.
    ...
```

Note the possibility here of using *virtual* (*deferred* in Eiffe subclass responsibility in Smalltalk) operations for classes. Th means that in the ancestor we only declare that a certain operatic will exist, whereas the implementation is done in a descendant. Th enables different implementations for different classes, a facility tha is frequently useful.

We see that all concepts are directly translatable to propertie in the programming language. In Table 8.1 we have summarized th traceability for C++. Note that this is one alternative; there may b other alternatives in each specific case.

**Table 8.1**    Traceability for C++

| Analysis | Design | Source code C++ |
| --- | --- | --- |
| Analysis object | Block | 1..N classes |
| Behavior in object | Operation | Member function |
| Attribute (Class) | Attribute (Class) | Static variables |
| Attribute (instance) | Attribute (Instance) | Instance variable |
| Acquaintance ass. | Acquaintance ass. | Instance variable |
| Communication ass. | Communication ass. | Reference to a (member) function |
| Interaction between objects | Stimulus | Call to a (member) function |
| Use case | Designed Use Case | Sequence of calls |
| Subsystem | Subsystem | File |

For state-controlled blocks, we often need to keep track of th current state. The basis is often a description from a state transitic graph. One solution is to use CASE or IF statements to check on th current state; another is to use polymorphism, in which case th virtual procedure is frequently very useful. It should be noted he that we do not use CASE statements to check the type or similar (th should definitely be solved by using polymorphism instead), but on to implement state machines. In, for instance, Smalltalk we could als concatenate the state name with the actual stimuli to find the corre operation. An example of this is given in Chapter 14.

Instantiation is handled in the manner offered by the languag The instantiation is normally described in the interaction diagrams. this context we should also mention that memory management mu be considered, as previously discussed. In languages such . Smalltalk, Simula and Eiffel you normally use automatic garba collection, whereas in languages such as C++ and Objective-C th program must implement it.

Data hiding is an important property used in object-oriente contexts. All attributes should be made private unless there a special reasons for not doing so. Accessing these variables should be carried out by special operations of the form getX. This is standard in Smalltalk and normally also in Eiffel and C++, but in Simula you must indicate explicitly that they are hidden.

We can therefore see that we maintain the traceability all the way to the source code by means of these rules. Below is the actual implementation of the member functions specified above:

```
// File receiptbasis.cc

#include"receiptbasis.h"

void ReceiptBasis::insertItem(DepositItem *di) {
    if (itemList->isEmpty()) {
    Inserteditem *ii = new InsertedItem(di);
    itemList->addLast(ii);
    } else {
    int found = 0;
    Inserteditem *ii = (InsertedItem*)itemList->first();
    do {
        if (ii->getItem() == di) {
            ii->incr();
            found = 1;
            } else
                ii = (InsertedItem*)ii->nextLink();
            } while (ii && !found);
            if (!found) {
                Inserteditem *ii = new InsertedItem(di);
                itemList->addLast(ii);
                }
            }
    di->incr();
    }
void ReceiptBasis::printOn(ostream &os) {
    char *name;
    float value;
    float totalValue;
    Inserteditem *ii = (InsertedItem*)itemLisf->first();
    do {
        name = ii->getItem()->getName();
        value = ii->getItem()->getValue();
        totalValue = value * ii->getTotal();
        os << name << value << totalValue <<\ "n";
        sum += totalValue;
        ii = (InsertedItem*)ii->nextLink();
        } while (ii);
    os << sum << "n";
    }
```

**Non-object-oriented languages**

If our language is not object-oriented, we must translate the fundamental concepts, like inheritance and encapsulation, in another manner. Here we will survey some of these properties and concentrate on what differs from what has been said above about object-oriented languages.

The most common languages used include object-based languages such as Ada and Modula-2 and traditional programming languages such as C, Pascal, Fortran and COBOL. Here we will primarily discuss Ada, but this, together with what has been said earlier, should be adequate to indicate how to transfer the terms to other languages. The great difference compared with object-oriented languages lies above all in the inheritance concept.

An important term in Ada is the package concept. It offers the ability to express hiding. In Ada we translate each object module into a package. Since packages can import other packages (using the WITH construction) we can also use them here to group blocks and subsystems.

The most difficult problem is how inheritance should be translated. The simplest solution is to get a preprocessor where these terms have been added to the language. Such preprocessors exist for Ada (for example, Classic Ada), for C (for example, C++) and so on. With this solution the entire problem is solved, but it is not always possible to do this.

Another solution is to simulate inheritance. This can be done in several ways. The easiest way is simply to import the package placed above the one being implemented in the 'inheritance hierarchy' encapsulate its type definition and simulate the inheritance by linking together several calls. This is sometimes called **call-through.** It can cause performance problems for long inheritance hierarchies, but it could be a solution when the inheritance hierarchies are short. If you use generic packages this linkage can be made by using a specific routine as the relevant (generic) parameter when instantiating the package. In this case linkage is done during compilation and produces no overhead on execution. Another way is to use derived types.

One alternative to simulating inheritance is to use the inheritance hierarchy only as a method of grouping your information and thus avoid having to write the source code slavishly according to the hierarchy. The result will be that we will not see the inheritance structure in the source code and the abstract blocks will have no correspondence in the source code.

Attributes will normally be made into variables, sometimes of a predefined data type but often as a self-defined type, for example, composite data structure. Class and instance variables can also be expressed in Ada, but this may be more difficult in other languages.

Acquaintance associations normally become a reference to the object or a variable of the object's type. Cardinality [1] or [0. .1] can be expressed with a simple reference. Cardinality [M] or [1..N] is expressed by a vector of references or as a dynamic structure (for example, a list) of references.

Stimuli normally give rise to a routine call. In Ada communication associations normally give rise to a variable of the associated object's type. Instantiation is made in different ways depending on the nature of the object. For example, blocks can be instantiated by simply declaring new variables of the relevant type. Note that these objects do not survive in the same manner as objects in object-oriented languages. If you want to instantiate control objects, for example, this is normally done with one or several procedure calls.

Also in this case we can see that we maintain the traceability all the way to the source code. Table 8.2 summarizes this traceability. Please note that there may be alternatives in specific cases.

**Table 8.2**   The analysis concepts are treated in the design model and onward to the source code. The example shows this traceability for Ada.

| Analysis | Design | Source code Ada |
| --- | --- | --- |
| Analysis object | Block | Package |
| Behavior in object | Operation | Procedure or task |
| Attribute (class) | Attribute (class) | Variables (global in package body) |
| Attribute (instance) | Attribute (instance) | Variables (part of private type) |
| Acquaintance ass. | Acquaintance ass. | Variable reference |
| Communication ass. | Communication ass. | Existence of procedure call |
| Interaction between objects | Stimulus | Procedure call or entry call |
| Use case | Designed use case | Sequence of calls |
| Subsystem | Subsystem | Package |

### 8.3.5   Implementation of probes

The explanation of why the extension association gives rise to a communication association was given earlier. This association is associated with a probe which specifies where the sequence should be inserted. By a probe we mean a position in a use case description or its accompanying interaction diagram where, when a use case follows this description, another behavior can be inserted. Since the original description must be independent (have no knowledge) of the new, inserted behavior, all of the control structure should be placed in the block containing the inserted use case.

Unfortunately we cannot accomplish this with today's programming languages, and so we are forced to deviate from this ideal. Instead the probe must be implemented in the block where the sequence should be inserted. We thus must add one variable to hold a reference to the inserted functionality and also the stimuli that should be sent to this object. This is illustrated below:

```
class CustomerPanel {
public:

    . . .

    void stuck();
    void reset();

    . . .

private:

    . . .

    alarmist myAlarm;

    . . .

}
void CustomerPanel::stuck()
{
    myAlarm.alarm;
}

    . . .
```

We here assume that an instance of *Alarmist* (myAlarm) is created in, for instance, the constructor of the class.

In a more traditional language where we do not have the class concept, we usually implement the probe with a specific procedure. In the example this would look something like this:

```
procedure Receive_Item(measure:measure_type);

    . . .

DO
    Item := getItem;
    probe_Alarm; \\ here is the probe_procedure
    CASE Item : Item_type OF
        Can:     newCan(Item);
        Bottle:  newBottle(Item);
        Crate:   newCrate(Item);
```

```
        ENDCASE
    WHILE not Receipt;
      . . .
```

And the probe procedure would look like this:

```
    procedure probe_Alarm;
    BEGIN
      IF stuck THEN
        BEGIN
        alarm;
        wait_for_reset:
      END;
    END:
```

In this manner we have hidden what the probe really means. When a change needs to be made to the inserted sequence, we do not have to change the procedure that realizes the *Returning Item* use case, but only the probe procedure.

Today there is no other way of resolving probes in the most common programming languages. There are some indications, however, that similar problems have been solved in some systems, for example TMS (Doyle 1979) which is implemented in KEE3 from IntelliCorp Inc. Another solution can be found in the programming language LOOPS (see Stefik *et al.* (1986)). The problem is also discussed by Jacobson (1986).

# 8.4  Working with construction

We have now discussed how the ideal analysis model is refined and adapted to the implementation environment to reach, finally, the source code level. This process is seamless as it will lead to the implementation in a straightforward manner. We here discuss some topics that were briefly mentioned in the previous presentation.

As stated several times, our design must be adapted to the real environment in which our system works. All conditions for our implementation emanating from somewhere other than the analysis phase are called collectively the implementation environment. This environment comprises the conditions coming from the target environment in the form of, for example, existing hardware and its distribution, and also the requirements that come indirectly from the development environment in the form of the selected programming language and its conditions.

The implementation environment also includes requirements that can be traced to the requirements specification in the form of performance requirements and the use of existing resources. Also requirements such as the system using other systems are included in the implementation environment. This environment is, in short everything disregarded in the analysis phase that now must be looked at. We say that we **specialize** the construction process to these different environments. Specialization thus means adapting the design to the relevant implementation environment.

### 8.4.1   Existing products

A common requirement from the implementation environment is that the system must use **existing products**. Even if the limit for extending the existing product and thus making a further development is fluctuating, it is still two different problems. In one case the existing product is the same system, but in an older version, and in the other we build another (new) system that only makes use of the existing product because it already exists.

This situation is very similar to that of using completed components, which will be discussed in a chapter of its own, and the difference is above all the size and thus complexity of the existing product. Building with components also differs from this solution, components are used as powerful units that we combine into objects. Using an existing product is different; in this case we must first make an analysis of the product and adapt our design to it.

An assessment must be made as to whether you want to use an existing product, and thus are forced to adapt your design to it, or whether you will not use the existing product but decide to develop this functionality yourself. The advantage of the latter is that you have a homogeneous system that should be easier to maintain since everything is described in a similar manner, rather than having two systems that perhaps are described differently and thus look very different. The advantage of the former is that it requires fewer resources since you need not devote resources to developing this part; the only thing required is to adapt the interfaces between the two systems. Experience tells us that in the long run it is very expensive to change a system architecture fundamentally, and this should therefore be avoided as far as possible. You should use the same design idea for an entire system (see Lawson (1990)).

A common problem is that you want to develop a system that has not been designed according to an object-oriented method, and this involves great adaptations to the existing system. This problem is difficult and often requires much **re-engineering.** See the discussions on this subject by Dietrich *et al.* (1989) and by Jacobson and Lindström (1991).

One of the (most important) criteria when deciding whether you should use something old or develop something new yourself is to consider the testing costs. It is hoped that an existing product has been used earlier and it should therefore already be well tested, whereas our own new system must be tested thoroughly to minimize the number of faults in it. Another important decision is how well you know the existing product and how much resources are needed to get to know it. Perhaps some project members have been involved in its development and it may therefore be rather easy to become familiar with it. Otherwise it may take a long time, especially if the documentation is poor, before you have learned this product and how to use it.

## 8.4.2   Abstractions

When you develop systems on an industrial scale you must at all times be able to handle the system complexity. This is the important issue for abstractions on different levels. We have seen how we have used blocks to encapsulate and thus abstract actual implementation details. In this way we could group several classes in the actual system to one block in the design model.

The block structure used in the example is appropriate for smaller systems, but is by no means satisfactory for larger systems. So we must find some way of grouping these blocks into larger units. In a normal system it is not unusual to have hundreds of blocks. This becomes impossible to handle and assumes a complexity that is hard to manage.

To handle this complexity we use **subsystems** as discussed in Chapter 7. The subsystems defined in the analysis model should also serve as the base for a division into subsystems in the design model and in the implementation. To achieve flexibility for larger systems, we can have subsystems within subsystems.

These subsystems should become the management unit in the organization. A subsystem should thus offer a protocol to other subsystems. We do this by exporting or making certain blocks public to other subsystems, as previously discussed. The interface of these blocks then will form the interface of the entire subsystem.

The lowest level of the subsystem, **service package**, often groups a related functionality. This level is then used as a base for system configuration. Such subsystems will either be delivered in their entirety or not at all. The subsystems are thus indivisible. Subsystems can have a functionality that is optional in the system, so that the system can be delivered with or without certain subsystems.

This means that the subsystems are atomic units used, for example, in discussions with customers and for product planning.

The work flow illustrated in this chapter can be applied recursively to the subsystems. Hence it is entirely possible to draw interaction diagrams between subsystems on various levels. This is often an appropriate technique when further developing a system. Then you could design a subsystem using only the interfaces of related subsystems and only use the blocks or classes that are made public from these subsystems.

So, we have a technique to decrease complexity on the object level. In the same manner there may be times when you also need to reduce the complexity of the stimuli. In some of the interaction diagrams presented here we have used this technique. Normally a stimulus would be specified exactly as it will look in the source code but we could, for instance, postpone the definition of actual parameters until later when the stimulus picture starts to mature. Another way of reducing the complexity is not to show stimulus interaction encapsulated in a block, such as stimuli sent to components or predefined stimuli in a class structure. We could also but with some reservations, abstract the stimuli to have one abstract stimulus that when implemented will give rise to many stimuli being sent to the same block.

### 8.4.3   Development is incremental

The picture we have given here is that the process of construction is straightforward and an easy road to follow. However, this is not true. The development is an incremental process and many iterations must be done before all stimuli are defined and the interfaces can be frozen. Further, when implementation has started, changes to the definitions of stimuli will still occur. For example, you will find that you must now get a reference to an object as a parameter. These iterations will occur and there is no point in rejecting them. What is important is to find a way of handling them. We will disuss this topic more in Chapter 16. We will only give some good advice here:

- Start the construction early, preferably at the same time as you start working on the analysis model. The first step in construction is to identify the implementation environment and this could be done in parallel with analysis so you have it ready when the actual construction starts.

- You have surely noticed that the design model is a refinement of the analysis model with regard to a certain implementation environment. When should you do the transition? You could use the interaction diagrams in the analysis model as well as state transition diagrams. If you have done a very detailed analysis model, the degree of refinement needed may be very small, unless the implementation environment is going to give you problems. When to do the transition must be decided from project to project. It is important to decide this early, and the decision should be based on the result from the identification of the implementation environment.

- Try to take one shot through all the models initially, particularly if you are inexperienced in OOSE. In this way you will get a much better feel for how the models relate and how output from one process will work as input to another. By working in this manner you will also get some feedback which will help you to decide when to make the transition from analysis to design. Another advantage is that you will deal with potential problems early, that you may have to solve before going fully into construction.

Iterations may thus exist on several different levels of granularity. Work on the design may give rise to changes in the analysis model. Smaller iterations may occur when, after an inspection meeting, you decided to change something in the design, for example in which object some functionality will be placed. Iterations are also made on a less formal level where two designers perhaps agree to change the type of a parameter in a stimulus. The lowest level of iteration is probably an individual designer who simply makes changes in his or her own classes.

## 8.4.4 Further issues

We have now described briefly both analysis and construction. The presentation has been an overview to illustrate the central features and the flow of work. Among the simplifications we have made we can mention the following:

- Documentation rules have been entirely ignored. Real situations require such rules and in real projects we use document instructions that specify these rules. There are different document instructions for different types of activity.

- The discussion only reflects the method; process issues are left out. In real development there is of course much more interaction between different parts. This interaction has been formalized, as discussed in Appendix A, and the idea is illustrated in Chapter 15.

- Other activities also take place during these phases, such as configuration management and reviews. However, this has been omitted entirely here.  These issues are extremely important in a real development. We will discuss some of them in Chapter 15.

- We will devote a whole chapter to tests later in this book. Here we will only mention that the tests of the blocks and object modules are normally done by the designer who designed them, whereas testing of the use cases and the system as a whole is done by special testers, often in a special test department. Tests of classes, blocks, use cases and the system will be discussed in Chapter 12.

## 8.5 Summary

In construction we carry out the design and implementation of the system. This work is based on the output from analysis. The analysis model describes the system under ideal circumstances where no consideration is given to the actual environment. The purpose of this model is to achieve a robust and maintainable structure over the entire system life cycle. In construction, we must adapt this ideal model to the prevailing conditions.

In construction, we must first identify the actual implementation environment. Here we must investigate all prevailing conditions affecting the realization of the system. This includes considering for instance how the DBMS should be integrated, how processes and distribution should be handled, the constraints of the programming language, the components libraries that can be used, and the incorporation of any graphical user interface tools. It also includes organizational issues such as distributed development, the competence areas of the staff, and marketing issues such as early delivery of a subsystem. The result of this work should be a strategy for handling all these issues in advance. This work can be done in parallel to analysis.

When the analysis model starts to mature, the implementation strategy should be added to this model. This will give us the first design model. Here we show how the DBMS is incorporated, how the system distribution is solved and so on. This will give us the first real approach to the actual system architecture. Since we want this architecture to be stable and robust, it is important to make as few deviations from the analysis model as possible.

The design model is then refined using the use cases specified during the analysis. By doing use case design, using the special technique of drawing interaction diagrams, we will develop the complete interface specification of each object step by step. Here we will define each stimulus sent between objects in the system. These specifications can be further refined through a state transition graph for each object, showing the object behavior in more detail.

The objects are then structured and implemented using one or several object modules. These object modules correspond to classes in an object-oriented language, but if the language is not object-oriented they will correspond to the module concept in the current language. The use of software components is important in this structuring.

The implementation is straightforward in the chosen programming language. An object-oriented language is preferable since all important concepts used in OOSE are directly mapped onto these languages. If the language is not object-oriented, some deviations must be made. However, an object-oriented structure is entirely possible even for systems implemented in non-OO languages.

To handle the construction for real system development, we need abstraction mechanisms on several levels. The block is such an abstraction mechanism for the classes in the source code. Perhaps the most important concept involved in handling the complexity is that of subsystems. These subsystems will partition the design model and can be used to define explicit interfaces for the subsystems in terms of block interfaces or class interfaces.

# 9 Real-time specialization

## 9.1 Introduction

The development of advanced industrial real-time systems is one of the major areas of applicability for OOSE. As with all solutions, the problem philosophy established for the first version sets the tone for implementation. OOSE does not bind the solution space of real-time applications at the beginning of the development. That is, the problem can be analyzed, to a large extent, independently of the artifacts (operating systems, languages and so on) that will be used in its realization. The analysis phase proceeds from the requirements and the functionality to be provided (expressed via the requirements model). From this base, various alternative realizations can be obtained from the selection of appropriate operating system structures, programming languages and so on.

In order to establish a degree of commonality for our discussion of real-time systems, let us first introduce a model for the broad class of industrial real-time systems as portrayed in Figure 9.1.

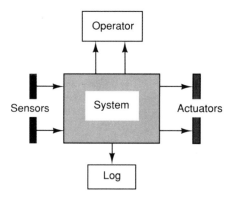

**Figure 9.1** Abstract model of industrial real-time systems.

In general we can state that the **sensors** and **actuators** provide respectively a view of the application behaviors in the external real-time environment and the means of controlling the external environment behavior(s). The **resource structure** (that is, hardware and system software processes) can be distributed or centralized. By process we mean, in this context, a structural and behavioral unit.

The real-time system may have some means of observing what is going on (externally and internally) as well as for controlling processing from an **operator** interface. Further, there may be some means of keeping a history of what has transpired via some form of **logging** medium.

## 9.2   Classification of real-time systems

In relationship to Figure 9.1, we can identify two major categories of industrial real-time system: those that have hard deadlines that must be met (otherwise a catastrophe can occur) and non-hard systems where services are provided in real time (while important, a catastrophe will not occur if immediate service is not provided for all requests by a certain deadline). The control of a modern aircraft belongs to the hard category, whereas a digital telephone exchange is a typical example of the non-hard category.

In the scale of application processes that are to be implemented we find critical processes, essential processes and non-essential processes as identifed by Ramamritham *et al.* (1989). The deadlines for **critical processes** must be met. **Essential processes** have deadlines, but missing these deadlines will not cause a catastrophe. **Non-essential processes** may miss their deadlines without any effect in the near future, but they may have an effect in the long term if not executed (for example, maintenance and bookkeeping functions).

We can also categorize processes according to their periodicity. That is, **periodic processes** are executed at regular intervals, whereas **aperiodic processes** are executed at any arbitrary point in time.

From these views of processes and taking into account the deadline requirements, we can further characterize hard versus non-hard real-time systems.

In **hard real-time systems**, deterministic predictability of processes' execution is the essential property. We must be able to guarantee processing of all critical periodic and aperiodic processes. While it is possible to dimension the system for periodic processes, the accommodation of aperiodic processes typically provides a major challenge. Further fault tolerance is essential in this type of system.

For more on hard real-time systems, see Stankovic (1988) and Stankovic and Ramamritham (1988).

In **non-hard real-time systems**, quality and performance is measured in terms of service provided. The execution properties are stochastically distributed based upon the quantities of resources available and the loading of the system. While it is quite possible analytically to place bounds on such systems, the development of an optimal scheduling strategy is impossible in the general case.

In applying OOSE to non-hard real-time systems, the specialization is based on the functionality and the degree of service achievable within the resource structure; in hard real-time systems, a more direct relationship between the execution properties of processes within selected or alternative resource structures and the deadline requirements must be taken into account. The timing requirements as well as the execution property parameters are taken into account during design and implementation.

## 9.3 Fundamental issues

In developing industrial real-time systems of the hard or non-hard variety there are three fundamental issues that must be considered: the view of **processes,** the means of **communication** and the method of **synchronization.** These issues are typically treated in the behavioral description of the problem as well as in the implementation environment and resource structure.

When strong semantics are provided at the behavioral description level for all of these fundamental issues, they radically affect the selection of an appropriate resource structure (hardware and system software processes). All programming languages and most formal methods, as well as most contemporary software methods, have explicit or implicit means of dealing with these three fundamental issues. When these views are congruent or at least congenial to the views of the implementation environment, all is well. However, when a semantic gap exists between the behavioral description and the implementation environment, typically long-lasting complexities are built into the solution; these complexities will affect its lifetime and its ability to continue to provide predictable results and satisfactory service as well as its maintainability and extendability.

A good example occurs in Ada, where the semantics of the rendezvous provides for a particular (orthogonal) view of processes (tasks), communication and synchronization. Matching Ada's strong semantics to the problem and implementation environment leads to difficulty (see Lawson (1990)).

In the area of software methods, we can for example consider HOOD (see Chapter 16), which is based on Ada. In this case, the solution domain that is reasonable from HOOD is affected by its Ada orientation.

While the concepts used in OOSE provide a useful means of identifying processes, it does not provide any *a priori* strong semantics for communication and synchronization. Thus, while the problem is addressed at a structured high level, specialization is necessary in order to match the semantics of the problem with those of the implementation environment.

The real-time requirements are passed from the requirements specification to analysis and are further used in selecting potential implementation environments (if there is a choice). Based on the execution properties of the resource structure(s) (hardware and software processes), parameters are extracted, fed into the construction process and used as a basis for determining whether predictability requirements can be met.

Varying real-time system requirements have an impact on the work to be performed in the various OOSE activities. We will consider the more important aspects of this impact here. The analysis process primarily involves the collection and structuring of the real-time requirements, while in the construction process the requirements are implemented in various ways. Based upon the degree to which the actual implementation environment can be influenced, different potential model modifications influence the actual system design. However, it is essential to retain a strong logical coupling between the application problem and the actual implementation environment in order to achieve the goal of traceability. The testing process is possibly the most problematic, since it is often extremely difficult to test a real-time system. Therefore verification methods should be applied in the preceding phases in order to guarantee that (especially hard) real-time deadlines are met.

## 9.4   Analysis

The use cases, specified in analysis, provide a very strong tool for capturing real-time requirements of various kinds. At this early stage, it is possible to attach both hard and non-hard requirements to use cases. An example of a hard requirement is a control use case that must be completed within 100 ms. An example of a non-hard requirement is that 10 000 subscribers should be able to use a telephone exchange simultaneously.

By associating a time attribute to a sequence in the use cases, we are able to document hard real-time requirements. These requirements will then naturally become relevant during later phases since the use cases form the thread through all activities of OOSE. We thus have traceability of these requirements and also a technique to verify that these requirements are built into the system.

Time attributes may be related to either periodic or aperiodic processes, as discussed earlier. In the periodic case, we also need to attach the period or frequency associated with the time attribute. In the aperiodic case we may want to indicate the maximum response time. In our previous example of the recycling machine, for instance, we may specify that when a customer pushes the receipt button it should take no longer than 1 s before the printing of the receipt is initiated.

We may wish to attach information on possible concurrency to the use case model. This may occur in two different ways. The first type of concurrency occurs *within* a specific use case, that is, multiple activities within a use case may be performed simultaneously. The second type concerns concurrency *between* use cases, that is, several use cases may be performed by the system in parallel. This form of concurrency actually involves instances of use cases, since it is possible that one type of use case may have several active instances at the same time.

Hence real-time requirements of a system are often naturally attached to use cases, thus making the requirements traceable during all phases of development. Further, the requirements information contained in the use case model can later be exploited in the verification of system behavior with respect to the specification.

In the analysis process, the use cases are further structured in the analysis model. Even for real-time systems, this structuring should be done from a logical perspective. That is, real-time requirements should *not* normally affect the structuring. Later, during construction, we may need to modify this structure to meet these real-time requirements. The reason for this is, as already stated several times, that we want the system structure to be stable and robust and this is best achieved by focusing entirely on the problem initially, and not on the circumstances for its realization.

When structuring the analysis model, the real-time requirements initially attached to the use cases, when meaningful, may be attached to the objects. Thus we provide traceability of the real-time requirements into the objects. This assists in verifying the requirements in later design and implementation phases. However, in some cases, the requirements may be attached to a sequence in the use case and this sequence may be allocated to several objects. The sum of the times it takes for the objects to carry out their tasks must then be less than or equal to the time associated with the sequence in the use case.

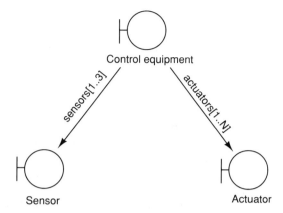

**Figure 9.2**  Modeling the interface with several associated interface objects.

Real-time requirements often come from the externals of the system. The sensors and actuators of the system are then often tightly connected to these requirements. These will normally be the interface to the actors of the system. Note here that we may have actors which only receive stimuli from the system in, for instance, a control application.

If the sensors and actuators of the real-time system environment are **external** to the system, we normally model the interface to them as interface objects. We then specify an interaction protocol between the system and its sensors/actuators. This protocol may be specified in advance (possibly standardized), but it may need to be specified as a part of the system development. Since interface objects may be built using a hierarchic structure of other interface objects, complex interfaces may be built principally as illustrated in Figure 9.2.

Alternatively, sensors and/or actuators as well as other hardware may be viewed as an **internal** part of the system, and this may be modeled using the techniques described in the analysis chapter. For example, we may view a temperature gauge as an entity object. Through this entity object we can read the current temperature value using an operation on the entity object.

## 9.5 Construction

During construction, we consider the real-time requirements in relationship to the target environment. Although the target environment is often given *a priori*, it is essential to consider how it can be adapted to fit the object structure, so that the structure is minimally distorted.

Real-time systems do not necessarily include concurrent processes. However, we will discuss processes in this context anyway since traditionally concurrent processes and real-time systems are often treated together. The reason for this is that real-time systems are often based on process concurrency in the target environment. Behaviors in the use cases are then mapped onto the individual concurrent processes. It is essential to note that it is behavior that provides the basis for this division and not the objects. In the general case, processes are orthogonal to the objects, that is, one process can involve several objects and one object may be involved in several processes (see Figure 9.3). However, in almost all practical cases one object will be allocated to only one process. Note that in the figure two executions occur in Block 3 in two processes. This means that either an object module has two instances, one in each process, or that two different threads use the same instance.

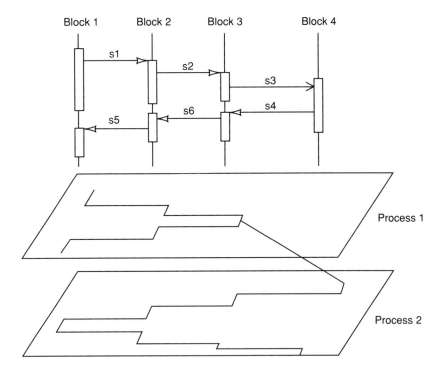

**Figure 9.3**  The behaviors in the objects are associated to certain processes. Note that objects and processes are orthogonal in the general case. s3 is a signal, while the other stimuli are messages.

To use different processes requires that the target environment supports the process concept. The processes are normally handled by the operating system which manages the process scheduling, synchronization and so on. Processes in the operating system context usually have separate memory address spaces. This means that execution in one process cannot directly access information in another process. Hence references to instances cannot be sent between processes, since only one process has the instance in its memory address space. To send an instance you therefore need to copy it and send the copy. So, in practice you will have only one process handling a specific instance in the system. This makes the orthogonality of objects and processes hard to work with in reality.

It is sometimes possible to simulate processes with a shared memory address space. These are often called **threads** or **lightweight processes**. The common address space is one of the benefits of such an approach. Additionally, since all threads execute in one 'heavyweight' process, the inefficiency coming from operating system overheads, for example replacing address translation tables or processor cache memory, is eliminated. Using threads, you handle scheduling and other process-related topics yourself. The use of threads is often an attractive approach in combination with object orientation since it is possible to share instances between different threads in a straightforward way.

If processes execute on one processor they will not be executed in parallel, even if the developer has this view of the execution. Processes may also be allocated to several processors which will give a true concurrent execution. However, so long as interprocess communication is handled over several processors, the developer can often view the processes irrespective of which processor they execute on.

Parameters from the target environment often strongly affect the semantics of the concepts of process, communication and synchronization. To ease the transition to implementation, the actual target environment's semantics of these concepts should be used; therefore OOSE needs to be specialized to use the semantics of the implementation environment. If concurrent processes should be used, the operating system must of course support this. Then the semantics used in the operating system should also be adopted in construction. Many operating systems support different views of processes. Not only may there be support for threads and processes, but also different kinds of these. The technique(s) should be chosen early on and then used subsequently in the construction.

When introducing the stimuli, we defined two types, messages and signals. The signal type is used for interprocess communication.

The exact semantics of a signal is not specified, but should normally be as used in the current implementation environment. This means that the signal type could be further specialized for expressing different semantics, like timeouts, balking or Remote Procedure Call (RPC).

Process synchronization should also be taken from the semantics used in the actual operating system. The use of properties such as mutual exclusion, semaphores, monitors, locks, different scheduling algorithms, process priority and so on that are available in the operating systems must be decided upon for each system. Here again, the concepts used should be adapted to fit the semantics of the actual implementation environment, for example rendezvous semantics when working with Ada and UNIX semantics when working with UNIX.

The modeling concepts used in OOSE can be used to **identify the processes** in the system. We will discuss here some of these approaches. Strategies for decomposition of the system into processes in an object-oriented system do not differ essentially from strategies in more traditional systems. Quite the contrary, an object-oriented structure is often more straightforwardly decomposed into processses than a structural decomposition. The reason for this is that processes fit very well into the general ideas of object orientation: internal states, well-specified interfaces, data abstraction, information hiding and the like.

The most obvious reason for introducing processes is that the system is in a *parallel environment*. Since events from the environment can occur at different speeds, frequencies and orders, we often need processes that receive these stimuli. Here we use the behavior of the actors, and also the specifications of the interface objects that receive stimuli from these actors, to identify these processing requirements. We could then assign one process to each interface object or each group of interface objects that must execute in parallel. Possibly one process for incoming stimuli and one process for outgoing stimuli is required. Buffering of stimuli must also be considered in this context.

This identification of processes from the interface objects must then be viewed with regard to the use cases. How should the use case continue its sequence in the system? There may be processing of the incoming stimuli that should not lock the interface processes and thus *loosen the coupling* between the interface and the processing. Then it may be necessary to assign new processes that can execute simultaneously with the interface process for this internal processing. A concrete example of this approach is the situation in a telephone exchange, where a common solution is having one process receiving digits from a subscriber and another process analyzing them.

Possibly, we must protect *shared objects*. The use case may continue and affect, for instance, an entity object that should be accessible in several different use cases and possibly from several different interface objects. Such objects must then be protected by some sort of mutual exclusion, that is, we must ensure that only one process can affect the object at a time. This problem can be solved in various ways. For instance, monitors or semaphores could be used in the operating system. The introduction of new processes that handle requests to the objects is another possibility. An even better solution is to let the operating system handle atomic transactions with mutual exclusion.

*Time-critical functions* are typical for hard real-time systems. To guarantee that we will meet these deadlines, use cases that involve them must often run as separate, high-priority processes. The scheduling of processes is done by the operating system and it is not always possible for the programmer to influence this. Additionally, the scheduling algorithms used often make it hard to guarantee that deadlines really will be met. However, **rate-monotonic scheduling,** (see Sha and Goodenough (1990)), is a scheduling algorithm in which it is possible to verify that processes will meet their deadlines under certain conditions. The processes must be *independent, periodic* processes that execute under a *pre-emptive* scheduler. Additionally, the processes must also have a *fixed* upper limit of *execution time*. The strategy is to set the process priorities in decreasing order of their process execution period. Hence the most frequently executed process will have the highest priority and less frequently executed processes will have lower priorities.

A *distributed environment* will of course also involve several processes, since we will execute on several connected processors. Usually, we must then allocate the objects to different processors as well. However, there are cases when one specific object must be represented on more than one processor, and thus in more than one process. The principal strategy should then be to encapsulate this distribution inside the block. The implementation of this block could be done using one object module at every node representing the object and classes that will handle the distribution (see Figure 9.4).

In the figure, objectAtHome represents the object that exists at the mother site, while objectAway represents the object at the distributed node. The Interface/Converter is the functionality that handles the packaging and unpackaging of stimuli between the nodes and also the transferring. These latter object modules are components that are used in all distributed blocks. Normally it is necessary to have different object modules at the host and at the distributed sites. An execution should then look as follows. A message is sent to the

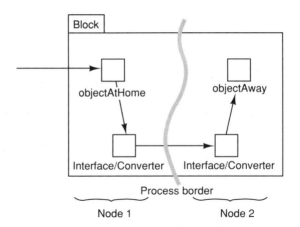

**Figure 9.4**   A distributed block with object modules at different nodes.

objectAtHome. This decides whether the processing must go to th
distributed node. If so, a request is issued to the Interface/Converter
that packs the message and sends it to the appropriate site. There it i
unpacked and a message is issued to the appropriate instance. When
the operation is complete a signal is sent back to the mother site
where the return parameters are unpacked and sent to the
objectAtHome which, in its turn, responds to the first message.

Here of course there are several detailed topics that must be
solved (how to find the correct instances at the sites, how to block th
first message, how to keep track of the transactions issued, what
happens when the distributed site does not respond). We have found
that the use of threads solves many of these (transaction-related
problems since we then have implicit support for transaction identity
blocking messages, finding the correct instances and so on. However
a discussion of all the details will take us too far and, since this matter
is not OO-specific, we will not discuss it any more here. We will only
mention the similarities of this approach to RPC (see Birrell and
Nelson (1984)). RPC has been implemented in some (UNIX) operating
systems.

Objects in a use case that are *tightly coupled* in the sense of their
having a large number of stimuli being sent between them should
preferably be placed in the same process. The reason for this is that
signalling between processes will have a high penalty in operating
system overhead in process communication. Note that this penalty
should not be heavy when using threads since we will not then have
the overhead of context switching in the processor. However, this

coupling between objects indicates that they are closely related and should therefore be placed close to each other anyway.

Use cases that have a *periodic behavior* could also be used as a base for process identification. Such periodic behavior can be grouped together and placed in one process that is activated periodically. However, if we have two behaviors that are not functionally related, but do have the same periodicity, it is not always certain that the best thing is to place them in the same process. The reason is that their periodicity may change over the system's life cycle, and not necessarily in the same way.

Use cases that involve *heavy computation* can also give us ideas for additional processes. Such behavior can normally be placed in low-priority processes and thus consume spare CPU cycles and not interfere with the more normal process execution.

To handle process **communication** and **synchronization** between processes may introduce additional processes. Examples of such processes are buffers, transporters and relays to loosen the coupling between processes (see Figure 9.5).

These different kinds of intermediate processes may also be combined to achieve a varying level of process coupling. This is especially interesting in Ada where the rendezvous mechanism between tasks is asymmetric. For instance, we may have a sequence like PBTC (see Figure 9.6).

This configuration will loosen the coupling to C. Here C does not have to wait for rendezvous with B since C will be called by T. When new processes have been introduced, we must decide for each

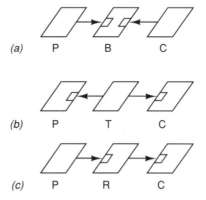

(a)    P    B    C

(b)    P    T    C

(c)    P    R    C

**Figure 9.5**  The principal functionality of processes for (*a*) buffers (B), (*b*) transporters (T) and (*c*) relays (R). P is the producer process and C is the consumer process.

Figure 9.6  A process configuration that loosens the rendezvous coupling between P and C.

pair of P and C which will be the caller and which will be the callee. For more on this topic, see Buhr (1984).

Owing to the problems of mapping processes onto existing hardware resource structures, an ideal process structure can very seldom be directly implemented. The real work involves the merging of the ideal process structure to an acceptable number of processes that can be conveniently implemented. For example, we may need to sequentialize behavior from several processes to a smaller number of processes. Thus it is important to differentiate between what *might* be run in parallel and what *must* be run in parallel. Using the guidelines discussed above may yield too many processes. Application knowledge is then necessary to decide which processes should really be used in the system.

Many of the process identification approaches discussed above are not unique to OOSE. This topic has also been discussed by Gomaa (1984, 1989), Ward and Mellor (1985) and Nielsen and Shumate (1988).

The introduction of processes will yield many problems of its own like deadlock, starvation and racing between signals. However, these problems are not unique to OOSE, but are well-known problems in the concurrent programming community. We therefore only refer to any ordinary textbook in this area, for example Ben-Ari (1982), Hoare (1985), and Peterson and Silberschatz (1985).

Other issues that may give problems when processes are introduced are the topics of *performance* and *memory management*. The introduction of processes will decrease the performance of the system since we have increased the operating system overhead, for example process scheduling, context switching, interprocess com-munication and memory spacing. We must therefore have a clear picture of the performance and memory requirements of the system and the cost of introducing new processes.

The processes introduced may very well change the design model. Normally we will introduce blocks that handle the interprocess communication and suchlike. Then the communication between the objects will change. Since the communications have been found from the logical relationships between objects, this must not be the actual way that the stimuli are implemented. Objects in different processes must access each other through objects supporting interprocess communication.

The use cases are described by means of **interaction diagrams**. This technique is very powerful since it conveniently maps the real-time requirements of the use cases to specific objects and specific processes. We can thus easily trace the requirements to sequences over the blocks thereby providing assistance in verifying time requirements. An example of this is shown in Figure 9.7 where a requirement of a maximum execution time of $T$ ms for the alarm in the recycling machine can be allocated to the participating objects.

The syntax and semantics of the interaction diagrams should be adapted to the actual implementation language. When we require special semantics, such as for synchronization and communi-cation, notation for this may be used in the interaction diagrams.

The interaction diagrams also assist in identifying behavior that may be executed in parallel. In the interaction diagrams we may specify which parts may be executed at the same time and which parts must be executed in a specific order. The interaction diagrams provide a visualization of how a certain series of tasks will be executed.

Interaction diagrams may also be drawn for processes only. Then the vertical lines represent processes and all communications are performed with signals.

To handle concurrency and racing problems we may use state transition graphs. These can also be drawn for processes. In these graphs we can see which stimuli can be received at what times. Hence

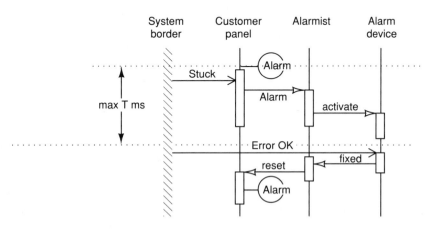

**Figure 9.7** A real-time requirement from a use case can be allocated to objects using interaction diagrams.

we can use this to detect erroneous stimuli received at the wrong times (states). This should be designed to get a more fault-tolerant system.

When the hardware resource structure provides for parallel/distributed processing, new criteria must be applied for process allocation and scheduling. In addition, owing to the availability of redundant resources, the possibilities for developing fault-tolerant responsive system solutions can be exploited. For a further discussion of these parallel processing issues for real-time systems, see Lawson (1991).

# 9.6   Testing and verification

The testing of real-time systems is extremely difficult. There are several reasons for this. To provide verification of hard deadlines we must test the system in the target environment and test it so that the probability of missing the deadline is sufficiently low. Often the verification of deadline requirements is impossible using normal testing techniques since the system may meet the deadline 99 times, but fail on the 100th time, for example when two processes use a common resource. Problems may not always arise because the processes using the common resource might seldom execute simultaneously and thus the problem will not occur. This means that failures can be very hard to reproduce since they can be time-dependent. Another consequence is that when the system is executed with debugging tools or traces on, it can behave correctly, while when these are switched off the system runs into a failure, or vice versa.

We will discuss testing in a later chapter, but we wish to say here that the ideas of automated testing, regression testing and stress testing are extremely important in real-time systems. Furthermore, since real-time requirements are often attached to use cases, use case testing becomes extremely important. All of these tests should be performed many times since the system may behave differently at different times (which motivates automation of the test).

Verification is not simply a question of the testing of the system, but must be an integrated part of the design process. An interesting approach to the verification of the timing properties of real-time systems has been presented by Shaw (1989) where minima and maxima for process execution as well as time for environment overhead are used to determine the predictability and loading of real-time systems. Techniques of this kind should complement the use of OOSE as a means of verifying timing properties during development.

# 9.7 Summary

A typical real-time system detects and/or controls events outside the system under timing constraints. If these timing constraints must be met to avoid catastrophes, the system is a hard real-time system. Otherwise it is a non-hard real-time system. Real-time systems add an extra dimension to the system, namely time, which makes them even harder to develop than other systems. Although it is not a rule, the fundamental issues of these systems include processes, synchronization and communication. OOSE does not have any *a priori* strong semantics for these concepts since various implementation environments provide various semantics. Instead the semantics of the actual implementation environment should be used. Therefore a specialization of OOSE should be created for each specific implementation environment.

During analysis the real-time requirements must be collected and analyzed. This is done mainly by associating these requirements with the use cases in the requirements model. The requirements are then traceable through all activities to implementation for verification at various levels. The development of the analysis model should not normally be affected by these real-time requirements since this model should be independent of the implementation environment.

However, during construction we must design and implement the system under these constraints. This often involves the design of processes, communication and synchronization of processes using the appropriate semantics. OOSE provides a basis for the identification of processes. Since the ideas of object orientation have many similarities with concurrent processes, it is often straightforward to make the identification. The use cases are a strong tool here since they express the execution in the system. Distribution of a specific object over several computer nodes can be encapsulated in the object itself. The interaction diagrams can also be used to handle real-time requirements and to allocate the timing requirements to different objects. Traceability of timing requirements is achieved to aid the timing verification. State transition diagrams can also be used for timing constraints.

Testing real-time systems is very hard, mainly because of the extra dimension of time. Since all executions are time-dependent, failures may be almost impossible to reproduce. Therefore it is even more important to have quality assurance and verification procedures during the entire development. The traceability in OOSE is then a fundamental property.

# 10 Database specialization

## 10.1 Introduction

The need to use a database often arises from the limited capacity of primary memory. Therefore databases are often stored on **secondary storage**, providing efficient ways to access the objects. Another need that arises is the ability to store objects longer than a program execution. Thus we want the object to survive the execution that created it. This ability is called **persistence.** Persistence often means that objects are copied from a fast and volatile primary memory to a slow and persistent secondary memory (see Figure 10.1).

Since the user of the database does not want to bother about how the storage is done, we often need a database management system, or DBMS, to handle this. The application programmer only wants a logical view of the database and does not want to take part in the decisions about how the physical storage is done. This is an important property of a DBMS. One alternative to this approach is to implement this functionality yourself using the file system and bury it in application code, but this would be a significant amount of work.

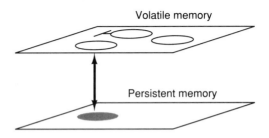

**Figure 10.1**  An object is copied from/to the volatile memory to/from the persistent memory.

A DBMS enables one to obtain such functionality in another, usually easier way.

Other features that a DBMS should provide are (see Atkinson *et al.* (1989)):

- Concurrency: allows multiple users to work with a common database simultaneously.
- Recovery: if a (hardware or software) failure occurs, the DBMS should be able to bring the database back to a consistent state of the data.
- Query facility: the DBMS should support an easy way to access the data in the database.

Database specialization means that a DBMS product is integrated in the development of a system. The specialization of OOSE will vary according to the type of DBMS being used.

Often it is obvious that a DBMS should be used in a development and usually it is already in the requirement specification of the system. If such a requirement does not exist, then the need should be discovered by studying the requirements model. Typical properties that indicate a need for a DBMS are:

- Information that needs to be persistent
- More than one application sharing (part of) the data
- Information structures with a large number of instances
- Complex searching in the information structure
- Advanced generation of reports from stored information
- Handling of user transactions
- A log for system restart

Therefore the requirement and analysis models can be studied to decide which objects are to be persistent. Since the entity objects typically hold information that survives the use cases, the entity objects are major candidates for persistent storage. In some applications there is also a need to store other kinds of object, such as objects to handle interface set-ups. Even if the information does not have to survive different executions, there may be a need to use secondary storage devices. This is typically the case if the number of instances (and/or the size of each instance) is very large compared with the primary memory space. Ways to solve this are to use the file system or to use a DBMS.

However, the main integration work is done in the construction process. Here we must decide how the DBMS should be incorporated in the design model and the implementation model.

Additionally, we must obtain information on how to optimize the storage of the object's state, for example, how a table structure in a relational database should be indexed in order to perform faster searches. Our discussion will focus on the design work involved in integrating a DBMS in the system.

DBMSs have evolved through a number of generations including hierarchic, network, relational and now object-oriented databases. The dominant type in industrial applications today is the relational model and that is why our discussion here will emphasize relational databases. For a thorough discussion on relational database systems see Date (1986). Object-oriented databases will be discussed briefly.

## 10.2  Relational DBMSs

### 10.2.1  Problem issues

In a relational database, information is stored in tables. The types to be used in the tables are mostly the primitive types such as characters, integers and the like. This yields some problems for our ambition of storing objects. Firstly, only data can be stored and not behavior and, secondly, only primitive data types can be stored and not the complex structures of our objects. Although many vendors add these capabilities to their RDBMS products, no standard or even consensus exists on how this should be done (see Bloom and Zdonik (1987)). We therefore assume that none of these capabilities exist in the products we are to use. In our discussion we will assume that our programming language is an object-oriented language, such as C++.

When a programming language is connected to a DBMS, a number of problems arise. The first problem is that in our system all information is stored in the objects. We therefore need to transform our object information structure into a table-oriented structure. This problem is sometimes referred to as the **impedance problem**. The problem is often that the program has too rich a set of types, including those created by the user. All these types must be converted to the more primitive data types of the RDBMS. The name of the problem has been obtained from similar problems of impedance when using transformers in electrical engineering.

The impedance problem yields yet another problem: it creates a strong coupling between the application and the DBMS. To make the design minimally affected by the DBMS, as few parts of our system as possible should know about the DBMS's interface.

A third problem is how to express inheritance in the database. If one object is inherited by another, how do we express this? Since all objects that are persistent have this ability (role) in common, the behavior of persistence can be inherited also. Hence we have similarities both in the data structures and in the ability to be persistent. The latter ability will be expressed in the programming language (we will look at an example later) and the former may be expressed in the database.

Other problems that arise include how to store operations, the transaction view (application view versus DBMS view), locking of the database during longer transactions, and distribution. Integrity problems between primary memory and the database must be handled, for example, references between objects might change in the system and hence must be updated in the database.

We will look at solutions to some of the problems mentioned above. The problems we will discuss include the impedance problem, how to isolate the DBMS from the system, how to handle inheritance and how to model the ability to be persistent abstractly. The other problems must of course also be solved, but we will not discuss them further here.

## 10.2.2   Objects into tables

The first thing to do is to decide upon which classes and which variables of the class must be stored in the database. Each one of these classes will then be represented by a table (at least one) in the database. A class is mapped onto tables in the following manner:

(1) Assign one table for the class.

(2) Each (primitive) attribute will become one column in the table. If the attribute is complex (that is, must be composed of DBMS types), we either add an additional table for the attribute, or split the attribute over several columns in the table of the class.

(3) The primary key column will be the unique instance identifier, namely the identifier by which the instance is uniquely recognized. The identifier should preferably be invisible to the user, since changes of the keys for administrative reasons should not affect the user; machine-generated keys should be used.

(4) Each instance of the class will now be represented by a row in this table.

(5) Each aquaintance association with a cardinality greater than 1 (for example, [0..N]) will become a new table. This new table will connect the tables representing the objects that are to be associated. The primary keys of these tables can be used in this 'aquaintance' table. In some cases, however, we may have the relation represented only as a column (attribute) in the associated object's table.

Let us turn to an example. In the recycling machine example we have the object *Deposit Item* yielding a table as illustrated in Figure 10.2. The attribute types are all very simple and thus will not yield any new tables.

This strategy will give us a first logical database design where we have defined tables to store the objects. Now what about normalization of the database? (Normalization concerns the issue of eliminating redundancy in the database and avoiding certain update anomalies. In most cases it is enough to reach the third normal form for the database design.) Actually, a database design based on an object model will normally end up in the third normal form from the start. The reason for this is quite obvious. The third normal form states, intuitively, that: if, and only if, for all times, each row consists of a unique object identifier together with a number of mutually independent attribute values, then the table is in third normal form (see Date (1986)). Hence we will have the third normal form if we have an object model where each object has a unique identifier and the attributes are mutually independent (that is, none of the attributes is functionally dependent on any of the others).

More intuitively, since object-oriented models are often models of reality, we tend to identify unique objects and also assign the attributes to the objects where they naturally belong. Hence, since reality is normalized as such, a good object model will also be normalized.

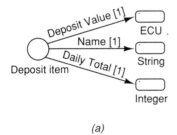

Deposit item

| Name | Deposit value | Daily total |
|---|---|---|
| Can33 | 0.25 | 142 |
| Can50 | 0.35 | 35 |
| Bottle25 | 0.30 | 173 |
| Bottle75 | 0.50 | 78 |

(a)                                                      (b)

**Figure 10.2**    In (*a*) the object and its attribute will yield a table as shown in (*b*).

Techniques for relational database design based on object orientation have evolved (see Blaha *et al.* (1988)). The experiences have been good and superior to other techniques and these authors state that: 'Building a data model from a small number of coherent entity objects is superior to the traditional approach of collecting all the attributes, ferreting out the functional dependencies, and synthesizing tables.'

However, when the database is normalized, the problem of low performance occasionally occurs. Low performance can in many cases be solved by special indexing tables. If this is not possible, the real problem is to *'denormalize'* the database to increase performance. The denormalization must be done with consideration as to how the database is used. This may take the database design as far as below the first normal form.

In this case we have redundancy problems in the database. However, here an object-oriented view will help us again. An object encapsulates the object's representation in the database. Then the only place where the knowledge of the redundancy exists is within the object, that is, in one place and not spread among several application programmers.

### 10.2.3   Inheritance

The objects that should be persistent will thus be mapped onto tables in the database. If classes inherit each other, there are principally two different ways to solve this:

(1) The inherited attributes are copied to all the tables that represent the descendant classes. No table will represent the abstract class.

(2) The abstract class is in one table of its own, to which the tables of the descendant classes refer.

We will illustrate this with some examples from the recycling machine. We want every *Deposit Item* to be persistent, namely to survive when we turn the machine off every night. In Figure 10.3 we show some of the entity objects with their attributes.

The first alternative is to have only tables for the *Can* and *Bottle* objects and copy the attributes from the parent class as shown in Table 10.1.

The second alternative is to store the common attributes in a table representing the abstract class *Deposit Item* as shown in Table 10.2. Please note that in this case the primary key must be unique in

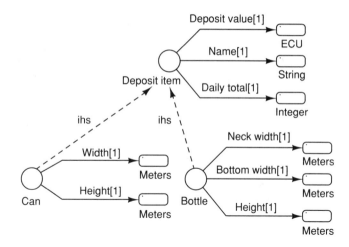

**Figure 10.3**    Some entity objects with their attributes.

the common table. Generally, primary keys should be generated by the system to guarantee uniqueness.

So which alternative is to be chosen? There is no best general solution for all cases, but let us illuminate some of the properties of both alternatives. The first alternative is normally faster since no joining, or searching in several tables, is necessary to get information about one object. However, the size of the database will increase since the inherited columns must be duplicated. Additionally, if changes occur in the inherited attributes, these changes will affect the tables of

**Table 10.1**    Only the descendant classes are represented by tables

| Can<br>Name | Deposit<br>value | Daily total | Height | Width |
|---|---|---|---|---|
| Can33<br>Can50 | 0.25<br>0.35 | 127<br>283 | 17<br>25 | 7.50<br>7.50 |

| Bottle<br>Name | Deposit<br>value | Daily total | Height | Bottom<br>width | Neck<br>width |
|---|---|---|---|---|---|
| Bottle25<br>Bottle75 | 0.30<br>0.50 | 173<br>78 | 23<br>32 | 6<br>9 | 2<br>3 |

**Table 10.2**  All classes in this alternative are represented by a table. The Can and Bottle objects refer to a common table where the common attributes are stored

Deposit Item

| Name | Deposit Value | Daily total |
|------|---------------|-------------|
| Can33 | 0.25 | 142 |
| Can50 | 0.35 | 35 |
| Bottle25 | 0.30 | 173 |
| Bottle75 | 0.50 | 78 |

Can

| Name | Height | Width |
|------|--------|-------|
| Can33 | 17 | 7.50 |
| Can50 | 25 | 7.50 |

Bottle

| Name | Height | Bottom width | Neck width |
|------|--------|--------------|------------|
| Bottle25 | 23 | 6 | 2 |
| Bottle75 | 32 | 9 | 3 |

all descendant classes. In this solution we have no knowledge of what type is represented in the table representing the abstract class. A specific table recording the various types would then be necessary. The second alternative includes less redundancy, but may lead to problems if the identifiers are common in the table of the abstract class. For instance, if we have an abstract class person and descendants teacher and student, then no person can be both student and teacher. Additionally, if we want to change the primary keys, these changes must be done in several places. Generally, the second alternative (to have tables for the abstract class) is to be recommended. It is then practical to have one common identifier for all tables. If this is not possible, use system-generated unique keys for the shared tables. What really is important is of course how the tables are used in the different use cases. Which specific search criteria need to be satisfied? What other requirements need to be considered?

## 10.2.4  Modeling the persistent object

We will now look at an example of how to handle persistent behavior in an abstract block. Since every object that should be stored in the database must have a persistence functionality in common, we create an abstract block, *ObjectToStore*, that has this functionality (see Figure

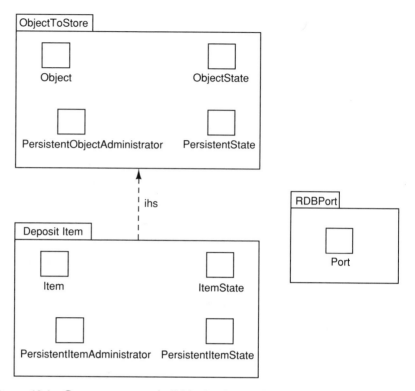

**Figure 10.4** Common parts of all blocks that will store their information in the database are put in an abstract block which is inherited by other blocks.

10.4). The classes in this block form a framework from which to build other blocks. The classes are not independent, but have a well-defined protocol that handles the persistence mechanism of the blocks. This block is inherited by all blocks that must be able to store information in the database and the framework is specialized for each particular block (see Deposit Item in the figure). The block *Deposit Item* thus inherits the block *ObjectToStore* which is a design framework. This means that the classes in *Deposit Item* each inherit a specific class from the framework in *ObjectToStore*. In this case Item inherits Object, ItemState inherits ObjectState and so on. We will thus reuse an existing design for the DBMS mapping, but all specific data must be added to the design. The classes in *ObjectToStore* are abstract (base) classes with mainly virtual functions, that is, they specify the interfaces but not the actual implementation. We also add a block *RDBPort* which is responsible for the actual interface to the RDBMS product, that is, all specific SQL statements are generated from this block. It thus works as an encapsulator of the RDBMS.

The classes of *ObjectToStore* are as follows:

- Object represents the object abstractly and Item is the actual object in the system.
- ObjectState represents the attributes of Object to be stored in the database in Object's data structure, hence ItemState contains the information of Item that is to be stored in the database.
- PersistentState represents the attributes in ObjectState, but in the type systems used in the DBMS.
- PersistentObjectAdministrator converts ObjectState into PersistentState. Hence, PersistentItemAdministrator converts ItemState to the attributes in the tables and stores it in PersistentItemState.

  PersistentItemAdministrator uses *RDBPort* to store this information in the database.

Initialization and the creation of tables must of course be done at the beginning. We do not discuss this here, but these issues should preferably be handled by *RDBport* since they are highly DBMS-dependent.

The flow will be as follows. When Item is updated, ItemState is also updated. To store this information in the database, Item tells PersistentItemAdministrator to store the information. PersistentItemAdministrator gets the information in ItemState and translates it into PersistentItemState. When this is done it stores PersistentItemState in the database via *RDBPort*.

Figure 10.5 shows how a creation and an update will look externally from a *Can* block. Note that none of the internal behavior in *Can* that stores information in the database is seen from the outside. We have thus encapsulated the function/data paradigm used by the DBMS and can now show an object-oriented interface to the application.

Let us take a look inside the *Can* block (see Figure 10.6). When the INCR stimulus is received, the Daily Amount is incremented. The operation also updates the corresponding attribute in CanState since the update should also be reflected in the database. When CanState has been updated, Can sends a reference to CanState to the PersistentCanAdministrator as a parameter to the Store stimulus. The PersistentCanAdministrator then maps the CanState attribute to DBMS-conformant attribute types in PersistentCanState through the stimulius Convert. When this is done, it is all stored in the database through the Print stimulus. The parameters then specify the table to store it in, that is, the table Can, and a reference to the data, that is,

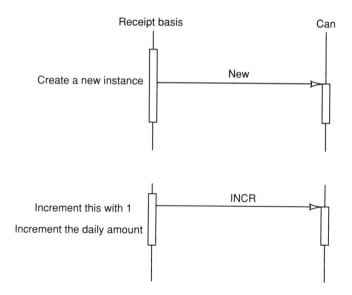

**Figure 10.5**    The external view of creating and updating a block *Can*.

the PersistentCanState. Note that all of this execution is invisible from outside the block Can, that is, the relational DBMS solution has been totally encapsulated. This will allow us to change database technology without affecting the entire application.

The impedance problem is handled by instances of ItemState, PersistentItemState and PersistentItemAdministrator. The independence of the DBMS (provided that it is a relational DBMS) is handled by the block *RDBPort*. The similarities of all persistent blocks are thus described in *ObjectToStore*.

If we want to use another type of DBMS, which parts must we then change? Obviously *RDBPort* must be changed. This block thus encapsulates the specific DBMS query language used. PersistentItemAdministrator and PersistentItemState are the only objects that know we use a relational DBMS, but they do not know the specific details of it (for example, its type system); therefore, a change in vendor, or a new release, would not affect these two (as long as it is still an RDBMS). However, different RDBMSs may have different type systems and possibly also different table semantics. Generally, avoid being tied to any specific vendor, and use only capabilities which are widely recognized. PersistentItemAdministrator knows the names of the tables which store the object's state and PersistentItemState knows the table structure, so if these topics also change, these need to be changed too.

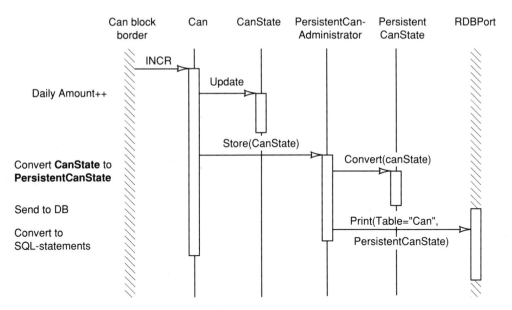

**Figure 10.6**   The behavior inside the *Can* block when updating the daily amount.

To summarize, to each block we assign a block description that includes descriptions of:

- Classes for the block's data and behavior
- Classes to handle persistency
- Tables in the database to store the block's information

A similar technique to encapsulate an RDBMS behind an object-oriented interface is described by Premerlani *et al.* (1990).

## 10.3   Object DBMSs

Relational systems were first introduced in the early 1970s. During the late 1980s they totally dominated the DBMS industry. They serve as a simple and logical view of the data stored in the database. The user views the data as stored in tables which he or she can manipulate. One important idea is that data be stored in as few places as possible. Different normalization techniques, as we have briefly mentioned, support the process of making the tables as independent of each other as possible.

Simplicity and data independence are the major features of a relational DBMS, but can also be a drawback in some applications.

The relational model cannot capture the semantics of complex objects. To model a complex object we often have to split the information into several tables; this makes each access to such objects slow since the DBMS must join a lot of tables to gather the object's information.

The idea of an Object DBMS (ODBMS) is to store the objects as such, and thus bridge the semantic gap all the way to the database. In this way we do not have to perform any slow joins to get access to a specific object. By storing the objects as such instead, it is possible to express the semantics of the objects in a much better way than is possible in relational systems. This implies that ODBMS is very useful in applications where complex objects must be persistent. Typical examples are different kinds of design support such as CAD, CASE, CAE and the like.

Most commercial ODBMSs do not use a specific data manipulation language to store and retrieve information, but use the programming language directly, for example C++ or Smalltalk. This means that a specific interface to the DBMS is not necessary, which is not the case with relational systems (that mostly use the language SQL). Hence the impedance problem is eliminated completely. This also means that the design of the database is integrated during the analysis and design of the application.

What criteria are there for an ODBMS? One of the more important papers written on this topic is by Atkinson *et al.* (1989), although there is far from being a consensus on the contents among the ODBMS community. They identify, besides the criteria discussed above for an ordinary DBMS, the following:

- **Complex objects**. It should support the notion of complex objects.
- **Object identity**. Each object must have an identity independent of its internal values.
- **Encapsulation**. It must support encapsulation of data and behavior in the objects.
- **Types or classes**. It should support a structuring mechanism, in the form of either types or classes.
- **Hierarchies**. It should support the notion of inheritance.
- **Late binding**. It should support overriding and late binding.
- **Completeness**. The manipulating language should be able to express every computable function.
- **Extensibility**. It should be possible to add new types.

The commercially available object DBMSs have evolved from two origins. The established DBMS vendors have built object-oriented features on top of their relational systems. These are often called extended relational DBMSs. Several new vendors start instead from the programming language and often support specific classes or other features to integrate the ODBMS in the programming environment.

We do not have sufficient experience to discuss fully the use of ODBMS in development using OOSE, but the projects where we have used such systems show that the construction process is much simplified in comparison with using relational systems. Mostly this does not affect the remaining construction, but is very straightforward to use during implementation. You just mark the classes whose instances should be persistent and define the transactions in some way, and that is all. However, since relational DBMSs have been used for a long time, these products are more mature and also have more extensive support for many complex issues included in the use of databases.

Hence the major benefits of using ODBMS include:

- The objects as such can be stored in the database (often the operations are not stored, but are only present in the class library in the primary memory).
- No conversion is needed for the DBMS type system; the user-defined classes are used as types in the DBMS.
- The language of the DBMS can be integrated with an object-oriented programming language. The language may even be exactly the same as that used in the application, which does not force the programmer to have two representations of his objects.

## 10.4  Discussion

The ease of incorporation of an ODBMS into the design often makes this an attractive solution. However, different application areas have different requirements. The tendency is therefore that different vendors optimize their product for different requirements, that is, application areas. The differences may involve the complexity of the objects, the length and frequency of the transactions (the checking out of information during longer periods such as days or weeks) and so on. What is obvious, however, is that all ODBMSs focus on more complex data structures than a relational DBMS is able to handle. This also means that for application areas where the information structures are very simple and are best expressed in tables, a relational DBMS may be a better choice than an object DBMS anyway. Typical of such application areas are banking systems where we have customers and their accounts, or a flight reservation system where we have flights and reservations on the flights.

Hence there is no general best choice. A choice must be made with great respect to the needs of the application to be developed. The best thing is to benchmark different databases with the specific application or to simulate the requirements of the applications. Then it is important to use real volumes of data and real use of the data. If this works, increase the amount of data since it is almost impossible to guess the amount of data to be stored in the future. In practice, all queries with a performance requirement must be verified in advance. More about ODBMS, maturity and benchmarking can be found in *JOOP* (1991). More comparisons between RDBMSs and ODBMSs can be found in Loomis (1990) or Stone and Hentchel (1990).

## 10.5  Summary

Databases are used to store objects persistently, that is, for longer than a specific execution. Using a DBMS provides support for this persistence and also other issues that raise the abstraction level for the database user. The main DBMS type in use today is the relational DBMS which stores data in tables. Object DBMSs are now evolving with great speed to support the complete persistence of entire objects.

Using a relational DBMS in combination with an object-oriented system raises many problems. However, many of these problems can be encapsulated; one strategy using a reusable framework is shown schematically in this chapter. Doing the logical database design from an object-oriented model is straightforward since it normally leads directly to normalized tables. Also, inheritance can be simulated using the tables.

Object DBMSs have been developed to store objects as such in the database. No standard, or even general consensus, exists on what defines an ODBMS. Different application areas have different requirements, and many vendors optimize their products for a specific application area. Using an ODBMS in an OOSE development is often easy. Generally, no extensive overheads are needed to incorporate the ODBMS in the application being developed.

# 11 Components

## 11.1 Introduction

### 11.1.1 Reusable software engineering

To be able to reuse code has long been a notion in the world of software engineering. This has been one of the major issues to increase dramatically the productivity of the programming community. However, although most people agree upon the importance of reuse, it has been practiced only very rarely in software development organizations. We will come back to the reasons for this.

When we speak of reuse in software engineering we mean everything that can be reused at a later time. This includes all the information and knowledge that has been developed, including experience from earlier projects (both human and by organizational experience); system architectures that have proved to be good; development methods that proved useful; and written program code or completed algorithms. This highlights the fact that code reuse is only one small part of reusable software engineering (see Freeman (1987)).

We have seen that the models developed in OOSE provide a good base for reusing information. As an example we see that the use case model is reusing for developing all subsequent models. Additionally, the analysis model is developed to get a robust structure with reusable objects for future changes. In that model, we try to identify a structure that is as much reusable in future changes as possible. However, in this chapter we will concentrate on the code reuse level, namely the reuse of **software components**.

### 11.1.2 Components as a reinforcement mechanism

When working with software components, we should view these as a part of the programming language. Just as we have primitive constructs in the language, we will have primitives at a higher level of abstraction. In this way components constitute a reinforcement mechanism for the implementation language; instead of working with primitive constructs, we will work with constructs of higher-level abstractions, like lists and windows. In this manner we can leverage the development from primitive constructs to more complex constructs. By having the components built on the programming language we will get a higher level of the application layer on which to develop our applications (see Figure 11.1). This implies that these components should be hidden in the design, that is, we do not include them in design diagrams, interaction diagrams and so on. The use of them is encapsulated. We call these component objects. However, the reuse of existing objects is not just limited to component objects. Higher-level objects may also be reused, and these objects are often necessary in the design documentation to make the design understandable. What distinguishes these objects is that they may not be changed by the current application; they typically exist in another layer below the current layer. Typically several applications share a common set of such reusable application objects.

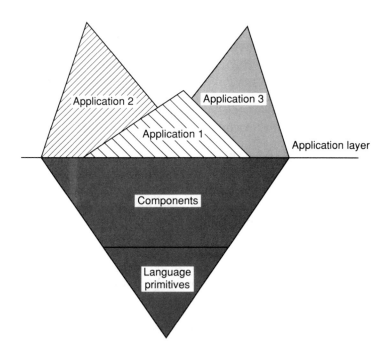

**Figure 11.1** Components are used to build bottom-up whereas applications are built top-down.

Building applications using such application objects is a key factor for improving productivity. Typically they may be identified as certain central entity objects in OOSE. This chapter will mainly discuss component objects.

Building with components and building with objects are two entirely different activities. With objects we start from the use cases and design the objects as our system is developed. Building with components, on the other hand, is a bottom-up activity. Furthermore, blocks will be managing units handled by the application developers and several applications may be developed in one organization. They are documented for this purpose. Components, on the other hand, will be managing units of a component system and are shared among several applications. They are normally documented in a completely different way.

Having to work with components is not unique to software engineering. Exactly the same mode of working is used in all the other engineering disciplines. Electrical engineers, for example, work with integrated circuits in their designs, mechanical engineers have standardized bolts, civil engineers have different types of girder to work with, chemical engineers have different solvents and process devices. Not least, VLSl designers base their work on complete module libraries in building their circuits. They only have to indicate the width and number of registers to have a complete register bank for their design; they do not put in each transistor by hand! Today software development is something of an art in which each programmer is more of an artist than an engineer, as discussed in Chapter 1. You can consequently say that the use of components is making the software industry into a fully fledged engineering discipline that should work on an industrial scale.

Many feel that components are one of the most important solutions to the software crisis. The crisis is that as the complexity of our systems grows, they become more expensive and more difficult to develop. The problem is that the productivity of the software engineers does not grow at the same pace. If we do not become more productive we will fail in building the systems that we are expected to build.

By means of components we thus hope to master the design of large systems. There are above all two important ways in which components are of great help: reducing the development time (cost) and raising the quality. We reduce the development time as we have more powerful components as a basis. This means that we reduce complexity and will thus have to write less code ourselves. As we use complete components this means that they are also well tested, both because we spend more time on their development and because they have been used in other applications. If we achieve these two aims it will lead us to less expensive and better software systems.

### 11.1.3  Why do we not have components today?

Now, if components are so good why are they not widely used to a greater extent today? We can identify a number of answers, as follows:

- Projects often have a tight budget and a tight time schedule. Designing good components takes time. Since it is not profitable to design components for one single project there is no incentive to do so.
- It is safest if I write the code myself: the 'not invented here' attitude. To trust the code of someone else makes one feel uncertain. If there is going to be a fault I want to have control over it and be able to correct it myself.
- There is no recognized component standard that is widely used. Such standards should specify the functionality and the use of components. To establish a standard for components is a gigantic task.
- Components already exist, but we cannot find them. Complete components may be designed in a project but they are not saved.
- You feel productive when writing source code. Since the most common measure of software is lines of code, you feel you are progressing when you produce code. This is an abuse of your task; you should solve the hard problems, not the easy ones. Instead you must accept what is available and go forward; you cannot spend time putting the finishing touches to a component to suit your purposes. This will lead to low productivity and a waste of resources.
- A component market must protect itself from the copying and distribution of good components without reimbursement. There are ideas today for distributing components freely and having a 'pay per use' strategy instead. However, this is not yet realized in a satisfactory way, although it may well be in the future.

An important reason why good components have not been designed is that engineers have tried to find them from functions. That means that every new feature had to go in the function call as a parameter. When it was discovered that something was to be stored, a function for this purpose was immediately designed; put (e). It quickly became apparent, however, that you had to store it in different ways so a parameter was added – put(e,queue) – and the variants proliferated rapidly. Then you wanted different parameters for the data structure – put(e,queue, preemptive, priority, length) – and you continued to add parameters for efficiency, and so on. You never found the correct abstraction, or to quote Gerry Weinberg (1971): 'Unfortunately, program libraries are unique; everyone wants to put something in, but no one wants to take anything out.' Tracz (1988) also discusses this topic. In an object-oriented structure, new features go in as new operations instead. Here we start with the object type and add the objects around it. This makes it possible to decrease the number of parameters since many of them will instead be variables encapsulated by the object which will be affected by the separate operations (for example, the priority mechanism in the queue); also the type of the object will now imply the body of the operation.

However, reuse in the software field *has* been practiced in different forms. If we want a sorting algorithm for a specific situation we normally find a good algorithm in the literature and implement it instead of inventing a simple algorithm ourselves. This shows that reuse of program code and algorithms is actually nothing new but it has existed for as long as we have been programming. A standard work that has been a source for many such 'components' is Knuth (1973, 1981).

## 11.1.4  A new approach

The area in which components have succeeded best is probably mathematics routines in Fortran. Here we have an abundance of routines to be used in a lot of applications that need some form of more advanced calculation, for example statistical or numerical. The reason why it has succeeded there is probably that it was easy to define the 'objects' that the routines were to operate on; representation of matrices or arrays is easy to standardize. That it was easy to design components where the data structure was well known is interesting. By having a defined and well-understood data structure with defined and well-understood operations on it, various applications could utilize the standard operations on matrices without specific knowledge of their implementations. However, this is a fact due to mathematics, not to computer science  But we can learn from this, define the data structures and their operations well, and utilize only the higher-level operations. This would indicate that information hiding in general and object-oriented programming in particular is a good road to take when it comes to components. This proves to be true; as we encapsulate the data structure completely and only offer operations on it in an object, the component becomes insensitive to the surrounding world that only knows certain operations. In the same way we have developed the theory about abstract data types which also provide an excellent basis for implementing components.

This also suggests another reason why it has been so difficult to design useful components: the development method has not stimulated it. A traditional development method often has the form of functional decomposition or at a least top-down process. This does not at all benefit the use of components; you need luck to end on a component at the very bottom. With object-oriented methods you build both bottom-up and top-down. Building with components is consequently much more natural with an object-oriented method than with a function/data method.

Components are today used in certain areas. An example is the Smalltalk world in which much of the programming is to find the correct class for your application. Here we already have the attitude that 'a good class is a reusable class'. Here it is a matter of pride to write such a good class that others will want to use it. Consequently, you can spend your efforts on solving the difficult problems instead of doing mechanical routine work. The challenge is raised by one level of difficulty.

Software components are also used in certain industries; several companies (among them Toshiba, IBM and NobelTech) have now formed special software component departments. Their purpose is to provide all other departments with components, and they have no direct profitability requirements. This means that work on designing a good and useful component will not detract from some critical project budget, but rather will be distributed over several different projects. Later in this chapter we will outline how such a department can work.

## 11.2   What is a component?

As stated before, here we will only deal with reuse consisting of already implemented software components. Once more we wish to emphasize that this is a considerable restriction of reusable software engineering. However, we need to define what we mean by a component and how to work with them. A component is a standard building unit in an organization that is used to develop applications.

To make a component reusable in various applications it is necessary that it be independent of the application for which it was designed. This is not always necessary to achieve; sometimes components that are application-dependent are of interest for reuse. We can consequently grade our components on a scale that ranges from complete application-independency (such as a binary tree structure) up to complete application-dependency (such as scanning a bar code reader). The more dependent the component is on a certain application, the more frequently you must adapt it in order to use it. Examples of components that may have to be adapted are browsers, windows and file handlers, but they are still very useful.

The requirements imposed on a component are much greater than on ordinary software. Using a component means that we can save time since we do not need to know how it works on the inside. We only need to use it from the outside. A complex component that is easy to use thus raises the *abstraction* level for the developer. It then forms a conceptual simplification of what is implemented.

Since the component must be used in various contexts we require it to be a general abstraction so that it can be used widely. This means that the component must be designed to be reused. Hence we need to include sufficient operations so that all reasonable use of the component is satisfied. However, we should not include too many operations, since that makes the component hard to understand and use. Thus the component should capture all operations that make it meaningful for any developer to use and no other operations. Note though, that this does *not* mean that we should give the component a *general implementation*. If this makes it ineffective, it should definitely be avoided (more about this later).

A critical issue is whether the developer trusts the component. If the components come with a bad reputation, no one will use them. Therefore the components must be of an extraordinary *quality*. They need to be well tested, efficient and well documented. Components are therefore normally more expensive to develop than ordinary software.

The components should also invite reuse. They must have a well-designed interface, easy retrieval and be accompanied by good, correct and easy to use documentation. The components should thus be *packaged for reuse*.

Generally speaking, there are two schools of thought on what primitive components should look like. One is that components should be *flexible*, which means that they should be easy to change in order to adapt them to your own needs (see Parnas *et al.* (1983)). This is for reasons of efficiency; general components are often inefficient.

The other viewpoint is quite the opposite, namely that components should already be *specialized* and you should *not* make changes in them (see Booch (1987a) where there are 26 different implementations of Set). Here you solve the efficiency problem by having several different types of the same component. We will here mainly follow the latter school for small-scale components, but for larger-scale components the former is of course of interest.

Designing useful components is not easy. The most well-known components include various data structures and window management systems. Today there are several libraries on the market for these kinds of components. However, more specialized components have been harder to define. Components are often developed gradually from several different examples where you can find a general behavior. From these you can extract something that is useful in several different places, an embryo of a component, that you frequently have to modify in order to make it fully useful. We have then a *white-box component;* that is, you have to look inside it to reuse it (see Johnson and Foote (1988)). These often have a tendency to be oriented towards a specific application domain. To develop these white-box components it is therefore necessary to have a good knowledge of the application domain.

When white-box components have been used and further refined it is often possible to reach an even further level of abstraction. Then it is possible to extract the essence of a component and design it as a *black-box component.* In this case you will not change the inside of it in order to use it in a new context.

Black-box components are often easier to use than white-box components since they are used as plug-in components and no modification is necessary. Additionally, they should be well tested and are often of a higher quality than ordinary software. Typical black-box components are the common abstract data types such as stacks, strings and search trees.

However, white-box components, although they are harder to work with, are of great interest anyway. The reason for this is that they often include reuse of much larger parts and thus they will increase the productivity significantly more than reuse of black-box components. A special form of white-box component is a design **framework** where you have an entire skeleton to build your application in. This is a reusable design in terms of an abstract block or subsystem that has been specified. This abstract block or subsystem may be adapted to another, concrete block or subsystem. Typical white-box components include a sorting algorithm where you might want to change the 'greater than' operator (this could also be done with a black-box component) and Model/View/Controller in

Smalltalk which is a class framework (one of the first) for interface construction.

Many problems still need to be solved for white-box components, although research is under way and experience is being gained. One example is the quality assurance of a white-box component, since they are only used as frameworks, that is, as a basis for other designs.

# 11.3   Use of components

## 11.3.1   Finding places to use components

Components should be viewed as an important part of the implementation language used. They should give leverage to increase productivity. This means that, just as the developer must have a good knowledge of and skill in the programming language, she or he must likewise have a good knowledge of the component library in order to use it effectively. This is taken to the extreme in Smalltalk, for instance, where the language vocabulary as such is very small and the actual programming is more a case of managing and using the class library.

Generally, everything could be implemented using components. However, often the right component does not exist and so is not available for use. We will discuss later how a component library could be built incrementally for more application-oriented components. Normally the 'classical' components exist as a base. These are obtained on the market and/or developed in-house, and implement classical abstract data types, often also offering windowing facilities. Today there are several such libraries for various environments. To give you an idea of how such components could be used, we will discuss some examples of how we can find places to use these components.

The analysis and design models provide a strong framework for finding such places. In particular, objects, associations and attribute types should be reviewed. If the component exists in the library we could use it directly; otherwise proposals for new components are needed. Here are some examples of places where components could be used:

- General **entity objects** that are used to develop other entity objects, for example, if they are inherited or accessed by other entity objects (see Figure 11.2). This is often an application-oriented component. If a certain kind of object will be

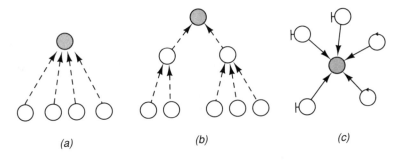

**Figure 11.2** Objects that are inherited by many other objects, either directly
(*a*) or indirectly (*b*), or are accessed by many others (*c*), could be a base for a
component.

implemented in the same way all over the system, such as an
entity object whose information should be stored in a
database, a general framework could be developed as
indicated in Chapter 10.

- **Interface objects** can often be implemented using components
  for windowing systems. Windows, buttons and scroll bars are
  typical components. In the same way, one application area
  could have similar interfaces which could be a general
  framework for all applications in the area. General frameworks for windowing systems and tools for GUIs should also
  be used when developing the system interfaces. Note here the
  conflict; if you use a modern UIMS, you normally do not need
  any components for window management. Another example
  is the reuse of an existing protocol stack for machine–machine
  communication.

- Some **control objects** will have general functions such as
  logging activities, data collection for statistics and on-line help
  functions. These are often modeled using an extension relation
  and are used in different places and possibly also in several
  applications. Thus we could have, for instance, a general on-
  line help function that is a reusable framework in various
  applications.

- An **acquaintance association** is often implemented with a
  reference. If the cardinality has a fixed interval we use a static
  structure such as an array or collection to hold these
  references. If fast searching is required, other structures or
  storing strategies could be possible such as binary searching

and/or tree structures. If the cardinality is variable (see Figure 11.3), we use a dynamic structure such as a list, dictionary or a collection, depending on what is available and which is most appropriate.

- Different **types** will occur at various phases, for example attribute types, types of parameter and local types when implementing the blocks. Some of these types may be general and thus can be implemented with components. The criterion is whether the type is a good abstraction, namely a conceptual simplification without involving implementation details. If the type only has read and write operations, this indicates that it is not a good abstraction. Thus it is not a potential component. To make it a component you should raise the conceptual level of the operations.

- During construction we mentioned that our system should be robust against changes in the **implementation environment**. This was achieved by encapsulating the environment. This encapsulation could be done using components as discussed in Chapter 8. By using these components whenever a service is to be used in the environment, we only need to change these components when changing the underlying system.

To be able to use components, it is essential that it is clear early in the development which components are available. The best case is when the components are available from the beginning. Then the developer can view them as a natural tool during all the development work. In some larger projects/organizations it is sometimes appropriate to start with the development of application-oriented white-box components and frameworks. Then what is essential is a good application domain knowledge for developing components that will generally be used for different applications. Version handling, configuration management and the release of such systems to the developing organizations must be managed with care.

**Figure 11.3**   An acquaintance association with a cardinality greater than one will typically be implemented with a component that holds all the references.

### 11.3.2    Implementing with components

Components are used to construct blocks. The use of components is therefore not documented in the same way as the use of design objects is. When using components in the design model, various techniques can be used to document their use. The use of the most primitive components is normally not documented in the design model; these are used more like programming language primitives. Components are normally introduced as a special case of object modules, namely on the most primitive level in the design. However, for more complex components it is often meaningful to include them in the design model. In particular, frameworks and other components that involve major design decisions should be included in the design model. Blocks can also be reused, but they are reused to configure the system for different customers. Examples of reusable blocks are *Account* in a banking system and *Line* in a communication system.

It is often claimed that inheritance is fundamental to reuse since you can inherit components and thus reuse them. Although inheritance is a strong tool in many contexts, this is a misconception. Inheritance is not a prerequisite for reuse. It is entirely possible to reuse without inheritance. Actually, inheritance has frequently been misused for reuse issues. Imagine you want to implement a class with a list component. One possiblity is of course to inherit it as shown below:

```
class house:private list{
   head* doors:
   . . .};
```

Here the class house inherits list. This is in most cases an inappropriate use of inheritance as discussed in Chapter 3; a house is not a subtype of list – it only uses list for its implementation, that is, it uses it as a client and hence from the outside. So when implementing the class you should have an acquaintance association to the component instead, as in the following code segment:

```
class house{
list* doors.
   . . .};
```

In this example it is obvious that inheritance should not be used but, as we stated when inheritance was first introduced, it is not always obvious how to differentiate between the use of inheritance and acquaintance. However, as a first rule, use composition when implementing with components.

A common need when you use components is to adapt or specialize them to the application in question. This should not normally be done by making changes in the component; instead you should either encapsulate the component in another object that acts as an interface between the application and the component, or make a specialization of the component. The former technique can also be used when you want to solve naming problems or encapsulate components to make the application independent of the component's implementation (language, software, hardware and so on). When you encapsulate you should be careful to avoid efficiency losses.

Another problem in using components is that they are written in another language or for another environment and not for the relevant development environment. This will probably be of less importance in the future when it becomes easier to bridge such gaps.

The use of components leads to better code. This is a consequence of their frequent use and the fact that they have been thoroughly tested; it is also a result of the fact that more work has been put into designing the component than is normal for ordinary program code. Components should be looked upon as 'fault free' by the application developers. This means that faults should not initially be looked for in the components.

Components should be used in the implementation. It is important for any manager to be serious about the use of components. You should encourage the use of components and question any design or implementation that does not use components. Hence it is obvious that to judge a developer's productivity in terms of the number of lines of source code is detrimental to this idea. The more you reuse the less you will write yourself. Thus a better productivity measure is the number of components used in the design or implementation. This will also increase the quality of the system.

## 11.4  Component management

A **component system** is normally not profitable for only one project. Such systems should be shared among several projects. The reason is that the development of components is often more expensive than the development of ordinary software and this makes it unprofitable in terms of a project horizon. The real benefits come when a component can be used in several projects and products. Therefore component management should be based on multiple projects.

A special component management department or group is therefore necessary, to be responsible for building a specially made component library for the organization. This department should also be responsible for obtaining components from the market. Additionally, they should encourage and enforce the use of components in projects.

Besides such a component department, and especially if it does not exist, a spontaneous component activity will evolve. We have seen that this is particularly true when working with an object-oriented programming language which encourages the use of components. These activities will be on the individual, group and project level and they are often done as a developer adds some extra effort for the design of a specific class or module that she or he sees will be usable in other contexts too. This should be encouraged by the project management since it could form a source of good components.

There are two types of activity for component management: one for the design of a complete component system and one for construction of individual components. We will discuss both of these and we start with the latter.

## 11.4.1  Construction of components

The construction of components is fundamental to their use. Reuse does not come as a side-effect. Specification, construction and testing must all be done for reuse. This makes a component more expensive (up to 10 times) to develop than other software.

Several different criteria for a good component have been suggested. These criteria can be summarized in the following areas:

- The first is **understandability**. The component should represent an abstraction. It should have high cohesion and offer only the operations needed to make it useful in an efficient manner. It must also have a well-defined interface, both syntactically and semantically. If two operations in two different components have the same name, they should act in a similar manner. Their style should be similar to facilitate understanding.

- The component must be **independent** of surrounding entities; it should be loosely connected and thus have low coupling to other units. An object-oriented philosophy leads to this independence.

- The component should be a **general** abstraction which is useful in several applications without having to undergo changes. It is standardized with respect to name, fault handling, structure and so on.

Understandability must be internal as well as external. Since good components will have a long life, they will be maintained for a long time. This means that it is especially important that they are written so that they are easy to maintain, even if people should not make changes in them. One problem in the maintenance of component systems is the need for (backward) compatibility. Even if we improve our component system, perhaps in performance or interfaces, it must be possible to use the new version or use an earlier version. This means that we must also be able to handle versions of components, just as for all other products. This requirement is a great problem but must be solved in order to create a working component library.

The most important criterion for reuse concerns the interface of the component. It must be general and complete enough to make the component easy to reuse.

A trivial but very common problem is the name. Generally it takes a long time to get a good name, a task that is often underestimated but extremely important. The most obvious need here is to have standards. Naming standards can be specific for a project but should be applied more widely to be really useful.

As mentioned before we can use inheritance in our component design. The inheritance mechanism is very useful for building up a powerful component library. However, the use of inheritance is also fundamental to the quality of the component system. Booch and Vilot (1990) note that the trade-off between different inheritance hierarchies is a fundamental design issue.

Time and/or memory performance of components is also a critical issue. As stated earlier, a general implementation that leads to an inefficient component should be avoided since it will probably not be used. So different implementations for various requirements should be used. For instance, Booch (1987) offers several different implementations of each abstract data type.

Several criteria for good and reusable component designs have been proposed (see Johnson and Foote (1988), Meyer (1990), and Lieberherr and Holland (1989)). These criteria include:

- Reduce the number of parameters; fewer arguments will lead to more cohesive operations that also imply more primitive operations.
- Avoid using options in parameters; any options should be set by the creation procedure, and special operations should be used to change these options.
- Prohibit direct access to instance variables; to access instance variables, special operations should be used, as this frees the implementation from the actual interface.

- Naming should be consistent; operations in different components should have similar names if they perform the same task.

## 11.4.2  The component system

A component library is something that all mature development organizations should have. The construction and evolution of such a library does, however, involve many questions and we will discuss some of these here. This activity includes selecting, classifying and managing the components included in the library and also the development of new components. Somebody should also be responsible for making sure that information about the component library is available and spread throughout the development organization, and that the components are accessible.

We have stated that a component library should preferably be shared between several different products. This means that the component system should serve several projects. Proposals for new components normally come from the projects that the component system supports. It is important not to be passive in the search for new components by merely waiting for proposals; you must also actively search for new components that could be suitable. All our experience shows that to have a component system working well, the people working with it should actively search through the actual projects. Figure 11.4 proposes an organization for a component system.

The proposals should be reviewed by a group consisting of experienced designers and also someone from the component department, forming a software component committee. They should judge whether the proposed components are to be developed or not. If they decide to construct the component, it is forwarded to component construction with a deadline. When ready, it is added to the software component library which then takes a new revision state.

As the component system is being used, the software component group should analyze its value. Which type of component is used most? Which are not used at all? How much can you gain from using the components? This analysis helps to develop the component system. A similar manner of handling the component library is described by Matsumoto (1987).

When you decide to delete components from the library, great care must be taken. Since applications that have already been designed can be built on these components it is important not to remove the basis for these designs; thus you must make sure that the documentation will not be removed completely. It is not until all

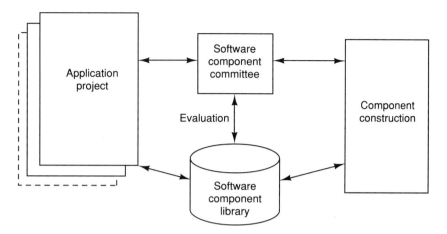

**Figure 11.4**   An organization for component management.

users of a component have stopped using it that a component can be deleted. A component will thus have a life cycle as illustrated in Figure 11.5.

When you start the design of a component system you are faced with some important questions:

- In which programming languages and development environments (for example, compilers) will the components be offered? How should various environments be handled? Does this work for the target environment?

- Are components already available internally? How are they used? Can we use them for our component system? Should they be integrated?

- Which external component systems can we use? Should we purchase them or use them as a source of ideas?

- How will the components be used? Which classification method should we use? How can we simplify the use of components? What should our component survey look like?

When you have obtained a basis for your component system this should not be a static library, but quite the opposite. It should evolve continuously and be extended gradually.

So, which components should be included in the library? Initially, a study of existing, mainly external, libraries should be performed. The basic components, such as data structures and graphics facilities, should exist in the library. These are normally bought from an external vendor or accompany the development environment used.

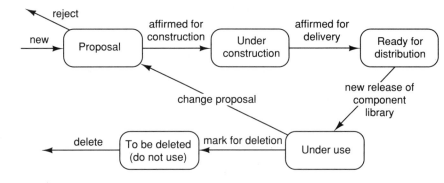

**Figure 11.5**    The life cycle of a component.

The most essential factor is that the components should be profitable for the organization. Here the most important criteria are the potential reuse of the component and its size. The more places it is used, the greater its profitability.

A component proposal consists of the desired functionality (interface and characteristics), its reuse potential (how and where it will be used) and a date for delivery. The proposal can concern development of a new component, purchasing a component or a proposal to change a component.

Whether a new component should be developed or not is determined by the software component committee. The value of it should then be judged. A technique for this is discussed below.

Purchasing a component is often cheaper in the beginning, but may involve trouble in, for instance, maintenance and support. The purchased component should be incorporated in the structure used and should also be documented in the standardized way used in the component system.

A change proposal could be of three kinds. An *error report* is always accepted. A *change of the implementation* is accepted if it is reasonable, such as an optimization change. A *change of the interface* is accepted only if there are very good reasons, since it affects everyone dependent on the component, both application developers and other components.

To determine the value of a component, a cross-reference table could be used which points out where a certain component could be used. Such a table will help in justifying which components should be developed. This table also serves as a tool for determining when components must be ready for use. Many proposals will not become components. This is essential to note early so that the development of these parts can be carried out on a project basis.

Statistics should be collected continuously concerning the use of components. Every use of a component should be noted. Then the software component commitee can see which components are reused and use this as a base for the evolution of the component library. As the library grows it may be necessary to restructure it.

A more active way of finding components has been proposed by Caldiera and Basili (1991). Various metrics of what is typical for a reusable component are used to identify components. A program that calculates these measures for existing source code has been developed and produces candidates for components. Hundreds of thousands of lines of C source code have been analyzed. The result looks promising. The metrics used include:

- **Size**. This affects both reuse cost and quality. If it is too small the benefits will not exceed the cost of managing it. If it is too large, it is hard to have high quality.

- **Complexity**. This also affects reuse cost and quality. A too trivial component is not profitable to reuse and with a too complex component it is hard to have high quality.

- **Reuse frequency**. The number of places where a component is used is of course important too.

The release of a new version of a component library must be timed in cooperation with the projects. The projects should of course also know which components are included in the forthcoming releases. Since many components will be used in different versions, it is essential to keep track of where a certain component is used. As we have stated earlier, only when no product uses a component can it can be deleted from the library.

One problem that will occur when several different class libraries are to be joined is that they will not be compatible with each other. Today this is a big problem since many different component libraries have components with the same name and they are not disjoint. One possibility is to split each library into parts and then to merge the relevant parts from the libraries into a new library. Unfortunately, it may be almost impossible to split a library, since the components of a library often use other components in the same library. This is a major problem today when a component library grows, and here standards are necessary.

## 11.4.3    Documentation of components

Although we do not discuss documentation in this book, we think it may be appropriate to mention it in this context since the documentation of components must be provided from several viewpoints. Since the components are used in various ways we need different kinds of document for different purposes.

Firstly we have the projects which use the components. A component is documented for use by a **component data** sheet. This sheet has the same purpose as a data sheet for hardware components, namely it describes what a user needs to know in order to use the component. To find the correct component we use a (possibly automated) **component survey**. This document presents the entire component library and the developer searches this document to find the correct component to use. This document should be generated from characteristic information attached to each component. Different organizations of the component survey will be discussed shortly. For maintenance purpose, we also have a **component description**. This document describes the implementation of the component and is used by the organization maintaining the components. The relationships are illustrated in Figure 11.6.

The thing that differentiates industrial software development from other programming is above all the large scale. To get the real benefits of reuse we therefore need a large number of components. We have previously discussed some problems with a large component library. Another problem is the structure of the library. To have too many components in a library is not recommended today; the technology to handle them simply does not exist. The problem of classification is one part of such a technology. We can compare this with hardware components. There are many different types of circuit with a certain functionality. They have different sensitivities to temperature, they have different power consumption, and they can

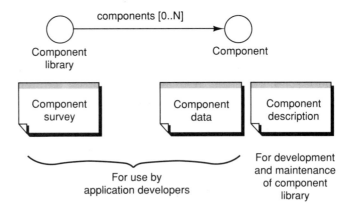

**Figure 11.6**    Documentation for a component system.

drive different types and numbers of circuits and so on. Here you search for the desired logical function and also for the properties. This must also be done for our software components; the question is which criteria are important. We should include criteria such as efficiency, speed and storage requirements.

Today's classification methods can be characterized as hierarchical methods and keyword-based methods. In **hierarchical** methods the components are classified in a tree structure where you start searching from the root and as you get down into the tree you indicate which properties the component should have. When you have reached a leaf node in the tree, you have found your component. An example of a hierarchical method is suggested by Booch (1987). His taxonomy starts by first classifying components into *structures, tools* and *subsystems*. Structures are components that can be described as abstract data types or abstract state machines. Tools are components that describe an algorithm abstraction. Subsystems are components that are built of structures and tools (see Figure 11.7).

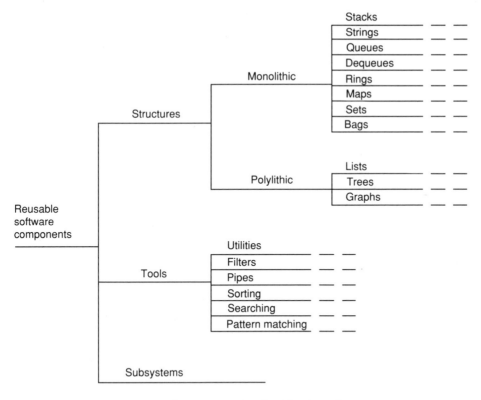

**Figure 11.7**   Booch taxonomy for classification of components.

Structures are in turn divided into monolithic (the structure must be treated as a whole in order to be meaningful) and polylithic (it is meaningful to speak of parts of the structure). On the next level you find your abstract data types. When you have reached this far, you continue searching to indicate exactly which properties the component should have. Should the component work in a concurrent environment? Is the size of the structure static? When you have answered all these questions you have found your component in a leaf in this tree.

The other classification method is built on **keyword-based** searching. Here we try to describe our component in descriptive words that we then can search for in a database. It is self-evident that it is important to have a standardized terminology that everyone can use. Examples of methods to name components have been proposed by Prieto-Diaz and Freeman (1987) and by Cox (1987). The first is based on the fact that each component can be described in terms of its function, how it is executed and its implementation details. Each component can then be described with a 6-tuple (function, object, medium, system type, application, application field). A word list of synonyms is an aid to using standardized words.

Of course both methods have advantages and disadvantages. A hierarchical method is good since it is simple and logical to use, and it is also relatively easy to introduce new components if the structure is good. The problem is that you cannot describe many-to-many relations with it, which means that if you have entered the wrong subtree in the taxonomy you will never find the right component. If you find the taxonomy is not very good, it becomes difficult to work with, and if it appears that the structure should be changed then it is a big job to rebuild your component library. The keyword-based method has its advantages as it is very flexible when it is controlled by ordinary language. You can also select the resolution you want since you can make a selection on different words (indexes). The disadvantages are that you are forced to change, or at least extend, the search keys as the library grows. The method also requires a uniform vocabulary. To cope with the deficiencies of both methods, new methods have been suggested in which properties from these two methods have been mixed (see Browne *et al.* (1990)).

However, to get a working reusable library, the size of it is not critical. For one product using Objectory, the team developed about a dozen components. Most of them are quite primitive, but some are larger frameworks. These components are very reusable and increase the productivity significantly. The system is built using C++ and in almost all operations (member functions) at least one component is used. Additionally, the components are used to make the code look cleaner and easier to read than plain C++ code. These components, together with the system structure, help the team to do further development very rapidly. One new use case is typically developed in one or two weeks. The lesson to learn is to start using a small and carefully selected component library today, and add new components as they are needed.

# 11.5  Summary

Reusability in software engineering is not a new idea and it is a critical issue for a substantial increase in productivity. Still, it is not widely applied in the software engineering community and there are several reasons for this. Object-oriented technology is a promising approach for enhancing reuse. The reusability concerns more than code alone, although this is the main topic of this chapter. Reuse of components should raise the abstraction level of our programming efforts and thus increase our productivity.

A component is an implemented abstraction that is general and of a high quality; it is developed and packaged with the aim of reuse. A component could either be white-box, which means that you have to modify its internals to reuse it, or black-box, which means that you do not change the inside of it. A special kind of white-box component is a framework, which is a larger skeleton of a design that is reusable.

The models used in OOSE provide a strong tool for finding places to use components. Components should be used widely in the implementation. A construction not using components should be reviewed with skepticism and discriminated against in favor of constructions that use components widely.

Component management should be based on multiple projects. Since the construction of components does have greater requirements in terms of quality and documentation than ordinary software, the construction of components should not burden a project.    For component construction the fundamental issues are understandability, independence and generality. All of these issues should be highlighted in the component interface.

Component management includes management of the component library. This should evolve in an ordered fashion and support increasing reuse in the organization. Proposals for new components come from the projects; these proposals are then implemented by the component department. It is of great importance that the component department is active and actively promotes the component library. Documentation of components should satisfy both the use and the maintenance of components. Various methods exist for structuring the component library for easy retrieval.

# 12 Testing

## 12.1 Introduction

Testing a product is relatively independent of the development method used to develop it. An object-oriented approach to development gives some new possibilities, but also some new problems. In this chapter we focus on aspects that are specific to an object-oriented approach. Of course, many traditional techniques are still valid and we refer to Myers (1979) as the standard work on testing.

The test activities are normally divided into **verification** and **validation**. Verification checks whether the result agrees with the specification. However, this alone does not guarantee customer satisfaction. Validation checks whether the result really is what the orderer actually wanted. This focus on customer satisfaction is concerned with getting the specification *and* the result right. The two terms are usually summarized as two questions:

- Verification: are we building the system correctly?
- Validation: are we building the correct system?

In this chapter we will focus on verification. Validation is mainly captured by a thorough requirements analysis including active involvement of customers, use of prototypes and so on. We have found the use case concept in particular to be a very strong tool for validation purposes. Testing is not the only activity necessary to obtaining a qualitative product, however. Apart from continous validation during the development process, activities such as reviews and code inspections should also be performed, that is, someone inspects the developed code and assesses its quality. This is a very expensive method, but it produces high quality code. We will discuss some of these other quality assurance issues in Chapter 15.

The fact that we discuss testing in a chapter of its own does not mean that the test activities commence only when analysis and construction have been completed. Testing is integrated into all activities and test work can begin at the same time as the analysis work is started. The more the testing is integrated, the better.

The most important aspect of testing is actually the attitude adopted towards it. You must be aware that testing takes time and the cost must be allowed for. The test activities take up perhaps 30 % of the entire development cost, but may exceed 50 %. Testing is consequently a large part of the work and must of course be planned in the same manner as analysis and construction. Testing should be included in the project plan like all other activities. We must obtain the best possible result for our resources invested.

Traditionally, testing is an activity that occurs after other development efforts. This indicates that assuring quality is something you do as the last activity in a development project. But we all know that it is not possible to arrive at high quality software just by testing and debugging. Although most people agree that this attitude is not sound, this is the typical situation in most software development projects. This is only one indication of immaturity in the software engineering community, as discussed in Chapter 1. To arrive at a more mature engineering process most software developers need to change their attitude. Our terminology does not capture what is important. Words like 'bug' and 'debugging' don't reflect the seriousness of our work. Debugging gives a completely faulty impression. It is as if we know that we will introduce faults and then just remove them. It should be as serious to make errors in software as in other engineering disciplines. Therefore quality must be introduced from the beginning, that is, we should do it right the first time. The purpose of the final testing activities is then only to ensure a quality certificate for the product, which is why this is sometimes called **certification** to distinguish it from other types of quality activity. Testing can thus be done on analysis and design documents by verifying through reviews that they have been developed appropriately. Any faults introduced should be eliminated as early as possible. That it is possible to develop zero-fault software is well known. As an example, the primary author of this book was in 1970 the manager of 13 people who developed object-based software implemented in assembler. The development team decided that we did not want any faults during unit or integration testing. We decided that every fault would be considered as a personal failure. We reviewed one another's code and I myself reviewed all interactions between the objects. We found three faults during unit testing and two faults during integration testing. Although this required thorough review efforts, we were much more efficient than our colleagues. Such ideas also form a major part of an approach called **Cleanroom Software Engineering** (see Mills *et al.* (1987)). Major techniques in this approach include frequent reviews, formal specifications, teamwork, statistical usage profiles as a base for testing, incremental development and stepwise refinement. Although it is not developed to support an object-oriented approach, it focuses much on interfaces and externally visible behavior.

We will first discuss testing in general. Then we illustrate how the testing of individual units is done and how integration is done and we discuss testing on the system level. We will see that the use cases give us much help in integration testing. Finally we will give some comments on the testing life cycle.

## 12.2  On testing

### 12.2.1  The purpose of testing

Let us first define some important concepts following the IEEE (1983) standard. A **failure** occurs when a program misbehaves. Thus a failure is a (statistical) property of the system in execution. A **fault** exists in program code. When the code is wrong, the fault can be fixed by changing the code. A fault, if encountered, may cause a failure. There is no fault if the program cannot fail. An **error** is a human action that results in software containing a fault. Thus an error may lead to the inclusion of a fault in the system, making the system fail.

The first lesson to be learned about testing is that you can never prove that the program will never fail; you can only show that it contains faults. We should therefore consider a test that has found many faults to be a successful test and not the opposite. Thus if we have developed a successful construction, we will have an unsuccessful test encountering no faults. For completeness, we will mention that active research into proving program correctness is in progress, but even if such techniques are used on a small scale today, we believe that it will be a long time, if ever, before they can be fully applied to the systems discussed here. A lower level of ambition concerns the use of formal specification techniques. We will not go into more detail here, but for information on such formal techniques, see Wing (1990) or Hall (1990).

The purpose of testing is to find faults. Testing is thus a destructive process to some extent; we must show that something is incorrect. It is therefore unwise for you to test your own construction since it does not feel natural to work only in order to prove that you yourself have made an error. Unfortunately, however, it becomes very expensive to have someone else test all you have done in detail; usually you can only afford to test major parts in a special test department. This is normally done during integration or at system test level. The developers should of course be given the opportunity of identifying these faults, however.

It is a well-known phenomenon that when you correct detected faults, you introduce new faults into the system. When a fault has been corrected, you may therefore have to retest your software, including the unit that is a client of the corrected unit. It is to be hoped that you introduce fewer faults than you correct. Levendel (1990) has noted that you generally introduce one new fault for every third fault you correct. He also notes that 'defect avoidance is more powerful than defect removal.' Defect avoidance, he claims, is achieved with a structured development method, and this is something we strive for in OOSE.

There are many types of test. In the box we discuss some of the more common types.

**Test types**

> Below is an overview of various test types. They are not independent of each other and when you test you should use several of them in combination.
>
> *Testing levels*
>
> - **Unit testing** means that one and only one unit is tested as such. In OOSE, the unit is typically a class, block or service package.
>
> - **Integration testing** involves testing with the purpose of verifying that the units are working together correctly. Integration and unit tests can be performed by the same test cases (for example, for a block); it is the testing purpose that differs. We use the use cases as a strong tool for this type of test. Blocks, service packages, subsystems and the entire system are tested in this manner.
>
> - **System testing** concerns testing the entire system or the application as such. This takes an end-user view of the system and the test cases perform typical end-user actions.
>
> *Testing techniques*
>
> - A **regression test** is done when you have made changes in the system, for example corrected a fault, and the test's purpose is to verify that the old functionality remains. This test is very important, but rather tiring and time consuming which is why you should try to automate the testing.

*Testing focuses*

- The **operation test** is the most common system test. Here the system is tested in normal operation for a longer time. The system is used in the intended manner. Only normal mistakes are made, that is, mistakes that the normal user may be expected to make. If the system is to be reconfigured during operation, then this should be tested also. This type of test also measures the reliability of the system, and thus statistical measures may be used, such as Mean-Time-To-Failure (MTTF).

- A **full-scale test** means that we run the system on its maximum scale. All the parameters of the system approach their limit values, all types of equipment are connected, and the system is used by many users, each executing use cases simultaneously. This test requires a lot of the system, but these requirements must be managed by it. The test requires that a full-scale system site is available and it is therefore often expensive, but experience shows that new failures arise with full-scale testing. An extreme of this is **stress testing** which means that the extreme limits of the system are tested.

- A **performance test** or **capacity test** has the purpose of measuring the processing ability of the system. The test is designed so that you can measure the performance with different loads. What you want to measure may include store allocation, CPU utilization or perhaps only the speed in a specific use case. The measured values are compared with the required values.

- An **overload test** goes one step further than the full-scale and performance tests. Its purpose is to see how the system behaves when it is subjected to overload. We cannot expect the system to manage the processing of these tests, but it should perform well and not go down thus permitting a possible catastrophe to occur. The system should survive load peaks. How much the system's performance drops is an interesting measurement and we consequently also have a performance test in this case.

- A **negative test** is a type of stress test intended to subject the system to stresses beyond what it has been built for. If there are any special barriers they should be tested and verified, use cases that normally will not be invoked simultaneously should be executed at the same time, and so on. The system is intentionally and systematically used in an incorrect manner. This maltreatment should be carefully planned so that especially critical places are tested.

- **Tests based on requirements** are those that can be traced directly to the requirements specification. They can be the same test cases as used in one of the earlier tests, for example a performance test or full-scale test, but they can also be a particular requirement that you want to check explicitly.

- **Ergonomic tests** are becoming increasingly important as computer systems come to be used by non-computer professionals. If the system has a man–machine interface then the ergonomic aspects should be tested. Is the interface consistent in a use case? Is the interface consistent between different use cases? Are the menus logical and readable? Are system messages visible? Can you understand the failure messages? Does the system provide the same conceptual picture that the end user has?

- **Testing of the user documentation** is a type of ergonomic test in which the system's documentation is tested. Both the user manual and the documentation for maintenance and service should be tested. Far too often manuals and system behavior are not consistent. The manual's readability should also be tested, the documents should be checked for language, the balance between chapters and the balance between text and pictures should be assessed and so on.

- **Acceptance testing** is normally performed by the organization ordering the system and it is the final check by the orderer. This is often also the validation of the system. The system is now tested in its real environment. This type of testing is often called **alpha testing**. This test can be done for a longer time when the system is working in the environment for which it has been developed. When the testing has been done, the decision is made as to whether the product is to be accepted or not. If there is no specific orderer, for example in the case of a compiler product, **beta testing** is often used. This means that the product is tested by specially selected customers who use the system and report the faults they detect. Beta testing is done before the product is shipped and is a form of pre-release.

### 12.2.2    Testing strategies

Testing may be performed in various ways. The most common way is to test in the reverse order to that in which the design and implementation is done (see Figure 12.1). Verification is then done at various levels, including integration of various units through use cases and finally system-level verification.

However, we have already mentioned that testing should be as interleaved as possible with other development efforts. This means that whenever a design at one stage has been completed, the testing for that stage should be done at that stage. This means that design, implementation and testing are very interleaved activities performed in an incremental fashion. Since we can do development in either a

**Construction**                                              **Testing**

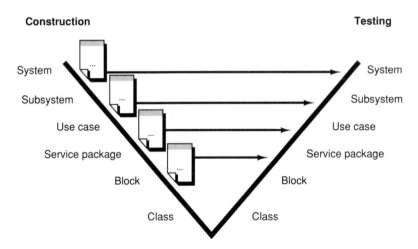

**Figure 12.1**  The test activities are usually performed in reverse order relative to the construction activities. Documents prepared on one level are used on the corresponding test level.

top-down fashion, a bottom-up fashion or in a per use case fashion, we can also do these increments using the same strategies.

Assume a top down-approach in design. This means that initially we develop the interfaces between the subsystems. These interfaces are implemented using stubs for the various subsystems. The underlying stubs may return random values, and they are subsequently replaced with the real code. This now makes it possible to test the overall flow at the highest level first before going into the lower levels.

Testing may also be done bottom-up or on a per use case basis. A bottom-up approach may be preferable at the lower levels, so that when the first unit is certified its direct clients can be certified. Then the next level of clients can be certified and so on. This technique minimizes the need to implement class stubs just for testing, as the already certified units will work as servers. This gives a smooth merging of unit and integration testing. However, the detection of faults in server units may force the process to start all over again. Additionally, it is difficult for a developer who is dependent on the objects of other designers to test his or her own objects. Then special test beds are needed. They are used as for traditional programming, namely to simulate the world surrounding the tested unit. Often you are forced to introduce special test operations in your classes to instantiate the test bed. In the extreme case you must build up an entire shadow object structure that simulates all the objects of the surrounding system. Normally, though, it should be enough to have a test bed that is one magnitude smaller than what you are testing; one test class for each block, one test block for each service package and so on.

### 12.2.3  Equivalence partitioning

**Equivalence partitioning** is a technique for reducing the number of test cases that we need to perform. The objective is to select a reasonably small number of test cases, out of a large number of possible test cases, so that the probability of finding faults is high. An **equivalence set** (we deliberately avoid the term 'equivalence class') is a set of conditions for which an object is supposed to behave similarly. The idea is then to write test cases to cover all equivalence sets. For every equivalence set we identify one test case. For example, if we want to test a *Stack*, we may write three test cases: for when the Stack is empty, loaded and full. Often it is at the boundary values of these equivalence classes that failures occur.

The technique of equivalence partitioning should be used in all testing. Then we select typical test data for each of the equivalence sets. Most important of course is that the unit under test works with normal input values. Ordinarily it works for them, whereas limit values tend to cause problems, for example when a queue is empty or if a parameter is on the verge of forbidden values. If our unit expects values in the range 0 to 100, then we should test, for example, with 0, 1, 56, 99 and 100. We should also test with values outside the range, for example −1 and 110, to see that the unit will not break down. The selection of test cases should be made so that failures do occur.

Equivalence sets for the output should also be made. From these we can select test data (input) so that we will verify all output equivalence sets.

### 12.2.4  Automatic testing

Since testing is an expensive activity it must be efficient. One consequence of this efficiency requirement is that we must be able to do regression testing without any great effort. Otherwise the risk that regression testing may not be done in a satisfactory way is too high, owing to project pressure. This means that all tests should be stored, including ergonomic tests, in order to perform regression tests in a simple manner. The goal should therefore be to **automate** as much as possible of the testing. This can be done through special test programs with associated test data. It is then simple to do regression tests, either in new versions or when some part has been changed since the preceding test. The principle of automatic testing is illustrated in Figure 12.2.

The test program fetches sequences and data from the input data. Then the unit or the system is fed with the sequence and the tested system's response is observed by the test program. This output can be stored directly on an output file or compared with some expected output. Hence a (primitive) failure analysis can also be done automatically. The test data consists of sequences of stimuli to be sent. An example of such an instruction could be 'send stimuli X with parameters A B C, receive response Y'. The sequences indicate which data will be sent and received.

The test program and data are placed in separate files, and can therefore be reused with several different test combinations. The test program is usually bound to the environment where it is executing, but this does not apply to the test data. It is easy to modify a test case; we only change the test data files. The goal is to have the test program as general as possible and independent of the test data. We should be able to reuse it for several different tests, and if we can reuse it for several different products so much the better. Test data, on the other hand, can seldom be reused in other tests, but it should be possible to reuse it if we want to make a regression test. We can modularize our test data, however, so that it can be combined in different ways and thus provide different tests. For example, use cases with extensions can use the test data for the use cases that are to be extended.

Other issues that should be considered include the automatic generation of test data. For example, test programs to test different

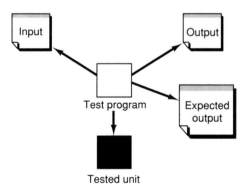

Input

Output

Test program

Expected output

Tested unit

**Figure 12.2** Schematic illustration of automated testing.

classes will have similar structures. It may be worthwhile to write a specific program that takes a given class and generates a skeleton for a test program or test data for that class.

When you test the entire system you need several different test programs. To obtain a simple interface to the system and to make the test program independent of the system, you normally build an interface simulator or test driver (see Figure 12.3). The test may now be performed in the target environment. This simulator often saves work since the handling of the interface of the system does not have to be described in each test program.

When you develop the test programs and test data you should of course use the same techniques used for all other development. Modularity and reusability are the guidelines. By writing good test programs we can build up a store of reusable tests, both test programs and test data, in the same manner as we do for components. These test programs, however, must be developed at the same time as our system is developed. Once more we see that testing must be part of the regular development process.

A question that quickly arises is whether the test programs are part of the tested product or whether they are a separate product. We should regard them as part of the product and they should be placed in a separate block. This block can be used for maintenance of the system and it also simplifies failure finding and fault localization when the system has been installed.

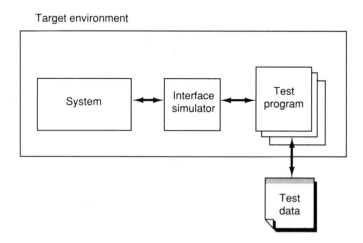

**Figure 12.3**  Use of an interface simulator.

# 12.3   Unit testing

A unit test is the lowest level of testing and it is normally done by the developer himself, mainly due to costs. Unit tests are performed for classes, blocks and service packages. The larger the unit, the more formal the testing will be.

In a traditional system a unit test is often a test of procedures or subroutines. In object-oriented software it concerns classes, which implies that unit tests in object-oriented systems are carried out at a higher level. Doing a unit test of object-oriented code is therefore more complex than testing ordinary (procedural) code. This is a result of the object-oriented approach; a unit is not just a set of routines, but also has an encapsulated state which may affect the behavior and correctness of the unit. Also, concepts like inheritance and polymorphism lead to additional complexity in testing. Perry and Kaiser (1990) have discussed the problems of unit testing object-oriented programs.

The requirements for debugging tools are also greater for object-oriented systems. Normally the environments contain support for inspecting the object structure during execution. This is (usually) a standard in environments for Smalltalk, C++, Simula and Eiffel. These tools are invaluable for fault finding. For more on debugging tools for object-oriented systems, see Purchase and Winder (1991).

Traditionally a unit test consists of **structural testing** (or white-box testing), which means that we use our knowledge of how the unit is designed internally for the testing, and **specification testing** (or black-box testing) which means the opposite: we base our test cases only on the specification of the externally visible behavior of the unit. Normally both are needed since they complement each other. This is also the case in object-oriented systems. But additionally we may need to perform tests based on the encapsulated state of the object and the interaction of the operations. This is sometimes called **state-based testing** (see Turner and Robson (1993)). This may be done both as specification and structural testing.

Since the structural test cases are dependent on the code structure, and the state-based testing and the specification testing may modify this code structure, it is preferable to do the structural testing last. If a fault is encountered in any of the first test types, the code needs to be altered, affecting the structural test cases. Additionally, many test cases required for structural testing may already be performed by the other two test types and thus need not be executed again. Since the specification-based test cases can be defined first, and may also use stubs for interacting operations in the same class, it is often advisable to start with specification testing. These test cases may now overlap other test cases in the structural and state-based testing and thus should not be performed again (unless during regression testing).

## 12.3.1 Specification testing

Specification testing, or black-box testing, has the purpose of verifying the input/output relations of a unit. The goal is to verify the specified behavior in the interface of the unit, that is, what the unit does, but we are not interested in how the unit solves this. We send stimuli with different parameters to the unit and as output we receive responses or perhaps we see a change in some attribute. The selection of test data is based on the parameters of the operation. We may also test the input/output relation in different states of the unit, but this is done in the state-based test cases.

In traditional testing, the equivalence sets are based upon the parameters. Since parameters in object-oriented languages are often references to objects, these references may refer to no object (0 in C++ or nil in Smalltalk). This means that every parameter may be a reference to no object and this thus forms an equivalence set. In untyped languages like Smalltalk, we may also have the equivalence set where the object belongs to the wrong class. A technique for finding equivalence sets from object references is to 'flatten' the object. We then view all the attributes of the object and find equivalence sets for the combination of the values of these attributes.

As our units only communicate through a defined interface, specification testing is quite straightforward. We have defined which operations the unit supports and which behavior it will show for each operation.

A common mistake when you test the code is not to check the output data. Just to receive output data is not sufficient, we must also make sure that it is correct. This may involve much work, for example in mathematical applications when you must verify the calculation manually or by using another system that you know will produce correct results.

## 12.3.2 State-based testing

State-based testing tests the interactions between the operations of a class by monitoring the changes that take place in an object's attributes. Testing only one operation in isolation is not enough to

**Table 12.1** The state matrix for testing. Combinations of states and stimuli can be tested on the basis of this matrix

| Stim | State s0 | s1 | s2 | s3 | s4 |
|------|------|------|------|------|------|
| Stimulus1 | ok | ok | wrong response | ok | fail |
| Stimulus2 | | fail | ok | | |
| Stimulus3 | | ok | slow – check it | | |
| Stimulus4 | | | | | |

test a unit. We must also test with respect to the object's attributes, since they persist between invocations of different operations and possibly also across operation interactions. Thus you cannot view the operations of an object as independent, to be tested separately. We must also see how the objects are to be used, that is, their life cycle. This is especially important for state-controlled objects described using state transition diagrams. Then test cases should be selected so that every state is visited at least once and every transition is traversed at least once.

A very good tool for this type of testing is a state matrix (see Table 12.1). The matrix indicates all the states that can be adopted by the unit and all the requests that the unit is expected to receive in the various states. As the testing is performed you can fill in this matrix. One of the great advantages of this type of matrix is that it draws the attention of the designer to state/stimulus combinations that may have been neglected during the design.

In reality it is impossible to include all combinations of attributes of the object (all possible variable values!) and all variants of stimuli (different parameters!). The states identified when describing state transition graphs of the objects are sufficient as a base. Additionally, some specific combinations of attributes may be of more interest than others. These combinations thus form an equivalence set. Such an equivalence set is those combinations of attributes for which the code should behave in a special way or which have special significance. Other combinations are assumed to be behaviorally equivalent. Review attributes (in the design and analysis, not the code – it may be wrong) and decide upon particularly significant values; then allocate one equivalence set for each such possibility and one set for each group of related values.

Some operations do not affect the state; they may be purely read operations. These do not need to be considered in the state-based testing. All other operations should be executed for all possible starting states. Also it is reasonable that all operations can allow all legal attribute combinations as input parameters.

It should also be verified that all possible equivalence states can be reached from some combination of operations. Otherwise there may be a flaw in the design of the class.

### 12.3.3  Structural testing

The purpose of structural testing is to test that the internal structure is correct. Structural testing is sometimes also called program-based testing, white-box testing or glass-box testing. This means that you use your knowledge of how the unit is implemented when you test it. It would be desirable to cover all possible combinations of parameters, variable values and paths in the code during the testing, but this is almost always impossible since we would have an enormous number of test cases. To examine the effectiveness of our test cases we can use measures of **test coverage**. The least coverage is to exercise each Decision-to-Decision path (DD path) at least once. A decision is typically an IF-statement (that is, a DD path is a path between two decision statements). This coverage leads to the situation where all statements are executed and each decision outcome has been tested. The minimum requirement should be that all statements have been executed. Normally this is a reasonable goal for test coverage. However, most problems arise on unusual path combinations. A more ambitious goal is exercise all pairs of DD paths. We can then increase our ambition to cover a significant number of DD paths in combination. However, the number of test cases increases very rapidly. It is hardly ever possible to test all the possible paths in the system, regardless of parameters or variable values. Complete path testing can often only be made locally. Especially critical passages such as loops must be given extra care. Using debuggers is often a great help in these tests since they permit the user to inspect statements that are executed and run-time values of variables.

Consider the example shown in Figure 12.4. This describes a member function in C++ for a class intset to check whether a certain integer is a member of the set. This member function can be tested so that each DD path is tested at least once. The test cases are illustrated in the flow graph.

Theoretically, all possible paths in the code should be executed to test an operation completely. In the example we have three alternative paths inside the while loop. The loop can be executed zero or more times. If the loop is executed zero times we have only one

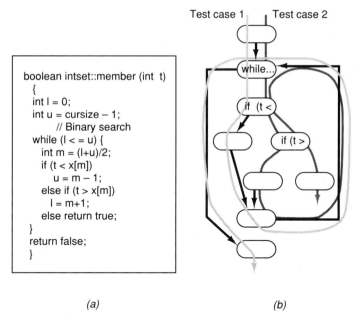

```
boolean intset::member (int  t)
  {
  int l = 0;
  int u = cursize – 1;
        // Binary search
  while (l < = u) {
    int m = (l+u)/2;
    if (t < x[m])
      u = m – 1;
    else if (t > x[m])
      l = m+1;
    else return true;
  }
  return false;
  }
```

(a)                                                      (b)

**Figure 12.4** The member function in (a) can be tested with only two test cases illustrated in (b) to do a full cover of each DD path.

path through the function. If the loop is executed once we have three alternative paths. If it is executed twice we have nine (3*3) paths, and so on. The total number of paths through the code is thus 1+3+3*3 + 3*3*3 +... , or $1+\Sigma 3^n$ ; $n > 0$, an infinite number of cases. We must therefore choose an appropriate number of test cases through equivalence partitioning. In this example two test cases will lead to execution of all statements, as can be seen in the figure.

Polymorphism is a very strong tool which often makes changes easier to incorporate. Polymorphism also helps us to isolate the test cases needed when changes are introduced. If you add a descendant class A and test A on its own, you do not need to test client classes again, as long as you have used inheritance for subtyping (see Chapter 3). In procedural code, however, you not only need to add and test the new functionality, but client codes must be changed and tested also, as we will indicate below.

One of the major strengths of polymorphism is that it hides the complexity of the code. However, improperly used it makes testing of the code more complex. Consider the class hierarchy shown in Figure 12.5.

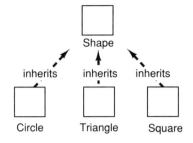

**Figure 12.5**  A class hierarchy of shapes.

We want every Shape object to be able to be drawn. Hence we have a virtual operation in Shape called Draw. This means that whenever a user of Shape wants to show the object on the screen, he or she can use the program indicated below:

```
...
figure: Shape;   // declaration of attribute figure
...
figure.Draw;     // invocation of Draw operation
...
```

Here we first declare a variable figure of type Shape. Then we can assign figure to an object of any of Shape's descendants. Since they all have a Draw operation, although differently implemented, we do not need to know to which class the objects belong. This is the polymorphism mechanism. In a traditional language we would need to know exactly to which type the object belonged, since we would need to call different procedures for different shapes. The code fragment would look something like:

```
...
figure: Shape;
...
CASE figure.type IS
    Triangle: DrawTriangle(figure);
    Circle: DrawCircle(figure);
    Square: DrawSquare(figure);
ENDCASE;
...
```

In this latter case we can see that we have three different paths to test. In the object-oriented code fragment this complexity was not obvious from reading the code. Test coverage based upon DD paths, as discussed above, is thus much harder because of polymorphism. You do not see in the code which unit is actually invoked, not even in a strongly typed language. It looks as if a stimulus is sent to an instance (of a specific type in a strongly typed language), but during execution, an instance of any class (of the descendants in a strongly typed language) can actually receive the stimulus. In traditional languages the operation to be invoked is made explicit. Hence every stimulus in polymorphic code corresponds to a CASE-statement in procedural code.

The discussion above about test coverage and paths to be tested illustrates that these concepts make testing of OO software much harder. In the discussion we have taken a traditional view based upon code being sequences to execute. This view, however, is not the view traditionally taken in the object-oriented community. Instead the focus is to write code for a class independent of any clients of the class so that every class is self-contained. The sequences are still there (refer to the use cases), but they are implicit over the classes. The interfaces are explicit, though, and this is one of the major strengths of object-orientation. The implicit sequences are tested during integration testing. Hence integration testing is an important activity and integration occurs throughout the development, as the object interfaces are focused upon early.

Another issue specific to OOSE testing is the use of inheritance. Inheritance often leads to less code, as operations defined in ancestors are also used in descendants. However, the amount of test cases for such code is not necessarily less. We must test that we can inherit the class and that we can create instances of the descendants. The test case should thus create instances of the descendants and then test these instances.

When a class inherits another class, the inherited operations may also need to be retested in the new context. That an operation worked well in an ancestor class does not necessarily mean that it will work well when it is inherited. There are at least two reasons for an inherited operation not functioning in a descendant:

- The descendant class modifies instance variables which the inherited operation assumes certain values for.
- Operations in the ancestor invoke operations implemented in the descendant, leading to self-calls.

The first case can be avoided by only using the ancestor class in such a way that it is always consistent, namely by not changing instance variables in an improper way. This can be accomplished in C++ by defining certain operations or instance variables as private, that is, they are not accessible to the descendants; otherwise this must be controlled by coding rules. The second case can be avoided by testing the operation in the descendants that are invoked to be sure that it really fulfills its specification. If the new descendant does not interact in any way with the instance variables or the operations inherited, we do not need to retest these in the descendant.

Overriding of operations in the inheritance hierarchy is also crucial for testing, as we may conclude from the above discussion. Of course, we must retest the overrided operation. We may then also need to develop new test cases as the implementation of the operation is changed. We can view this as the descendant class using the ancestor class just as a module uses another module.

Hence inheritance may lead to more extensive testing. As well as having to retest the descendants when we modify an ancestor class, we may need to retest the inherited operations when we add a new descendant. In the worst case, we may need to develop unique test cases for every level in the inheritance hierarchy. By designing the test cases optimally, several of the test principles discussed can be covered in the same test.

## 12.4  Integration testing

When units have been certified in unit tests, these units should now be integrated to larger units and finally to the system. The purpose of integration testing is to test whether different units that have been developed are working together properly. In integration testing we include the testing of blocks, service packages, use cases, subsystems and the entire system. There is consequently not just one integration test in a development, but rather integration tests are performed several times on different levels. In OOSE it does not come as a 'big bang' event, but is introduced smoothly.

If we test all units extensively, is there a need for integration testing, since all units will be correct as they are? Yes, there is definitely a need. When units are combined, new failures will be detected. The combination of units will increase the number of possible paths exponentially. Therefore, on testing the combination of units, failures may be detected that were impossible to detect when testing only a single unit.

When we have certified the blocks and possibly also the service packages, integration testing is best done on a per use case basis. Hence, the use cases now form the major tool that drives the integration testing.

Before we start the integration test the units included in it must of course be completely designed and certified. This does not mean that we must postpone the integration test until the entire system has been designed. On the contrary, as we have seen, we will start the integration test when we have only a few units. Additionally, we can test use cases as soon as the blocks required for them are certified and approved.

So what should you focus on during integration testing? For the first time, several classes, blocks, service packages and subsystems are brought together and therefore the testing should concentrate on this. The use cases constitute an excellent tool for the integration test since they explicitly interconnect several classes and blocks. The basis of the specification emanates from the interaction diagrams. In them we can see all the stimuli that are sent between the user and the system and between the objects in the system. If the testing is done manually this is often enough, and if it is performed automatically then the diagram is the basis of the test data (and to a certain extent the test program).

In a use case test you test the basic courses of the use case, that is, the expected flow of events. Since this is the first time the service packages are integrated, these tests should stress the interaction of the service packages. The tests for alternative courses cover all other flows of events, that is, the unusual cases of the use case. If we can trace something from this use case to the requirements specification, it is also identified during the tests based on the requirements specification. Here we also include tests of the user interface to the system in this use case. Normally we test all use cases one by one. Those use cases which extend other use cases are tested after testing the use cases where they are to be inserted.

Integration testing is thus performed by testing each use case one at a time, both from an internal viewpoint and an external viewpoint. The internal viewpoint is based on the interaction diagrams and the external viewpoint is based on the descriptions from the requirements model. Each use case then corresponds to a set of test specifications. During identification of tests we divide the testing into different test types. For a use case we may have the following tests:

(1)  Basic course tests

(2)  Alternative course tests

(3)  Tests of user documentation

Each test type is now divided into subtests with different conditions. We can describe these subtests according to Figure 12.6 and consequently decompose the test hierarchically. Figure 12.6 illustrates an example of how equivalence sets are used to do this decomposition for the use case *Returning Item* in the recycling system. Each node indicates some condition. The tests that are specified and

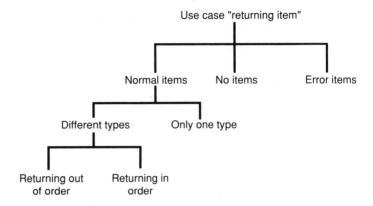

**Figure 12.6** Each subtest is divided according to different conditions.

performed are those placed in the leaves of this tree. The tests that we thus want to perform in this case are:

- Returning items out of order
- Returning items in order
- Returning only one item
- Just pressing the receipt button
- Returning erroneous items (incorrect size, not a can, bottle or crate, or whatever).

When we test the use cases, the machine could very well execute other tasks; it is actually an advantage to have background noise of this kind during these tests, but this should only be done when the basic tests are complete. When we test the use cases it may happen that one of them perhaps cannot be tested alone, but requires several other use cases to be meaningful (for example, a use case for supervision).

Test cases that must not be overlooked include different configurations of instantiations of classes, as well as different configurations of the final system. Above all we must test to ensure that no block is dependent on other blocks that are not certain to be delivered.

Normally integration testing (at subsystem level and upwards) is done by a special testing team. Here the documentation is more formal than in the unit tests. The testing done by the test team should usually be performed in the target environment, that is, the environment in which the system will execute when in operation.

## 12.5 System testing

Each use case is initially tested separately, from an external viewpoint. These tests are thus based on the requirements model. When all use cases have been tested separately, the entire system is tested as a whole. Then several use cases are executed in parallel and the system is subjected to different loads. The system tests may now be divided into the following tests:

(1) Operation tests
(2) Full-scale tests
(3) Negative tests
(4) Tests based on the requirements specification
(5) Tests of the user documentation

When we test the system the use cases should be tested in parallel, both synchronized and unsynchronized. We should also stress the system by running several use cases at the same time. All these tests appear from our division into subtests; the operation test is a run of the entire system, the full-scale test increases the parameters of the system to their specified limits, and the negative test has the purpose of breaking the entire system by pushing through these limits.

The performance test, which may be of extra interest for object-oriented systems, is placed among those tests based on the requirements specification if it is mentioned in the requirements specification; otherwise it is placed under the operation tests. In the same way we place the overload test either under those tests based on the requirements specification or under the negative test.

## 12.6 The testing process

It is important to plan the testing; testing is not something that is done on an *ad hoc* basis. The testing process is a process that, to a great extent, runs in parallel with the other processes. The testing process is a set of activities that we can describe as shown in Figure 12.7. We start by planning the testing. This plan is the basis for identifying what will be tested and then specified in more detail. This specification is the basis of the actual test performance.

### 12.6.1 Test planning

As mentioned before, the activity of testing begins early in the development process. The planning can begin when we start the

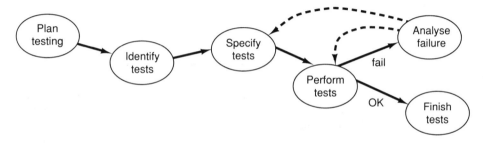

**Figure 12.7**    Activities in integration testing.

development. We can work on it in general during analysis, but we cannot seriously start preparing the testing until we start construction.

The testing guidelines are established early. By determining the method and level of ambition we have created the foundation of the testing. It should be determined whether the testing will be done automatically or manually, and we can also make an early estimate of the resources that will be required. These decisions should be reflected in the project plan.

When our requirements model is ready we can start the test planning in earnest. We study whether existing test programs and data can be used, whether they must be modified or whether we must develop new ones. Using the guidelines as a basis we can determine what degree of coverage our tests should have. We can also define the surroundings for the test. By looking at which parts will be ready first, we can decide which tests can be defined first. Never start the integration test until the unit test is ready; deviations will prove crucial! Faults on underlying levels will usually prevent further tests. You can test incrementally, however, by adding new functionality to the blocks as you go along.

The test planning must also consider any standards for the testing and the resources required for each subtest. The plan should not control the testing in detail, but only function as a basis for the test activities.

A **test log** is kept during the entire test process. A log should be connected to a version of the system. The purpose of the log is to give a brief history of all the test activities, both successes and setbacks. Setbacks often require a longer explanatory text indicating the reason for the failure and explaining what action has been taken. The log is filed after the testing has been done and is the basis of the refinement of the test process and the planning of new tests.

## 12.6.2   Test identification

When we identify what should be tested, we can also estimate the required resources. This is a more detailed estimate than that done earlier and it now acts as the guiding principle for the specification and execution of the test.

Since the integration test is normally performed in the target environment, the need for testing equipment can be identified at an early stage. This equipment can then be purchased or developed within the company and can be installed in good time. Usually this picture becomes clearer with time, but if we can identify the testing needs, then we also increase the probability that the appropriate equipment will be available when we need it.

When the test resources are restricted, each test case must maximize the statistical probability of the detection of a failure. We should strive to find the major failures first.

## 12.6.3   Test specification

When we have identified which subtests are to be made, they are specified on a functional level, where we describe the test and its purpose in overview form, and on a detailed level where we describe exactly how the test case is to be executed. The latter part includes a complete procedural description of each step in the test. Here again the use case descriptions are very powerful tools. The purpose of the test specification is to give a detailed run instruction so that people not familiar with the application, or even the system, can execute the test case. In the ideal case, the design specifications should also act as test specifications.

Each test case to be done, with the exception of the most low-level unit tests, should be documented. Remember that we want to reuse them in regression testing, possibly in other system versions. The conditions for the test should be specified, for example whether the test should be done in a development or target environment, test beds, system software, hardware, test equipment, and different versions of these. It also includes how the test should be performed, in what order, the expected outcome and the criteria for an approved test.

When you write the test specification you also prepare the test reports required to report the result of the tests. The reports are used for notes when the test is being made. Since the report skeletons are prepared prior to the testing, they control the testing instead of the test outcome controlling how the reports are written. It should be possible to document the actual outcome together with the specification, although it should be treated separately since we may want to reuse the specification.

If the design documentation is written in the form of specifications, these could be used as test specifications as well. A test specification is also often a proper design specification. This also helps in finding the faults. If a fault is encountered at some level, then it should also be corrected at that design level, not only in the code, hence the two-directional arrows in the figure.

When writing a test specification, you should reflect the system as it will function during operation. Then weaknesses may be discovered in the design, and these should of course be forwarded to the designers. The earlier a design error can be detected, the cheaper it is to correct it.

As previously discussed, each test should aim to detect a failure. If we have a view that we should detect all faults present in the system, we may aim at trying to minimize the number of faults per 1000 lines of code or something like that. This view implies that we are striving for defect-free software, that is, that all faults will be found. However, all experience shows that we are far from this situation. What is actually more interesting is to view the system as having faults, and instead focus on how many hours of operation are needed to detect new failures. Thus, operation tests at least should also be performed with this statistical view in mind, to measure metrics like Mean Time Between Failures (MTBF).

The test specification is used for the planning and execution of the tests. From the specification we can identify the need for equipment together with the test programs and test data that must be prepared. What we prepare and what we do not prepare is written down, with reasons, in the log.

### 12.6.4    Test execution

When performing tests we use the test specification and the prepared test reports. When the test bed has been installed we start the tests of the use cases, which are tested one by one. The strategy is to test as much as possible in parallel, even though this may be difficult.

The testing is done by executing the automatic tests and by doing manual tests according to the specifications. The test specification indicates the expected result. If some subtest should fail, the subtest is interrupted and the result is noted, and the defect is analyzed and corrected if possible. Then the subtest is performed again.

By means of a decision table, see Table 12.2, we can get an assessment of the result of the test. The table includes all the subtests,

**Table 12.2**   An example of a decision table

| Test nr | Importance | Outcome | Evaluation |
|---------|-----------|---------|------------|
| 1 | 5 | 1 | 5 |
| 2 | 4 | 1 | 4 |
| 3 | 2 | 0 | 0 |
| ... | ... | ... | ... |
| n | 5 | 0 | 5 |

$\Sigma 53 > 50 =>$ Test is OK

weighted according to their importance, and we can determine whether the test is approved or not by its outcome. The importance denotes the weight of the test. The outcome is 1 for OK and 0 for fail. Evaluation is calculated from importance*outcome. The evaluation is summed up and compared to a limit (in this case 50). If the sum exceeds this value, the test has approved the test object, otherwise not. This table should of course be prepared in good time so that the result will not influence the weighting. The table shows a survey of the total test result. The evaluation of the entire test depends upon which tests are approved and their weight.

When the tests have been made, we analyze the result. Is it approved or not? These analyses result in test reports. A test report contains a summary of the test and is also the final report from the test. It consists of a summary and the result of the individual subtests. The summary should be brief and must contain conclusions, the resources spent and whether the test is approved or rejected. The result of each subtest is also shown in this report with the result, resources spent and the action taken, if any. Any bottlenecks that have been discovered are also written down and shown in the log.

### 12.6.5   Error analysis

If faults are detected when the test is done, the test must be analyzed and the reason for the fault identified. The fault need not be due to the system, but may have other causes:

- Has the test been performed correctly?
- Is there a fault in the test data or the test program?
- Is the failure caused by the test bed?
- Does the underlying system software behave properly?

If the failure was not due to the test object it should be corrected and the test done again. If it was caused by the system, the basic principle is that deficient blocks or service packages should be returned to the designers. However, there can be some fault detection in the test activities, for example to identify the defect block. This fault finding is helped if the blocks offer suitable built-in facilities, for example fault counters for stimuli or a fault log. When a tested unit is changed, we may need to change the test specification if the design specification is changed.

### 12.6.6    Test completion

When all the testing has been completed, the equipment and the test bed should be restored so that they can be used again for later testing. All the documentation prepared for the test should also be saved; it is just as natural to save the test documentation as it is to save the source code and all other documentation.

The experiences of the testing activity are collected and discussed in order to learn for future test activities. Since experience is always highly coveted and always costs so much, it is important to make use of it. Concluding notes are made in the log which is also filed.

## 12.7    Summary

Testing is an activity to verify that a correct system is being built. Testing is traditionally an expensive activity owing to the fact that many faults are not detected until late in the development. A qualitative and well-organized approach to system development is necessary in order to increase the quality of the system and to decrease testing costs. To do effective testing, every test should aim to detect a fault. Therefore we must have a disciplined approach to testing. There are several different testing types and testing techniques, some of which have been discussed in this chapter.

Unit testing is performed to test a specific unit, where a unit can be of varying size from a class up to a specific service package. The unit is initially tested using its specification. We do specification testing of a unit primarily from the object protocol. Here we use equivalence partitioning to find appropriate test cases. Then we take into consideration any states of the object that may affect the behavior of the unit. In structural testing, we use our knowledge of the inside of the unit to test it. We then have different coverage criteria for the test where the smallest ambition is to cover all statements. However, these coverage criteria may be hard to define since many branches in an object-oriented system are made implicit, due to polymorphism. Polymorphism also emphasizes the independence of each object, making them easier to test as stand-alone units. The use of inheritance makes the testing harder, since we may need to retest operations at different levels in the inheritance hierarchy. On the other hand, since we normally have less code, we do not need to test as much code as in traditional systems.

Integration testing starts early in OOSE. Here we integrate instances of different classes continuously throughout the development. When the system has been integrated we test the entire system. Both for integration testing and system testing, the use cases provide a strong tool for guiding these activities.

Testing activities are performed throughout the development. Test planning should be done early, as should the identification and specification of the tests.

# Part III
# Applications

# 13 Case study: warehouse management system

## 13.1 Introduction to the examples

In this chapter we will give an example of using OOSE in a larger system. Our goal is to illustrate the use of the concepts we have discussed earlier. Of course, the entire process cannot be fully illustrated within these few pages (the documentation alone would cover more pages than this entire book). We will focus on certain especially interesting things and we will go fairly deeply into some details and skip others, rather than give a complete overview.

The discussion will be more detailed in the earlier phases and less complete in the later phases. This is due to the fact that complexity increases fast during construction, and thus needs more explanation in some areas. The implementation environment in particular needs much discussion that is unique for every development. However, we hope to give a feeling for the use of OOSE in large and complex systems. Our coverage of examples will initially give a brief introduction to the problem domain and the requirements of the system, and then we will discuss the different activities applied in this domain.

## 13.2 ACME Warehouse Management Inc.

The system will support warehouse management. The company ordering the system, ACME Warehouse Management Inc., specializes in supporting its customers with warehouse spaces all over the nation. Examples of customers are companies that need space to store their products before they are shipped or companies that need local warehouses without having local offices. ACME is already a specialist in storing different kinds of items and in the use of trucks to redistribute the items. ACME plans to grow and now needs an

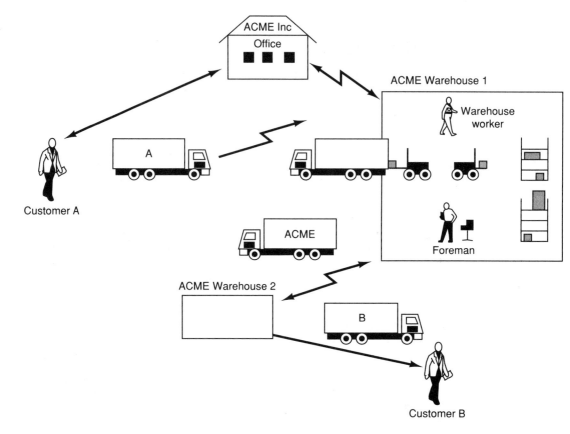

**Figure 13.1**   Overview of the ACME Warehouse Management Inc. The company consists of several different warehouses where the customers can store their items.

information system with which they can grow. The idea is to offer the customers warehouse space and redistribution services between different warehouses with full computer support. The service includes redistribution both within a warehouse and between warehouses, all dictated by customer needs. All kinds of items may be stored in the warehouses, which means that it is important to differentiate between certain kinds of items; for example some items must not come into contact with other items (such as industrial chemicals and foods). In Figure 13.1 the idea is illustrated schematically.

The following people will be using the system in some way or another:

- Foreman        responsible for one warehouse;

- Warehouse worker works in a warehouse, loading and unloading;
- Truck driver drives a truck between different warehouses;
- Forklift operator drives a forklift in one warehouse;
- Office personnel receive orders and requests from customers;
- Customers own the items in the warehouses and give instructions as to where and when they want the items.

It is fundamental to the ACME system that it should be as decentralized as possible and that all persons involved should be reachable at all times. Therefore the truck drivers should have communication devices for getting their orders and they must be able to communicate with the foreman or the office. This means that we also need a radio communication network, a system that should not be developed by us but bought separately. The warehouse workers loading and unloading should use a barcode reader when handling the items in order to be as efficient as possible. This means that all items must be marked when inserted in the warehouse system by a warehouse worker; this marking must at the same time give information about the item to the information system. The foremen should be able to work with several items at the same time, so they will probably need a window-based terminal. They are responsible for effecting the redistribution orders from the office.

When a customer wants to do something with his items, he will contact the office, which in turn submits redistribution orders to the system. Eventually, if the system is to work well, ACME plans to give their customers terminals so that they can interact directly with the system.

The system should use a relational database (since ACME has all its information in relational databases already and does not want to change) and the application should be coded in C++. The system should have a distributed implementation.

## 13.3 The requirements model

The first model to be developed is the requirements model. This model is used to gain a better understanding of the system and analyze the requirements of it. In Section 13.2 we described the ACME warehouse management system. Although requirements specifications are usually more thorough than the description given there, they are seldom complete and consistent. Generally, it is very hard to identify the right objects from the initial requirements specification. Usually, a far better understanding of the system is needed before objects can be identified which will result in a robust maintainable system.

The actors may be identified as roles played by people (or other systems) interacting with our system. An often appropriate strategy is to identify organizational roles in the system domain. We know that we have foremen, employees (warehouse workers, truck drivers and forklift operators) and office personnel. In the future we may also have customers as actors. Our picture of the system will initially look like that in Figure 13.2.

Thus we will have the following actors interacting with the system.

- Foreman
- Warehouse worker
- Truck driver
- Forklift operator
- Office personnel

To start identifying the use cases, and especially when specifying them later, it is often appropriate to have a first picture of

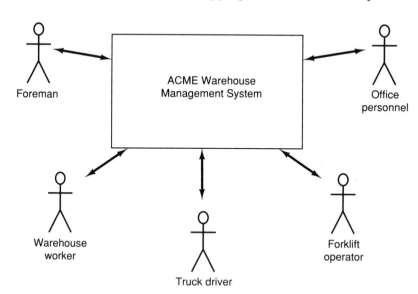

**Figure 13.2**  The initial system with interacting actors.

the system in terms of some problem domain objects. This picture should only function as a support for identifying and specifying the use cases. If too much detail is put into this sketch, it can later be hard to liberate ourselves from this model. When looking at the description of the system to be built with the accompanying picture of it, we can directly find the problem domain objects.

The system should manage items stored in certain places in the warehouses. Every item has an owner who is a customer of ACME. The transporters can be either a truck or a forklift. They are transporting some items from a customer order and they should all be reachable over the radio. The initial picture of the internal view of the system may thus be as shown in Figure 13.3. Here we have chosen not to devise an exhaustive object model complete with behavior and so on, but rather a support to help us understand and formulate the problem.

To identify the use cases, we look at each actor and investigate what that actor wants to do to the system. We will here only look at some of the primary use cases (use cases that support the main functionality of the system). In this system there will also be secondary use cases (use cases that support the primary use cases). When investigating these we will probably find at least one new

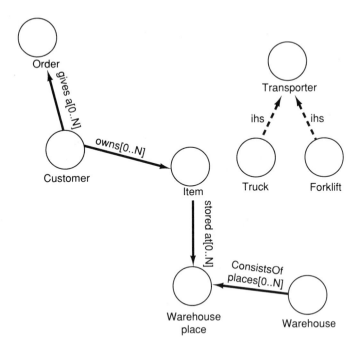

**Figure 13.3**   The first intuitive picture of the objects in the system.

actor, a system manager, that will administer the system.

We will from here on concentrate on the actors Foreman and Warehouse worker.

A Foreman has to be able to move items between warehouses with or without a customer order. We call this use case *Manual redistribution between warehouses*. He or she also wants to check how far a customer order has been handled. This use case we may call *Check status of customer order*. Other use cases that might be interesting are:

- *Manual redistribution within a warehouse*
- *Insertion of a new item into a warehouse*
- *Check status of a truck driver*
- *Check items in a warehouse*

The actor Warehouse worker is concerned with performing the following use cases:

- *Customer ordered withdrawal of items*
- *Check items in a warehouse*

among others. We see that some use cases can be performed by both actors. This is an indication of a separate role that is common to both actors. Are they in fact identical? No, they are not. We want the Foreman to have more privileges than a Warehouse worker, thus he or she should be able to do more. To avoid specifying the same use case twice, as the above example indicates, we might identify a common abstract actor that both Foreman and Warehouse worker inherit. While thinking further about this abstract actor, we realize that it will actually be identical to the Warehouse worker; everything that the Warehouse worker should be able to do the Foreman should also be able to do. Thus we might instead let the Foreman inherit the Warehouse worker (see Figure 13.4). This is actually a technique used when modeling different levels of privileges for the actors.

Before concentrating on some of the use cases, we might do a review of the use cases mentioned. We see that many of them will have a particular sequence when moving an item inside a warehouse. This sequence will be carried out when moving items between warehouses (to move the item from the loading platform to a place in the warehouse), when carrying out a customer withdrawal (to move the item from the warehouse to the loading platform) and when performing a manual redistribution within a warehouse. We here might identify an abstract use case that redistributes an item within a warehouse; this abstract use case could be used by use cases that might need this sequence as a sub-sequence (refer to Figure 13.5).

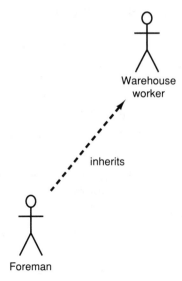

**Figure 13.4**   Actor Foreman inherits actor Warehouse worker.

We will from now on focus on two use cases for a more detailed discussion:

- *Manual redistribution between warehouses*
- *Customer ordered withdrawal from warehouse*

The first use case is performed by the Foreman when he or she wants to redistribute an item in one warehouse to a place in another warehouse. The second is performed when a customer wants to withdraw some items from the warehouse.

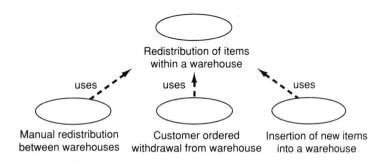

**Figure 13.5** An abstract use case of redistribution of items within a warehouse has been identified.

### 13.3.1   Manual redistribution between warehouses

A common question when identifying use cases is the extent of a use case. A use case should be a logical cohesive sequence of events, but what does this mean? If we analyze what will happen when a Foreman performs a manual redistribution of items between warehouses, we see that it has at least four phases:

(1) Initialization, when the Foreman gives the request to do the redistribution;

(2) Planning, when the system does the planning to coordinate the transports and issue transport requests;

(3) Loading, when a truck fetches the items from the warehouse;

(4) Unloading, when a truck delivers the items to the new warehouse.

When specifying a use case which is to be performed in a window management system, it is often appropriate to do sketches, or even better prototypes, of the view the users will have. Our experience shows that to do effective user-interface prototyping you need first to have identified the major use cases and also to have developed a first intuitive picture of the objects in the system. This is because you need to have thought about the system for a while, what information it should hold (the intuitive objects) and how it should be used (the major use cases), before you can do effective user-interface prototyping. Starting with the user interfaces may end with the prototypes determining what the system should do, instead of the other way around.

We will here use interface descriptions as seen by the users when specifying the use case. In the use case description we have numbered each line so that we can refer to it in the text later. With a tool support this can be appropriate. We have also used headlines to indicate the different phases in the use case, a method often appropriate also in real cases.

---

*Initialization*

(Words in italic refer to words from the noun list.)

(1) The Foreman gives a command for redistribution between warehouses.

(2) The window in Figure 13.6 is presented to the Foreman.

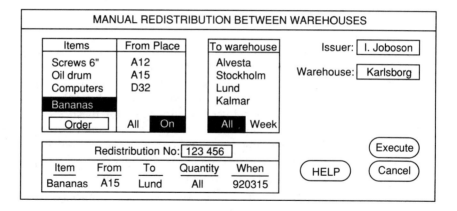

**Figure 13.6** Manual redistrubtion between warehouses window.

(3) The *items* can be ordered in a number of ways. This is selected with the ORDER menu. The following orders are possible:

(a) Alphabetical order

(b) Index order (each item has a unique number)

(c) Turnover of the items

(d) Storing order.

(4) In the 'From place' table we might choose to view either all *places* in the current *warehouse* or, if we have selected an *item*, the *places* where that *item* exists.

(5) In the 'To warehouse' table we might select all *warehouses* or the *warehouses* that we have a transport to this week.

(6) The 'Issuer' and 'Warehouse' fields are automatically filled when the window pops up, but they might be changed. (This is the way to do a redistribution from another *warehouse* to our own *warehouse*.)

(7) The Foreman selects an *item* by pointing to it and dragging it to the Redistribution form. He or she then selects from which *place* to take the *items* and to which *warehouse* to transport them. This information is automatically shown in the form.

(8) The Foreman then gives the quantity to be moved (a possibility is to choose 'ALL') and a date by when it must be done.

(9) It is possible to change the information when the form has been edited. When the Foreman EXECUTES the redistribution, the transport is planned. It is also possible to CANCEL the redistribution. Selecting HELP shows a window of information about the current window.

*Planning*

(1) When the redistribution is executed the *items* to be moved are marked as move-pending.

(2) The planning should minimize the use of *trucks* on condition that all delivery dates should be held and the *trucks* should be compatible with any delivery requirements for the *items* (for example, in size). This should be done by adjusting existing, already planned redistributions to take account of the new redistribution requirements.

(3) This may render new transport requests and may also change existing transport requests already in the system.

(4) The transport requests are connected to a specific *truck's* transportation plan.

*Loading*

(1) A *Truck* driver asks for a transportation request. The request is marked as ongoing. He or she also gives the expected time of arrival at the warehouse.

(2) Give an appropriate request to the *Forklift* operators to have the *items* ready when and where the *truck* is expected.

(3) When a Warehouse worker gets a request to fetch *items* he or she, at the appropriate time, orders *Forklift* operators to move the *items* to the loading platform.

(4) When the *Truck* driver arrives the *items* are loaded. The *Truck* driver tells the system when the *truck* is loaded and when it is expected to be at the new *warehouse*.

(5) Decrease the number of *items* in this *warehouse*. Mark the transport request as on transport.

*Unloading*

(1) When the *truck* has arrived at the new *warehouse*, the items are unloaded.

(2) The *Truck* driver tells the system that the transport to this *warehouse* has been done.

(3) The Warehouse workers receive the *items* and determine a place for them in the *warehouse*.

(4) *Forklift* operators are told to move the *items* to the new *place* in the new *warehouse*.

(5) When the *Truck* driver confirms the insertion, the system updates the new *place* for the *items*.

(6) The transportation time is recorded and stored in the system.

(7) The Redistribution and the transport request are marked as performed. (It is deleted by a Foreman or the system manager later.)

**Alternative courses**

*A request is not executable*

The execution is interrupted and the Foreman issuing the request is informed.

*Redistribution is wrong*

When the redistribution is filled in and executed by the Foreman, the appropriateness is checked immediately and returned to the Foreman. Possible errors may be:

(a)   The *warehouse place* does not have enough *items* to move.

(b)   The destination *warehouse* is not appropriate to the *item* (for example, because of size or storing circumstances).

*No truck available*

When performing the planning, there may not be any *trucks* available at an appropriate time. Then notify the Foreman who should either delete the request or change it.

The use case has some alternative courses that may change its flow. As many as possible of these alternative courses, often erroneous courses, should be noted. Although many of them will not be noticed or even identified at this stage, the more of these alternative courses that are noted in advance, the more robust the system will be. It is valuable to have these courses noticed at this early stage since they may be taken into consideration in the later work on the system.

Before discussing use cases more generally, we will first look at the other use case, *Customer ordered withdrawal from warehouse*, which is smaller than the first one.

### 13.3.2   Customer ordered withdrawal from warehouse

This use case covers the case when a Warehouse worker does a withdrawal at the request of a customer. The use case starts when the customer request is inserted into the system by the office personnel. It lasts until the customer has signed out the items from the warehouse.

(1) The Office personnel insert a request for a customer withdrawal at a certain date and from a certain warehouse. The window in Figure 13.7 is shown to the Office personnel when a customer withdrawal command is issued.

(2) The information filled in by the Office personnel is Customer, delivery date and delivery place. The name of the Office personnel person is filled in automatically but it is possible to change it. The Office personnel person selects items from the browser and adds the quantity to be withdrawn from the warehouses. The browser can here show only the items of the current customer.

(3) The following criteria are checked instantly:

    (a) The customer is registered.

    (b) The number of items ordered exists in one warehouse or across several warehouses.

    (c) The customer has the right to withdraw the items.

(4) The system initiates a plan to have the items at the appropriate warehouse by the given date. If necessary, transport requests are issued. The items are reserved three days in advance. (The longest possible time for a warehouse redistribution has been measured to take three days.)

(5) On the date of delivery a Warehouse worker is notified of the withdrawal.

(6) The Warehouse worker issues requests to the forklift operators to get the items to the loading platform. The forklift operator executes the transportation.

(7) When the customer has fetched his items the warehouse worker marks the withdrawal as ready. The items are removed (decreased) from the system.

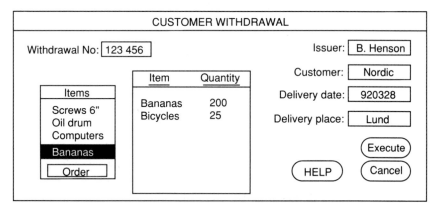

**Figure 13.7** Customer withdrawal window.

---

**Alternative courses**

*There are not enough items in the warehouses*

The Office personnel are notified and the withdrawal cannot be executed.

*Customer has no right to withdraw an item or Customer is not registered.*

Notify the Office personnel. The withdrawal cannot be executed.

---

When writing use cases, an active form should be used from the system perspective. When mentioning actors in the use case the formal names of the actors should be used. This means that when changing the formal name of an actor, it should be changed everywhere the name is mentioned.

It is the basic course that should form the foundation when specifying a use case and this should be described first. The basic course is the course which gives the best understanding of the system, not necessarily the one which is executed most often. The reason for this is that the use case aims to achieve understanding of the system.

Alternative courses are described separately. These are often written under a special headline *'Alternative courses'*. Here references are made to the basic course where the alternative course may happen. The reason for this is to build as much as possible on what has already been specified and to avoid redundancy in the descriptions. An example of this is in the *Customer withdrawal* use case when the system notices that there are not enough items in the warehouses.

When the requirements model has been specified, it is possible to check the model with the orderer or the end users. We see that there is no need to understand system development in order to understand the use cases. We have often seen in real projects that use cases are an appropriate basis for discussion when analyzing the system for requirements. The requirements model as a whole may form part of the contract between the orderer of the system and the deliverer – the use cases are then the commitment made by the deliverer regarding the system's functionality.

### 13.3.3  Abstract use cases

We noted earlier that several use cases have one thing in common, namely that they should move an item from one place to another inside a warehouse. This is also seen in the two use case descriptions above. In *Manual redistribution between warehouses* we see it in Loading step 3 and Unloading step 4, and in the *Customer withdrawal* use case we see it in step 6. This sequence may be described in an abstract use case *Redistribution of items within a warehouse* which covers the sequence relevant when a forklift operator receives an order to move an item from one place in the warehouse to another (including the loading platforms).

In the use case descriptions, we see that this step is not formulated in exactly the same way. This is very common since often several people are involved in the use case descriptions and it often takes some time to write the use case descriptions. Therefore it is essential that someone with a very good overview of the system performs an analysis of common parts in the use cases. The reason for separating this part out to form an abstract use case is so that we need only design this part once and can then reuse it in several use cases.

Experience shows that you should postpone identifying abstract use cases until you have described several concrete use cases. The reason for this is that the abstract use cases should evolve from the concrete ones and not the other way around.

## 13.4  The analysis model

When the requirements model has been developed, a large milestone has been reached. The requirements model has been checked by external reviewers, maybe the future users, and is now approved. Our aim now is to develop the first preliminary structure of the system. This should be a logical structure that will be stable over the system life cycle and that does not take into account the actual implementation environment.

The use cases will now be broken down into the analysis model and we will thus identify the objects that offer the use cases. When we have done this structuring of the system, we will identify the subsystems into which we may divide the system. First, the interface objects, entity objects and control objects will be identified. These objects are normally identified in an iterative manner over a use case and then over all use cases offered by them.

### 13.4.1  Analysis objects

When identifying the **interface objects** we focus on where actors interact with the use case (that is, the system). Everything in the use cases that implies some interaction with the system should be offered by an interface object.

In our example we do not have any examples of communication with other information systems. This version, at least, will be a stand-alone system that does not interact with any other system. This means that all interface objects will be interfaces to humans. These interfaces will be of three kinds: firstly, the window systems whereby the actors interact with a user interface based on a window management system; secondly, hardware devices like push buttons and barcode readers used by the warehouse workers; and thirdly, the radio communication network. Let us discuss the last one first.

The radio communication network is bought from another vendor. The network will thus be *outside* our system. This means that we may view it as an existing product that will be connected to our system. Therefore we should not describe the network in detail. What we need to model is an interface between the network management system and our system. Hence, in the analysis model we will model the interface to the network, in only one interface object. If we were to develop the network also, this would not be enough. Then we should analyze the entire network too. We have thus now identified the first interface objects which we may call Truck radio and Forklift radio. They are modeled by two objects since they will be different networks: inside a warehouse for the forklift operators and outside the warehouse for the truck drivers. If we were to have the network inside our system, we would not have an interface object to it.

To model the hardware devices in the warehouse, we model each different device with an interface object. This encapsulates everything in the device and converts external signals to stimuli inside the system.

The window systems and terminals will also be modeled by interface objects. Three actors will have such interfaces to the system. These are the Office personnel, the Foreman and the Warehouse worker. When considering which use cases each of them will be able to perform, we have already noticed that the foreman will inherit all the capabilities of the Warehouse worker. The Office personnel will perform quite different use cases from the Foreman and the Warehouse worker. User interface prototypes or sketches of the interfaces have been made during the requirements modeling. Since they are part of the requirements model which forms the contract between user and developer, many of the problems with user interface design are avoided. Users can now give their opinions on the interfaces before the actual development work starts and thus avoid much of the changing of user interfaces in late phases of the system development. This is one of the major strengths of OOSE since the development is driven from the actors' needs and the users have an important role to play during the requirements modeling when defining the tasks of the system. The sketches and/or prototypes form a rigorous base from which the interface objects are now to be modeled.

We see that many of the use cases start with one window which is filled with information and then executed. New windows may also show up at later stages in the use case. Hence we can use these to identify the interface objects.

The modeling of the interface objects can be done at several different levels of granularity. The usual level is to model each window that should be displayed by an interface object. When doing this we use the sketches or prototypes already developed. Refer to Figure 13.8. This was the first window to be shown to a Foreman who wanted to perform the *Manual redistribution between warehouses*.

To model the structure of the window we use the widgets that are needed. How these really look in the User Interface Management Systems (UIMSs) or other class libraries which we shall use when implementing does not show here. That will be taken care of during construction. The structural description describes only what the user interface should comprise. We use a central interface object which represents the entire window and other interface objects to model the widgets. A structural view of the window is shown in Figure 13.9.

Many modern UIMSs support the modeling and creation of windows from the external view shown above. Some of them also support the adding of dynamic behavior behind the windows. In

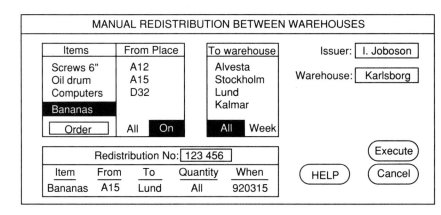

**Figure 13.8**  The window from the use case *Manual redistribution between warehouses*.

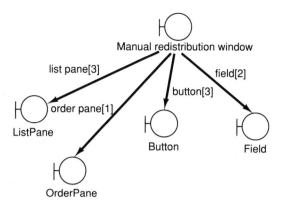

**Figure 13.9**   A structural model of the window for *Manual redistribution between warehouses*.

some projects, such UIMSs have been used in a successful manner, but since the above description of interface objects composed of other interface objects has much redundancy with the external view of the UIMSs, these projects have used another technique to model interfaces. In this technique interface objects are lifted one step. The central interface objects then represent all the windows that a certain actor will be able to view, while each window is represented by an interface object beneath it. An example for the Foreman view is shown in Figure 13.10.

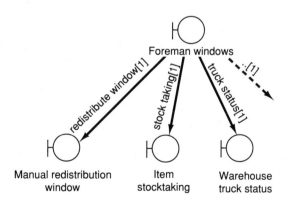

**Figure 13.10**   The possible windows of the Foreman.

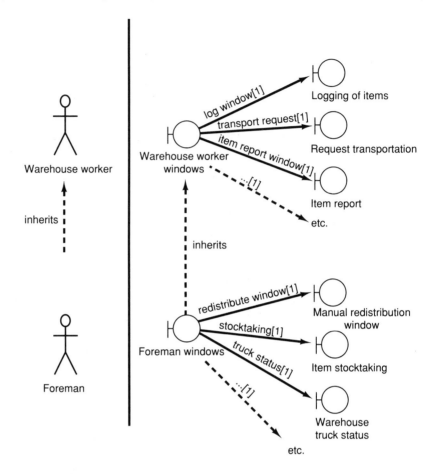

**Figure 13.11**    Inheritance of interface objects to reuse interface descriptions.

Here we suppose that we have a modern UIMS and thus follow the second strategy. With this technique we may therefore have one central interface object corresponding to each actor using a window system. To model the fact that the Foreman should be able to do everything that the Warehouse worker can do, we used inheritance between both actors – the Foreman inherited the Warehouse worker. When modeling the interface objects we may also reuse all the windows defined for the Warehouse worker when defining the Foreman's interface object. This may be expressed with inheritance between the interface object descriptions as shown in Figure 13.11.

To summarize, we will thus have the following central interface objects:

- Warehouse worker windows
- Foreman windows
- Office personnel windows
- Forklift radio
- Truck radio
- Barcode reader

The functionality of the use cases is thus placed in these interface objects. If we later want to change any of this functionality, for example when the foreman wants to relocate an item he could drag the icon representing the item and drop it on the icon representing the new location, such changes should only affect the interface objects associated with this functionality. Hence the objects 'behind' will not be affected.

Although the identification of the objects is normally an iterative process, it is often easiest to start by investigating the interface objects, since they are often evident in the use case specifications (pictures). Thereafter the **entity objects** often come naturally. We will now discuss the identification of the entity objects involved in the use cases previously discussed.

Basically we find the entity objects by reading the use case descriptions and looking for information that needs to be stored over a longer period of time. The problem domain objects are very good candidates for this, but are seldom enough. Entities are often quite easy to find and even if different people perform the identification, we have seen that the result is often very similar. We see that the system should manage information about Customer, Items, Warehouses, Truck, Warehouse places and so on. This is also confirmed when reading the use cases.

From the *Manual redistribution between warehouses* use case we also see that we need to store information about the new redistribution and the transport request (either an already existing one or a new one). A Redistribution entity object is thus identified in Initialization steps 2 and 7–9, Planning steps 1–2 and in Unloading step 7. The Transport request is noted in Planning step 24, Loading steps 1 and 5 and Unloading step 7. In Planning step 4 a Transportation plan is mentioned which should contain the Transport requests planned for a certain truck. One possibility is to have this as an attribute of the Truck entity object, but since the Planning part will use all these transportation plans to coordinate the transportation we choose to have it as a separate object. We need some entity object to hold this information as well. This is a typical example of what we discussed in Chapter 6 about an object model. Objects must be identified in the light of how they will be used, not as a stand-alone process. In another system the Transportation plan could very well be an attribute in the Truck entity object. Now Transportation plan is a complete list of all planned transportations relating Trucks with Transport requests.

When we identify the entity objects we notice that they have certain relations to each other. These relations are static in the sense that they are stored for a longer time. These static relations are modeled by acquaintance associations. Every such association has a name and a cardinality. An example of such an association is that we may say that a Redistribution should be performed by one Transport request. The entity objects and static associations identified in this use case are shown in Figure 13.12. Note that all associations are one-way only. If an acquaintance is needed the other way around too, a new association is needed. This is a significant and often subtle difference from many kinds of data modeling techniques.

Attributes cannot be attached to associations. Therefore we must model these attributes in some other way. Here we have such examples. Refer to the association Item–place [0..M]–Warehouse place. How many of the items have we stored at the Warehouse

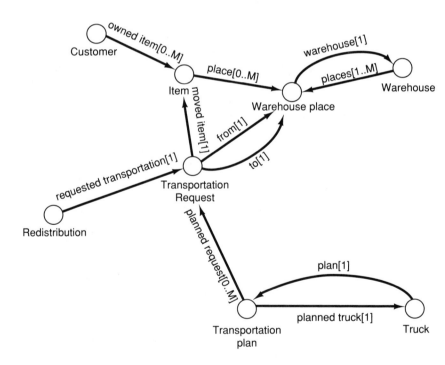

**Figure 13.12**    A first attempt at the entity object model for the use case *Manual redistribution between warehouses.*

place? We cannot have it as an attribute in the Item entity object since Items may be stored at several different places. Neither can we have it as an attribute in the Warehouse place entity object since several different kinds of Items may be stored at the same Warehouse place (the requirements have not defined how big the warehouse places are). So where should we store the information on the number of Items in a specific place?

There are two possibilities. If we think how this is likely to be coded, we will probably have a list to store association to the warehouse places. In this list we could add an attribute to each element to store the number of items in a specific place. If we consider the relational database and how the information should be stored, we will have one extra table for the association since it is of cardinality [1..M] (see Chapter 10). In this relation we could add an attribute to hold the number of Items at a specific place. Hence, when doing the design later on, it will be no problem to realize this attribute. The first alternative is therefore just to note down the attribute in the Item entity object description when describing the association.

If we also want to be able to check how many items are stored at a specific Warehouse place, this numerical information needs to be accessible from the Warehouse place entity object. The above solution would then not be appropriate, since we would need to store the number information in the Warehouse place entity object as well. Then we would have redundant information in the system and thus have difficulties in maintaining and updating the information. We should only store the information in one place and so we have to add a new entity object Number of to store this information, which the other two refer to as shown in Figure 13.13.

We choose to use the latter technique since we would probably want to know how many Items are stored at a specific Warehouse place in another use case. The problem of connecting information to associations also occurs in another place in the model. Between Tranportation request and Item we need to store how many items this request covers. But since we only have a cardinality of [1] and we do not need the inverse relation, there is no need to add an extra entity object in this case. Instead we note that this information should be stored at Transportation request. In this example there are no more cases of this problem. Thus the final entity object model will look like Figure 13.14.

The entity objects are thus:

- Item. The entity object holds information on its identity (name), any special storing or transport requirements and the total number in all warehouses (this may be calculated). It also

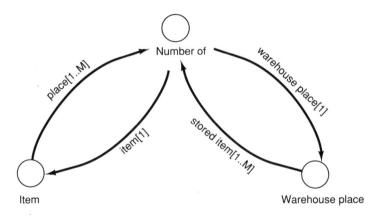

**Figure 13.13**  The entity object Number of represents the attributes of the relation between Item and Warehouse place.

has acquaintance with the owner (Customer) and where it is stored and how many are stored at that place.

- Number of. This holds information on how many items are stored at a specific Warehouse place.
- Warehouse place. This holds information on the name of the place and any special characteristics of it and also knows to which warehouse it belongs.
- Warehouse. This holds information on the identification (name) of the warehouse and its address and knows its associated warehouse places.
- Customer. The address and the customer number are attributes. It associates the Items that the customer owns.
- Transportation request. This keeps information on the number of Items to be moved, delivery dates and the status of the transport and associates what item to move with a source and destination for it. Concerns only one Item.
- Transportation plan. This is a list of Transportation requests that are planned for a certain Truck.
- Truck. This has information on the identification of the truck, its radio address, the driver of the truck, its maximum load and any other special characteristics of the truck, and associates its Transportation plan.
- Redistribution. This handles a redistribution order. It has information about the issuer and a redistribution log number and is handled by a Transportation request.

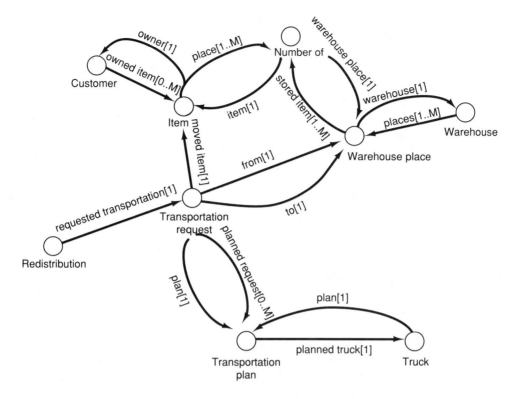

**Figure 13.14**   The final static entity object model covering the current use cases.

The description of an entity object includes its attributes, associations and possibly also operations identified for it (that is, the dynamic behavior of the entity object). The operations express how entity objects perform their task. They can also use operations on other entity objects. An example is when the truck wants to know from where to fetch an item. This may be an operation on Transportation plan which asks Transportation request to get a reference to the current warehouse. This may be fetched from the Warehouse place entity object. A reference to the Warehouse may thus be returned to the Transportation plan which asks the Warehouse for its identi-fication and then returns this to the Truck.

The acquaintance associations are used to model static references between entity objects. The dynamic relations between them are modeled by communication associations. In the previous example, there is a communication association from Transportation plan to the Warehouse (to get its name), but we do not need a static relation between them.

The acquaintance associations are also used to show how certain entity objects play different **roles** in the model. An example of this can be seen in the associations from the Transportation request to a Warehouse place. A specific Warehouse place may act as both the source and the destination of a transportation. Using associations to indicate different roles played by some objects is very effective since it significantly decreases the number of objects in the model and thus decreases the complexity of the model.

The **control object** is the third and last of the analysis object types. Its main purpose is to get a maintainable system and to increase the reusability potential of the model.

Control objects are also identified from the use cases. They mainly consist of behavior that we do not want to place in the entity objects, so as to get a looser coupling between different parts of the system. One reason for this is that the behavior placed in the control objects may change in a different way from the behavior associated with the entity objects.

The control objects are generated in two phases. The first is a rough attempt and generates one control object for each (abstract and concrete) use case. The reason for this is that every concrete use case represents behavior that should be tied together and the abstract ones represent behavior that will be shared by different use cases. In the first phase we name the control objects and it is often easiest to give them the same names as the use cases. In our example the initial control objects will thus be:

- Manual redistribution between warehouses
- Customer ordered withdrawal of items
- Redistribution of items within a warehouse

When this first attempt has been made, which can be done mechanically, we will allocate the behavior from the use cases to the objects identified so far. This forms the second phase of the identification of control objects and is much harder than the first phase. Now we see whether a control object is really needed or whether we need to add new ones. Often trade-offs must be made between the potential reusability of the model and the effort you want to put into it. In the second phase better and more appropriate names should be given to them. These are often more noun-like.

Let us look more closely at the use case *Manual redistribution between warehouses*. The Initialization part will be handled completely by the interface objects which will directly access the entity objects that have the information to be shown. Here a control object will not be needed since there is a simple correspondence between presentation and information. The interface object will also create a Redistribution object when the actor executes the redistribution (see Figure 13.15).

The Planning part of the use case is more complex, though. Planning step 1 will be performed by the Redistribution entity object. Steps 2–4 coordinate the activity of several entity objects not naturally associated with any special object in the model. One possibility is to assign it to one of the control objects already introduced, namely Manual redistribution between warehouses, but it seems more like a special activity that can be used in several different use cases. Therefore we introduce a new control object, Planner, that performs this planning activity.

The Loading part of the use case starts when a Truck driver gets his current Transport request (step 1). He then starts an activity to coordinate the withdrawal, transportation and insertion of items. This activity is naturally performed by the control object identified for this concrete use case. We see now that there are actually two activities going on here – one inside the warehouses currently storing the items and one to coordinate the entire transportation to another warehouse. So it seems that our first attempt at the control objects will fit very well into this use case. Hence the control object Redistribution of items within a warehouse will handle all activities inside a warehouse (that is, steps 2 and 3). This will now be a general and reusable control object that coordinates one transportation request inside a warehouse. This means that the original idea of having it as an abstract reusable use case was correct. It will be a

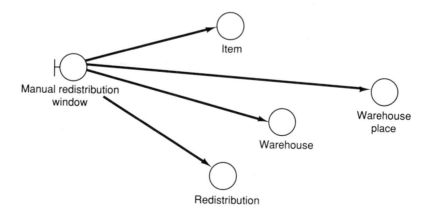

**Figure 13.15**   The Initialization part illustrated schematically.

special part of the system that can be used in several different use cases. To have a shorter, more noun-like name for the object, we rename it *Local warehouse transporter*. The other steps in this part of the use case (that is, steps 1, 4 and 5) can be handled by the other control object. (Possibly the behavior of step 1 will not need any control objects. This we will see more obviously later.) Thus the control object initially called Manual redistribution between warehouses will handle all activities that coordinate the transport between warehouses. This may now be renamed Interwarehouse Transporter.

The Unloading part of the use case will be provided by these objects. Steps 1, 2, 5, 6 and 7 will be managed by Interwarehouse transporter while steps 3 and 4 can reuse the control object Local Warehouse Transporter.

Thus the following control objects have been identified as participating in the use case *Manual redistribution between warehouses*:

- Interwarehouse Transporter, which handles the transportation of items between warehouses including some parts of the coordination of trucks and forklifts;
- Local Warehouse Transporter, which manages transportation inside a warehouse including some part of the coordination of trucks and forklifts;
- Planner, which plans and issues transport requests and inserts them in the appropriate truck's transportation plan.

We have stressed the coordination of the trucks and the forklifts. This is because two different control objects (actually three since Local Warehouse Transporter will be instantiated twice in every use case) must interact with each other, which is quite complicated. In the design they will probably be distributed and thus communicate over a computer network. We will focus more on this during the construction.

When **allocating behavior to the simple objects**, important decisions are made concerning how the objects will depend on each other. Refer to Figure 13.16 where we have used the interaction diagram technique to illustrate the relationships between objects. In case (*a*) the control object Interwarehouse Transporter knows of the existence and the protocols of both the entity objects Transportation request and Truck. The control object here accesses the Transportation request to get a reference to the right Truck. The Transportation Request knows about the existence of the Truck (actually indirectly, since it uses its Transportation Plan to get the reference – see the entity object model), but not about the Truck's protocol since it doesn't access it. In case (*b*) the control object does not need to access the

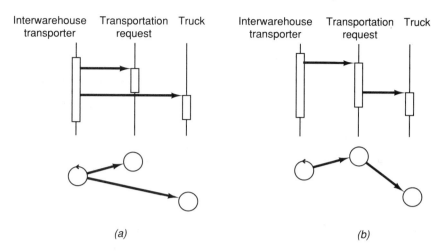

Figure 13.16   Two alternative ways of allocating the use case behavior to simple objects.

Truck directly, hence it is not dependent on its protocol or even its existence. When to use which approach was discussed in the analysis and construction chapters.

To illustrate schematically how the behavior of a use case is distributed over the objects, **use case views** over the objects are often drawn. In these views we include the objects and associations that participate in the specific use case. The union of all such views should become the entire model. Since, for instance, only the acquaintance associations used in the specific use case exist in these views, it is essential not to become confused when two objects that apparently should be associated are not associated in the view; they may very well be associated, but the association is not used in this particular use case.

We have drawn such use case views over objects for the use case *Manual redistribution between warehouses*. Since it is a large use case, we have drawn one view for every part of the use case instead of one for the entire use case. The initialization part of the use case is shown in Figure 13.17, Planning in Figure 13.18, Loading in Figure 13.19 and Unloading in Figure 13.20. In some views only communication associations are shown.

We will describe the Loading part in more detail to explain how we have arrived at this picture. The loading part starts when a truck driver asks for a Transportation request. The Interwarehouse Transporter asks the Truck for its next Transportation request which is found via the Transportation plan. The request is marked as ongoing.

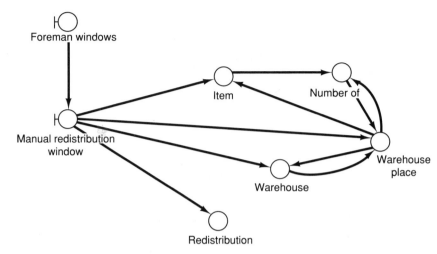

**Figure 13.17** The initialization part of the *Manual redistribution between warehouses* use case. We have used communication associations to illustrate the dynamic flow over the objects.

It also returns the Warehouse name. The time that the truck driver estimates he or she will be at the new place is attached to the Transportation request. The Interwarehouse Transporter then initiates the Local Warehouse Transporter which finds an unoccupied Forklift. The Forklift also gets information on what items to move, from where and how many. When all the prerequisites are ready, the commands

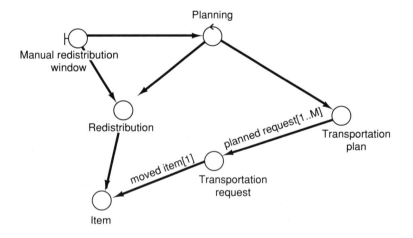

**Figure 13.18**   The Planning part of the use case.

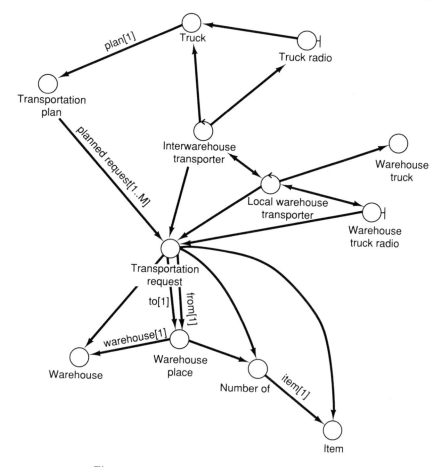

**Figure 13.19**  The Loading part of the use case.

are returned to the Interwarehouse Transporter. That object waits for the truck to arrive. When the truck driver signals that the items have been loaded, the expected arrival time at the destination warehouse is stored in the Transportation Request. The number of items shipped is then decremented at this warehouse.

The use case views are quite extensive. It can be quite hard to find all the dynamic associations.

A structure that often appears is shown in Figure 13.21. A control object or an entity object hands a reference to an object over to another object. This object then accesses the referenced object. This structure often encourages reuse since the accessing object does not need to know which object it is sending messages to; the only

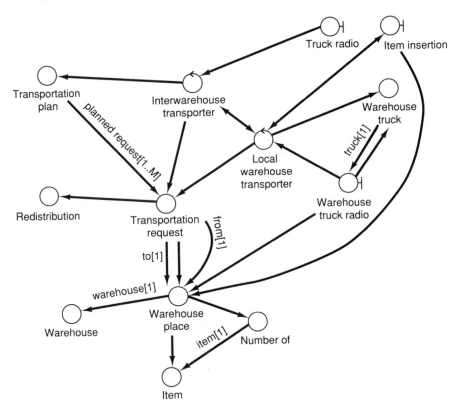

**Figure 13.20** The Unloading part of the use case.

requirement is that the accessed object can respond to these messages. For instance, the interface object Forklift radio asks for radioNetworkAddress and is not interested in which kind of object answers.

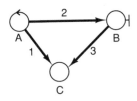

**Figure 13.21** A common structure to facilitate reuse is when an object A gives a reference of an object C to another object B. Then B accesses C.

### 13.4.2 Subsystems

The lowest level of subsystem is a unit of configuration designed for management purposes. It contains a group of objects that represent a self-contained piece of functionality. It also represents a part of the system that a customer either wants in its entirety or does not want at all. As an example, a subsystem of a wordprocessing program could be a tool for spell checking or for hyphenation.

Subsystems are also used as a basis for change; each change proposal should ideally affect only one subsystem. Furthermore, they are used as a basis for the transition from analysis to construction. All these different uses complicate the task of deriving subsystems from the objects.

From the objects, we can see quite clearly that some of them are needed for transportation between warehouses while some are only needed within one specific warehouse. When considering ordering criteria, we may want to be able to deliver a part which deals with adding another warehouse to the system. Other changes in the system can come from changes inside a warehouse or changes that affect interwarehouse communication. Hence there seem to be good reasons for using these considerations as our first basic criteria when dividing the system.

When further reviewing the objects (including other use cases), we see that some objects are used mainly to manage the system information while some objects are used to perform the transportation. Since these two areas are very much 'self-contained pieces of functionality' and also may have a different frequency in their changes, we should also use this information as a criterion for the division. Thus we now have four subsystems, namely:

- Single Warehouse Management
- Multiple Warehouse Management
- Local Warehouse Transportation
- Interwarehouse Transportation

Attaching the objects to these four subsystems is now quite easy, but when reviewing the objects once more in view of potential changes in the system, we see one object which will probably be changed quite often initially. That is the Planning object. We have not discussed the planning strategy here, but there are many ways of creating a fast and effective planner. One possibility is to use techniques from artificial intelligence to do the planning. We will probably need to simulate and prototype the planner to make it effective, but even then we will probably want to optimize it when we have had some experience with the system in operation. Additionally, since the system will execute in a dynamic environment, many of the plans will be inexecutable because something which invalidates them has happened in the environment. Then we may need to replan to adapt to the new circumstances. The areas of planning and replanning are currently evolving fast in the AI community. Hence there are many reasons to isolate the planning object so as to handle future changes more easily. Therefore we add one subsystem object to handle the planning.

When attaching the objects to a specific subsystem, we must be aware of one thing. If the system is to be used only within a single warehouse (a quite reasonable guess), we will only deliver the subsystems that are local to a warehouse. Therefore all objects that are fundamental to the system should be placed in the single warehouse subsystem to be sure that they will always be delivered.

Hence the subsystems will be as follows, each containing the objects listed.

(1) Single Warehouse Management
   (a) Item
   (b) Number of
   (c) Warehouse place
   (d) Transportation request
   (e) Item insertion
(2) Multiple Warehouse Management
   (a) Warehouse
   (b) Redistribution
   (c) Manual redistribution window
(3) Interwarehouse Transportation
   (a) Interwarehouse transporter
   (b) Transportation plan
   (c) Truck
   (d) Truck radio
(4) Local Warehouse Transportation
   (a) Local warehouse transporter
   (b) Forklift
   (c) Forklift radio
(5) Planning
   (a) Planning

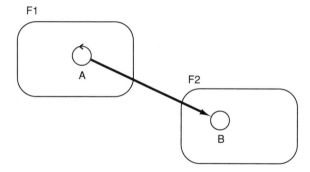

**Figure 13.22**   An example of a dependency between subsystems. The control object A accesses the entity object B. This leads to a dependency between the subsystems F1 and F2.

Almost all the other subsystems use objects in Single Warehouse Management. It contains the basics of what we need to run the warehouse management system (from the perspective of the use case *Manual redistribution between warehouses*). All different configurations of the system must have at least this subsystem.

Different subsystems have different purposes. The subsystem Interwarehouse Transportation contains the objects needed for transportation between warehouses. Local Warehouse Transportation contains the objects needed for transportation within a warehouse. Multiple Warehouse Management's purpose is to handle the functionality that makes it possible to manage many warehouses. Planning takes care of using the trucks as economically as possible.

A subsystem is said to be dependent on another subsystem if at least one of its objects is dependent on an object (that is, associates it in some way) in the other subsystem. In Figure 13.22 we see an example of a dependency between two subsystems. The dependency originates from the association between the two objects.

Dependencies between subsystems limit the number of possible configurations of the system. The dependencies between the subsystems in the example are shown in Figure 13.23; they are derived from the associations in the use case *Manual redistribution between warehouses*.

Figure 13.24 shows one of the possible configurations of the system.

We have here identified subsystems when the object model has been completed. Sometimes it is more appropriate to identify them earlier, often before you identify the objects.

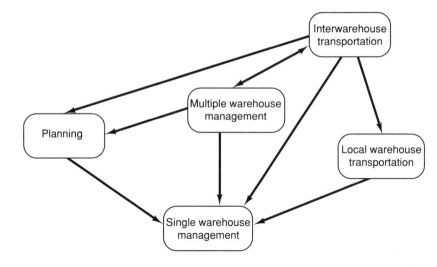

**Figure 13.23**   Dependencies between the subsystems of the example system.

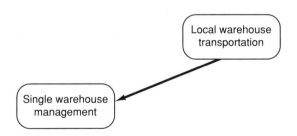

**Figure 13.24**   A possible configuration given the dependencies between the subsystems.

## 13.5   Construction

The analysis model has now been developed under ideal conditions. It is mainly a logical model of the system which takes no acount of the current implementation environment. The main purpose of the construction and implementation process is to customize this logical model for a specific implementation environment and to implement the system.

### 13.5.1   Identify the implementation environment

To do this customizing we need to analyze the current implementation environment. This analysis should aim to clarify strategic questions for the implementation and draw conclusions on how to implement certain tasks. In our example we need to clarify how to handle the distributed environment, the relational database, distribution of the database, the radio network, and incorporation of results from the UIMS, for example. Many of these questions have several answers and it is important to choose one before starting the actual design. This is to avoid redoing things later and having different solutions adopted by different developers.

Ideally, the implementation environment should be specified from requirements that have evolved from the analysis work and the implementation analysis. Then we will have the implementation environment that is ideal from our perspective. However, this is seldom the case in practice. In our example we had the prerequisites of using C++ and a relational database. These prerequisites are actually quite good. C++ is one of the more efficient and widespread OO languages and is also appropriate here. A relational database is also quite appropriate in this case. The data structures in the example are quite simple and thus an RDBMS will probably give better performance than an ODBMS. However, we would need support for a distributed database.

How to handle all the specific parts in the implementation environment is not something that OOSE controls. Normal software engineering practice should be used and techniques used elsewhere are often also appropriate here. In this book we have illustrated some examples of how to handle these issues (for example, databases, programming language and real-time systems). However, our experience shows that you should strive to encapsulate consequences of the implementation environment as far as possible. This is in order to spoil the logical structure as little as possible and also to encapsulate potential changes in the implementation environment. In this example we will not do an entire analysis of the actual implementation environment, but rather give some examples of how to reason when analyzing and handling it.

When analyzing a system like this it is often appropriate to start from the major structure of the system, namely the system **hardware configuration**. In the example we see that the system will be spread over several sites, namely the warehouses and the office. We can then either have one central mainframe to serve all these users or have a decentralized structure using several computers. Since there is no natural central site, but rather the system has a very decentralized nature, we choose a decentralized structure. Thus the office needs one server and each warehouse also need a server. The office personnel and the foremen will be clients of these servers. The warehouse workers and the forklift operators will also be clients of the servers located at the warehouse sites. The truck drivers will communicate with the system from several different places. Choosing one specific server for them is harder since they will not be tied to any specific warehouse. One possibility is to give them the office computer as a server; another is to allow them to be distributed and to connect to the server which is closest at any particular moment. Since many network facilities today support this latter facility, and also because the future in telecommunications is going in this direction, we choose to allow the truck driver to use the closest site as his or her server. In the future customers should also be able to use the system as clients. Then it should be possible for them to use the closest site as their server. Thus it is appropriate now to prepare for dynamic use of the servers. Our client/server model and structure will thus look like Figure 13.25.

The distributed nature of the system must be supported by some kind of network. This network would probably be the public telecommunication network. There are existing products to handle this distribution which can very well be used here. In our system we use such facilities and do not develop this part ourselves, but instead use an existing product. What we do need, however, is to design an interface to this product so that our system will not be too dependent on the chosen product. It should also be possible to change the communication product with as few changes as possible to our system.

In larger systems it is also essential to consider how the system should be configured, managed and delivered. When identifying the subsystems we did the first analysis of this. If it is not done before, it is essential to do a final analysis and decide upon the product structure here. In our example we see that the subsystems identified earlier are still appropriate  here. The subsystem Single Warehouse Management must be delivered to each specific warehouse. The other warehouse subsystems must also be delivered to each warehouse with the capability to communicate with other warehouses. Although the office should only need the subsystems that are needed for distribution, we see from the dependency between them (see Figure 13.23) that the single warehouse subsystem is also needed. We have not identified subsystems especially for the office, but some subsystems will only be needed at the office site.

When discussing the distributed nature of our system let us also discuss how to distribute the database; first the realization of it.

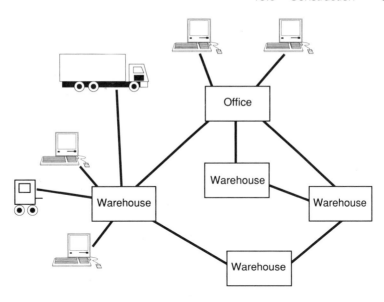

**Figure 13.25** An example of the physical configuration of the sytem. The boxes represents servers in the systems while the trucks and terminals represent clients to these servers.

Commercial *distributed databases* exist. The best solution is to use one of them to avoid developing and maintaining this facility yourself. It is often best to build a homogeneous database initially, that is, one with all sites running the same DBMS; but during further development, when extending the network, it is seldom possible to maintain this situation. Then we will have a heterogeneous system, that is, we might have different kinds of DBMS in the network. This is a likely change to the system and we should therefore prepare for it in the design.

A major benefit of a distributed database is that data is stored close to the place where it is most frequently used, thus giving high performance at the same time as increased accessibility of information in the entire system. One of the major drawbacks when using a distributed database is that the network is often far too slow. Therefore how you structure the database is very important. The goal is to minimize the communication over the network. We must therefore analyze how frequently the objects will be used at different sites. When considering the analysis model, we see that it does not provide a direct map from a particular object to a specific site where the object will be used. For instance, the Item object will be used from almost all sites. The same goes for almost all objects in the system.

This means that almost all objects in the system must be distributed and thus dependent on the communication product discussed earlier. We will discuss how to handle this shortly.

To incorporate the relational database in the object-oriented structure of the system we will use the guidelines given earlier in Chapter 10. For a discussion on the topic, please refer to that chapter.

To communicate with the truck drivers, a radio network will be used. This network is also an existing product that we should use. There are products that can be programmed to adapt them for the messages to be sent and displayed. The interface objects should therefore be designed as interfaces to this network. This means that we will not have any problems with the distributed nature of the network – the network will handle that – but we do need to cope with unique radio addresses; however, that will surely be a part of the interface to the network at every site. This is also true for the forklifts; they will also be handled by a commercially available radio network. This means that a truck needs a unique identification not only within a certain site, but also within all warehouses and offices connected to the system.

### 13.5.2    The block structure

We have discussed some of the preconditions to consider when developing the preliminary block structure. We will now look at some examples of ways to handle the implementation environment in order to keep a logical, and thus stable, structure as far as possible.

The ideal block structure would be to take the complete analysis model and map it directly onto a block structure: but is that possible in this case? Let us look at the consequences from the implementation environment analysis. We start with the distribution. One example of blocks that should be spread over several sites is the block corresponding to the Item object. Since the Item objects each belong to a specific warehouse it is natural to place the particular instances at the site where the item is stored: but how do we solve the distribution? The first intuitive picture is to have one block at every site, with the blocks communicating with each other when they need to do so: but this means that when another block needs to communicate with the Item block it needs to know at which site the block exists. This knowledge is not natural for other blocks, but should belong to the Item block itself. Hence we should encapsulate the distribution of the block as discussed in Chapter 9. One way of doing this is to use the classes in the blocks. We then have an instance of one class that represents the existence of the items at this site. This instance receives stimuli from other parts of the system at this particular site. If the information does not exist at this site, we have to go out on the network and fetch the information. This means that we should have one class that looks up a particular instance of the Item, either at this site or on the network; one class that represents the existence of the Item at this site; one class that works as the interface to the network; and one class that receives signals from the network to this particular Item (see Figure 13.26).

We see that this design idea can be applicable to all blocks that share the same property of being distributed. Therefore we may very well form an abstract block that all distributed blocks may inherit. Such a reusable design is often called a **framework.** The distributed block thus consists of the network classes NetworkOut and NetworkIn and a general LookUp class, possibly having only virtual member functions (in C++). The network classes will then be the only classes dependent on the current network; a change in the network will only affect these two classes. This block, called the Distributed block, is shown in Figure 13.27.

By designing the distribution in this manner we can design the use cases without having to think about how to find a particular instance in the network. All this behavior will be encapsulated inside the block.

To incorporate the relational database in the system we will use the design discussed in Chapter 10. This gives us a block which will function as the interface to the DBMS. The design framework used also has an abstract block that specifies how the conversion from the OO system to the RDBMS functions. This block should be

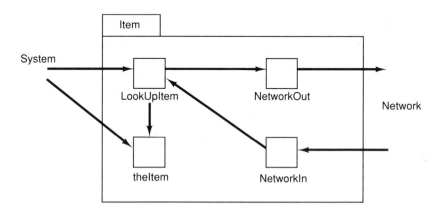

**Figure 13.26** The initial design of the Item block. Classes are used to encapsulate the actual distribution of the block.

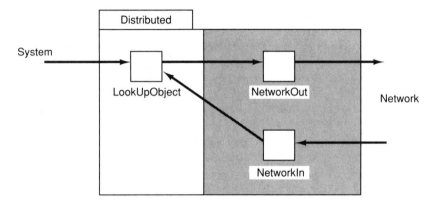

**Figure 13.27**   An abstract Distributed block that will be inherited by all blocks that should be distributed in the system. This block forms a framework for the design of other blocks. Note that some classes are private.

inherited by all blocks that will have the ability to store their information in the database. This means that blocks that should be both distributed and stored in the database need to inherit both the Persistent block and the Distributed block. Can we solve this with only single inheritance? We can, if we have an inheritance hierarchy as shown in Figure 13.28(*a*) or (*b*). However, each of these produces unwanted consequences: in case (*a*) all Distributed blocks must be persistent; and in case (*b*) all Persistent blocks must be distributed. In case (*c*) we can have these two abilities independent of each other. Case (*c*) is an example of subtyping (see Chapter 3) with multiple inheritance. Here there are two roles which we want to reuse in several blocks, the roles of distribution and persistence. We choose to use the last alternative here.

Since the Distributed block and the Persistent block may have a general integration which can be made independently of the actual concrete block, we add a new block which incorporates these two blocks. This block is called the Distributed Persistent block and it inherits the two blocks Distributed and Persistent, as shown in Figure 13.29. Since some blocks may be only persistent or distributed but not both, we also need to retain the two blocks just as they are. This will also be a benefit when we want to modify the persistence or the distribution; the modification will be local and easy to isolate.

We also need to cooperate with the radio network. Since the main functionality will come from an existing network system which will be used in our system, we need to design the interface to the network system. This may very well be designed as a component to

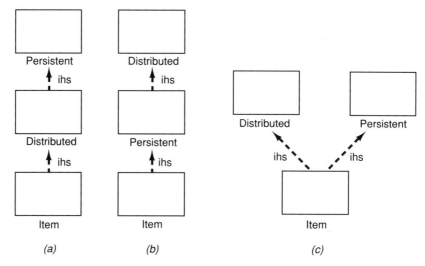

**Figure 13.28** Inheritance hierarchies to get both the ability to be stored in the database and the ability to be distributed. In case (a) all distributed blocks must be persistent while only some blocks (those inheriting Persistent) may be persistent. In case (b) all persistent blocks must be distributed since the Persistent block inherits the Distributed block. In case (c) it is possible to have both abilities independent of each other.

be used in the network block. The actual network will thus be encapsulated in the radio network block.

The block structure has now grown to constitute a first attempt at considering some of the consequences of the implementation environment. All blocks that should be distributed and persistent will inherit from the Distributed Persistence block. This accounts for practically all blocks that come from entity objects.

We will here continue to focus on the use case *Manual redistribution between warehouses*. The block diagram for the first part of the use case will look like Figure 13.30. Here we have used the analysis model with very small modifications; the only change is that we have removed the Number of entity object which was used to express how many Items are stored at a specific Warehouse place. Instead, we have drawn the communication associations as bidirectional since both blocks will initiate stimulus sending. The reason that the Number of block is excluded is that the attribute will be a column in the table connecting Item and Warehouse place since the association between them is [0..M]. In that table we can include the information. The information can also be attached to the references between the classes in the blocks in C++. Thus it would be overkill to have a block for this information.

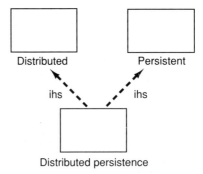

**Figure 13.29**  Since many blocks will both be distributed and persistent, we add a new block that integrates these two features. All blocks that need these two abilities will inherit from this particular block.

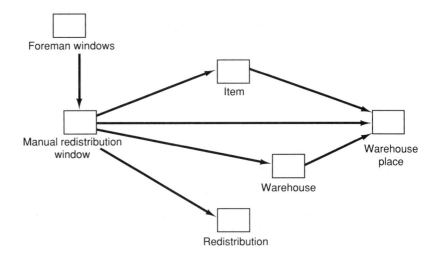

**Figure 13.30**  Block diagram for the first part of the use case *Manual redistribution between warehouses.*

Block diagrams over the other part of the use case will be discussed when we design the use cases over the blocks.

### 13.5.3  Use case design

We will now look at the design of the use case *Manual redistribution between warehouses,* for which we will use interaction diagrams. The division into four parts will also be used here. To recall the Initialization part of the use case, we give it here again.

---

*Initialization*

(1) The Foreman gives a command for redistribution between warehouses.

(2) The window in Figure 13.31 is presented to the Foreman.

(3) The items can be ordered in a number of ways. This is selected with the ORDER menu. The following orders are possible:

    (*a*) Alphabetical order

    (*b*) Index order (each item has a unique number)

    (*c*) Turnover of the items

    (*d*) Storing order

(4) In the 'From place' table we might select to view either all places in the current warehouse or, if we have selected an item, the places where that item exists.

(5) In the 'To warehouse' table we might select all warehouses or the warehouses to which we have to transport items to this week.

(6) The 'Issuer' and 'Warehouse' field are automatically filled when the window pops up, but they might be changed. (This is the way to do a redistribution from another warehouse to our own warehouse.)

(7) The Foreman selects an item by pointing to it and dragging it to the Redistribution form. He or she then selects from which place to take the items and to which warehouse to transport them. This information is automatically shown in the form.

---

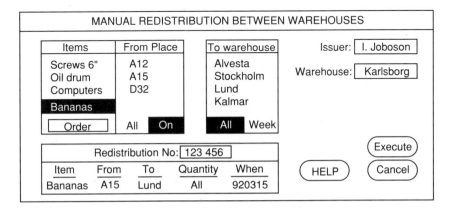

**Figure 13.31** *Manual redistribution between warehouses* window.

8) The Foreman then gives the quantity to be moved (a possibility is to choose 'ALL') and then a date by when it must be done.

(9) It is possible to change the information when the form has been edited. When the Foreman EXECUTES the redistribution, the transports are planned. It is also possible to CANCEL the redistribution as such. Selecting HELP shows a window of information about the current window.

This sequence will now be distributed over the blocks participating in the use case and we will now define the stimuli sent between the blocks. The interaction diagram corresponding to the Initialization part of the use case is shown in Figure 13.32. This diagram shows the typical behavior of external events. Many events may happen in an arbitrary order. Every external event gives rise to some action inside the system.

In the interaction diagram we see that almost all events are directly triggered from an operation on the window. We thus have no complex sequences in this diagram. This we could have guessed, since we do not have any blocks originating from a control object which are typically found in more complex sequences. Let us continue by looking at the next part of the use case, namely the Planning part. The first use case description looked like this:

*Planning*
(1) When the redistribution is executed, the items to be moved are marked as reserved.
(2) The planning should minimize the use of the trucks within the terms of the condition that all delivery dates should be held and the trucks should fit any item delivery requirements (for example, size). This should be done by adjusting existing, already planned redistributions to take account of the new redistribution requirements.
(3) This may give rise to new transport requests and may also change existing transport requests already in the system.
(4) The transport requests are connected to a specific truck's transportation plan.

To draw the interaction diagram we first look at the block diagram. Since all objects in this model will be substantial, the block diagram will be a direct map of the analysis model. The diagram is shown in Figure 13.33.

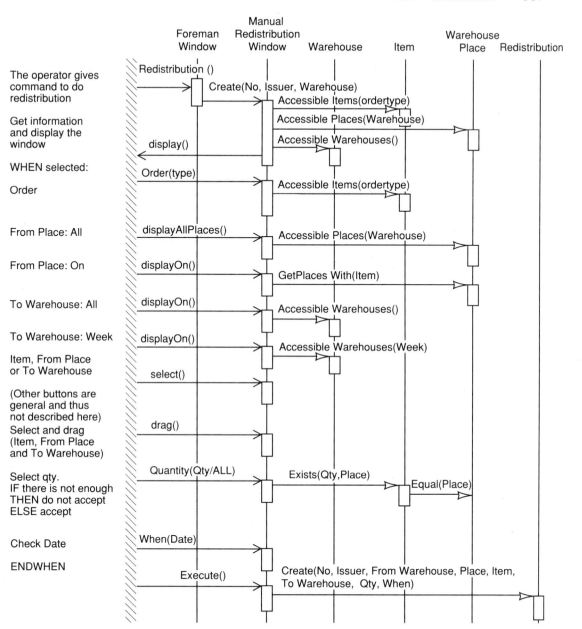

**Figure 13.32** The interaction diagram for the Initialization part of the use case. Note the typical structuring from external events coming into the window block.

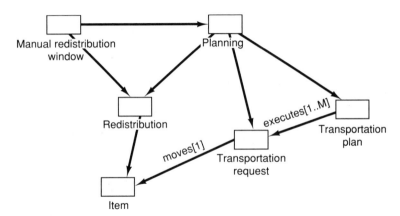

**Figure 13.33**   The block diagram for the Planning part of the use case. This is a direct mapping from the analysis model.

The interaction diagram of this part of the use case is shown in Figure 13.34. Note that much of the behavior has been centralized in the Planning block. The reason for this is the changeability of the planning routine discussed earlier; we believed that it would change and be optimized quite frequently. Therefore the behavior is not distributed, but rather kept together. Note also how the stimuli have been designed to be reusable. The Add(...) stimulus to Transportation Request has been used twice. It would be possible to include this behavior in the Create(. . .) stimuli, but since we might like to do creation separately from the addition of information in a request, we have designed two stimuli for this. Additionally, if the Create(...) stimuli involved the Add(. . .) information, a change in this information would affect two stimuli instead of one. The other parts of this use case are designed in the same way.

In this fashion all use cases are designed, the behavior is distributed over the blocks and the interfaces between the blocks are specified. This is an iterative process where use cases are designed and the block structure and stimuli are modified. In practice it is very hard to design the use cases in detail without having any simulation tools. One possibility is to design a use case and simultaneously implement the interfaces of the classes. In C++ this means that the header files will be developed during the use case design. The body files may be implemented with stubs in this phase. Then you are directly able to simulate your use case design and thus develop the interaction diagrams close to the code in an incremental manner. The use case design then helps you to find the interfaces to the classes while the classes help you to verify your design incrementally. We will now look at how the blocks are designed from this.

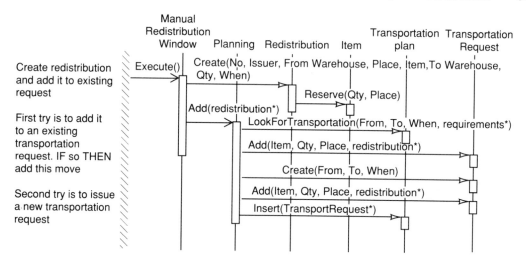

**Figure 13.34**  The Planning part of the use case distributed over the blocks involved in the sequence.

### 13.5.4  Block design

Block designation can start when the design of the use cases becomes stable. From the use cases we will have detailed specifications of the protocols of the block and the behavior associated with these protocols. The task is now to decide upon an implementation of the block. The first sketch has already been made when making the first attempt at a block structure under the contraints of the implementation environment. This design will now be refined and finally implemented.

We will here focus on the Item block and only take into consideration the protocol identified in the use case design described above. When doing the design of all use cases we would have a much larger protocol, but the idea should be clear. The rest is a straightforward realization in the same manner as described here. From the use case design described above we can identify the following signatures of the Item block:

AccessibleItems(ordertype)
Exists(Qty, Place)
Reserve(Oty, Place)

This identification is done merely by looking at the column representing the block Item. This is a mechanical extraction which can be automated.

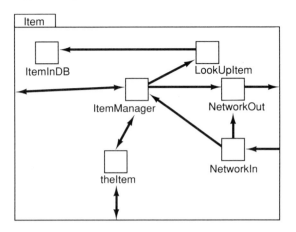

**Figure 13.35**   The detailed structure of the Item block.

To realize the block let us look at the first attempt at the structuring of the block. Since Item will be both persistent and distributed, the block will inherit from the Distributed persistent block. We will thus have a structure that looks like Figure 13.35.

The classes are explained below:

- ItemManager manages all Item instances at this site and also can give requests on the network to other sites. It inherits from the abstract class Manager.

- theItem is the actual Item object with state and operations. It inherits from the class Persistent.

- LookUpItem finds the item in the database from a specific key.

- ItemInDB: when LookUpItem finds an Item it creates instances of this class. When the Item is needed in the system an instance of theItem is created by ItemManager and information from this instance is converted to instances of theItem. The reason for having two classes for this is that not all instance variables of theItem will necessarily be stored in the database. It inherits from the class ObjectInDB.

- NetworkIn and Out are interface components to handle the network.

When looking at the protocol we can assign the signatures to specific classes. The AccessibleItems() and Exists() functions will handle several instances of the Item while the Reserve() function will be called on a specific instance of theItem. We thus have the following header files for the classes of ItemManager and theItem:

```
enum ordertype {alphabetical, index, turnover, storing};
class ItemManager: private Manager {
public:
    list AccessibleItems(ordertype order);
    boolean Exists(int Qty, storePlace Place);
    //.  .  .
private:

    .  .  .

    };
class theItem: public Persistent {
public:
    status Reserve(int Qty, storePlace Place);
    //.  .  .
private:

    .  .  .

    };
```

This is a direct mapping onto C++ member function definitions from the interfaces extracted from the interaction diagrams. The implementation of these functions may initially be done using stubs, as discussed above, and later refined into the actual code. The benefit is that you are able to simulate the use cases in the code as you develop them. The final implementation may then evolve from these stubs.

When implementing the blocks, new stimuli will arise from sequences not described in any interaction diagrams. In particular, flows that are internal to the block and not shown outside will be added. These flows are internal and thus hidden from the outside, that is, they describe the internal implementation of the block and are up to the block designer to implement. Other additional flows that often arise are error flows, namely flows that will arise when errors occur. These will also be added later to make the system robust.

Here we have only outlined the analysis and construction of the system. The real system includes many more use cases and interaction diagrams. The use of existing products has also only been outlined. Since this is not unique to OOSE, but common to all larger system developments, we have not described it in detail. Also, we have discussed implementation in outline only. This is due to the fact that this book does not cover programming techniques; there are other excellent books on this topic. We hope, though, that the strategy for reaching the code is clear. Neither have we mentioned anything about how to organize the system into files and file structures. This must also be handled. Components have been mentioned briefly while testing has been omitted. Quality assurance, metrics and bad design decisions have also been left out. The reader should understand by now that the development of real software systems needs extensive support from a well-defined development process, something that is only touched upon in this book. For real system development a far more comprehensive process description is needed.

# 14 Case study: telecom

## 14.1 Introduction

This chapter describes the development of a telecom switching system. The focus is on the parts handling a local phone call between two subscribers connected to the same switch. We first discuss the functionality of switching systems in general and the specific requirements of the parts on which we are to focus. We then develop the different models concerning this functionality. We use Smalltalk to illustrate the imple-mentation, although Smalltalk is not (yet) widely used in this application area.

## 14.2 Telecommunication switching systems

Before looking at the requirements of the functionality to be developed, we will give a very short and simplified introduction to the world of telephone exchanges. An exchange connects subscribers with each other. The subscriber that calls is called the **A-subscriber.** As she or he dials the number, the exchange analyzes the digits and looks up the line to the subscriber to be called. This subscriber is called the **B-subscriber.** The exchange then connects the lines of the two subscribers so that they can talk to each other. When they have finished, they put their telephone handsets down (called on-hook in the telecommunications world; picking up the phone is called off-hook) and this makes the exchange disconnect the two lines. Normally, a subscriber can be both an A-subscriber and a B-subscriber, but in a specific phone call he or she can only play one of the two roles.

Every unit connected to the switching system is called a **device**. A line to or from a subscriber, for example, is a device. This implies that each specific subscriber is connected to a certain exchange. Each subscriber has two associated physical devices, an **A-subscriber line** and a **B-subscriber line**. These devices are used to make outgoing calls and to accept incoming calls. Since a larger telecommunication network cannot be handled by one exchange alone, devices can also be **incoming lines** or **outgoing lines** to other exchanges (see Figure 14.1). An incoming line is connected to an A-subscriber in another exchange, while an outgoing line directs the call to a B-subscriber in another exchange. When a subscriber wants to call a subscriber connected to another switching system, she or he uses outgoing lines on the system to connect to the other system's incoming lines.

A **route** is a collection of outgoing lines, all in one specific direction, such as all lines from one exchange to another. To communicate with the other system, our system will choose one outgoing line from the route in that direction. It is of no interest which line in the route is used; so long as it is not busy, the system can use any free line in the route.

Before we start defining the requirements of the functionality, we will make some general assumptions:

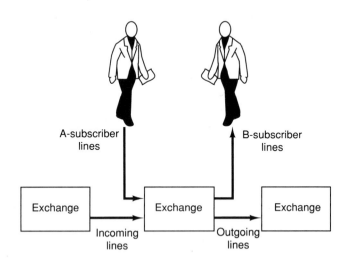

**Figure 14.1**    A schematic picture of a telecommunication network.

- A subscriber is assumed to have two identities: a subscriber number known among subscribers and found in the telephone directory, and a physical external identity used by the maintenance personnel.
- It is assumed that hardware associated with each subscriber will recognize whether an off-hook is performed as the beginning of a new call or as an answer to a call.
- All devices have an external physical identity.
- Each route has a unique identity.
- In our example system, for simplicity, we will not directly include the application hardware, but instead consider the hardware as part of the underlying system.

Now let us turn to the actual functional requirements. The requirements specification is separated into two parts:

- Call handling
- Operation and maintenance

**Call handling**      *Call between A-subscriber Line and B-subscriber Line.* When an A-subscriber lifts his handset, it results in the following actions being taken by the system. First the subscriber category is checked to see whether the subscriber is allowed to make outgoing calls. If so, the system marks the subscriber as being busy for incoming calls, and returns the dial tone. The dialling tone indicates that the system is ready to receive digits. The dialling tone is disconnected when the first digit is received. After dialling all digits, the A-subscriber will be connected to the B-subscriber.

If the B-subscriber is idle and if her category allows incoming calls, she will be marked busy and the A-subscriber and the B-subscriber will be connected. When the connection is performed, the B-subscriber will get a ringing signal and the A-subscriber will receive a ringing tone. Both these signals will be interrupted when the B-subscriber answers. In a normal call, the two subscribers talk to each other for some while before disconnection. The call will be disconnected when both the A-subscriber and the B-subscriber have cleared. Then both subscribers are marked idle and they are disconnected.

If one of the parties clears, the call is continued if the party that has cleared lifts his or her handset again. The A-subscriber may clear the call at any moment during the call set-up.

*Call between A-subscriber Line and Outgoing Line.* This function is similar to the *Call between A-subscriber line and B-subscriber line* with a few exceptions. The direction of the call will now be to an Outgoing line. This will be chosen from the free lines in the route between this switching system and the other system. The line will be marked busy during the call in the same way as the B-subscriber line. The system does not need to check the category of the outgoing line since it is always allowed to receive calls.

*Call between Incoming Line and B-subscriber Line.* This function is similar to the *Call between A-subscriber line and B-subscriber line* with a few exceptions. The function will be started when another switching system starts communicating with this system. In this case all the digits will be received directly and there is no need to check whether calls are allowed to originate from this line. The function will then behave like the function *Call between A-subscriber line and B-subscriber line.*

*Call between Incoming Line and Outgoing Line.* This function is similar to the previous functions but in this case the line from where the call originates in this switching system is an Incoming line and the direction of the call is to an Outgoing line.

**Operation and maintenance**

*Subscription Changes.* An operator can connect a new subscriber to the system or disconnect an existing subscriber. When a new subscriber is connected to the system, the system is informed by the operator of the phone number, the external identity and the category of the subscriber.

*Changes of Digit Information.* An operator can change the digit information for the system. This information is used for each call in the system so that proper action can be taken. The information is normally structured as a tree where each node represents a digit and a leaf node represents a direction.

The result of a digit analysis is associated with a leaf node. The result consists of three components: the name of the outgoing function to which the call is directed, an external route identity object (not required for a call to a B-subscriber line) and the expected number length (dependent on the direction of the call). The number length is used to decide when all digits for a call have been received.

*Connection of Devices.* This function is used to connect new devices and to delete existing devices from the system. For each connected device the system is informed of the external identity of the device and the external identity of the route to which the device belongs. The external route identity is used outside the system and for communication with the system.

## 14.2.1  An overview of the system

Before going into the development work we will now give a brief overview of how the system works. When a new subscriber is to be connected to the system, an operator uses the function described as *Subscription Changes*. The operator gives the subscriber's number, external identity and category to the system. Then the operator uses *Changes of Digit Information* and the system is informed about the new subscriber, the number of the subscriber, the direction of the call and the length of the number. The number of the subscriber is used to find the other information, such as the direction of the call. It is now possible to make a call to and from this subscriber if the subscriber is physically connected to the telecommunication switching system. This should be done before the operator connects the subscriber to the exchange.

When the subscriber lifts the handset to make a phone call, the external identity of the subscriber is sent to the system. Then, depending on the destination of the call, the subscriber uses one of the functions described as *Call between A-subscriber Line and B-subscriber Line* or *Call between A-subscriber Line and Outgoing Line.*

An operator removes a subscription by giving the number of the subscriber whose subscription should be removed, or for another type of device by giving the external identity of the device to the system.

## 14.3 The requirements model

In the use case model we will describe what functionality each actor should be able to perform. Therefore we start by identifying the actors. From the above description, we see that the system is primarily developed to serve subscribers. A subscriber is thus a candidate actor. However, we see also that the subscriber can play either of two roles: an A-subscriber or a B-subscriber. We have previously discussed the importance of describing roles played in the system. These two roles will therefore be perfect to model with two actors: A-subscriber and B-subscriber. To model incoming and outgoing lines we also use actors since they will show behavior external to our system. Here we see an example where other systems (in this case even the same kind of system!) are modeled with actors. Let us call these actors A-remote and B-remote. In this example these four actors will be the primary actors. We also have secondary actors, namely actors that will service the functionality for the primary actors. From the description above we see that we have a secondary actor, namely an Operator to perform the functionality described under Operation and Maintenance above. In this example we will not have any more actors. We thus have the picture in Figure 14.2.

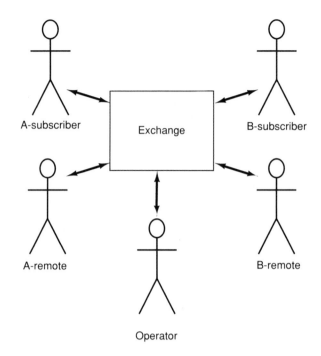

**Figure 14.2**    The actors of the switching system.

From these actors we will now identify and specify the use cases. In this example we have a much more extensive requirements specification than in the example of the warehouse management system. The requirements specification is here quite detailed and can actually work well as a base for the use cases.

To understand the requirements specification, we will draw a conceptual picture of the system using the domain object model. We have seen that Subscriber is essential to everything that will be done. Additionally, we notice that we have different kinds of devices; A- and B-subscriber lines, incoming and outgoing lines. These are all devices. We also need to group outgoing devices in a Route. To direct a certain call we also need some sort of Directory to keep track of all the Subscribers and Routes. We thus have a domain object model as shown in Figure 14.3.

Some of the objects and their attributes are as follows:

| | |
|---|---|
| Device: | physical id |
| A-line: | – |
| B-line: | – |
| Incoming line: | – |

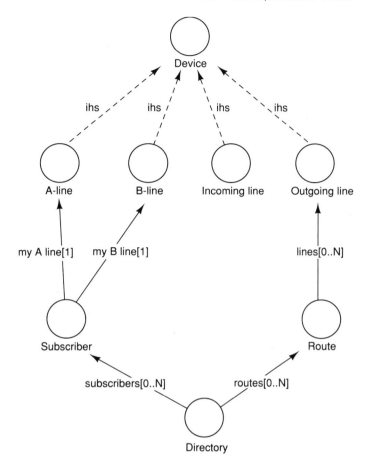

**Figure 14.3**    The domain object model of the telecom example.

| | |
|---|---|
| Outgoing line: | – |
| Subscriber: | number, category, busy |
| Directory: | – |
| Route: | external id |

This domain object model could be further refined to include operations and stimulus paths. We could even use interaction diagrams to show how they interact. However, we believe that normally this is overworking the model since this model will not form the direct base for implementation. The domain object model is, for now, at a sufficient level of detail to ease the understanding of the domain. However, there may be cases when it is worth refining this model, for instance if you just want to do a system specification and not implement the system based on this model. For very simple systems, where robustness is not a major concern, it may also be worthwhile to base the implementation on such a model. We will later show that it is possible to execute an entire use case using only these objects.

The call handling functionalities described above have great similarities since each is described in terms of the others. Here there should be great potential for reuse. However, we will postpone the reuse issue until we look at the abstract use cases. We now focus on the actors.

The A-subscriber should be able to call a B-subscriber and an outgoing line. This yields two use cases: *Local Call* and *Outgoing Call*. The A-remote actor should in the same way be able to call the B-subscriber and an outgoing line giving us another two use cases *Incoming Call* and *Transit Call*. The B-subscriber and B-remote actors will not initiate any use cases and thus not give us any more use cases. The four use cases are the same four alternatives for call handling as we found in the requirements. Such a direct correspondence between a requirements specification and use cases is not uncommon, quite the opposite; often use cases can be found directly from the requirements.

In the requirements we do not have anything about how to charge for the phone calls. However, it is likely that the calls should be charged. To be able to charge for the calls we therefore need to specify how the charging should be performed. Since it is not in the requirements, this question would have to go back to the people responsible for the requirements. Let us say that we want the caller to be charged for the phone calls he or she is making. This means that charging should only be included in the use cases *Local Call* and *Outgoing Call*. *Incoming Call* and *Transit Call* will not be charged in this switching system, but in the system to which the A-subscriber initiating these use cases is connected. Charging could be described in the two use cases that require it, which would mean that we have to define it twice. Another possibility is to describe it as an extension use case common to these two use cases. This alternative is better since we only have to describe it once and also it is separate from the other two use cases. Additionally, these two use cases can be described independently of how they should be charged. That is good because they are now independent; a change in one of the use cases will not affect the other. Changes in how the charging should be performed will now be local to only one use case. We thus identify the use case *Charging* that can extend *Local Call* and *Outgoing Call*. We now have the use cases shown in Figure 14.4.

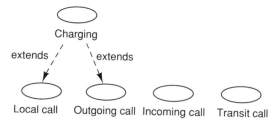

**Figure 14.4**   The use cases in the exchange system when the primary actors have been analyzed.

The secondary actor Operator will have to perform use cases to manage the functionality offered to the primary actors. Turning again to the requirements we see that we need a use case for adding and deleting subscribers; this we call *Subscription Changes*. Additionally, we need a use case for managing and changing the digit information; this use case is called *Change Digit Information*. Furthermore, to handle the devices we need a *Device Connection* use case. These use cases are directly found in the requirements. The *Charging* functionality must also be managed by the operator. The operator must be able to change a charging factor and investigate the amount a subscriber has been charged. We thus have two new use cases: *Changing the Charging Factor* and *Reading the Charging Register*. We cannot find any more potential use cases in the functionality specified in the requirements. We thus have the use case model shown in Figure 14.5.

The use cases are summarized below:

- *Local Call*: A call between an A-subscriber and a B-subscriber both connected to the same switching system.

- *Outgoing Call*: A call between an A-subscriber connected to this switching system and a subscriber connected to another system.

- *Incoming Call*: A call from another switching system to a B-subscriber connected to this system.

- *Transit Call*: A call between two subscribers connected to other switching systems and using this system for transiting.

- *Charging*: The use case includes the behavior related to charging a subscriber, namely time measurement, deciding which charging factor should be used and incrementing the subscriber's account.

- *Subscription Changes*: Connection or disconnection of a subscriber to/from the system.

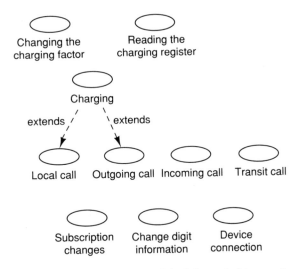

**Figure 14.5**   The use case model of the switching system.

- *Change Digit Information*: The use case changes the associated digit result for a direction in the system.
- *Device Connection*: The system is informed of a device that is connected or disconnected to/from the system and its corresponding route.
- *Changing the Charging Factor*: The system is informed of a new charging factor for a certain direction.
- *Reading the Charging Register*: The amount a subscriber has been charged is presented to an Operator together with some additional statistics.

    From now on, we will focus on the two use cases *Local Call* and *Subscription Changes*.

### 14.3.1   The use case *Local Call*

*Local Call* is started by the A-subscriber when he off-hooks. The B-subscriber will also be involved in the use case even if she does not answer. Specific interface descriptions are not very interesting here since they will mainly be handled by the hardware which we do not discuss. Below is the detailed description of the *Local Call* use case. Note how the items in the noun list, extracted from the domain objects, are used as predefined concepts.

(Words in *italic* refer to words from the noun list and the Helvetica font indicates actors.)

**Basic course**

When a Subscriber makes a call, namely lifts his handset, a stimulus is sent to the system carrying the external identity object of the calling Subscriber (the A-subscriber) which is used for identifying the Subscriber in the system. The system checks if the Subscriber is permitted to make calls. If so, the Subscriber is marked as busy to prevent other calls being connected to him. Finally, a dialling tone is sent to the A-subscriber.

A digit from the A-subscriber results in the disconnection of the dial tone and storing of the digit. Then the system checks in the *Directory* if enough digits have been received for analysis, and, if so, requests the outgoing function. In this case the outgoing function request must return a call to a B-subscriber.

Furthermore, if all digits have been received, the system uses the number for translating the number of the B-subscriber to the corresponding internal Subscriber representation. This is used to check in turn if the B-subscriber is idle and if she may receive incoming calls. If so, the Subscriber is marked busy and her external identity object is found. Then the system operates the switches between the A- and the B-subscriber, sends a ringing tone to the A-subscriber and starts ringing the B-subscriber.

When the B-subscriber answers the call, the ringing signal to the B-subscriber and the ringing tone to the A-subscriber are disconnected. The two Subscribers are now in conversation mode.

Finally, when the B-subscriber clears the call, the new event is registered in the system. Then, when the A-subscriber also clears the call, the system marks both Subscribers idle and terminates the call by releasing the switches between the two *subscribers*.

**Alternative courses**

*Termination order*

If the call is first cleared by the A-subscriber then the system waits for the B-subscriber to clear. When the B-subscriber clears the call, the use case continues as in the basic course when both Subscribers have cleared the call.

*Termination point*

At any time when the B-subscriber has not answered, the A-subscriber can clear the call. The system marks the calling *subscriber* idle, terminates the call in case connection has taken place and releases the switches between the two *subscribers*.

In this use case we also specify two alternative courses: if the A-subscriber on-hooks before the B-subscriber, and if the B-subscriber does not answer when she is called.

We stated earlier that it is possible to express the computation as having the domain objects interacting. We will here show that this is possible, although we do not recommend it in the normal case. The reason is that this work will not be used in subsequent phases. However, we could draw a figure like Figure 14.6.

The use case starts when a subscriber off-hooks. This will invoke an off-hook operation in the object A-line. A-line tries to make a call using the appropriate Subscriber object. Then a dial tone is sent. When digits are dialled, they are analyzed and the Directory is used to find the B-Subscriber. When the B-subscriber is found the call is connected. Hence it is fully possible to describe the use case flow over these domain objects but, we repeat, normally this should not be done since this model will not be used again in the development and it forces the developer to get used to a structure which is not made for robustness.

How the objects are related by the stimulus paths is shown in Figure 14.7.

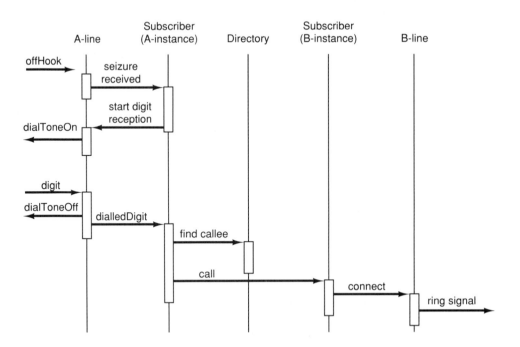

**Figure 14.6**   The first part of the use case *Local Call* using the domain objects.

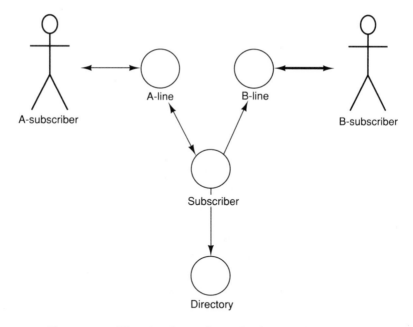

**Figure 14.7**   The stimulus paths in the domain object model.

## 14.3.2   The use case *Subscription Changes*

This use case is performed by the Operator when he or she wants to connect or disconnect a subscriber to/from the system. The specification is as follows.

---

**Basic course**

A new *Subscriber* is connected by an Operator through a command which presents a form on the screen. The Operator completes the information requested, namely a *Directory* number, the *subscriber's* category and the external identity object of the new *Subscriber*. The information is stored in the *Directory*. Finally, the Operator is informed of the success of the subscription.

**Alternative course**

*Disconnection of Subscriber*
Disconnection of a *Subscriber* follows a procedure similar to the basic course. First the information representing the *Subscriber* is found by the *Directory* number of the *Subscriber*. If the *Subscriber* is idle, its internal information is removed and deleted. The Operator is informed of the success of the disconnection. If the *Subscriber* is not idle the Operator is informed and the disconnection is not performed.

---

We do not describe here the details of what the window presented to the operator looks like. For a more detailed discussion of window systems see Chapter 13.

Before going into the analysis model we will briefly discuss the topic of abstract use cases in this example.

### 14.3.3    Abstract use cases

When specifying the rest of the use cases we notice similarities between them. We will have this situation in the call use cases especially. In the *Local Call* use case we see that there are functionalities to take care of the A-subscriber and also the B-subscriber. The A-subscriber behavior (and thus functionality) will be similar whether the A-subscriber makes an Outgoing call or a Local call. Likewise the B-subscriber functionality will be similar whether the call is local or an incoming call. A Transit call can be composed of an incoming part and an outgoing part. All use cases also have a common part where the system analyzes the digits that are received and determines how to connect the call. This is also a potential abstract use case. We thus have five abstract use cases for calling, as shown in Figure 14.8. The *Charging* use case should only be inserted in those use cases where the A-subscriber participates. This can be

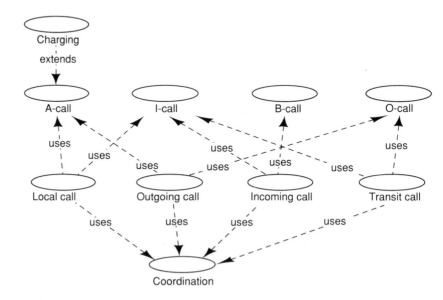

**Figure 14.8**    The use case model with abstract use cases.

modeled by having this use case extend the *A-call* use case as shown in Figure 14.8.

The abstract use cases are:

- *A-call*: This use case includes the behavior related to an A-subscriber, that is, communicating with the calling subscriber by receiving its hook signals and dialled digits, and sending a dialling tone and ringing signals.
- *B-call*: This use case includes the behavior related to a B-subscriber, namely receiving its hook signals and sending ringing signals.
- *I-call:* This use case includes the behavior related to communication with an incoming trunk line.
- *O-call*: This use case includes the behavior related to communication with an outgoing trunk line.
- *Coordination*: This use case includes the behavior related to the analysis of the direction of the call and the connection of the subscribers.

The reasons for identifying abstract use cases are actually threefold. Firstly, they give us a tool for reusing descriptions of use cases. Secondly, we can guarantee that certain parts of several different use cases will execute similarly, for example we do not want the A-subscriber to bother whether it is a local call or an outgoing call; his behavior should be similar. Thirdly, they will be a tool when developing the analysis model, especially when identifying the control objects.

## 14.4   The analysis model

We will here discuss how the analysis model is developed from the use cases. We then take one part of a use case at a time and discuss the objects needed for that part.

### 14.4.1   The use case *Local Call*

Based on the use case descriptions, we will now develop the objects in the analysis model. We will start by looking at the use case *Local Call*. By identifying the analysis objects we will illustrate further how a real development works. Then we go through the use case and identify the objects one by one, independently of their type. Let us take a closer look at the first section.

> When a *subscriber* makes a call, namely lifts his handset, a stimulus is sent to the system carrying the external identity object of the calling *subscriber* (the A-subscriber) which is used for identifying the *subscriber* in the system. The system checks whether the *subscriber* is permitted to make calls. If so, the *subscriber* is marked as busy to prevent other calls being connected to him. Finally, a dialling tone is sent to the A-subscriber.

From this we see that some sort of interface object is needed for the A-subscriber; let us call this interface object A-subscriber line. The external identity object of the subscriber comes to this object. We then need to process this information and find the correct subscriber information in the system. Information about a subscriber is something that should be kept and handled in the system. Therefore we identify an entity object Subscriber to handle this. We now have an interface object and an entity object. There is some processing (such as finding the right subscriber instance, checking whether that subscriber is allowed to make phone calls, marking him as busy and so on) that should be done on the subscriber; however, it does not seem suitable that the interface object should be responsible for performing these operations, since this should be done independently of the kind of interface object being used (for example, a pay phone). New use cases would then require changes to the interface object. An alternative is to allocate this processing to the Subscriber object instead. However, the Subscriber object should not know which decisions are taken as the result of a test, for example, checking whether he is allowed to make calls. Thus far in the use case this processing could be an alternative, but we will see later that there will be more processing like this. To handle this processing, we therefore initially identify a control object A-subscriber Call Handler. This control object could also be found from the abstract use cases; we had an abstract use case *A-call* which corresponds very well to the control objects just identified. From the first section we thus have the objects shown in Figure 14.9.

The next section in the use case was as follows.

> A digit from the A-subscriber results in the disconnection of the dial tone and storing of the digit. Then the system checks in the *Directory* if enough digits have been received for analysis, and, if so, requests the outgoing function. In this case the outgoing function request must return a call to a B-subscriber.

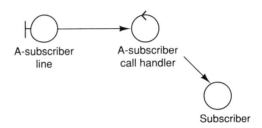

**Figure 14.9**   The analysis object identified from the first section of the use case *Local Call*.

Here we start to analyze the digits and try to find the direction of the call. The direction of the call must be determined from some stored information concerning how to interpret the digits dialled by the subscriber. The processing of the digits is something that is common to the different kinds of call use cases we have, that is, the abstract use case *Coordination*. Let us therefore assign a control object Coordinator. The Coordinator receives the digits entered and checks them against a directory which explains how to interpret digits. This information should be handled by an entity object; we call it Digit Information. Whenever a new digit is received the digits are checked against Digit Information to see whether more digits are necessary. Digit Information then identifies that this call is a call to a B-subscriber and thus can return this to the Coordinator. How to handle a call to a B-subscriber is part of the use case *B-call*, so we will have a corresponding control object for the B-subscriber also. Hence there is a control object B-subscriber Call Handler. In this section we thus have the objects shown in Figure 14.10.

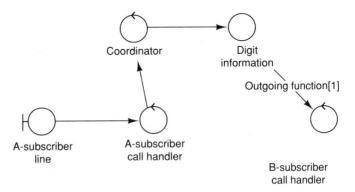

**Figure 14.10**   The analysis object identified from the second section of the use case *Local Call*.

The third section of the use case is as follows.

---

Furthermore, if all digits have been received, the system uses the number for translating the number of the B-subscriber to the corresponding internal *subscriber* representation. This is used to check in turn if the B-subscriber is idle and if she may receive incoming calls. If so the *subscriber* is marked busy and her external identity object is found. Then the system operates the switches between the A- and the B-subscriber, sends a ringing tone to the A-subscriber and starts ringing the B-subscriber.

---

Initially we must find the internal representation of the B-subscriber. This is stored in a similar way to that of the A-subscriber, that is, in an instance of the entity object Subscriber. The handling of finding, checking and allocating the B-subscriber is performed as operations on Subscriber done by B-subscriber Call Handler. From the external identity we have now found which devices (lines) should be connected for the call. Now we should find a free path and connect these two devices. This can be represented in the system by an entity object Connection that connects subscribers. All connections in the system are aggregated and handled by another entity object Network. When the connection is made, a ringing tone should be sent to both the A- and B-subscribers. This part of the use case can now be offered by the objects shown in Figure 14.11.

The fourth section of the use case reads as follows.

---

When the B-subscriber answers the call, the ringing signal to the B-subscriber and the ringing tone to the A-subscriber are disconnected.

---

This part can be offered by the objects already identified and will thus not yield any new objects. Hence, from this use case, we have identified the following *interface objects*:

- A-subscriber Line: The A-subscriber Line communicates with an A-subscriber, transforming the subscriber's actions into stimuli recognizable to the interior of the system and vice versa.
- B-subscriber Line: The B-subscriber Line communicates with a B-subscriber, transforming the subscriber's actions into

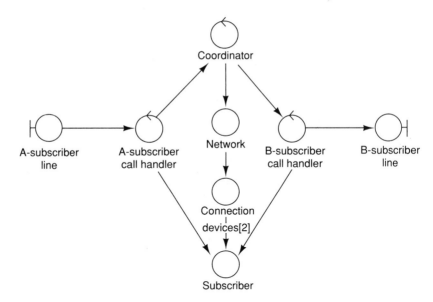

**Figure 14.11**   The objects offering the third section in the use case.

stimuli recognizable to the interior of the system and vice versa.

We have also identified the following *control objects*:

- A-subscriber Call Handler: The A-subscriber Call Handler communicates with the calling subscriber, that is, receives its hook signals and dialled digits, sends a dialling tone and ringing signals and cooperates with the Coordinator.

- B-subscriber Call Handler: The B-subscriber Call Handler communicates with the called subscriber, that is, receives its hook signals, sends ringing signals and cooperates with the Coordinator.

- Coordinator: The Coordinator cooperates with the caller, analyzes the dialled digits and decides the direction of the call. It also cooperates with the callee. Finally it communicates with the network for the physical connection of the subscribers.

Finally, we have the following *entity objects*:

- Subscriber: The Subscriber entity object represents subscribers internally to the system. For each subscriber there is an instance of the entity object keeping the information of the subscriber's state, the directory number, the external physical identity and the category.

- Digit Information: The Digit Information entity object keeps the information about what kind of outgoing function there is for a number, how many digits there are in a complete number and what route the corresponding line belongs to. There can only be one instance of this object in the system.

- Network: The Network entity object includes the network switches and retains information about what devices are for the moment connected to each other. There can only be one instance of this object in the system.

- Connection: The Connection is an aggregation of Devices connected together in the network.

### 14.4.2    Further refinements

So far, we have only focused on objects in one calling use case. As the reader may guess, many of these objects can be reused in other use cases. Furthermore, these objects will be similar to objects participating in other use cases. This means that the object model developed here will be refined and enhanced when investigating the other use cases. We will not go into a detailed discussion on this here, but only give some results of such an analysis.

Similar to the control objects representing the A- and B-subscriber Call Handler, we will identify corresponding control objects for the other use cases as well, giving us four different kinds

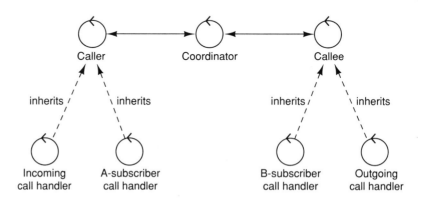

**Figure 14.12**    The control objects participating in the different kinds of call use cases.

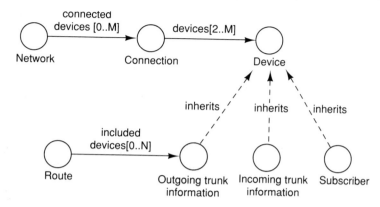

**Figure 14.13** Entities participating in the different kinds of call use cases.

of call handler. When examining these further we will notice that there are great similarities between the caller party and the callee party. It is mainly the interaction with the Coordinator object that is similar. We will therefore get a control object view as shown in Figure 14.12.

When analyzing the devices connected to other switching systems we will have a similar situation. We will have entity objects representing these devices that are similar to the devices for subscribers, as shown in Figure 14.13. (The reason that we have the cardinality [2. .M] on the acquaintance association between Connection and Device is that we may actually allow more than two parties to be involved in a call, that is, a multiparty call.) The knowledge of the Outgoing Trunk Information object is also held by a Route object.

### 14.4.3 The use case *Subscription Changes*

The use case *Subscription Changes* is far simpler than the *Local Call* use case. The basic course in the description reads:

A new *subscriber* is connected by an Operator through a command which presents a form on the screen. The Operator completes the information requested, namely a *directory* number, the *subscriber's* category and the external identity of the new *subscriber*. The information is stored in the *Directory*. Finally, the Operator is informed of the success of the subscription.

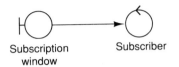

Subscription          Subscriber
window

**Figure 14.14**    The objects offering the use case *Subscription Changes*.

This part thus creates instances of the object Subscriber as identified in the *Local Call* use case. We also have a form on which to fill in the information. This form will be a direct mapping onto the entity object, which is why there is no need for a control object to handle this part. We thus have the objects shown in Figure 14.14. These objects will also be sufficient for the alternative course, namely when a subscriber should be disconnected from the system.

### 14.4.4    Subsystems

In this manner all objects required to offer the use cases are identified. When all objects have been identified and described we will have a large number of objects that we are not able to handle at one level. These objects are therefore grouped into different subsystems.

From the use cases we have reviewed here we will have the objects shown in Figure 14.15. Note that we have a direct pairing between interface object and entity object; one interface object for Incoming Trunk Line and one entity object for Incoming Trunk Information. The reader may ask, why not place the entity object functionality in the interface object? This is fully possible, but again we have the robustness motive for modeling as we do. There are certain kinds of information for each associated line that are independent of what type of line it is. However, there are several different types of line and thus many different types of interface object to interface the lines. All of these interface objects will have the same information functionality, so this is modeled in the entity object. In fact we have an association between each interface object and entity object pair, an association not shown in Figure 14.15.

We see that this results in a large number of objects and also a large number of associations. For real systems, the number of objects must be grouped in order to get a manageable structure. Subsystems are the normal grouping concept of OOSE. Subsystems should group objects with related functionality. We see that some objects concern traffic control. These will form the Traffic Control Subsystem, which includes the following objects: Coordinator, Caller, Callee, Digit

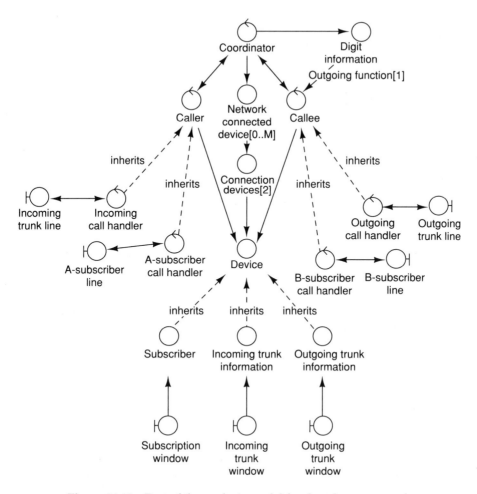

**Figure 14.15**  Part of the analysis model for the telecom example.

Information, Network and Connection. Some objects are involved with the lines to the subscribers and to other switches. These constitute the Trunk Subsystem which includes Outgoing Trunk Line, Outgoing Call Handler, Outgoing Trunk Information, Incoming Trunk Line, Incoming Call Handler, Incoming Trunk Information, A-subscriber Line, A-subscriber Call Handler, B-subscriber Line, B-subscriber Call Handler and Subscriber. We will also have one subsystem for Operation and Maintenance which includes objects like Subscription Window, Incoming Trunk Window and Outgoing Trunk Window.

## 14.5   The design model

In the design model we will adapt and refine the analysis model so that we can implement the system in a seamless and straightforward way. The adaptation will be made to the current implementation environment and the refinement will be made by explicitly expressing each stimulus sent between the objects.

We will continue to focus on the *Local Call* use case and see how we incorporate the implementation environment in the object model offering this use case. We will then refine this object model and also look at how the implementation is done for some objects. We will use Smalltalk as our implementation language.

### 14.5.1   The block structure

Let us start with the block structure. The first attempt at such a structure is to do a one-to-one mapping from the analysis model, that is, for each analysis object we assign one block. The use case view of the analysis model for this use case looks like Figure 14.16.

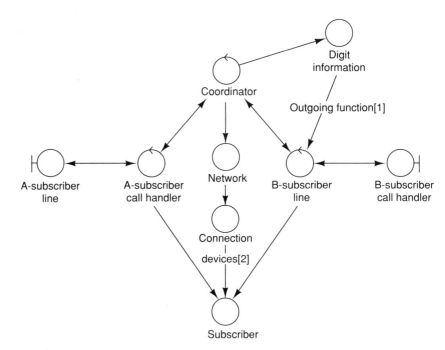

**Figure 14.16**   The use case view over analysis object in the *Local Call* use case.

The ideal design model starts by converting the analysis objects into blocks. This means that the first design model would be as shown in Figure 14.17.

Let us discuss some of the blocks. The interfaces A- and B-subscriber lines are actually interfaces to the hardware (lines) going to every subscriber attached to the system. We do not discuss the hardware here, but in a real switching system there is only one circuit handling I/O to each subscriber. Therefore we must develop software that handles this interface. It is not interesting to differentiate here between different kinds of lines when preparing for the implementation. We therefore only have one block Subscriber Line. This means that we merge the A- and B-subscriber line into one block. However, in every use case there will be two different instances of this class participating in the use case. It can therefore be interesting to have both these instances shown in the design model when approporiate.

The different kinds of call handlers will have different behavior, though. Therefore it is not possible to join these to make one block; both are needed. Recall that during analysis we discussed

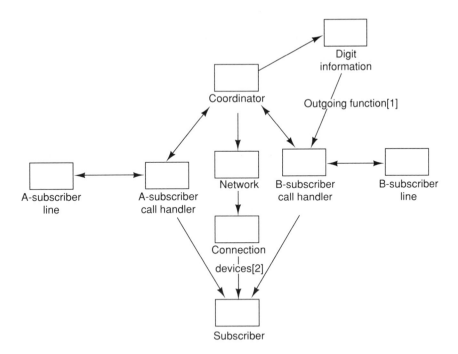

**Figure 14.17**  The first attempt at a design model is a direct conversion of analysis objects into blocks.

whether to place this behavior in the interface objects or in the entity object Subscriber. If we had done the latter, it would be harder to combine the interfaces in one block and we would have an unnecessarily complex Subscriber.

The network block will have control over all switches connected in the system. There will only be one instance of this class in the system. However, the connection through the switches was modeled by an entity object Connection in the analysis model, which gave rise to a corresponding block. The network can very well be implemented with, for instance, an array or a list that, in each element, has two (or more) references to a Subscriber object. Thus Connection can actually be encapsulated in the Network block to hide the actual implementation of the representation. We can therefore eliminate Connection from the design model and have a block in terms of classes of Network as outlined in Figure 14.18.

The Digit Information, which again only has one instance in the system, will match the number dialled and find which outgoing function should be offered. It will also check that the number dialled is a valid number and, for outgoing calls, find an outgoing route. Finding the outgoing function can be done after only a couple of digits (usually the first three digits in a telephone number determine which switch to turn to), while we may need the entire number to determine whether it is a valid number. To handle this matching, a tree structure is appropriate, where each level is determined by a digit. That is, we start in the root and when the first digit is dialled we can descend one level in the tree to the appropriate node and from there analyze the next digit. At some node we will discover whether it is a local call or a call to another exchange. When a leaf is reached we can determine how to handle this call, namely what outgoing function to use. In the leaf we have information on the outgoing

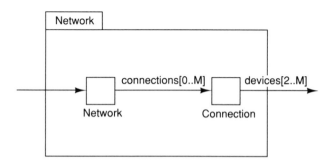

**Figure 14.18**   A first sketch of the inside of the Network block.

function, the length of the entire catalog number and how to direct the call. The outgoing function refers to a B-subscriber Call Handler if the call is internal to the exchange, or to an Outgoing Call Handler if it is to a remote B-subscriber. If the call is internal we have a Subscriber object; if the call is outgoing we are referred to a Route object. The Digit Information block can thus be designed in a similar manner to the Network block, but with a tree structure of Digit Nodes. A node could thus possibly refer to both an outgoing function and a route (not used in the use case studied). The Digit Information block design thus looks like Figure 14.19.

The matching of the received digits to the digit tree is also worth discussing. The Coordinator block will receive the digits from the A-Subscriber Call Handler. These digits should be stored at the Coordinator and when a new digit has been received, a new check should be made against the Digit Information. Additionally, the entire number dialled should then be passed to the B-subscriber Call Handler. This indicates that we need some form of unit to store the dialled number in. We thus identify a class Register to store this information. We could use some kind of string, collection or some other class from the library, but we will need a little more functionality from this unit when it is sent to different objects as a parameter. The Register can however be encapsulated in the Coordinator block, since it is mainly this block which handles it. The first sketch of the Coordinator looks like Figure 14.20.

This analysis of how to handle different aspects of the design cannot, of course, be decided all at once. Many aspects will not be noticed until the model has been detailed further. This work thus has a strongly iterative character. We have given here just a few examples of what such a refinement of the design model can involve. We have thus far reached a design model as shown in Figure 14.21. Note that

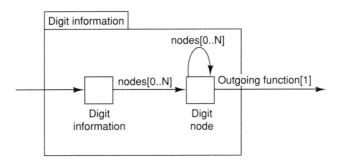

**Figure 14.19**   A first sketch of the interior of the Digit Information block.

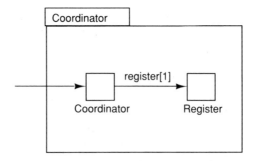

**Figure 14.20**    A first sketch of the design of the Coordinator block.

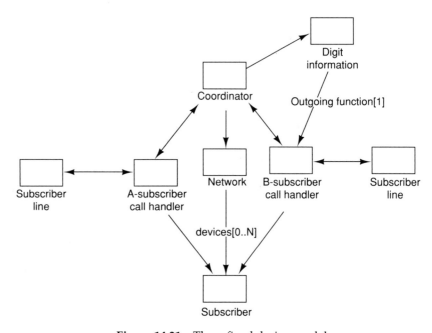

**Figure 14.21**    The refined design model.

we have included the Subscriber Line block twice to make Figure 14.21 easier to draw. This should be done if it clarifies things. Semantically, however, it is the same Subscriber Line block.

## 14.5.2    The process structure

A telecommunication switching system is a typical example of a real-time system in which processes are a natural ingredient. Let us now, from the design model developed, discuss how processes should be identified and handled in this switching system. Taking the guidelines given in Chapter 9, we will start identifying candidate processes. There it was stated that one should initially focus on the interface blocks and see which of these could receive events in a nondeterministic way. In this example, and now we only focus on the *Local Call* use case, we see that actually both the A- and B-subscriber can generate events possibly independent of each other. We can therefore allocate one process to handle each party of the Local Call. Let us call these processes the A- and B-processes. In these processes we allocate the behavior of the appropriate instances of Subscriber Line and of A-Subscriber Call Handler and B-Subscriber Call Handler respectively. Additionally, we need something to handle the processing of these events independently of the events themselves, something which is typically handled by the Coordinator. This is also a process candidate which will include the Coordinator block. Instances of these processes will be created for each Local Call. (How this is actually done is dependent on the operating system used; since it is not a subject of this book, we will not go into detail.) The blocks Network, Digit Information and Subscriber will be shared by several instances of the processes just discussed. This was also discussed in the chapter about real-time, where entity objects must often be protected from simultaneous access by some form of mutual exclusion. This can be implemented with semaphores, monitors or even separate processes, or some other feature existing in the programming language or operating system. Here we assume that they will be protected by some kind of semaphore.

A process view of the design model may thus look like Figure 14.22. Note that here we have been able to fully allocate each block (instance) to a certain process. These processes, as we will see, are explicit in the interaction diagrams.

### 14.5.3   Use case design

We are now ready to describe how the interaction between the different objects will look in the *Local Call* use case. All of the blocks previously discussed will participate in this use case. We will thus specify each stimulus sent between the objects. Since different processes are involved, we must also differentiate between the types of stimulus sent: messages for normal operation invocation (closed arrows) and signals for interprocess communication (open arrows).

To show explicitly how the use case descriptions are used, we will partition the interaction diagram as for the section on the

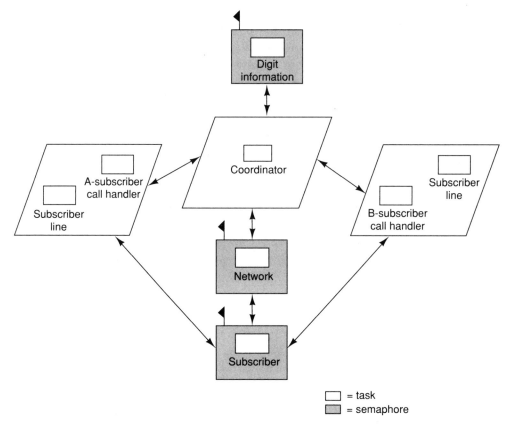

**Figure 14.22**  A process view of the design model involved in the *Local Call* use case.

descriptions. This is not normally done in real systems, but is done here for clarity.

Let us start with the first section of the use case description.

> When a Subscriber makes a call, namely lifts his handset, a stimulus is sent to the system carrying the external identity object of the calling Subscriber (the A-subscriber) which is used for identifying the Subscriber in the system. The system checks if the Subscriber is permitted to make calls. If so, the Subscriber is marked as busy to prevent other calls being connected to him. Finally, a dialling tone is sent to the A-subscriber.

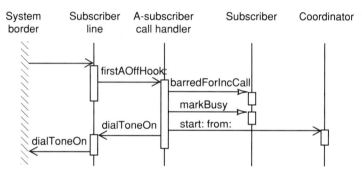

**Figure 14.23**   Interaction diagram for the first part of the use case.

From this we will be able to define the stimulus sequence as shown in Figure 14.23. The correct subscriber will normally be stored in the database. We have not explicitly discussed the database issues in this example. However, we have here different possibilities. We could add a new object which represents the database to which we would send a stimulus createObjectFromDBref: aDBref. This would then return an instance of the correct subscriber. However, the handling should rather be encapsulated in the Subscriber object since we do not want other objects to be dependent on how it is actually done, for reasons of robustness. This encapsulation is implemented using the framework discussed in Chapter 10.

We thus have defined several stimuli sent between the blocks. Note that when we specified the use case we did not have any idea which blocks should participate in the use case. The domain objects were then our logical view of the system. Neverthless, it is quite easy to allocate the behavior over the objects, and the stimuli come naturally. Let us continue with the next part of the use case (see Figure 14.24).

A digit from the A-subscriber results in the disconnection of the dial tone and storing of the digit. Then the system checks in the Directory if enough digits have been received for analysis, and, if so, requests the outgoing function. In this case the outgoing function request must return a call to a B-subscriber.

We thus have now found the correct outgoing function, in this case a B-subscriber Call Handler. The stimulus enough: checks whether enough digits have come to determine which outgoing

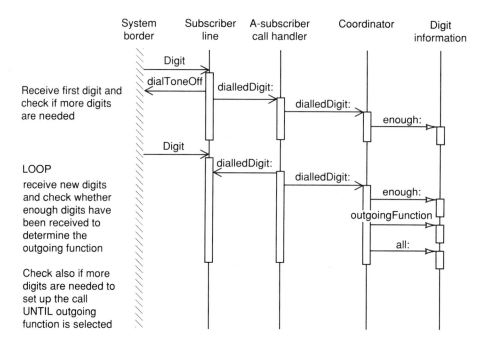

**Figure 14.24**   Continuation of the interaction diagram for *Local Call*.

function is to be selected. The colon indicates that the stimulus carries a parameter (we use the notation used in the current programming language, which is Smalltalk in this case). The parameter for enough: is the current instance of Register where the received digits are stored. Digit Information uses this instance to check the number against the digit tree. Now we are just waiting for the final digits before the call can be connected. This is described in the next section.

Furthermore, if all digits have been received, the system uses the number for translating the number of the B-subscriber to the corresponding internal Subscriber representation. This is used to check in turn if the B-subscriber is idle and if she may receive incoming calls. If so the Subscriber is marked busy and her external identity object is found. Then the system operates the switches between the A- and B-subscribers, sends a ringing tone to the A-subscriber and starts ringing the B-subscriber.

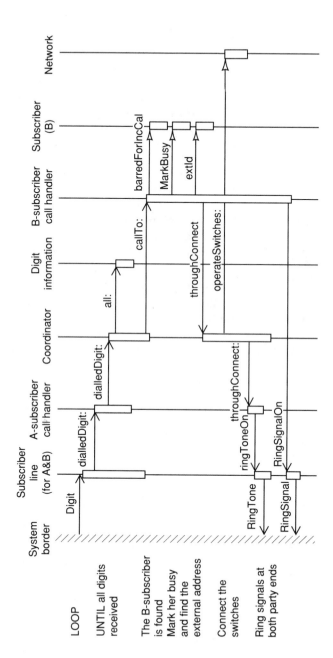

**Figure 14.25** Continuation of the interaction diagram for *Locall Call.*

Here the Coordinator initiates the processing of handling the B-subscriber (see Figure 14.25). She is marked as busy and then the connection between A- and B-subscribers is connected and dialling tones are given at both ends. In the next section of the use case the B-subscriber answers her phone.

> When the B-subscriber answers the call, the ringing signal to the B-subscriber and the ringing tone to the A-subscriber are disconnected.

Here we have used a notation where we actually have two lines representing the system border (see Figure 14.26). One represents the A-subscriber and the other represents the B-subscriber. With this notation we can more clearly see where and to whom the stimuli are really sent. In the same spirit we also have two lines for Subscriber Line. One represents the instance of the A-subscriber and one represents the instance of the B-subscriber. This notation is also used in order to gain more clarity in the interaction diagram. However, remember that the aim of doing the interaction diagrams is to obtain the interfaces of the objects. Since both Subscriber Lines belong to the same class, we will define stimuli on the same class. Therefore this notation will not give us any more (or less) information; the only reason for using it is for clarity in the diagrams. Let us look at the last part of the use case (see Figure 14.27).

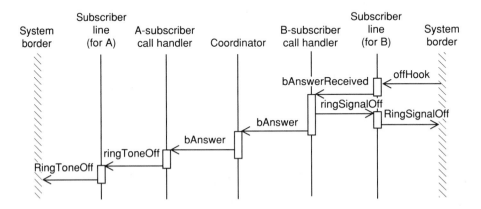

**Figure 14.26**  The part of the use case when the B-subscriber answers the telephone call.

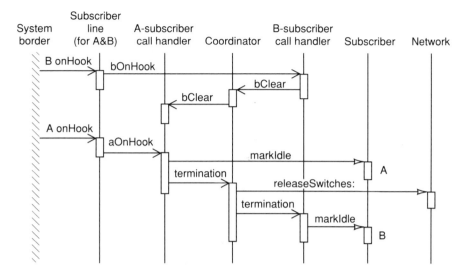

**Figure 14.27**   The final part of the use case *Local Call*.

> Finally, when the B-subscriber clears the call, the new event is registered in the system. Then, when the A-subscriber also clears the call, the system marks both Subscribers idle and terminates the call by releasing the switches between the two Subscribers.

The basic course of the use case has thus been designed. The alternative courses are designed in the same manner. This will give us the stimuli sent in this use case.

### 14.5.4   Block interfaces

When all use cases have been designed we will also have the interfaces to each block. We will here focus on the Coordinator block. To get the complete interface of the object we investigate all interaction diagrams in which Coordinator participates. From the use case just designed we will have the following interface for the Coordinator object:

| | |
|---|---|
| start: *ald from: aCaller* | 'ald – ShortNumber, aCaller – Caller' |
| dialledDigit: aDigit | 'aDigit – ShortNumber' |
| throughConnect: bld | 'bld – ShortNumber' |
| bAnswer | |

bClear
termination

Here ShortNumber and Caller denote the intended types of parameter. This is not the only information that we can extract from the interaction diagrams. We also have a sense of the objects' states and what will happen when these stimuli are received. Thus, before going to implementation, we can describe the objects with a state transition graph, describing the dynamic behavior of the object. We continue to focus on the Coordinator block. From the rules given in Chapter 8, we know that each input stimulus is a potential state transition. With the notation described earlier we can produce the state-transition diagram shown in Figure 14.28.

The state transition diagram gives a picture of the behavior of an object. The figure only includes the basic course for one use case. As the other courses and more use cases are analyzed, we will refine this diagram. Hence the diagram will be further refined as more specified behavior is incorporated into the diagram. In this case the basic structure will remain as above; some more alternatives will be added, though. As an exercise, the reader can try to design the alternative courses of the use case and incorporate this behavior into the diagram.

We will now discuss the implementation of the Coordinator block.

## 14.6  The implementation model

Since the system is to be implemented in Smalltalk we have used Smalltalk syntax in the design model. This will ease the transition to the actual code, as we will see. We will focus on the Coordinator block.

When viewing the state transition diagram in Figure 14.28, the first question is how to implement the states. In most object-oriented languages, this must be implemented explicitly by the programmer. However, there are class libraries to handle state machines. We will not assume any such predefined classes, but instead illustrate two alternatives for an explicit implementation.

The first design of the Coordinator block looked like Figure 14.29. This design still seems to be appropriate; we have not encountered anything that will make this design implausible. In the state transition diagram, the behavior specified should mainly be implemented by the Coordinator class. To implement and handle the different states, we can do this in either of two ways. The first and

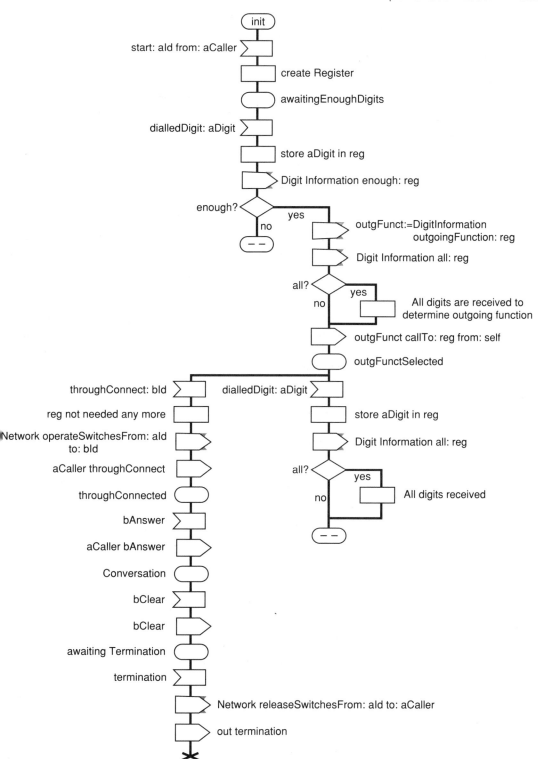

**Figure 14.28**   A state transition diagram for the Coordinator block.

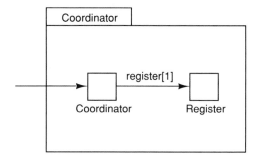

**Figure 14.29**   The overall design of the Coordinator block.

most obvious solution is to have an instance variable for the state that we test whenever we receive a stimulus. The second is to implement different operations for different states and, when a stimulus is received, a concatenation of the state and stimulus names will give us the correct method to invoke. We will look at both these solutions. In the code we have also included the alternative courses. The fork message is used to handle processes and signals in Smalltalk. Signals do not return anything in Smalltalk and this is why we return nil everywhere this is used.

## 14.6.1   If-clause implementation

```
class: Coordinator
superclass:  Object
instance variable names: 'in out inId outId reg outgFunct state'
```

The instance variables used are:

| | |
|---|---|
| in | refers to the caller |
| out | refers to the callee |
| inId | external id for the caller |
| outId | external id for the callee |
| reg | stores the digits received |
| outgFunct | holds the current outgoing function |
| state | the state of the call |

*class methods*
**start: aId from: aCaller**

'Create a new Coordinator and connect it with the corresponding
Caller.'
↑super new start: aid from: aCaller

*instance methods*
**start: aId from: aCaller**
  'Initialize the coordinator.'

  inId := aId.
  in := aCaller.
  reg := Register new.
  state := 'awaitingEnoughDigits'
**dialledDigit: aDigit**
'Receive a dialled digit, store it and and analyze the received digits.
If enough digits have been received, create an instance of the
Callee.'

state = 'awaitingEnoughDigits'
  if True:
    [reg store: aDigit.

(DigitInformation enough: reg)
  if True:
    [outgFunct : = DigitInformation
       outgoingFunction: reg.
    (DigitInformation all: reg) if True: [reg allReceived.]
    [out : = outgFunct callTo: reg from: self] fork.
    state : = 'outgFunctSelected'].
    ↑ nil].
state = 'outgFunctSelected'
  if True:
    [reg store: aDigit.
    (DigitInformation all: reg) if True: [reg allReceived].
    ↑ nil]
**throughConnect: bId**
'If the call is successfully through-connected with the Callee, the
network switches are connected and the Caller is notified.'

state = 'outgFunctSelected'
  if True:
    [outId := bId.
    reg notNeededAnyMore.
    Network operateSwitchesFrom: inId to: outId.
    [in throughConnect] fork.
    state := 'throughConnected'.
    ↑ nil]
**bAnswer**
'The Caller is notified when the Callee has answered the call.'

```
            state = 'throughConnected' I (state = 'awaitingTermination')
               if True:
                  [[in bAnswer] fork.
                  state := 'conversation'.
                  ↑ nil]
```

**bClear**
'The Caller is notified when the Callee has cleared the call.'

```
            state = 'conversation'
               if True:
                  [[in bClear] fork.
                  state := 'awaitingTermination'.
                  ↑ nil]
```

**termination**
'When the call is terminated the network switches are disconnected and the Callee is notified.'

```
            state = 'awaitingEnoughDigits'
               if True:
                  [state := 'terminated'.
                  ↑ nil].
            state = 'outgFunctSelected'
               if True:
                  [reg notNeededAnyMore.
                  [out termination] fork.
                  state := 'terminated',
                  ↑ nil].
            state = 'throughConnected' (state = 'awaitingTermination')
               if True:
                  [[out termination] fork.
                  Network releaseSwitchesFrom: inId to: outId.
                  state := 'terminated'.
                  ↑ nil]
```

## 14.6.2   Perform: clause implementation

```
class: Coordinator
superclass: Object
instance variable names:  'in out inId outId reg outgFunct state'
```

*class methods*
**start: aId from: aCaller**
'Create a new Coordinator and connect it with the corresponding Caller.'

↑ super new start: aId from: aCaller

*instance methods*
**start: aId from: aCaller**
    inId := aId.
    in := aCaller.
    reg := Register new.
    state := 'awaitingEnoughDigits'
**dialledDigit: aDigit**
    'Receive a dialled digit.'

    self perform: state 'dialledDigit:' with: aDigit.
    ↑ nil
**throughConnect: bId**
'The call has been successfully through-connected with the Callee.'

    self perform: state , 'throughConnect:' with: bId.
    ↑ nil
**bAnswer**
    'The Callee has answered the call.'

    self perform: state , 'bAnswer'.
    ↑ nil
**bClear**
    'The Callee has cleared the call.'

    self perform: state 'bClear'.
    ↑ nil
**termination**
    'The call has been terminated.'

    self perform: state 'termination'.
    ↑ nil


**awaitingEnoughDigitsdialledDigit: aDigit**
    'Store the received digit. If enough digits have been received, create
    an instance of the Callee.'

    reg store: aDigit.
    (Digitinformation enough: reg)
        if True:
            [outgFunct := DigitInformation outgoingFunction: reg
            (DigitInformation all: reg) if True: [reg allReceived].
            [out := outgFunct callTo: reg from: self] fork.
            state := 'outgFunctSelected']
**awaitingEnoughDigitstermination**
    'The call has been terminated before enough digits had been
    received.'

state := 'terminated'

**outgFunctselecteddialledDigit: aDigit**
'A new digit has been received after the outgoing function has been selected (the Callee).'

reg store: aDigit.
(DigitInformation all: reg) if True: [reg allReceived]

**outgFunctselectedthroughConnect: bId**
'If the call is successfully through-connected with the Callee, the network switches are connected and the Caller is notified.'

outId := bId.

reg notNeededAnyMore.
Network operateSwitchesFrom: inId to: outId.
[in throughConnect] fork.
state := 'throughConnected'

**outgFunctSelectedtermination**
'The call has been terminated before it had been through-connected.'
reg notNeededAnyMore.
[out termination] fork.
state := 'terminated'

**throughConnectedbAnswer**
'The Caller is notified when the Callee has answered the call.'

[in bAnswer] fork.
state := 'conversation'

**throughConnectedtermination**
'The call has been terminated before the Callee had answered.'
[out termination] fork.
Network releaseSwitchesFrom: inId to: outId.
state := 'terminated'

**conversationbClear**
'The Callee has cleared the call.'

[in bClear] fork.
state := 'awaitingTermination'

**awaitingTerminationbAnswer**
'The Callee has lifted his handset again.'

[in bAnswer] fork.
state := 'conversation'

**awaitingTerminationtermination**
'The call is terminated.'

[out termination] fork.

Network releaseSwitchesFrom: inId to: outId.
state := 'terminated'

A comparison of these two implementations shows that the first gives fewer but longer methods. The second implementation gives more methods and this solution also has a more direct map from the state transition diagram to the code, being more structured with respect to the possible use case. Note that the second solution is not possible in a language where it is not directly possible to evaluate strings or values, as in, for instance, C++ or Ada. Which of these alternatives should be chosen is up to the developer. We have included both alternatives here to illustrate that one design model can be implemented in various ways. Hence several decisions remain for when the actual implementation is done.

We see here that the transitions between the different models have been seamless and do not involve any major distortions. This is a typical feature of OOSE, namely to develop the system incrementally from initial informal and ideal sketches to a more formal model, ending the transition with the actual code.

# 15 Managing object-oriented software engineering

## 15.1 Introduction

Introducing a new development process into an organization is seldom painless. Getting all the people involved to accept all the ideas in the new process involves a lot of work from pedagogical methodologists.

It is essential to persuade the development staff to adopt an organized way of working and thinking, as fast and as painlessly as possible. No one will accept any delays caused by a new process being introduced. On the whole it is the standard problem of getting an old organization to adopt a new way of working. The organization is often, at least initially, a specific project. That is often the best form for system development.

In this chapter we will discuss some of the experiences we have had introducing and working with Objectory in real projects during the past few years. To date (Summer of 1993) Objectory has been used in about 20 projects of varying size (3–50 man years), and is currently in use in more than 50 projects, principally in Europe and North America. We will first discuss some of the preparations necessary for introducing a new process and then carrying out projects.

## 15.2 Project selection and preparation

### 15.2.1 Introducing a new development process

Most organizations we have worked with that have chosen to use a new development process already have a significant method maturity. Most have worked with one or several development methods earlier, and they have also developed a sound skepticism against introducing new technology or new ways of working too fast.

Five levels of process maturity for a software development organization have been defined by people at the Software Engineering Institute (see Humphrey (1989) or Yourdon (1990)). This classification is gaining wide acceptance. The levels are as follows.

(1) **Initial level**. No documented method is being used. Every software developer is doing it his or her own way.

(2) **Repeatable level**. A method exists, but has not been formalized or written down. However, there is a consensus about 'the way we do things around here'. Often this level is reached after lengthy experience of system development. However, when new methods and tools are introduced, the organization can very well be thrown back to level (1).

(3) **Defined level**. A formal, documented process for developing systems exists. The process is continuously refined by a software process group.

(4) **Managed level**. Formal measurements of different characteristics of process and product are continuously performed. Not only time and cost are measured, but also productivity, effectiveness, quality and so on.

(5) **Optimizing level**. The measurements from level (4) are systematically used as feedback to optimize the process.

There also seems to be general agreement that an organization is not ready to adopt new methods or tools effectively unless it is at or above level (3). Investigations in the late 1980s showed that 85 % of the large software development organizations in the USA were still at level (1), 10–12 % were at level (2) and only about 3 % were found at level (3). In 1990 no organizations were found at levels (4) or (5) in the USA.

These observations from the USA are very interesting. However, from our (European) perspective, they seem a bit odd. Method maturity, we believe, is greater in Europe. In practice, all of the projects that we have been involved in are with organizations at levels (2) or (3). About half of the projects have been in organizations at level (3) (which is said to be only 3 % of the large USA data processing organizations in the late 1980s). Our observations are also that certain organizations at level (2) have been mature enough to adopt the new technology. An especially important observation that we have made is that there can be a significant difference between the maturity of the organisation and the maturity of the individuals.

Hence a big effort and much preparation are needed when introducing a new way of working. The new way means that the organization needs to be retrained and to develop new routines. This will, in a period of transition, result in lower productivity. If an organization has maintenance responsibility for several systems which have evolved during their life cycle, each system should be studied individually in order to decide whether it really pays to change technology for that particular system. With a mature system, which requires limited resources for maintenance and will be replaced in the near future by a new system, there is probably no reason for changing the maintenance strategy.

It is often practical to introduce the new way of working stepwise. A suitable first step is to select a smaller project for new development or limited re-engineering of an existing system. We will discuss how to select the right project in the next section.

There are certain factors that increase the likelihood of making the transition to the new way of working successful, as follows:

(1) The selection of a new development method is a very important strategic decision which must be supported by upper management. The entire organization should be aware of the importance of the decision.

(2) The first development project using the new method will be exposed to much attention. Thus there is a great need for success. There will always be critics who will exploit every sign of failure to discredit the new method. The first project must therefore be selected with much care and must have all the attention and resources needed to guarantee an appropriate result.

(3) The people working on the selected project must have a feeling of a positive change. This requires, for instance, that they must have sufficient training that they feel comfortable with the new situation. Further, they should have tools (for example, CASE support) which stimulate the new way of working.

(4) Introduce the method prior to any CASE tool supporting the method. Method and tool are distinct, but both are desirable. You can use a method without a tool, but not a tool without a method. Far too many people have a hard time in realizing the difference between methods and tools.

(5) The new way of working must be integrated with other routines, for example project and product management. This integration should be ready when the new order of working is introduced widely.

(6) Have reasonable expectations of the first project. It will take some years to reach a significant increase in productivity, but

increase in quality will usually come from the start. OOSE will normally not be profitable in one project; the first project will be more expensive than traditional technologies, but the quality will be better. The profits will come in subsequent projects with experienced people and also in maintenance of the first system.

(7) Do not have high expectations of components and reuse initially. The benefits will come in two or three years.

## 15.2.2   Selecting the first project

The first project using a new working method is often an evaluation project. It is not only a matter of evaluating the new method as such – there may be well-documented experiences from other organizations; it is also a matter of evaluating the method used in this particular organization. This involves examining how inclined the staff are to change their working method and what is involved in doing it effectively. Therefore how the first project is selected and which staff should be involved in it are essential considerations.

We suppose here that the overall decisions have already been made. By this we mean that upper management believes that the selection of the method is a crucial and strategic decision which they are ready to support both financially and with careful attention. There should be a person in upper management who has a special interest in following and supporting the project. This person we call a **sponsor**. He or she should have a good professional reputation and be respected in the organization.

When selecting the first project there are certain things to consider. Generally, it should have the optimal conditions possible, so that the method can be evaluated without any disturbances such as unnecessary shortage of staff or problems in defining the system responsibility. We summarize this in the following recommendations:

(1) Select a real project that is important, but not with a tight time schedule or any other hard constraints.

(2) Select a problem domain that is well known and well defined.

(3) Select people experienced in system development who have a positive view of changes. The management should have confidence in them.

(4) Select a project manager with a high degree of interest in the task.

(5) The staff should work full time within the project and not be distracted by other projects.

(6) Base your work on a detailed plan developed in advance. Perform evaluation at all stages with criteria established in advance.

### 15.2.3　Education and training

All personnel involved in the new order of work need education and training. Given a strict method and process definition, more emphasis can be put on formal education and training. Therefore more material can be taught, and staff will need fewer projects on which to learn how to work in an orderly way. In a less formalized method, staff need several learning projects before getting familiar and highly productive with the method.

The scope and amount of education needed varies according to each person's role in the project. Everyone should have a basic education, so that there is a common basis of concepts and way of working. More specialized education and training is needed for individual roles within the project.

In Table 15.1 we have summarized our experiences of the need for education.

An example of the contents of the courses is given below:

- **Concepts**. Basic concepts of object orientation and the fundamental concepts of the method. Chapters 3–6 in this book may form a basis. 1–2 days.

- **Project management**. Specific characteristics for the new method. Appropriate metrics for the management within the new method. 1 day.

**Table 15.1**　The need for education when introducing a new development process: × = necessary, + = preferably

| role<br>issue | Project manager | Analyst | Constructor | Tester | QA | Upper management |
|---|---|---|---|---|---|---|
| Concepts | × | × | × | + | × | + |
| Project mangement | × | | | | | |
| Overview | × | + | + | + | × | + |
| Analysis | + | × | × | + | + | |
| Construction | + | + | × | + | + | |
| Testing | + | | + | × | + | |

- **Overview**. An overview of the method using examples to introduce the entire method in the system life cycle and the underlying ideas. This entire book may form a basis for this course. Attendees should be familiar with object orientation. 3–4 days.
- **Analysis**. A thorough and detailed study of the entire analysis process. Emphasis should be on applying the method and process to a larger example, possibly on the current system. 3–6 days.
- **Construction**. A thorough and detailed study of the entire design and implementation process. Emphasis should be on applying the method and process to a larger example, preferably the system to be built. The course does not cover the specific programming language, but rather how the language is incorporated within the process. Those attending should be familiar with the programming language used. 3–6 days.
- **Testing**. A thorough and detailed study of the testing activities and principles. 2–3 days.

If CASE tools are to be used in the project, additional training is needed. Our experience shows that the CASE tool should be well separated from the process and method issues. The attendees will otherwise have difficulties in distinguishing between method, process and tool and too much time is spent on getting acquainted with how to use the tool.

Any other technical aids that are new and going to be used may also pose additional education and training requirements. Examples are the programming language, DBMSs and operating systems. Other examples of new areas that also require education and training are component management and use and quality assurance.

Besides these courses we also need training in order to become familiar with the new technology. This can be done by developing a part of the system or by introducing new people for simpler tasks in projects with experienced developers. Altogether, about three months should be allocated for a developer to become productive in the new environment. Hence it is quite expensive to introduce a new development process, but it normally pays off in a few years.

## 15.2.4 Risk analysis

Introducing new technologies always brings potential risks. The number of new technologies introduced simultaneously increases risks exponentially. The introduction of a new development process often involves other changes as well: a new point of view – object orientation; a new programming language – OOP; a change of documentation techniques; new CASE tools, new development environments, new QA techniques and so on. Not only does the technology introduce risks, but the maturity level of the development organization could also be a large risk. Are we mature enough to treat system development as an industrial process? Can we introduce the discipline needed? All of these changes at the same time do involve a large risk. It is therefore essential to be aware of these risks and to have a way of handling them. To have progress one must take risks, and awareness of the risks is a prerequisite to managing them.

We will here give a simple technique for detecting and managing risks in introducing OOSE. The method is divided into three steps.

(1)  Risk identification

(2)  Risk valuation

(3)  Managing the risks

In **risk identification**, we define the potential and foreseeable risks of the project that, if they occur, may seriously injure the project. The starting point should be the goal of the project. What risks may occur that will make us fail to reach the goal? These risk areas could involve OOSE-specific risks, but also other risks. Examples of risk areas involved in OOSE projects are:

- *Paradigm shift*
  - Are we mature enough to adopt a new development strategy?
  - Will the team be mature enough not to start coding too early?
  - Is the project manager familiar with the new paradigm?
  - Are the team members familiar with the new paradigm?
  - Are we familiar with the programming language to be used?

- *Process*
  - Is our process well defined and well documented, and can we work through it?
  - Is the process mature?
  - Does the documentation produced fit our purpose?
  - Do we have sufficient training capabilities?

- *Tools* (analysis, design, implementation, DBMSs, configuration tools, purchased component libraries and so on)
  - Are we familiar with the tools to be used, and with the learning threshold?

  − Are the tools to be used mature and stable?
  − Will we have the tools when they are needed?
  − Are the tools compatible? Are they integrated?

- *The system*
  − Are we familiar with the application domain?
  − Are the requirements clear, consistent and stable?
  − Can or must we integrate existing systems? Is it possible?

- *Organization*
  − Do we have a tight schedule?
  − Will time-to-market be critical? Will the pressure from the market change?
  − Does the organization have realistic expectations for the project?

These are just a few examples of potential risks. There are of course many more, and the risks must be identified for each project's circumstances. About 15–20 risk factors could be identified in a normal sized project (5–15 persons). Risk identification is best done on a group basis, and it is better to identify too many risks than too few. The risks should be broken down into concrete situations or events.

The next step is **risk valuation**. Now the potential risks should be evaluated to assess the consequences (disturbance or damage) if they occur. We then initially judge the *probability* that the risk will occur. A scale from 1 (very improbable) to 5 (very probable) could be used. Then we assess the *consequences* of each risk. A scale from 1 (negligible) to 5 (catastrophic) could be used. Now multiply the probability and the consequence factor for each risk (see Table 15.2). We will now have a relative measure of the size and potential threats of the risks.

The third step is **managing the risks**. From the first two steps, we establish a prioritized table of the most serious threats to the project. For each of these serious threats we propose active actions to prevent them from occurring or to reduce their consequences. This could be done by decreasing the probability of the risk occurring or decreasing the consequences, or both. In this example we see that the major threats are that the project team are not used to OOSE and we are not sure about the delivery of the DBMSs. The measures to avoid these threats could be to put in place an education program for the team members and not to use the DBMS proposed.

Since some risks may be hard to detect initially, we should identify warning signals that we should look for during the project. We could also issue alternative plans to be put into action should any of the risks occur.

**Table 15.2**   A table for risk valuation

| Risk | Probability to occur (P) | Consequence (C) | P*C |
|---|---|---|---|
| Development tools not mature | 3 | 4 | 12 |
| Not familiar with application domain | 2 | 4 | 8 |
| Project team not used to OOSE | 5 | 5 | 25 |
| Weak support from upper management | 1 | 4 | 4 |
| Delayed delivery of stable DBMS | 4 | 5 | 20 |
| . . . | . . . | . . . | . . . |

Risk analysis should be done at the start of the project, but it is also important to do it throughout the project, since new risks may show up or their probability/consequence may vary during the project.

Introducing OOSE in an organization involves risks. It normally also involves a large paradigm shift with far-reaching consequences. It is important to be aware of this and, as stated, not to have too high expectations of the first project, especially not with respect to reuse. As previously mentioned, OOSE stimulates reuse, but to be able to reuse, we need something to reuse. Depending on existing reusable software, the first project will normally have varying levels of reuse. However, the first project will usually yield reusable software for future projects.

This simple method of risk analysis could be used if no other method exists in the organization. The important thing is to think about potential risks prior to the project and to prepare activities to manage potential problems. Please note that we cannot compare projects with this method. Neither should we mechanically conclude that any project with high-risk threats should be stopped. As stated, preparing mentally for potential risks strengthens the project. A more advanced method for risk analysis is the **Lichtenberg** method (see Glahn and Meland (1985)).

Since a project introducing a new working method involves large risks, a risk analysis often sets danger signals flashing. To balance such a risk analysis, a **benefit analysis** could also be made. What are the advantages of introducing this new working method? We will not go into details here, but just mention some major benefits of OOSE. Firstly, traditionally more than 50 % of total development time involves information search and retrieval and coordination of activities, thus not directly effective development time. An ordered way of working, introducing a defined method and tools, typically decreases the information search and retrieval time. Additionally, a well-defined process decreases the coordination time overhead. Hence more time can be spent on actual development. Secondly, since OOSE models the way people think, the models are much easier for non-OOSE practitioners to understand than models produced by other classes of method. Thus managers and customers can take a more active part in the actual development. These are just two benefits of OOSE, and there are many more, such as higher quality and decreasing future maintenance costs.

## 15.3 Product development organization

When developing a product, the basic organization of a project should be built around the product and the activities associated with the development of the product. Since the product (one hopes) will be developed in several versions, we must have the **product life cycle** in mind when discussing this topic. Here we see the important difference between method and process as discussed in Chapter 1. Thus let us discuss briefly the processes for developing a product.

Product development with OOSE is built around different models that are developed in sequence. All these models must be maintained during the entire product life cycle; every further development should be accomplished by modifying these models. This means that all changes in the requirements specification should first be analyzed in the requirements model and inserted there. These should lead to modification in the analysis model and later in the design, implementation and testing. Hence all of these models must be up to date at all times during the product's life cycle. In these models, all objects will be documented individually. The whole model will hold all of these documents together. We have earlier discussed the importance of traceability between these models and the documents. It is important to be able to do this continuous revision smoothly.

The first model to be developed in OOSE is the requirements model. This model is developed by the activities shown in Figure 15.1. Here we have one coordinating process that lays the foundation and one specification process for each use case. The identification of domain objects, actors and use cases is done in the coordination process while the specification of the use cases, objects and subsystems and their interfaces is done in the specification processes.

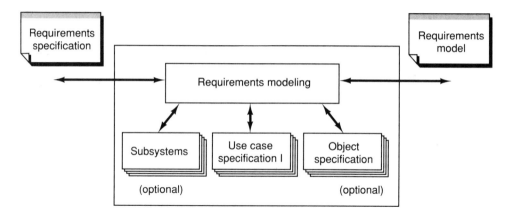

**Figure 15.1**   The process of requirements analysis.

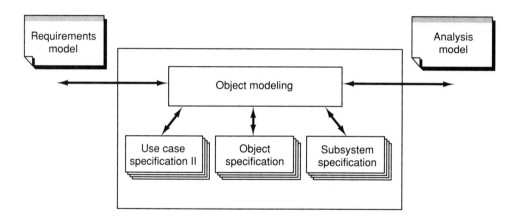

**Figure 15.2**   The process of robustness analysis.

The requirements analysis process delivers a well-defined result: the requirements model with the use case specifications. This forms the input to the object modeling for the analysis process (see Figure 15.2). The main process here coordinates three different kinds of activity: the identification of analysis objects from the use cases; the specification of each object; and the specification of each subsystem. All of these subprocesses have one subprocess instance for every such activity.

The analysis model forms the well-defined result after this process. This forms the input to the construction process (see Figure

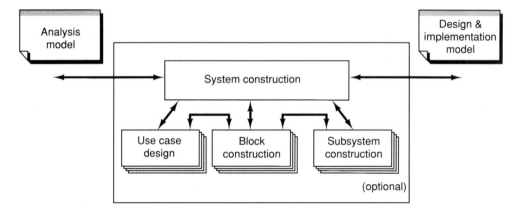

**Figure 15.3**   The process of construction.

15.3). Here it is the system construction process that is the coordinating process. It has three classes of subprocess. The first is the design of the use cases, where each use case is designed over the blocks. These activities will result in the interfaces of the blocks. The second class of process is the block construction process where each block is designed, implemented and unit tested. The third is an optional subsystem construction process for a top-down approach. As you will have noticed, we keep the design and the implementation encapsulated in the block construction process.

The well-defined result delivered by the construction process is the design model and the source code for the unit-tested blocks. This result is the input, together with the requirements model, to the testing process (see Figure 15.4). In the testing process the system is integration tested and system tested. Here the coordinating process is the system test itself. The integration testing is performed by two subprocesses, use case tests and subsystem tests.

In addition to these three main processes we also have the component process. This process is normally not coupled to any specific product, but is a multi-product process, that is, it is shared by several product processes. It mainly interacts with the construction processes. The component process and its subprocesses are shown in Figure 15.5. The coordination process here is the component system construction process; the actual design, implementation and unit testing are done in a component construction process, one for each component.

We have now discussed the main activities as processes in the product life cycle. The processes start when the development of the

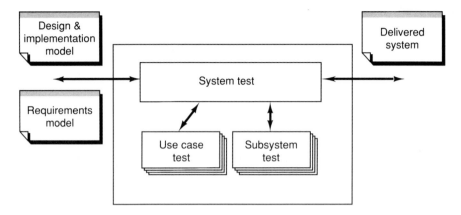

**Figure 15.4**    The testing process.

first product version starts. They last as long as the product is maintained. Note that these processes will be unresourced when no development is being done on the product, but when a further development is to be performed the processes will be resourced again. The processes may also be concurrent activities. In this fashion we can define responsibilities for these processes in terms of, for instance, documents to be maintained. Additionally, all work that is being done on the development of a product can be associated with one of these processes. Note here that we have generalized the development to interacting, long-lasting processes and that we will have very similar behavior both in new development and in further development. These processes do not just participate in pure development projects, but also in tendering projects, error handling projects, and so on.

A **development case description** specifies one set of processes and models and how they should be used in a project. The most fundamental task of the development case description is to tell you:

- Which processes and models to use
- How to use the processes and models in a project.

The first decision is then to decide which models are necessary for the development work. When you know which models you need, you should decide which processes are necessary. It is advisable to use only a few simple models and corresponding processes when introducing OOSE as a new technique. Most people have a limit as to how much they can and want to change their way of working within

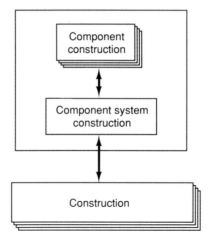

**Figure 15.5** The component process interacts with several construction processes, one per product being developed.

a limited time. It might for instance be a good idea to introduce only the use case model and one of the oject models in the first project.

Having decided which models are appropriate, it is possible to decide which architectural concepts are suitable. The organization must for instance decide whether or not to describe operations in the domain object model. Many such decisions come down to basically the same pros and cons:

+   By using a certain concept we gain clarity.
−   By using a certain concept we may need to allow more time for the developers to learn how to use the concept.
−   By using a certain concept we may make understanding the models more complicated for those not fluent with them.

A typical example of such a decision is whether or not to use inheritance between actors.

When the architecture has been decided, it is possible to decide which documents to use when describing the different models. When documenting operations for domain objects it might be a good idea to provide a separate document for each domain object; in other cases it might be sufficient to have a catalogue document containing all the domain objects.

The different processes must now be adapted to work with the architecture and documents chosen for the project. This involves leaving out work steps associated with the documents and architectural concepts which have not been selected. But there are other process adaptations which are necessary. It is for instance necessary to decide how to handle components, operating system processes and database management systems in the design. There are also some major adaptations which must be made early in the project, for example, adapting the OOSE process to the way configuration management and version control is treated.

The **project organization** problem is now reduced to the question of resourcing these processes. Note also that the processes are similar during the entire product life cycle, that is, each new project for changing the product also uses these processes. The first version of the product will thus have the responsibility for initiating the processes, while subsequent projects just reactivate them by resourcing them. From these processes we can also identify roles played by different people during development; we shall discuss the importance of this later. Another benefit of this process model is that it is easier to encompass different kinds of development. Incremental development, which we shall discuss more later, is a very sound and common strategy and is easily expressed in this process model. Also, the iterative nature of development is supported by the process model. Let us now discuss the allocation of development staff members to these processes, that is, the actual project organization and management.

## 15.4 Project organization and management

Managing and organizing any software development project requires a thorough understanding of the pitfalls of the trade. A necessary, but not sufficient, condition for successful software development is good **project management**. There is an abundance of literature on how to manage software development projects. This is not, however, the subject of the current book and we therefore refer the reader who wants a comprehensive treatment to any of the standard works, such as Metzger (1981). Instead we will concentrate on how to combine common project management practice with OOSE and how to organize the project with respect to the product processes discussed in the previous section. We will also consider what implication object orientation and OOSE will have on project management and what project management should especially consider when working with this new technology.

All projects will have a technical aspect and a management aspect. The purpose of the management aspect is to control, steer and follow up the project. The technical aspect covers what should be done and how you should work to develop the current system or product. It is here that we will find the process model discussed in Section 15.3.

The managerial and technical aspects of a project must, however, fit together and it is common to achieve this by defining a number of **milestones** that should be achieved. A milestone is a concrete, objectively defined or determinable event or precisely defined deliverable. The milestones are often combined with **reviews** and **audits** of the work done so far. Between these milestones the work is performed. This division aims to give better control of the project.

Figure 15.6 shows a typical project model for the overall management of a project. Each specific phase is delimited by a well-defined milestone.

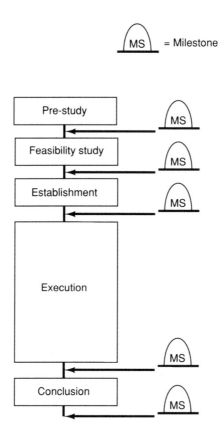

**Figure 15.6**   The management part of a project.

We will here give a short overview of each phase:

- **Pre-study**. Aims at defining the task by developing and evaluating different kinds of requirements, needs and ideas in order to judge, technically and economically, whether the project is practicable.
- **Feasibility study**. Different technical alternatives and their consequences are investigated. A main time and resource schedule is planned and an evaluation of potential risks in the project is made.
- **Establishment.** The project is organized, planned and quality assured. Detailed time and resource plans are developed.
- **Execution**. The project is developed in accordance with the plans previously prepared.
- **Conclusion**. The project is completed and proposals to improve the project and development methods used are summarized.

To this project model we should add the technical aspects of the project. These include what to do in the specific phases. OOSE will be used mainly during the execution phase, although it is also possible to do the pre-study in the same way as a simplified execution phase and thus also use OOSE there. However, work that is part of the technical aspect will also be done in the other phases. One example of this is prototyping. It is very important to achieve an early understanding of the system to be developed. The first two phases typically use prototypes. During the pre-study the purpose is mainly to evaluate technical aspects of the system to be built, often in the form of simulating certain critical parts. During the feasibility study, the prototyping is often more focused in its purpose to investigate certain technical alternatives or to support the requirements specification to be written. The purpose of these prototypes is to increase the precision and quality of the requirements, not to skip or short-circuit later phases. Often prototypes can result in new prototypes to investigate certain tasks further. This is shown schematically in Figure 15.7.

The prototyping technique may also be used during later phases to improve the quality of the system. It is extremely important to be aware of the purpose of the prototype; should the prototype be further refined to bring it closer to the system or does it just aim to investige certain questions? Both aims are good, but far too often a good experimental prototype 'becomes' the real product and is not what was aimed for originally. Prototyping should aim to increase the quality of the product, not decrease it.

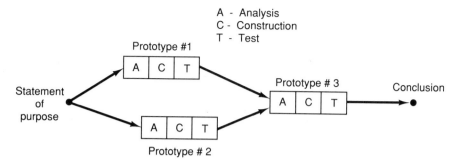

**Figure 15.7**  Prototypes are often an effective way of testing the validity of product ideas and preliminary system requirements. They may very well result in new prototypes to refine the ideas.

The models developed in OOSE are good for supporting the steering of the project. All models have a well-defined result and it is appropriate to use them in combination with milestones. Hence the models can be mapped onto the project model. An ideal mapping of the models is shown in Figure 15.8.

This ideal mapping gives a sense of an early waterfall model where the entire analysis model should be developed, reviewed and frozen before starting work on the design model. It is essential to realize, though, that the models will be modified when work is started on subsequent models. It is therefore essential to understand that there is no point in thinking that there will be no changes; rather, it is important to have a way of handling these changes. A model which is not updated will be out of date and thus not show a consistent picture of the system. An often appropriate way is to give each model a new version at the different milestones. In the following we have used an alphabetical versioning technique starting with A, B, ... Any technique could be used; we just want to illustrate the idea here. In Figure 15.9 an example of how to version the models at different milestones is shown. To handle this versioning a tool is often needed. Examples of different kinds of documents that evolve during the project are also shown in Figure 15.9. It is notable that the actual coding normally starts quite late in the project. We have seen that this is often an uneasy time for the team members since progress is often measured in terms of lines of code produced. Additionally, since the first project is often an evaluation project, several parties are interested in its progress. However, we have also seen that when the actual coding starts, it is done quite fast, often yielding a high productivity in the overall project. Larger projects often need a more incremental development, achieved by developing the system in layers. Incremental development is further discussed in Section 15.4.1.

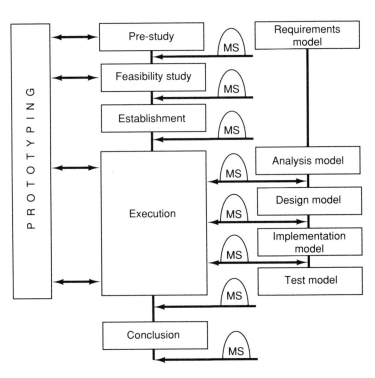

**Figure 15.8** Prototyping may be used during many of the phases in the project. The models in OOSE may be used as milestones that should be achieved.

The requirements specifications should be approved by both supplier and orderer and should contain a complete list of all requirements on the system. The requirements should be ranked by the orderer and the cost should be estimated by the supplier. Additional requirements may involve delivery date, resources and quality. The quality of requirements specifications varies tremendously. It is usual in technical systems to have detailed specifications, while information systems seldom have such detailed specifications as discussed in Chapter 1. The requirements model could very well act as the final requirements specification.

Since the requirements specification is something that may be used as the basis of a contract, it may seem odd that the document will be updated and modified as the version table indicates. The

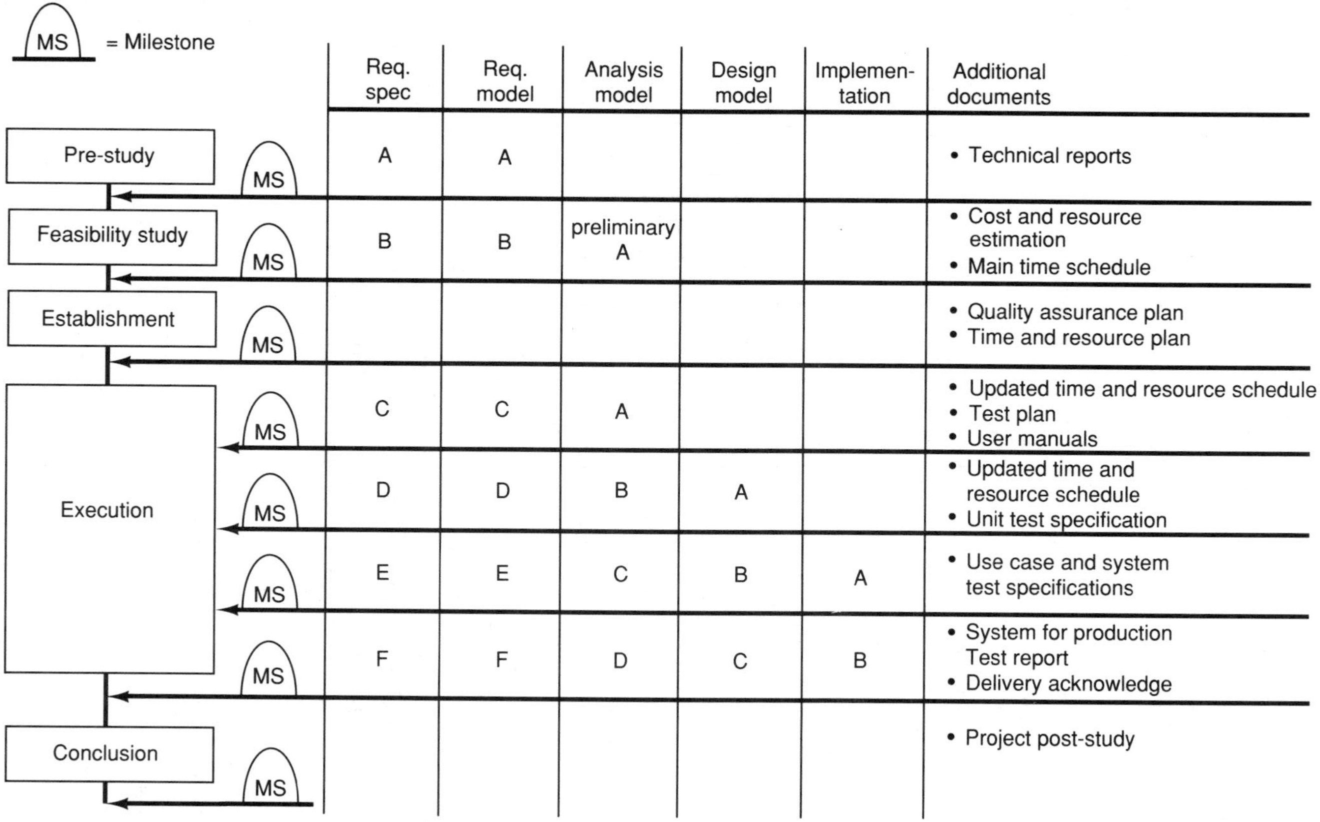

MS = Milestone

| Phase | Req. spec | Req. model | Analysis model | Design model | Implementation | Additional documents |
|---|---|---|---|---|---|---|
| Pre-study | A | A | | | | • Technical reports |
| Feasibility study | B | B | preliminary A | | | • Cost and resource estimation<br>• Main time schedule |
| Establishment | | | | | | • Quality assurance plan<br>• Time and resource plan |
| Execution | C | C | A | | | • Updated time and resource schedule<br>• Test plan<br>• User manuals |
| Execution | D | D | B | A | | • Updated time and resource schedule<br>• Unit test specification |
| Execution | E | E | C | B | A | • Use case and system test specifications |
| Execution | F | F | D | C | B | • System for production<br>Test report<br>• Delivery acknowledge |
| Conclusion | | | | | | • Project post-study |

**Figure 15.9** An example of how versions of the models may arrive at different milestones. Examples of documents that may be appropriate at each milestone are also shown.

hardest part when defining the requirements specification is often to formulate it so that the orderer and the end users can understand what will be delivered, while at the same time giving the developers a complete and well-defined support for the coming development. This document will therefore almost always be updated as the development proceeds and hence the requirements specification (version A) that is written early on will have to be changed during the project. These changes are often aimed at eliminating uncertainties that are noticed as work goes on and also often require additional functionality to be added. Since the contract is often based on this specification, it is important that all modifications of it are approved by both parties. This also enables the orderer to follow the development and to check that no misunderstandings occur. There are three main reasons for modifying the requirements specification during later phases. The first is that the requirements are not distinct enough and need to be clarified. The second is that the project notices that the time or resources available will not be enough to fulfill all requirements and thus wants to delete certain requirements. Finally, certain user groups will wake up when the system is soon to be delivered and then want to insert requirements that actually should have been in the first version of the requirements specification.

A point that is too often forgotten is that new or changed requirements will inevitably generate new costs and possibly also delay the project. Remember also that it gets more expensive to add new requirements the further you progress in the development cycle. A requirement that would have been estimated at 200 man-hours in the specification phase, but was left out, may very well cost 1000 man-hours if introduced in the design phase.

When talking about timing we will only mention an obvious fact that is too often forgotten. If you delay one phase of the project, it will inevitably delay the delivery date also. The subsequent phases will not suddenly be done faster just because one phase took longer. Here we see the importance of following up the project plan and schedule.

### 15.4.1  Incremental development

Although it is possible to carry out a development as discussed above, experience shows that an incremental approach is often more appropriate. Since the models are developed in a very seamless way, it often feels natural to 'investigate' what will happen to an object in one model when continuing to the next model. Object-oriented modeling is often connected to an iterative way of working, probably because of the strong traceability between different models; a problem domain object may exist all the way to the code. However, working too iteratively is not good either. Then you will use later models to correct earlier models in much the way that compilers often are used to debug programs. The solution lies of course in between: first develop one part of one model and continue this part to the subsequent models and then continue with the next part of the first model.

When using OOSE it is often appropriate to develop the requirements model quite extensively as a first step. One reasonable goal is at least to have all use cases *identified* for the entire application. The reason for this is that it is important to have an understanding of the entire system before starting to structure it. It is then possible to start with a couple of use cases, specify them, and then continue with these use cases into the analysis model and also the design, implementation and testing phases. In this way we take the use cases of highest **rank** not yet designed and refine the later models with the new use cases. The rank denotes the importance of a use case – the use cases that perform the main tasks of the system have the highest ranks. Supporting use cases have lower ranks. Here it is evident that the use case is the thread running through all the activities. Each use case ends up in the testing activity and, when all use cases have been tested, the final system test is performed. This development is illustrated in Figure 15.10.

Each increment should be of reasonable size, not too small and not too large. Increments of about 5–20 use cases are often appropriate. It is also important that each increment covers a limited time; often 3–6 months is a reasonable turnaround time, preferably with an upper limit of 12 months. We have seen that project members are often unsure how much work is to be done in one model and how that work is to be used in later models. When this is the case, it is often appropriate to have a fast turnaround, in order to gain experience from work in all models early. Working this way, the developers will have a better understanding of the whole development process early on and can thus optimize the process.

In this way the different phases may also overlap. For instance, while doing construction of one increment, analysis can be performed on the next increment (see Figure 15.11). Since one increment may modify results from previous phases in the same increment, it is important to have a very controlled way of handling different versions of the models. Additionally, you must be able to handle the modification and updating of models in a dynamic way, for example modifications in the analysis model in the first increment should be incorporated smoothly into the analysis model for the second increment.

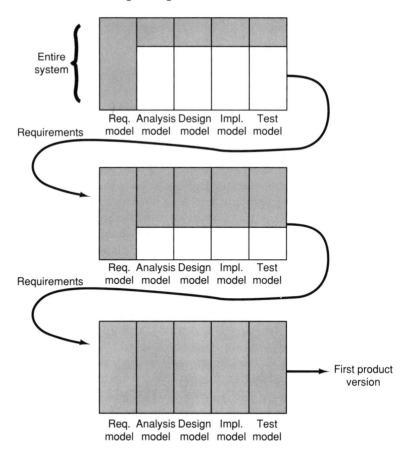

**Figure 15.10**  Incremental development in OOSE.

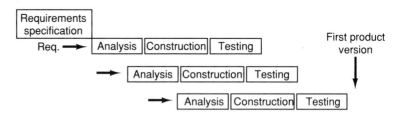

**Figure 15.11**  Work in different phases may very well overlap. Then it is essential to have support for handling different versions of the models.

It is essential to minimize the work needed to deliver results from one phase to another. The deliverables from each phase are defined by the process outputs. A way to solve this is to have some developers follow one increment through all phases and other developers follow one process over several increments; that is, to have some developers specializing in a couple of use cases and others specializing in, for instance, analysis.

# 15.5   Project staffing

The number of people involved in a project varies greatly in different phases. Different phases need different competences. Also, the project organization needs to be changed over these phases in order to manage the project. This is due to the fact that in some phases work can be done in parallel while this is harder in other phases; also, some phases require more resources than others.

Generally, it is valuable to have people participate in both analysis and construction and thus ease the transition between different models. Therefore a nucleus of development staff can be the core of the entire development. However, we may have people specializing in analysis, construction and testing. Integration and system testing in particular is often performed by a special group. The test specifications, though, are developed from the use case descriptions from the design and are based on which blocks are involved in the use case and when those blocks will be delivered to testing. Design and implementation should thus be planned so that the blocks can be delivered to testing when they are needed. In this way much of the work can be done in parallel. This means that even if other people are involved during testing, they must collaborate intensively with the construction personnel.

We will briefly discuss some typical ways of organizing a project and also illustrate some specific points in an object-oriented development. We here assume a medium-sized project which involves 5–20 people during analysis, construction and testing. Staffing in phases other than the ones we have discussed in this book will not be covered.

When assigning development staff tasks in a project, we use the processes discussed earlier. After all, since the processes describe what is to be done, a specific project is actually a flow over these processes. The problem is thus to resource the processes for a specific project. Let us start with the coordinating processes. These are summarized in Figure 15.12.

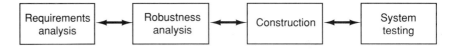

**Figure 15.12**   The coordination processes in OOSE.

These main processes coordinate the entire development. The identification of use cases is performed in requirements analysis, while the specification of them is done in specific subprocesses for each use case specification. These main processes will structure the system robustly (in robustness analysis) and make the final architecture (in construction). Hence the important structuring of the system is performed within these processes. The people staffing these processes should therefore be the core of the development and thus should be the same in at least the first three processes. We may call this group the **system architecture group**. Their responsibility is to make sure that the system architecture, and its coherent idea, is maintained during the entire development. It is essential that these people are highly qualified and have a strong influence on the project members and that the rest of the project members have confidence in them. The project manager should be tightly coupled to this group.

The initial analysis (mainly requirements analysis) should be done by quite a small group with much interaction with the end users. Not all of the people involved in requirements analysis need to know the technology used in later phases; the concepts used are quite intuitive. These people should have close contact with end users, customers, marketing people, experienced developers and so on.

The subprocesses for the more detailed work should be resourced by development personnel who have special skills for the activity. Here it is often a good idea to have the same person responsible for the same group of objects in all activities. For instance, the person specifying a particular use case should also specify the objects that offer the use case, design the use case and implement the corresponding blocks. However, since the complexity (that is, work) increases, especially during implementation, this is not always possible. Nevertheless, the person responsible for the specification in analysis should work as a senior designer when implementing the blocks. However, there are often people involved in modeling the requirements model who will not participate in the subsequent work.

The main reason for having the same person in all subprocesses that manage a group of objects is to minimize the work of collecting and understanding information. Additionally, you will avoid the conflict of not agreeing with the specification (the 'not invented here' problem). However, this may also involve drawbacks.

When doing it this way, reviews will be more important. Other people must also be able to understand the documentation, for further development.

In larger projects it is often appropriate to divide the development into several project groups. Each group is then responsible for one subsystem and/or a specific task in the development. It is far better to have one group responsible for one part of the system than to have one group responsible for a specific phase. The reason for this is that the domain knowledge, for example the knowledge of the subsystem's task, is more important for the result than detailed knowledge of a specific phase. In each project group, the activities are divided further. All these activities are cooperating subprocesses in the development.

When the construction phase is reached, typically more people are involved. This may be managed by adding more people to existing groups or by adding new groups to the project organization. When you add new groups you will also reduce the responsibility of each group. It is often more appropriate to keep the initial groups. Generally you should not let the resources affect the system structure. Block testing is done during construction and thus is usually an activity within each and every project group. These groups also need a coordinating architecture group, preferably the same as during analysis.

The component activity is responsible for maintaining and developing components. This is an activity that should be shared among several projects and is thus not a part of the project under consideration. It is essential that upper management realizes this important distinction.

Integration testing is done in a separate testing phase, often by a separate group. This group can very well start its activities by writing test specifications when use cases are specified during analysis. When all use case tests have been performed, the final activity within the development is the system test. This test involves testing the functionality of the system, documentation and tutorial material. The system test cannot start before all the parts in this version have been delivered by the construction phase.

During or after the testing phase, it is sensible to do a post-study of the project where positive and negative experiences are collected and documented. It is better to do this study directly after the project (when the members are available and their picture of the project is still clear) and to complement this study with a study of operational experiences of the system after about 3–6 months, rather than to do the whole post-study then. The risk then is that the post-study will never be done and hence valuable experiences are never documented.

Besides the actual development groups there may be a need for other roles or groups in the project. Examples are listed below:

- **Methodologist**. A person or group responsible for the method used. He or she or they should be experts in the method and support the development team in applying the method. It is often useful for these people to understand 'both sides', namely to be able to explain the new techniques in terms of the techniques already used. This means that the methodologists must be experts, not only in the new method, but also in the language, operating system, product structure and development organization of the team where the new method is to be introduced.

- **Quality Assurance (QA)**. People responsible for both the product and the process to develop the product so that it is of high quality. This involves guaranteeing that all software delivered is of high quality and that documentation is consistent. Reviews are a useful tool here and we will discuss this issue later.

- **Documentation, manuals and training**. Documentation of the system should be produced by the developers. It should of course be consistent with the system developed. Manuals, both for maintenance and for users, should be written by people with special skills for this. Planning for system training must also be done. People who should be trained include users, maintenance and operation people and sales staff.

- **Reuse coordinator.** This person or group is responsible both for encouraging reuse and for evaluating how much the project is reusing, as well as for investigating the reuse potential of the code and designs developed. Code, designs, documents and models may be reused. This person or group should work intimately with the architecture and QA groups. Reuse might not give a pay-back in one specific project; the real gain comes in subsequent projects that reuse what has been developed in this project. Therefore the cost of this function should not burden the project cost, but rather be considered as a multiple-project cost. Note that the coordination and management of the reuse library should be done on an inter-project basis (see Chapter 11).

- **Prototyper**. This role is necessary to investigate different solutions at an early stage in order to prepare for later development. Typically it is interesting to prototype user interfaces in early phases, but simulation of certain designs in later phases may also be interesting.

- **Support environment.** This is to function as a service to the project as a whole. Typically system managers play this role.

- **Staff.** Staff may be needed to help the project manager. One example is a special project administrator responsible for following up cost and time schedules. This is often needed in larger projects. Some of the above roles may be part of the staff supporting the project manager

- **User interface coordinator.** A specific individual or group should be given overall responsibility for user interface design. This is important in order to ensure consistency. The user interface coordinator(s) have final responsiblity for all matters concerning the content, shape and form of the entire user interface. There is a natural connection between the work to ensure a consistent user interface and the work with the use cases since the use cases define how the system is going to be used.

- **Help system coordinator.** Because it is such a crucial and potentially complex part of the user interface, the help system should also be made the responsibility of a specific individual or group. This help system group should include at least one technical/programming member and at least one documentation or technical writing specialist. Technical writers will have final responsibility for the actual text in the help system. The help system design coordinator works with and is subordinate in responsibility to the user interface coordinator. The help system coordinator(s) have responsibility for the development of the software (subsystem) necessary for the help function, as well as final responsibility for the contents of all help system text. This responsibility has a strong relation to the documentation, manuals and education responsibility mentioned above.

It is often effective to have people with these special roles also working in the project groups. If so, it is important to give them time to fulfill their double roles.

# 15.6   Software quality assurance

Software Quality Assurance (SQA) aims to ensure that the final product will have an acceptable quality. It is mainly a management activity to identify quality problems early in the development. Cost and time schedules are often tracked in the early stages, rather than quality, but quality problems appearing late in development involve large risks for any project. Therefore tracking quality is just as important as tracking cost and time.

Quality assurance focuses on both the product and the process. The **product**-oriented part of SQA (often called Software Quality Control) should strive to ensure that the software delivered has a minimum number of faults and satisfies the users' needs. The **process**-oriented part (often called Software Quality Engineering) should institute and implement procedures, techniques and tools that promote the fault-free and efficient development of software products.

What then are the characteristics for high quality in a product? In Figure 15.13 some of the characteristics are shown.

These characteristics are not exhaustive and not even independent of each other. Additionally, they often tend to conflict in a development. Therefore, when starting a development, it is often a good idea to decide which characteristics are the most important for this specific product and then focus on these throughout the development. In OOSE the focus is on maintainability characteristics. As we have discussed, the maintenance of the product is the major objective when developing the structure of the system. However, this will of course also have effects on the suitability criteria; if it is easy to introduce changes to the system, it will also decrease the number of faults introduced when the system is modified and thus give the product a higher reliability.

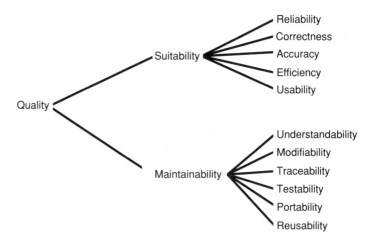

**Figure 15.13**  Some characteristics of software product quality.

The material to work with when doing SQA is mainly the documentation produced during development. No new documents should be needed for SQA. Therefore it is essential that everything important that is done should be documented. The (far too) common picture in software development is first to do the work and then to document it. The right way is first to document what should be done and then to do the work. When working with OOSE this philosophy is permeated throughout. The requirements model will be developed first and followed by the analysis and design models, before the actual code is written. Each of these models will be developed and documented concurrently. Therefore OOSE gives a good platform for carrying out quality assurance in an accurate way.

The main tools for quality assurance are the development process itself, reviews and audits, testing and metrics. The development processes of OOSE, including testing, have been surveyed in this book. Metrics will be discussed in the next section. Here we will discuss very briefly the integration of reviews in OOSE. First some terminology: a **formal** review's objective is to decide whether or not to proceed to the next phase. Such a review is held at every major project milestone. A quite large review team is often involved and customers or orderers also participate. An **informal** review's objective is to discover errors that have been made. These reviews can be held at any time during development, such as when something is completed that ought to be checked before continuing the development. Informal reviews often have a quite limited participation, typically involving some of the developers.

Where to use different kinds of reviews when working with OOSE depends on the size of the project. In a small-to-medium sized project, typical formal review points are between the main activities, that is, each model when it has reached its first version. Informal reviews may be used after each subprocess, possibly grouping some subprocesses in one review.

Different kinds of reviews have also been defined by IEEE (1983) in a standard glossary. Three different kinds of reviews are given:

- **Review.** A formal meeting at which a model is presented to the user, customer or other interested parties for comments and approval.

- **Inspection.** A formal evaluation technique in which models are examined in detail by a person or group other than the author to detect errors, violations of development standards and other problems.

- **Walkthrough.** A review process in which a developer leads one or more members of the development team through a segment of a model that he or she has written while the other members ask questions and make comments about technique, style, possible errors, violation of development standards and other problems.

Of these we may characterize review as formal and inspection and walkthrough as informal. Although every review is unique and focuses on a specific model or object, they have some points in common. We will not give exhaustive lists here of what to review in the OOSE models, but rather just highlight some examples.

Common to all reviews is checking of things like consistency with requirements, completeness of model, redundancy, structure, naming, correct associations, understandability, versioning of documents, standards and views. The importance given to each item in a particular review depends on the purpose of that review.

When reviewing each model there are specific things to focus on. Here we only give some examples of points to review in the requirements model, as follows:

- Is the delimitation of the system's boundaries appropriate?
- Do the use cases match the requirements specification?
- Has the requirements specification been updated?
- Is it possible to understand the use cases?
- Are all roles interacting with the system identified as actors? Do all actors have the correct set of use cases?
- Has the requirements specification been covered?
- Are the interfaces described in a satisfactory way?
- Are the use case flows correct and complete?
- Have enough alternative flows and error flows been described?

Of course, the actual questions may vary from time to time, but the intention should be clear from the examples given above. When reviewing the other models the intention should be the same: to find errors as early as possible in the development process and similarly to guarantee a high quality in the product.

When performing the review, different methods and techniques can be used. A systematic approach to this is necessary in order to achieve a delivered system of high quality. Methods and techniques for this are described in the literature (see Weinberg and Freedman (1982), Myers (1987) and Yourdon (1989b)).

When performing reviews, management has an important role to play. It is important that the management shows commitment to the process and results and also budgets time for performing reviews; more than 5 % of the overall development time is not unusual. Likewise it is important to get good people as reviewers in order to guarantee high product quality and to ensure high confidence in the review process among the development staff. The manager should also reward reviews which are well conducted, thorough and achieve their purpose, particularly of products which are not going well, and punish ineffective reviews of any product. There will always be errors to detect. Some hard facts about defects are the following:

- A defect introduced during requirements specification will cost 100-1000 times more to correct when the system is in the testing phase than it would cost to fix during requirements specification.
- The number of faults introduced by different programmers may vary by as much as a factor of 10 when producing 1000 lines of code.
- During normal testing only about 50 % of the faults will be detected.

To achieve good quality discipline, and high quality awareness, an independent quality group responsible for quality assurance in the development department may be needed. This group can review how well the project members follow the prescribed development process; they can also assess the project's probability of achieving its goals and illustrate potential risks. However, the QA group should not function as policemen, rather, together with the development team, they should increase the quality of what is being done.

Finally, we want to give some advice concerning quality:

- Follow the development process thoroughly, and note what goes wrong.
- Eliminate the faults as quickly as possible by reviewing all specifications thoroughly.
- See that the review groups have the right composition of people.
- Note in the review protocols the number of pages reviewed and the number of faults of different types found.
- Follow up the review protocols and identify, and possibly rewrite, extremely error-prone objects. Try also to identify any individuals who seem to produce many defects in specifications or code.

- Have an independent testing group testing the system and also writing the test report.
- It is always cheapest to *do it right the first time.*

## 15.7  Software metrics

'If you can't measure it, it's not engineering' is often stated in the (software) engineering community. We partly agree, and therefore it is essential to introduce quantitative values in the software industry. These are mainly lacking today, but some first steps on this road have been taken. We will discuss some of them here.

A necessary method for controlling a development is to use metrics. The metrics can measure either the process of development or various aspects of the product. Metrics in software engineering have been discussed for a long time, but not used widely as a means of increasing the quality of the product or process. The real problem is that we cannot measure exactly what we would like to measure; we must assume that there are relationships between what we can measure and what we would like to measure. Process-related metrics have been used much more than product-related metrics, so let's start by discussing these.

**Process-related metrics** measure things like man-months, schedule time and number of faults found during testing. To learn to handle and manage a development process such as OOSE it is important to start collecting data on these measures as methodically as possible. Below are examples of a number of process-related metrics that should be collected when working with OOSE:

- Total development time;
- Development time in each process and subprocess;
- Time spent modifying models from previous processes;
- Time spent in all kinds of subprocesses, such as use case specification, object specification, use case design, block design, block testing and use case testing for each particular object;
- Number of different kinds of fault found during reviews;
- Number of change proposals for previous models;
- Cost for quality assurance;
- Cost for introducing new development process and tools.

These measures may form a basis for future planning of development projects. For instance, if we know the average time to specify a use case, we can predict the time to specify all use cases when we know the number to be specified. Statistical measures (such as averages) should always be accompanied by an indication of the certainty of the measures (such as the standard deviation). Otherwise you will have no sense of the accuracy of the prediction. We have also noted that these measures may vary greatly between different projects, organizations, applications and staffing. Therefore it is dangerous to draw general conclusions on existing data without looking at the circumstances. For instance, in one project a typical complete use case design including all alternative courses and error courses could take about five days. In another project where the use cases are smaller a typical use case design may only take two days.

Several different kinds of **product-related metrics** have been proposed. None of these has been demonstrated to be generally useful as an overall quality predictor. However, as we discussed in the previous section, some quality criteria can be used to predict a certain quality property. One example to measure traceability is to measure how many of the original requirements are directly traceable to the use case model.

Traditional metrics on products (including code) may to some extent also be used in object-oriented software. However the most common metric, lines of code, is actually less interesting for object-oriented software. The less code you have written the more you have reused and that often (but not always!) gives your product a higher quality. To get a feeling for the actual code the following are examples of metrics that are more appropriate for object-oriented software:

- Total number of classes
- Number of classes reused and the number newly developed
- Total number of operations
- Number of operations reused and the number    newly developed
- Total number of stimuli sent

  Some metrics that are more specific are:

- Number, width and height of the inheritance hierarchies;
- Number of classes inheriting (or using) a specific operation;
- Number of classes that a specific class is dependent on;
- Number of classes that are dependent on a specific class;
- Number of direct users of a class or operation (the highest scored are candidates for components).

It is often also interesting to measure more statistical metrics. When this is the case you should measure both the average and the deviation. Some examples of such metrics are:

- Average number of operations in a class
- Length of operations (in statements)
- Stimuli sent from each operation
- Average number of descendants for a class
- Average number of inherited operations

When measuring code it is important that things like comments do not disturb the metric. Therefore it is often appropriate to differentiate between lines of code, lines of comments and lines of documented code (the sum of the two previous items).

Other common source-code metrics can be used with various degrees of usefulness in object-oriented software. For instance, the **McCabe cyclomatic complexity** (McCabe (1976)) measures the complexity of a graph (see Figure 15.14). The idea is to draw the sequence a program may take as a graph with all possible paths. The complexity, calculated as connections – nodes + 2, will give you a number denoting how complex your program (sequence) is. Since complexity will increase the possibility of errors, a too high McCabe number should be avoided. Some standards require that no module should have a McCabe number greater than 10. Note that the McCabe number also gives you the number of test cases to do path testing.

In object-oriented software the McCabe number as defined above will be of less interest. There are several reasons for this. The first is due to polymorphism. As we noticed in Chapter 12, every stimulus sent is a potential CASE statement in a procedural language. Since we do not know about the receiver's class, any stimulus statement could hide a number of operations – in an untyped language, in principle, as many as there are classes in the system. Typically CASE statements increase the McCabe number rapidly. Thus we must decide how to handle polymorphism when using the McCabe metric; in its traditional application it is usually not very interesting.

Another issue is that you would only measure the complexity of an operation, since that is where you find a program sequence. It is very unusual to have operations with a high McCabe number, and definitely not over 10 (except in very special circumstances), if we do not count polymorphic statements.

However, the McCabe number could be used in OOSE. The use cases connect together several objects in a specific sequence. This sequence will have a complexity that is of great interest. Calculating

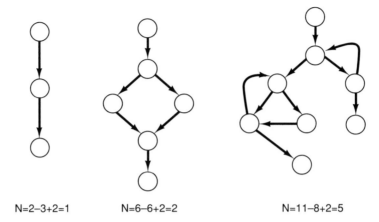

N=2–3+2=1          N=6–6+2=2                    N=11–8+2=5

**Figure 15.14**    The McCabe complexity metric. N = Connection–Nodes+2.

the McCabe number for a use case gives a complexity measure for that use case. Here the interaction diagrams are used as a tool to calculate the metric.

We have thus far mainly discussed metrics of code. What is often more interesting (and much harder) is to develop metrics to measure the quality of the design and analysis. Today we do not have any such generally applicable metrics. However, it is interesting to collect data and measurements even for these models. This is mainly for project management, where you are interested in quantitative metrics for project planning and control. Here we will give some suggestions of what to measure:

- Number of requirements
- Number of use cases and actors
- Number of objects of each type, namely entity objects, interface objects and control objects
- Number of subsystems
- Number of blocks
- Number of classes

Besides these absolute metrics, it is also interesting to measure:

- The number of objects offering a use case
- The correlation between analysis objects and blocks
- The number of blocks participating in a use case
- The number of classes in a block

- The number of operations per block
- The number of stimuli sent in one use case
- The number of parameters in every stimulus
- The locality of requirements expressed for subsystems and/or use cases

The metrics that we have discussed above should not be viewed as the only interesting measurements to be taken, quite the opposite; they are only proposed metrics and should inspire you to develop your own. We are not yet ready to give clear recommendations as to which metrics should be used when working with OOSE for quality assurance and project management.

The number of different kinds of metric is very large, and which to choose must be reviewed from time to time. It is important, though, to use metrics and collect data in an organized way. Actually the real problem with metrics is that they are not used. Since they are not used we will not collect any data and thus cannot validate or calibrate the metrics: therefore we do not have any really useful metrics. To start to break this vicious circle we must start to collect metrics and then refine the metrics as we learn about them. However, even if we have metrics it will not be the final answer. To quote Albert Einstein: 'Not everything that counts can be counted and not everything that can be counted counts.' More on software metrics can be found in Boehm (1981) and Grady and Caswell (1987).

## 15.8  Summary

The introduction of a new development process into an organization must be done with great care. Such changes are normally part of a long-term plan for the development organization. It is essential to introduce the new process smoothly; often a pilot project is selected to try out the new process in the organization. To give the organization and the project a fair chance, a special education and training program should be planned. Risk analysis should be done prior to starting the project to increase awareness of the risks involved, and steps should be taken to manage these risks.

The focus of each project must be on the product developed. The subprocesses of the development process describe this handling and these are therefore appropriate to use for the organization of the project. The project organization is thus mainly a matter of resourcing all the subprocess instances. A project model should be used to steer the project. This should support the idea of milestones to follow up the project and to check that the project is on the right track throughout. Prototyping is normally an integrated part of all development work in order to increase the quality of the final product. It is essential to keep track of the documents produced and a versioning strategy should be coupled to the development process. A more complex but often better strategy is to use incremental development. Then we have shorter turnaround times for each phase and we also have the chance to gain experience early.

Project staffing for OOSE involves some new roles, but also several roles that are important in traditional development. It is essential to have a core group that is responsible for the overall architecture and philosophy of the system throughout the entire development. It is also important to have knowledge about the system in all phases. The use cases provide this common thread in all phases. It is therefore often appropriate to have certain team members following some specific use cases throughout development. Other roles in OOSE involve methodologists, reuse coordinators and prototypers. The team responsible for reusable components is shared among several projects and thus is the concern of upper management.

Software quality assurance should focus both on the development process and on the product developed. The fundamental techniques include review, testing and metrics. Review is the best known technique today that gives the highest increase in quality early in development. Metrics should also be used to start collecting data to increase quality. However, today there are no well-known direct metrics that we can use to increase quality in advance. The indirect metrics include the number of faults identified or the number of changes in a review. Nevertheless, to gain quality in an ordered way tomorrow, we must start using metrics today.

# 16 Other object-oriented methods

## 16.1 Introduction

Most of the methods used in the industry today, for both information and technical system development, are based on a functional and/or data-driven decomposition of the system. These approaches differ in many ways from the approach taken by object-oriented methods where data and functions are highly integrated. In Chapter 4 we discussed the problems with a function/data approach.

Combining function/data methods with object-oriented methods in the same development cycle has been discussed; see for instance Ward (1989). In a panel discussion at OOPSLA'90 on this topic (see OOPSLA (1990)) the conclusion was that any such combination should be avoided. In general, we share this view. However, some of the diagramming techniques used in function/data methods may also be used in object-oriented methods. One example of this is state transition graphs which can be used to model objects. As we discussed in Chapter 4, a paradigm shift occurs when converting from one point of view into another. Such a paradigm shift is very complex and should in general be avoided.

In this chapter we discuss at an overview level some other object-oriented development methods. We make no claim to completeness. All of the methods aim at modeling systems in terms of objects which will form the basis of the system realization. The central problem in all object modeling techniques is to find an appropriate object structure.

It is very hard in a systematic comparison to do justice to all methods. There are so many aspects that have to be compared and real comparisons should involve parallel projects with equal members and under equal conditions. What is really interesting is to compare how the method has helped to achieve a better and more competitive product in terms of quality, productivity, ability to be modified and so on. What is much easier to compare is notation, concepts and easy-to-define strategies; most comparisons are made on this level, including this one. We will only be able to give some *ad hoc* comments on the methods.

The techniques discussed here are all what we defined as methods in Chapter 2. They are all described as step-by-step procedures. Although we have not discussed it substantially in this book, Objectory focuses on the product life cycle instead of on projects only. The Objectory process is thus actually described in terms of process descriptions where we focus on how the product is changed during its life cycle and the activities connected to these changes. Large-scale industrialization is thus essential. To compare methods with processes is, in our view, to compare an industrial process with craftsmanship. For instance, an industrial car manufacturer has a completely different approach from that of a craftsman car developer. If we only compare the fact that both put a steering wheel on, and both put seats in the car, we have missed the point. Then we do not understand the difference in the properties of the cars given by a process on the one hand and the craftsman on the other. Hence properties other than concepts are the most important.

As to the methods we will highlight in this chapter, there are some fundamental differences between OOSE and these methods. We emphasize some of these here:

(1) Working with *three object types* in the analysis model to help get a robust structure, which we have called robustness analysis, is unique. None of the methods discussed here use different object types to aid the robustness of the system. Some methods use several object types, but they are not primarily intended to find the actual structure of the system.

(2) The formalization of *models*: in OOSE we develop different models that are related. Our experience shows that different models are needed for different purposes; different models are needed for discussing the requirements with the customers, for the designer's use, and for testing. Models of the system are also needed in order to maintain it. These models are documented and revised separately. They are all under configuration management and version control. The other methods discussed in this chapter only work with one model or, in some cases, with different views of the same model.

(3) The need for a *use case concept*: the use case concept is central to OOSE. It is used for many different purposes. If not earlier, the need for such a concept comes when the system is to be

tested or when the manuals are to be written. Some of the methods discussed here have started to see the need for a use case concept, but none have formalized it as clearly as in OOSE.

(4) The difference between *process* and *method*: how appropriately a method fits into a larger organization and the scalability of a method are important. None of the other methods described here claim to have a supporting process.

(5) The degree of *formalization*: software engineering is as yet not very formal but there is a clear degree of difference between the formalization of the methods discussed here. Formalizing the concepts is essential, especially to develop CASE support that is more than a documentation tool, for example consistency control, dynamic and automatic relations between models, automatic generation of information or 'intelligent' support.

Most comparisons between methods compare only concepts and notations and thus do not cover some of the points above. Some also compare the actual advice and rules given by the methods. In this chapter we too restrict our discussion to the easiest level, namely a discussion of concepts and ideas about how to work with the methods. As stated, however, we believe that the 'industrialness' of the method is the most important consideration when selecting a method for an industrial organization. For academic purposes, however, the conceptual aspects may be the most interesting.

First we shall give a very brief overview of some object-oriented methods and then we will focus on some of them. The basis of this overview is publicly available references. Most methods used in the industry are not publicly available. The references we use may be old and new material which extends the methods may exist. Furthermore, several other methods do exist.

## 16.2 A summary of object-oriented methods

There are several object-oriented development methods around. Some are given generous attention in textbooks while others have only been described in articles. Still others are in-house developments that are only used within an organization. We know of several different OO methods that are not easily accessible for public use. It is natural to expect that the number of methods will increase as a result of the current high interest in object-oriented techniques.

Many of the earlier attempts were object-based methods, that is, supporting objects but not inheritance or classes. One of the early pioneers was Grady Booch (1983) whose early method was based on the ideas of Abbot (1983) and evolved in several steps (see Booch (1986, 1987)) to his latest version, **Object-Oriented Design (OOD)** (see Booch (1991)). The method has evolved continuously and in the latest version, earlier versions are criticized because 'it definitely does not scale well to anything beyond fairly trivial problems' (see Booch (1991)). We shall discuss OOD in more depth later.

Other early attempts include **Object-Oriented Systems Analysis** (OOSA) by Shlaer and Mellor (1988). This is essentially information analysis based on data modeling. OOSA fails to capture behavior and does not contain inheritance or classification. Rather, the focus is on describing relationships between objects.

The **Object Modeling Technique (OMT)** by Rumbaugh *et al.* (1991) (earlier drafts were presented by Loomis, Shah and Rumbaugh (1987)) is based on entity/relationship modeling with extensions to modeling classes, inheritance and behavior. The technique has been extended, to focus on relational database design, by Blaha, Premerlani and Rumbaugh (1988). We will discuss this method in more depth later.

**Object-Oriented Analysis (OOA)** by Peter Coad and Ed Yourdon (1991a) is a step-by-step method for developing object-oriented system models. OOA will be discussed in more detail later. A design method following the analysis approach has also been published (see Coad and Yourdon (1991b)).

**Hierarchical Object-Oriented Design (HOOD)** (see HOOD (1989a,b)) was initially developed for the European Space Agency (ESA) by a consortium consisting of CISI Ingéniere, CRI A/S and Matra Space. It has been further developed by the HOOD Working Group. HOOD has been selected by ESA as the design method for architectural design in projects like Columbus and Hermes, that is, for large real-time systems. HOOD assumes that the software will be coded in Ada. HOOD will be discussed in more detail later.

**Object-Oriented Structured Design (OOSD)** by Wasserman *et al.* (1989, 1990) is actually only a notation for object-oriented designs, and is an extension to the structure charts used in structured design and Booch notation techniques for Ada packages. OOSD does not include a method of its own, hence designers are expected to develop and use their own techniques.

**Responsibility-Driven Design** by Wirfs-Brock *et al.* (1990) is a method which models an application in terms of classes, their responsibilities and their collaborations. Initially the system's objects and classes are identified. The system's responsibilities are analyzed and allocated to the classes of the system. Finally, the collaborations between classes of objects that must occur in order to fulfill the responsibilities are defined. This gives a preliminary design which is further explored through hierarchies, subsystems and protocols. The method uses CRC (Class, Responsibilities and Collaboration) cards as described by Beck and Cunningham (1989). We will discuss this method in more depth later.

The **Object-Oriented Role Analysis, Synthesis and Structuring (OORASS)** method by Reenskaug *et al.* (described by Wirfs-Brock and Johnson (1990)) involves several steps in the system development cycle. Analysis focuses on different **roles** played by objects in the system. *Synthesis* defines new objects by inheriting behavior from several simpler ones. *Structuring* uses a meta-model to specify how objects may be bound to each other during system instantiation.

Other, more or less fully worked out, methods that are based on ideas from object orientation include **Object-oriented Systems Analysis (OSA)** by Embley *et al.* (1992), **Object Behavior Analysis (OBA)** by Goldberg and Rubin (1992), and **Synthesis** by Page-Jones and Weiss (1989) and Buhr (1991).

We will now discuss some of these methods in more detail. The methods we will focus on are:

- Object-Oriented Analysis (OOA), by Coad and Yourdon
- Object-Oriented Design (OOD), by Booch
- Hierarchical Object-Oriented Design (HOOD)
- Object Modeling Technique (OMT)
- Responsibility-Driven Design

For each of these methods we will discuss the architecture, method and deliverables, and we also compare the approach with OOSE. We will focus on the properties that differ from OOSE. Note that the comparisons are only approximate. Many of the relations are not clear. We have then chosen a concept  which is close to OOSE and also used parentheses where the relation is not clear.

In Figure 16.1 we have tried to compare what phases these methods cover as compared with OOSE. Note that comparing phases like this hides very many important aspects. For instance, in the requirements analysis phases the methods discussed here only use domain object models and no use case model, which is central in OOSE. The depth of the methods also varies tremendously. Some method descriptions only have a couple of pages of substance in each phase, while others only provide tools for the phases. The ambitions of the methods also vary greatly; we will comment on some of these issues below.

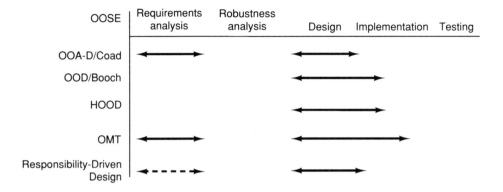

**Figure 16.1**   The activities of OOSE related to the methods discussed in this chapter.

# 16.3   Object-Oriented Analysis (OOA/Coad–Yourdon)

## 16.3.1   Architecture

In OOA an analysis model is developed to describe the functionality of the sysem. In Table 16.1 we have related some concepts used in OOA to OOSE. The idea in the Coad–Yourdon design is to extend this model with respect to processes (tasks), human interfaces and DBMS issues. We do not consider the design technique to be worth further discussion here.

The term **Class&Objects** is introduced to mean the class and the objects in that class. The word 'object' in OOSE is sometimes used to mean a class or a specific instance of a class. It should be obvious from the context of each occurrence what is meant. Also, in views we draw objects. This usually means the class and all instances of this class. We differentiate between the class' associations (dashed lines) and the instance's associations (drawn as full lines). This is to draw one view instead of three. Otherwise there is a simple mapping of concepts from OOA to OOSE. The term **subject** means a specific grouping of Class&Objects to help and guide the reader of a model. No direct correspondence to OOSE exists. Instead, we use different views for this purpose. Subjects may also be used as subsystems in OOSE, but this is not the normal case since subjects may overlap. Subjects are not treated as formally as subsystems.

**Table 16.1**   The concepts of OOA related to OOSE concepts

| OOA | OOSE |
| --- | --- |
| Class | Class |
| Object | Instance |
| Class&Object | (Object) |
| Gen-spec-structure | Inheritance |
| Whole-part-structure | Consists-of |
| Instance Connection | Acquaintance |
| Message | Stimuli |
| Message connection | Communication |
| Attribute | Attribute |
| Service | Operation |
| Subject | ~ View, (Subsystem) |

## 16.3.2   Method

OOA uses basic structuring principles and joins them with an object-oriented point of view. The method consists of five steps; it is proposed that the following order should be adopted:

(1)  Finding Class&Objects

(2)  Identifying structures

(3)  Defining subjects

(4)  Defining attributes

(5)  Defining services

**Finding Class&Objects** specifies how classes and objects should be found. The first approach is given by starting with the *application domain* and identifying the classes and objects forming the basis of the entire application; in the light of this, the *system's responsibilities* in this domain are analyzed. Investigating the system environment may produce further classes and objects that the system should know about. Notes are made of information that needs to be saved about each object and what behavior each object must provide.

**Identifying structures** is principally done in two different ways. The first, the *generalization–specialization* (gen–spec) structure, captures the inheritance hierarchy among the identified classes. The other structure, the *whole–part* structure, is used to model how an object is part of another object and how objects are grouped into larger categories.

**Identifying subjects** is done by partitioning the Class&Objects model into larger units. Subjects are groups of Class&Objects. The size of each subject is selected to help a reader to understand the system through the model. It is appropriate to use the structures identified earlier to define subjects. For example, a gen–spec structure can be grouped into one subject. When useful in guiding the reader, subjects may overlap.

**Defining attributes** is done by identifying information and the associations that should be associated with each and every instance. For each object, you identify the attributes needed to characterize it. The identified attributes are placed in the correct level of the inheritance hierarchy. Any instance connections are also identified by checking previous OOA results or by mapping problem domain relationships. The attributes are specified by names and descriptions. Any special constraints on the attributes are also specified.

**Defining services** means defining the operations of the classes. This is done by identifying the object states and defining services such as create, access, connect, calculate, monitor an external system and so on. How the objects communicate with messages is identified using message connections, which are similar to the communication associations of OOSE. These are used to specify each operation. Here 'threads of execution' is used as a technique to follow a message sequence. Finally, services are specified by a graphical notation similar to a flow chart.

### 16.3.3   Deliverables

The outcome of the OOA method is documented in a special graphical notation (see Figure 16.2) and special templates for the textual documentation of classes and objects. The model is presented and reviewed in a top-down manner in the following order:

- Subject layer (only subjects are presented).
- Class&Objects layer (Class&Objects and subjects are shown).
- Structure layer (structures are added to the previous layer).
- Attribute layer (attributes are added to the previous layer).
- Service layer (services are added to the previous layer).

### 16.3.4   Discussion

OOA is essentially an object-oriented approach and concepts like class, instance, inheritance, encapsulation and communication between objects are essential ingredients. The Class&Objects concept is introduced to avoid ambiguities that sometimes arise when there is an unclear combination of classes and objects.

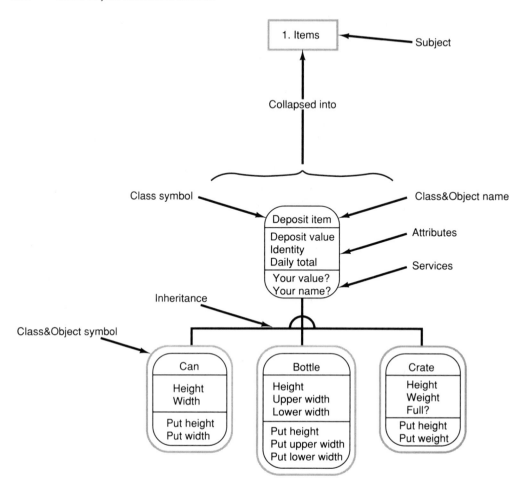

**Figure 16.2**   Graphical notation of OOA applied to part of the recycling system described earlier.

The techniques for finding the objects are very heuristic. There is a lack of a distinct method to follow step by step in order to identify the Class&Objects of a system. OOA is designed for small systems, even though today it is being used even for large systems. The objects found using OOA appear to be the initial problem domain objects found when using OOSE. There is nothing in the method that tackles the presentation of the user interfaces of the system during analysis; this is handled by the design part.

Neither has the method any specific support to capture systematically all the dynamic roles played by the objects (compare the use cases in OOSE). 'Threads of execution' is one approach to this, but this is done late, to verify that the correct operations have been identified. Here use cases and an interaction diagram can be supportive tools. In larger systems a tremendous effort is needed to capture the total interface of an object by an *ad hoc* strategy. In our experience it is hard to define exactly which objects are essential in a particular system without going through, in detail, how the system is to be used. For example, in one registration system it may be essential to keep track of the pilot of an aircraft, but in another it may be totally irrelevant to have that information. We also think that it is extremely hard to tell which attribute relations an object should have without knowing how the object will be used. Thus it is natural to model the attributes and the relations after (or while) the operations are defined. Otherwise the result will be that you find a lot of attributes initially which later must be removed when you find that they are not being used.

The subject concept is similar to the views or subsystems used in OOSE. However, the subsystems are a configuration unit and a way to manage large-scale systems. In particular, the service packages used in OOSE are used to make changes to a system local. A change in one functionality of the system should only affect one service package. This is not the intention of the subjects in OOA, where they are more a guide to a reader of the system model. Additionally, subjects may overlap, whereas this is not the case with the subsystems in OOSE. Views in OOSE are used to partition the model into different perspectives to guide the reader. In Table 16.2 we have related OOSE concepts to OOA.

**Table 16.2**   The concepts of OOSE related to OOA

| OOSE | OOA |
|---|---|
| Class | Class |
| Object | Object |
| Inherits | Gen-spec structure |
| Acquaintance | Instance connection/whole-part |
| Communication | Message connection |
| Stimuli | Message |
| Operation | Service |
| Attribute | Attribute |
| Actor | (User) |
| Use case | (Threads of execution) |
| Subsystem | (Subjects) |
| Service package | – |
| Block | – |
| Object module | – |
| Public object module | – |

# 16.4  Object-Oriented Design (OOD/Booch)

## 16.4.1  Architecture

Although the OOD/Booch method has great similarities to the OOA/Coad–Yourdon method in finding objects, the aim is to establish a grounding for implementation. In Table 16.3 we have related some OOD concepts to OOSE concepts in a summarized form.

The concepts and techniques used in OOD are many. We will here only mention the more important aspects. Booch gives a large number of concepts, but suggests that only some of these should be used when appropriate. What is interesting to note is that the relationships **uses** and **instantiates** (which can be further specialized) are drawn between classes, that is, this is a static view of the system. Between the dynamic objects there are only lines, with the messages sent between the objects attached to these lines. The technique for working with metaclasses has not been described in OOD. A metaclass is a specific class' class. In OOSE these are only used by the people defining the architecture of the method, and thus not normally directly available to the practitioners of the method. Booch also focuses on the interfaces at various stages. He uses different kinds of visibility of various grouping concepts. The **class category** is a grouping of classes for presentation and abstraction purposes, very similar to the subjects in OOA. The physical grouping is done by

**Table 16.3**  The concepts of OOD related to OOSE

| OOD | OOSE |
|---|---|
| Class | Class |
| Object | Instance/object |
| Uses | (Communication) |
| Instantiates | (Communication) |
| Inherits | Inheritance |
| Metaclass | (Used by methodologists only) |
| Class category | (Block) |
| Message | Stimuli |
| Field | Attribute |
| Operation | Operation |
| Mechanism | (~ Use case/skeletons) |
| Module | Block |
| Subsystem | Subsystem |
| Process | Process |

using **modules**. In OOSE we use blocks for these purposes and views to guide the reader. The concept of mechanism is introduced as 'structures whereby sets of objects work together to provide the behaviors that satisfy the requirements of a problem'. It is not clear exactly what is meant, but the idea has some similarities to the idea of use cases. However, it seems more of a kind of framework of classes where classes can cooperate, similar to the skeletons presented in this book for RDBMS specialization.

## 16.4.2   The method

Booch strongly emphasizes the iterative process and the creativity of the developer as essential components in object-oriented design. The method is more a set of heuristics and good advice regarding this creative process. No strict baselines or order of work exist, but 'the process of OOD generally tracks the following order of events':

- Identify classes and objects at a given level of abstraction.
- Identify the semantics of these classes and objects.
- Identify the relationships among these classes and objects.
- Implement these classes and objects.

This process is recursive and Booch also states: 'The process of object-oriented design starts with the discovery of the classes and objects that form the vocabulary of our problem domain; it stops whenever we find that there are no new primitive abstractions and mechanisms or when the classes and objects we have already discovered may be implemented by composing them from existing reusable software components.' (Booch (1991)).

**Identifying classes and objects** involves finding key abstractions in the problem space and important mechanisms that offer the dynamic behavior over several such objects. These key abstractions are found by learning the terminology of the problem domain. This may be achieved by talking to domain experts.

**Identifying the semantics** involves establishing the meanings of the classes and objects identified earlier. The developer should view the objects from the outside and define the object protocol. To investigate how each object may be used by other objects is also an essential part of identifying its semantics. This is described as the hard part of OOD and may require the most iterations.

**Identifying relationships** involves extending the previous activities to include the relationships between classes and objects and to identify how these interact with each other. Different types of association are used, such as inheritance, instantiation and uses between the classes. The static and dynamic semantics of the mechanisms between the objects are also defined. The visibility between classes and objects is decided upon. This step also produces iterations in the design process.

**Implementing classes and objects** involves delving into the classes and objects and determining of how to implement them. A decision is made on how to use the particular programming language to implement the classes. This is also the step where components are used. The classes and objects are structured into modules. How this structuring is done is not made very clear by Booch (1991). This step may lead to the point where the whole process is performed again, but now only inside a specific class and on a lower level. We may thus end up with a hierarchy of classes or modules. This seems to result in a hierarchical structure similar to HOOD (see below) for each class or object.

### 16.4.3   Deliverables

The major strength in OOD is perhaps the richness of the diagramming techniques offered to the developer (is it too rich?). By viewing the model developed from different views, a rich set of perspectives is proposed that expresses different things about the model. The perspectives are summarized in Figure 16.3.

Firstly, a separation is made between logical and physical views. The **logical view** consists of the **class structure** and the **object structure**. The **physical view** consists of the **modules** of the system and its process structure. All these diagrams form the basic notation of OOD, which is a static description of the system. In addition to these static diagrams, Booch uses two dynamic diagrams. The first is

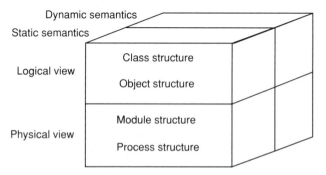

**Figure 16.3**   Documentation aspects in OOD.

a **state transition diagram** that describes the semantics of instances of a certain class. The second is a **timing diagram** that describes how events happen between objects.

### 16.4.4 Discussion

The method is not really developed into a process, but is rather a collection of techniques and heuristics that can be used when developing object-oriented systems. OOD does offer, though, a plenitude of diagramming techniques, although a complementary addition of rules for documentation is necessary; this is an activity that the project or organization can develop on its own.

The notation techniques have some similarities to those used in OOSE. For instance, the timing diagram has a similar purpose to the interaction diagram in OOSE, but is not yet as formally developed. The state transition diagrams are described using traditional notation (Mealy diagrams), whereas OOSE may use a different notation; in this book a notation similar to SDL is described. The operations are described in plain text or in (pseudo) code.

The discussion of OOA is in some parts also applicable here. OOD seems to be an outside-in method; starting from the outside and refining each class and instance until it can be implemented by components and code. Thus it is a kind of divide-and-conquer method. The great lack, as far as we can see, is of techniques for finding the operations of each object and class. How this actual work must be done is up to the developer. As to OOA, the use case concepts could be used together with OOD. In Table 16.4 we have related the concepts of OOSE to OOD.

## 16.5 Hierarchical Object-Oriented Design (HOOD)

### 16.5.1 Architecture

HOOD develops a model in a stepwise refinement that subsequently may be implemented directly in a target language. In Table 16.5 we have related HOOD concepts to OOSE concepts in a summarized form.

The concepts used in HOOD are intended to support an abstract view of the design and implementation which are aimed at Ada. This also explains the object-based approach, namely the lack of inheritance and pure classes. The objects are classified to support the designer. **Active objects** can execute in parallel, whereas **passive**

**Table 16.4**    The concepts of OOSE related to OOD

| OOSE | OOD |
|---|---|
| Class | Class |
| Object | Object |
| Inherits | Inherits |
| Acquaintance | (Uses relationships) |
| Communication | (Uses/instantiates relationships) |
| Stimuli | Message |
| Operation | Operation |
| Attribute | Field |
| Actor | – |
| Use case | ($\approx$ Mechanisms) |
| Subsystem | Class categories/subsystems |
| Service package | – |
| Block | Module/class category |
| Object module | Class |
| Public object module | (Visibility of class categories) |

**Table 16.5**    The concepts of HOOD related to OOSE

| HOOD | OOSE |
|---|---|
| Class | Class |
| Active object | Block that encapsulates a process |
| Passive object | Block that does not directly encapsulate a process |
| Environment object | Actor with specified interface |
| Class object | (Generic abstract object) |
| Virtual node object | – |
| Control flow | (Use case) |
| Use relationship | Communication |
| Include relationship | Consists-of |
| Operation | Operation |

**objects** can only execute sequentially at a certain level. The **environment objects** represent other systems with which the particular system must interact. **Class objects** are used to specify an object where some types are not fully described, namely a generic package. **Virtual mode objects** represent a node in a distributed system. The control flows are used to show how different objects at a specific level communicate. Different kinds of relationships between objects are used.

## 16.5.2   The method

HOOD is geared towards coding in Ada, but has been extended to support C++ coding also. This implies that the concepts in HOOD all have Ada semantics; for instance, inheritance is not supported. The method starts with the identification of one object for the entire system; this is called the **root object**. The root object is then divided into several internal objects that are further specified. This subdivision is done recursively inside all objects until a level is reached that can be directly implemented with Ada packages. A hierarchical structure was seen as a necessity in order to distribute the development work between different contractors. The order of work can thus be illustrated with Figure 16.4.

The phases are:

(1)  Problem definition

(2)  Elaboration of an informal solution strategy

(3)  Formalization of the strategy

(4)  Formalization of the solution

This is done recursively inside each object until the lowest object level is reached: the **terminal** object.

**Problem definition** means specifying the problem at the current level. First a statement of the problem is made to provide a context for the current object level. The requirements received from the parent object are then analyzed and structured. The purpose of the analysis is to make sure that the problem has been well understood.

**Elaboration of an informal solution strategy** means that a solution to the problem defined previously is outlined. This is done using natural language to explain the design for the current level of abstraction. This informal description should describe the design by means of real-world objects associated with the actions which may be performed on them. A maximum of ten sentences is recommended.

**Formalization of the strategy** aims at extracting the major concepts of the informal solution strategy in order to formalize a description of the solution. This is performed in five steps:

(1)  **Identification of objects** is done by extracting the nouns from the informal solution strategy and selecting the appropriate ones.

(2)  **Identification of operations** is done by extracting the verbs from the informal solution strategy.

(3)  **Grouping objects and operations** involves attaching each operation to an appropriate object.

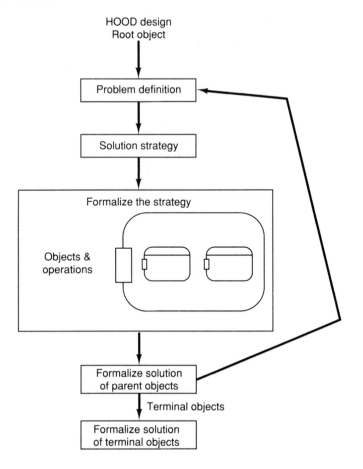

**Figure 16.4**   Basic design step in HOOD.

(4) **Graphical description** of objects and operation is done using the HOOD graphical formalism.

(5) **Justification of design decisions** is then performed by the designer, who explains the reasons for his or her decisions where they are not obvious.

This entire phase may involve several iterations with the former phase.

**Formalization of the solution** is done by developing a formal model of each identified object. This model is referred to as the *Object Description Skeleton* (ODS) and it contains interfaces, control structures of objects and operations, together with informal comments.

This sequence is thus performed recursively until the terminal objects are reached. The structure of the system will thus become hierarchical with child objects inside their parent objects.

### 16.5.3   Deliverables

Each object at every hierarchical level is documented in a HOOD chapter. Each HOOD chapter has subsections according to the steps described above. This provides a detailed object description which may be reviewed and further refined. Since the system will have a hierarchical structure, the documentation will also be hierarchical having the root object's documentation as its root document.

The formal description of the object, written during the step 'Formalization of the solution', is written using an Object Description Skeleton (ODS) which is thus a subsection of a HOOD chapter. The ODS is written using a special Programming Design Language (PDL). This language has a similar syntax to Ada and the ODS is also used to generate Ada code (and possibly also C++). In the ODS, pseudo-code or Ada may be used to specify each operation or each control structure (task). Further refinements, in the generated Ada code, of the object operations are performed by the designer. Each object generates a package in the Ada code and each child object is included in its parent object by the WITH clause in Ada.

The definition of the syntax used in ODS makes it possible for contractors using different development platforms to exchange design documents. The translation of ODS to Ada code can be automated and is normally part of the development tool.

### 16.5.4   Discussion

HOOD is fully geared towards Ada, which has both pros and cons. The advantages are of course that, during the design, Ada syntax and semantics may be used in the descriptions and thus no new language has to be learned by the system developers; this also helps code generation later. The existence of an Ada standard is thus essential since many developing organizations may be involved in a development. Support is also given in defining process communication and synchronization and the terminology of this is also based on Ada concepts.

If any programming language other than Ada is to be used, major changes in documentation techniques and possibly also of the method need to be made. For instance, the inheritance mechanism is not supported by HOOD. Additionally, there is no analysis view which is independent of the implementation environment. However HOOD could, of course, be extended by an analysis technique.

The method gives the basic design step, but does not give any help in finding the appropriate object structure. Actually HOOD does give strong support for containment structures, but not for other structures such as use or inheritance structures. An earlier method proposed by Booch, namely to extract nouns and verbs from a textual description, now abandoned by Booch himself, is recommended to support the finding of objects and operations. It is natural to expect that this recommendation will evolve into other strategies. There is nothing to support dynamic flows over several objects.

The method may be characterized as object decomposition. This is a very complex task and it suffers from several of the flaws of the traditional functional decomposition methods. The major flaw is of course that the most important decisions must be taken very early in the development when dividing the entire system into its components. In Table 16.6 we have related OOSE concepts to HOOD concepts.

**Table 16.6**   The concepts of OOSE related to HOOD concepts

| OOSE | HOOD |
| --- | --- |
| Class | (Class object) |
| Object | Object |
| Inherits | – |
| Acquaintance | (Include relationship) |
| Communication | (Use relationship) |
| Stimuli | (Stimuli) |
| Operation | Operation |
| Attribute | (Type) |
| Actor | (Environment object) |
| Use case | (~ Control flow) |
| Subsystem | (Root) object |
| Service package | – |
| Block | ~ Object |
| Object module | Terminal object |
| Public object module | Provided interface |

# 16.6 Object Modeling Technique (OMT)

## 16.6.1 Architecture

The Object Modeling Technique (OMT) covers analysis, design and implementation. In Table 16.7 we have related OMT concepts to OOSE concepts in a summarized form.

The OMT technique probably has the greatest variety of concepts of all the methods described in this chapter. Table 16.7 only represents the more important ones. However, the concepts are in most cases well defined and are also related to each other. For instance, we quote, 'a **Link** is a physical or conceptual connection between object instances' whereas 'an **association** describes a group of links with common structure and common semantics'. Link may have attributes, which is an interesting property. In this book we have not defined the acquaintance association in this way, which, however, is sometimes a useful extension. **Aggregation** is used to describe how objects represent assemblies of other objects. **Events** are very similar to the stimuli used in OOSE. **Scenarios** are described in the book in terms of ideas similar to those we have used for use cases in OOSE. However, they are not as formalized and central as in OOSE. Attributes and subsystems are similar to the ones in OOSE, whereas **modules** are used to group classes for manageable purposes. These are also the lowest level of subsystem. There is no special notation for modules; they are merely listed on top of each sheet. A **sheet** is a single printed document that shows part of the model.

**Table 16.7** The concepts of OMT related to OOSE

| OMT | OOSE |
|---|---|
| Class | Class |
| Object | Object |
| Generalization/inheritance | Inheritance |
| Link | Acquaintance |
| Link attribute | – |
| Aggregation | Consists-of |
| Operation | Operation |
| Event | Stimuli |
| Scenario | ~Use case |
| Attribute | Attribute |
| Subsystem | Subsystem |
| Module | (Block/service package) |
| Sheet | View |

## 16.6.2    The method

The method consists of four phases: analysis, system design, object design and implementation. Three models of the system are developed initially and then refined in all these phases. The models are as follows:

- The **object model** describes the static structure of the system with classes and their relationships.
- The **dynamic model** captures the temporal aspects of the object model with events and states of the objects.
- The **functional model** describes the computation in terms of how output values are derived from input values, that is, mainly in terms of the operations of the objects.

The purpose of **analysis** is to model the real world so that it can be understood. The analysis model is composed of the three submodels mentioned above. Initially the requirements are stated in a problem statement. From this statement, the classes relevant in the domain are extracted and also their relations and attributes. Together with inheritance and modules this will form the *object model*. The *dynamic model* is developed by looking for events in the object model. The scenarios are used to develop event traces which are very similar to the interaction diagrams in OOSE. From these the events can be identified. From these events, state diagrams are developed for the classes. The *functional model* is a dataflow diagram of the actual transactions in the system. These diagrams show dependencies between the operations represented by the processes in the diagrams. Additional operations are found from the reading or writing of attributes, from events in the dynamic model and also from actions in the state diagrams. These models are developed in an iterative manner.

For **system design**, a high-level strategy is developed. The system is partitioned into subsystems and also allocated to processors and processes (tasks). Strategic decisions are made on the use of DBMSs, global resources and implementation of control. This is basically similar to the first activity in construction in OOSE, namely the identification of the implementation environment and the decisions concerning certain strategic questions.

The **object design** phase aims to define the objects in detail. This includes defining their interfaces, algorithms and operations. The objects discovered during analysis serve as skeletons for this activity. Here the three models are integrated to design the objects. New objects are introduced to store intermediate results. Optimization of the design is also done. The classes are packed into modules.

The last step in OMT is the actual **implementation** of the objects. This is done following a number of guidelines and coding rules for good object-oriented coding style. The implementation of both object-oriented and non-object-oriented languages is described.

### 16.6.3  Deliverables

The actual deliverable consists of the three models:

- Object model
- Dynamic model
- Functional model

These are related to each other. The notation used consists mainly of conventional techniques such as combinations of entity/relationship diagrams, dataflow diagrams, event traces and state transition diagrams. The overall system design is described in a document of its own together with high-level strategy decisions. The source code is also delivered, grouped into modules.

### 16.6.4  Discussion

The OMT method has very many different techniques and guidelines to support actual development of a system. It is the only method presented in this chapter that makes a serious attempt to support both analysis and construction as defined in OOSE.

The method is the most developed of the ones presented in this chapter. OMT includes several different concepts, which gives the method a high granularity for expressing different modeling situations. It is thus very powerful, but many concepts require that the notation used, and their semantics, be formally defined to develop a consistent model. Otherwise it will be very difficult to learn and use the appropriate method. It is not very easy to see how all the techniques in OMT can be used to form consistent models, and the relations between the three models are not obvious at all stages.

OMT is affected by relational database design, and several concepts essential for such work are introduced. The transition to a relational database design is presented in detail.

The method presents interesting ideas concerning the use of events which have many similarities with those used in OOSE. OMT

**Table 16.8**    The concepts of OOSE related to OMT concepts

| OOSE | OMT |
| --- | --- |
| Class | Class |
| Object | Object |
| Inherits | Generalization |
| Acquaintance | Link |
| Communication | (Data flow) |
| Stimuli | Event |
| Operation | Operation |
| Attribute | Attribute |
| Actor | – |
| Use case | Scenario |
| Subsystem | Subsystem |
| Service package | – |
| Block | Module |
| Object module | Classes |
| Public object module | (Service) |

also uses a technique to abstract states and to have states at several different levels.

The approach is thus the most ambitious of the methods presented in this chapter. It also gives a large amount of good and explicit advice that is needed in common situations. In Table 16.8 we have related OOSE concepts to OMT concepts.

# 16.7    Responsibility-Driven Design

## 16.7.1    Architecture

In Responsibility-Driven Design, a model which should be the basis for actual implementation is developed from the requirements specification. In Table 16.9 we have related Responsibility-Driven Design concepts to OOSE concepts in a summarized form.

Responsibility-Driven Design supports the basic concepts of object orientation, such as classes, objects and inheritance. For each class, different **responsibilities** are defined which specify the responsibilities or the roles of the objects and the actions of the objects. This corresponds to the part of a specific use case for which an object should be responsible. To fulfill these responsibilities, the classes need to collaborate with other classes using **collaborations** which show how the objects interact. The responsibilities are further refined and grouped into **contracts** which define a set of requests that

**Table 16.9**  The concepts of Responsibility-Driven Design related to OOSE

| Responsibility-Driven Design | OOSE |
| --- | --- |
| Class | Class |
| Inheritance | Inheritance |
| Responsibility | (Part of a use case associated to one object) |
| Collaboration | Communication, acquaintance |
| Contract | Public class |
| Subsystem | Subsystem |

objects of the class can support. In OOSE this is similar to defining the public classes of a block. These contracts are further refined into **protocols** which show the specific signature of each operation, just as the classes in OOSE are refined. To ease the design, subsystems are introduced. A **subsystem** groups a number of classes and subsystems of lower level, and thus abstracts a certain functionality. A subsystem also has contracts which should be supported by a class in the subsystem.

## 16.7.2    The method

The method comprises a number of phases where each phase is described as a number of activities. The **exploratory phase** consists of:

(1) **Classes**. These are found by reading the specification and extracting the essential nouns. More essential nouns are found from physical objects in the domain, conceptual entities objects, external interfaces and larger categories of classes. We find abstract classes that share properties from several other classes, such as from the categories of classes. We also state the purpose of each class.

(2) **Responsibilities of each class**. By looking for the verbs in the requirements specification we can find the actions of the objects in the system. Wherever information is mentioned, this could be allocated to one class. Furthermore, we refine the purposes of each class to specific responsibilities and look for relationships between classes. We try to distribute the responsibilities evenly and decentralize the behavior as much as possible over the classes.

(3) **Collaborations between classes**.  The actual collaboration between classes is found by asking questions like 'With what

does this class need to collaborate to fulfill its responsibility?', 'What other classes need the result?' and 'What needs to make use of the responsibilities of this class?' Also the different kinds of relationships, for example is-part-of, can yield new collaborations between classes.

The **refining phase** consists of:

(1) **Hierarchies between classes**. Here the inheritance hierarchies between classes are further refined. By using Venn diagrams over responsibilities, abstract classes can be extracted. It is also emphasized that one must develop a kind-of hierarchy, namely a type hierarchy as discussed in Chaper 3. The classes are marked as abstract or concrete, with no abstract classes inheriting any concrete class. Common responsibilities are placed as high up as possible. Contracts are also identified on the various levels in the hierarchy by grouping responsibilities used by the same clients.

(2) **Subsystems** are groups of classes and are identified to simplify the patterns of collaborations. The use of collaboration graphs is then essential. These show how the different classes and subsystems collaborate to fulfill their responsibilities. All possible paths between classes in the system could be captured in these graphs. We look for frequent or complex collaborations and also try to name the subsystems of a certain functionality. Some contracts are made public to the subsystem. The collaborations internal to and between the subsystems are simplified by minimizing the number of collaborations in the design and also by minimizing the number of classes to which a subsystem delegates.

(3) **Protocols**. Here the responsibilities and contracts are further refined to pure protocols of specific signatures of each operation. Emphasis is placed on making the protocols as simple and useful as possible by naming them carefully and giving them reasonable default values for parameters. A design specification of each class, subsystem and contract is written.

Responsibility-Driven Design thus produces a design specification to be implemented. The idea then is to do a straightforward implementation, that is, directly map the design onto the implementation. However, new classes will occur and also previously existing classes will be used for the implementation.

In all steps, walkthroughs of different scenarios (use cases) are highly recommended to aid understanding of the model, but also to check that behaviors required of the system are not omitted.

### 16.7.3   Deliverables

The output of Responsibility-Driven Design is a design specification consisting of:

- A graph of each class hierarchy
- A graph of the collaboration for each subsystem
- A specification of each class
- A specification of each subsystem
- A specification of the contracts supported by each class and subsystem

The result should be appropriate for direct implementation.

### 16.7.4   Discussion

Responsibility-Driven Design is a design technique that uses informal techniques and guidelines to develop an appropriate design. The strategy for finding classes and their properties relies greatly on the skill of the individual designer. Responsibility-Driven Design uses the informal, but straightforward, technique of CRC cards whereby classes, responsibilities and collaborations are captured in an iterative manner. This will probably make the technique hard to scale to larger developments. However, some new and interesting techniques are introduced, among them the concept of contracts and the use of the subsystem in combination with the contract concept. A thorough use of these concepts should make it possible to implement several objects in parallel.

The technique of identifying classes is the traditional technique of object-oriented development. We have previously discussed the drawbacks of such a strategy. Additionally, great emphasis is placed on evenly distributing behavior over these classes. Hence the method recommends a decentralized, or stair, structure or delegation of interaction in all cases. We have also discussed our view on this matter.

The use of collaboration graphs and contracts has similarities to the technique of interaction diagrams presented in this book. Also, the use case view over the objects is reminiscent of this. Since much

**Table 16.10**   The concepts of OOSE related to Responsibility-Driven Design concepts

| OOSE | Responsibility-Driven Design |
|------|------------------------------|
| Class | Class |
| Object | Object |
| Inherits | Inheritance/hierarchy |
| Acquaintance | (Collaboration) |
| Communication | Collaboration |
| Stimuli | Message |
| Operation | Method |
| Attribute | Attribute |
| Actor | – |
| Use case | (Scenario) |
| Subsystem | Subsystem |
| Service package | – |
| Block | – |
| Object module | Classes |
| Public object module | Responsibility/contract |

emphasis is placed on walkthroughs of scenarios without any formal technique, we think the introduction of use cases and the interaction diagram in Responsibility-Driven Design would strengthen the method.

Of the techniques presented here, Responsibility-Driven Design is the one that can most easily be related to formal techniques in computer science. Here OOSE and Responsibility-Driven Design are similar. A semi-formal computational description technique is used in both methods. The simple and formal techniques are also evident, since the method has been developed from a Smalltalk background and has many fundamental similarities to Smalltalk. In Table 16.10 we have related OOSE concepts to Responsibility-Driven Design concepts.

## 16.8   Summary

There are a large number of object-oriented methods around. Only a few of them are publicly available, but an increase in the number of methods available can be expected. Many of the methods can be classified as object-oriented in the sense that they fully support the core concepts of object orientation.

We have only mentioned some of the most well-known methods and studied some of them in a little more detail. Our

**Table 16.11**   The concepts of OOSE related to the concepts of the methods discussed in this chapter

| OOSE | OOA | OOD | HOOD | OMT | Responsibility-Driven Design |
|---|---|---|---|---|---|
| Class | Class | Class | (Class object) | Class | Class |
| Object | Object | Object | Object | Object | Object |
| Inherits | Gen-spec structure | Inherits | – | Generalization | Inheritance/hierarchy |
| Acquaintance | Instance conn./whole-part | (Uses relationships) | (Include rel) | Link | (Collaboration) |
| Communication | Message connection | (Uses/instantiates rel.) | (Use relationship) | (Data flow) | |
| Stimuli | Message | Message | (Stimuli) | Event | |
| Operation | Service | Operation | Operation | Operation | Method |
| Attribute | Attribute | Field | (Type) | Attribute | Attribute |
| Actor | (User) | – | (Environment object) | – | – |
| Use case | (Threads of execution) | (≈ Mechanisms) | (~ Control flow) | Scenario | (Scenario) |
| Subsystem | (Subjects) | Class categories/subsystems | (Root) object | Subsystem | Subsystem |
| Service package | – | – | – | – | – |
| Block | – | Module/class category | ~ Object | Module | – |
| Object module | | Class | Terminal object | Classes | Classes |
| Public object module | | (Visibility of class categories) | Provided interface | (Service) | Responsibility/contract |

comparison is very simple and confined to a concept-based comparison between them and OOSE. This is actually not the most interesting comparison from a large-scale perspective, but it is the easiest one to make. Other areas to consider include:

- How the method enforces production of a robust structure
- The model concept
- The use case concept
- The degree of appropriateness for large-scale development
- The degree of formalization of concepts

The model developed in OOD/Booch is similar to the domain object model in OOSE, but also to the design model. However, there is an unclear mapping from domain objects (logical view in OOD) to the design model (physical view in OOD).

The model developed in HOOD is similar both to the domain object model and to the design model of OOSE. The domain object(s) are refined in a hierarchical manner into descriptions that can be further translated into code.

The object model developed in OMT/Rumbaugh *et al.* is similar to the domain object model in OOSE. Related to this is the dynamic model describing the interaction between objects (like interaction diagrams in OOSE) and their internal states (like state transition diagrams in OOSE), and the functional model which describes the actual operations. These models are refined and implemented.

The model developed in Responsibility-Driven Design/Wirfs-Brock *et al.* corresponds to the domain object model and the design model in OOSE.

Table 16.11 relates the concepts of OOSE to the concepts of the methods highlighted in this chapter.

# Appendix A:
# On the Development of
# Objectory

## A.1 Introduction

Here we briefly describe our work with the development of
Objectory, of which this book has described the fundamental
techniques. It is by no means complete, but we hope to give you an
idea of the way we are thinking.

Underlying Objectory are some basic assumptions and
problems, as follows:

- System development projects will involve a great number of
  people who will have to cooperate in an efficient manner.
  Sometimes as many as several thousand developers may be
  needed to develop and maintain a single system.

- Software cannot be viewed or touched but is much more
  abstract than corresponding components in other types of
  engineering. In the building industry it is always possible to
  'see' how the component parts fit together. In a computer
  system it is very difficult to understand how the different
  parts interact.

- Software development is a very young branch of industry,
  only a few decades old. However, in the future it will be
  necessary to view it as an engineering discipline with
  industrial techniques.

- System development is a very complex task involving very
  many significant details.

Competence, as well as good tools, is necessary to carry out
something complicated. Only poets and dreamers dare 'go for the
moon' without years of preparation and training. Obviously this also
holds true for other activities of large complexity, such as system
development. A system development process should offer the aid
that the developers need.

The system development techniques that were known to us when this work began (around 1978) were rather simple and limited, at least in comparison with techniques used in more mature disciplines such as civil engineering and electrical engineering. Most development methods, if described at all, are still described only in textbooks. To someone who is going to learn the basics of a technique, a textbook, in combination with teaching, will be necessary. A textbook will give a good introduction to the technique; moreover, it can constitute a 'management overview'. This book is structured more or less like a textbook. Below are a few properties that most textbooks have (and should have):

- Description is geared towards new development, that is, it covers only the first part of the life cycle.
- The theoretical substance fills some 50 pages even if the whole text may be up to 500 pages. The rest of the material consists of supporting examples and general information about software engineering.
- Rules and criteria for how the work should be carried out to yield a good analysis, a good design and so on, usually take no more than a few pages.

Anyone can understand that there is an imbalance if the development of a software system, which may cost millions of dollars, is based on instructions whose substance covers only some 50 pages. When the textbook has fulfilled its mission, the developer should therefore have a description, practically at once, of how he or she is to work in practice. He or she will also need a full description of his or her role in the development work, for example:

- The developer has to know what different tasks he or she is to perform and with whom he or she is to cooperate: for each step, information must be available about what input will be needed, what output will be required, what is to be done and how it can be *done well*.
- The developer will also have to learn which tools he or she can utilize, and find out how these tools should be used in the project.

In other words, the developer will need to have access to a large set of descriptions of different aspects of the system development process. The necessary descriptions will together make a text of some 1000 pages – a volume of considerable size. Not all developers take part in all the phases of the development, however. Therefore they do not all need to be familiar with the details of all the steps, even if knowledge of the whole process is stimulating and necessary for efficient work.

## A.2   Objectory as an activity

The system development process is therefore a very complicated **activity.** Moreover, this activity is continually being developed and improved, just as with any other system. In other words, it must be possible to maintain the process. We have therefore viewed the process as an activity of an enterprise and used enterprise modeling to describe the process. The enterprise modeling technique is in turn based on Objectory itself. We will here illustrate how we have used these concepts to develop Objectory. Then we will briefly introduce the Objectory enterprise modeling technique (which is conceptually very similar to the system development technique).

Instead of viewing a system, we consider an enterprise or an organization. A specific flow through the organization we call a **development case**, analogous to a use case. What the enterprise develops we call **development entity objects**, analogous to domain objects or entity objects. The actual activities in the enterprise we call **processes**, somewhat analogous to control objects. These concepts will not be further defined here. Moreover, this is a simplified description of Objectory enterprise modeling, in which not all the object types are used.

When analyzing a system development process, we use a similar method for our work as in the analysis of any other system. Thus the system development process can be applied to itself.

### A.2.1   Development cases

That which is to be performed by an enterprise is defined through its development cases. A development case is a way for the enterprise to function in order to attain a goal. Which development cases are included in an enterprise is thus determined by the goals of the enterprise.

In an enterprise where computer systems are developed, the two basic development cases, *New Development* and *Further Development*, will soon be found, and so will the development cases *Produce an offer* and *Handle errors*.

Figure A.l shows how the system development organization can be modeled as a number of development cases cooperating with the external entity objects Customer, Producer and Customer support.

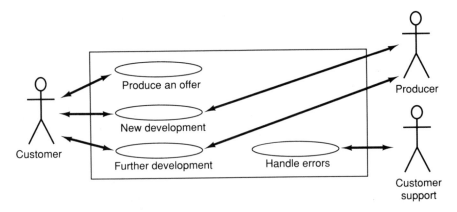

**Figure A.1**  In system development there will be a number of development cases that offer their services to external users.

A study of the development cases *New Development* and *Further Development* will reveal that these development cases have many parts in common. An abstract development case *Development* can therefore be identified which both *New Development* and *Further Development* will use. In it can be described all the common parts, such as how an interaction diagram should be drawn.

Further study of the development cases will reveal excellent chances to incorporate reviews. Reviews really have nothing to do with the development work as such, but they are vital to achieve high quality. It is possible to describe a review as a development case with

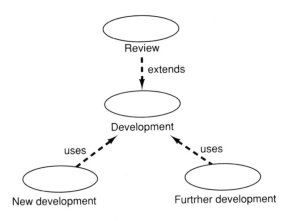

**Figure A.2**  *Review* is performed as extension to *Development*, which is used by both *New Development* and *Further Development*.

an extension association to the development case *Development* (see Figure A.2). *Review* will then be performed at a number of well-defined points in the development.

In the development case description it is possible to read how the activity will attain its goals, but for a full understanding it is necessary to see how the development case is performed by cooperating processes operating on development entity objects. We will return to this after we have discussed development entity objects and processes.

## A.2.2   Development entity objects

In system development, entity objects are primarily used to model information about objects known to the system. This also holds for development entity objects used in enterprise development. The development entity objects required to model a system development process are principally the concepts used in system development. Thus the following development entity objects are found in analysis: **use cases, systems, subsystems** and **objects**. Actors are not development entity objects since we do not describe them. The development entity objects are either simple or composite (see Figure A.3). Composite objects are packaging objects which contain other development entity objects. This containment hierarchy ends with the

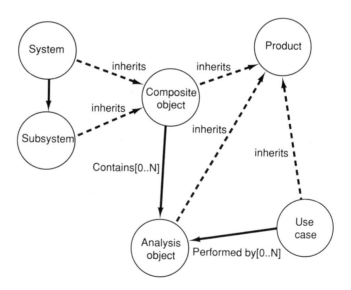

**Figure A.3**   A development entity object can be a simple or composite object.

analysis objects (entity objects, interface objects and control objects). Each use case is expressed in terms of the objects that cooperate to perform the use case.

All of these concepts will be handled as **products** in an organization. All the development entity objects have certain parts in common. There is one person or position responsible for each development entity object, for instance. Only this person is allowed to make changes in the development entity object. Others can suggest changes, but it will always be the person responsible who sees that the changes are made. Such common properties and rules can be formulated in the development entity object Product, which all the other development entity objects will inherit.

In construction, a system will be modeled as a hierarchy of blocks and object modules. Here we also have composite objects that can contain blocks and object modules. Normally it is the low-level blocks (simple blocks in Objectory) that contain object modules, but it is perfectly possible to have, for instance, subsystems containing object modules directly. Components are a special type of object module which can be used in several blocks to support the application object modules of the block (see Figure A.4).

When a system is to be delivered, we say that an **instantiation** will be made of a subset of the blocks in this system (a customer may not want all the parts of a system). Which blocks will be instantiated

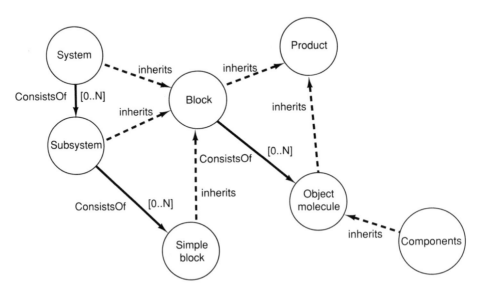

**Figure A.4**   All types of block can contain classes.

will depend on what **service packages** the customer has ordered. The delivered system thus consists of a set of block instances which contain those classes, namely the executable code, which have been obtained from the corresponding descriptions.

Once the system is installed with the classes that form part of the block instances, the objects that really perform the execution of the system will be created (instantiated). This is what instantiating means in traditional object-oriented programming. The relationship is shown in Figure A.5. We thus use the instantiation concept on two levels.

Like entity objects, development entity objects have associations, attributes and operations. Some associations have already been illustrated above. All the information that a development entity object must contain can be modeled by means of the attributes. Information stored in the attributes should be homogenized so that there is no redundancy between the attributes.

The most common way to view the attributes of a development entity object is in some form of **document.** It would be easy to make the mistake of saying that document types are equivalent to attribute types or, even worse, to development entity objects; this would be wrong because the content of different document types can and

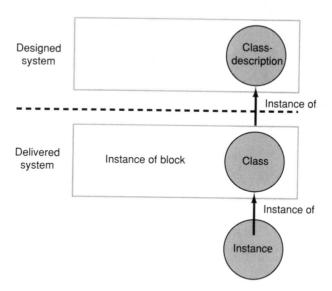

**Figure A.5**   Instantiation takes place at different levels: the delivered system will be instantiated from the designed system, and the executing object instances will be instantiated from the classes.

should show redundancy. The name of a certain subsystem, for instance, will be found in at least three document types: in the description of the subsystem, the overview of all the subsystems and in any diagram containing the subsystem. A document is, rather, a compilation of information from the model of the development entity objects, a compilation adapted for a particular type of reader. The same information can therefore be presented in different ways to different categories of reader, that is, we can define semantic views or perspectives of the model.

A subsystem, for instance, must have at least four attributes: Name, Introduction, Description and Special requirements (see Figure A.6). The attribute Name is only a String while the other attributes consist of a text that can contain arbitrary subsections, namely chapters. The subsystem development entity object contains objects (which the subsystem, so to speak, consists of) and it can have at least one association to another subsystem object, namely contains.

When a subsystem is presented in the **overview** of all the subsystems, only the Name and the Introduction of the object will be presented. This document is meant for those who only need a summary of the subsystems. In the **description** documents of the subsystem, meant for those who are developing the subsystem, all the

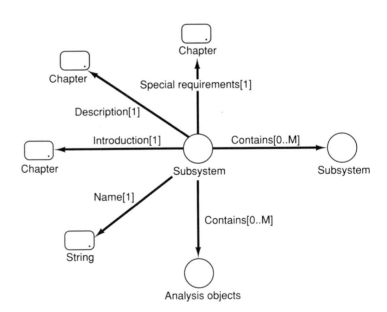

**Figure A.6**   The development entity object subsystem with attributes and associations.

information will be found, as in the model above, including the names of the associated objects. When the subsystem is shown in certain **diagrams**, only its name and the contained objects will be shown. The essential point here is that a document is only a kind of report with certain information from a set of development entity objects.

Each document has a unique identity. There will always be an appointed person who is responsible for the document. These are typical further attributes of a subsystem. There are, moreover, established rules for how changes to a document should be handled. Documents will have to be changed whenever the state of the development entity object is changed, because the attribute information will change.

A system consists of a number of development entity objects. These form a structure with the development entity objects as nodes. A set of documents goes with the development entity objects, and together with the structures they give a total view of the system. A system can therefore be said to be described by a number of documents that constitute part of a document structure.

The development entity objects' counterparts to operations are called **procedures.** A procedure thus defines some work on a development entity object. For instance it must be possible to *create, change* and *remove* development entity objects. Any change must be *registered* and form part of a new revision state for the system as a whole. In other words, there must be procedures which register state changes in the documents belonging to a development entity object. There are also procedures which apply to groups of development entity objects; it should, for instance, be possible to produce all the documentation that concerns a particular revision state of a system. In addition, there are procedures that are specific to a particular development entity object. For the development entity object subsystem it must for example be possible to add new objects.

### A.2.3   Processes

Well-defined activities within an enterprise can be described in terms of processes. Each type of process can then be made responsible for any work related to a particular type of development entity object. Detailed specification of an interface object, for instance, will be performed by a process responsible for that particular object.

Each process describes how to perform the activities for which the process is responsible. The description of a process can therefore be said to be a kind of work description.

In principle, a process is needed to specify each development entity object. In this way there will be a pair of objects that cooperate throughout the whole activity, a process and a development entity object.

## A.2.4  Development cases in terms of development entity objects and processes

Each development case is performed by a number of interacting processes and development entity objects. This implies that a development case is distributed among the different objects. Normally, the main part of the 'intelligence' of the development case will lie in the process. This is where it is described how the work should be carried out and how decisions are to be made about various steps.

In the development case *New Development*, a number of subcourses can be identified. Each of these subcourses can be described separately. One such subcourse comprises the steps that are to be taken when describing how a particular use case is to be realized in terms of blocks. That course is driven by a process for use case design. The process for use case design starts from the analysis description of a development entity object use case and the involved objects, and it transforms this into a description of how blocks are to cooperate in the use case. What happens, in practice, is that a designer, starting from the analysis description, draws a set of interaction diagrams for the blocks in the use case. In other words, this activity formulates requirements on the blocks participating in the use case (see Figure A.7).

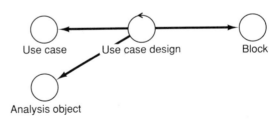

**Figure A.7**  The subcourse 'design of a use case' in terms of processes and development entity objects.

## A.2.5   Enterprise construction

With an enterprise analysis of system development behind us, we can now understand the activity at a logical level. In other words, we know what needs to be done in the activity in order for the goals of the activity to be attained. We also have an idea of how these tasks should be split up into well-defined activities. Now this should be implemented, that is, the logical picture should be translated into an organizationally functioning activity. We call this phase of enterprise development **enterprise construction**.

We will now introduce the term **activity block**, which corresponds to the term 'block' in construction. An activity block is a well-defined part of the activity, often corresponding to organizations or groups within a corporation. When we define an activity, we start from the development entity objects and processes we have identified. The different blocks can then be grouped together into larger activity blocks, until the subsystem activity blocks are reached. If Objectory is divided into subsystem activity blocks, four different blocks will be found: analysis, construction, testing and component management (see Figure A.8).

## A.2.6   Development cases in terms of activity blocks

It will now be possible to describe each development case in terms of the activity blocks. Each development case will then be realized as a number of cooperating activity blocks. The dynamics in the activity block model will be described by means of interaction diagrams, which show how the activity blocks communicate to realize the

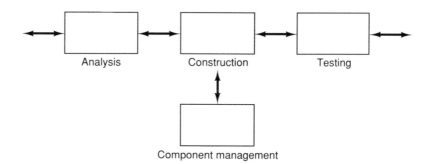

**Figure A.8**   System development can be divided roughly into four subsystem activity blocks.

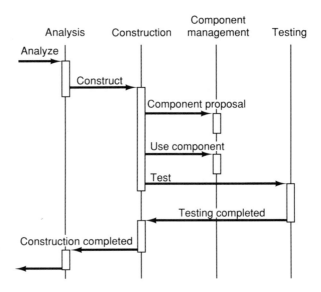

**Figure A.9**  A global interaction diagram for the development case *New Development*.

development cases. Figure A.9 shows a rough interaction diagram for the development case *New Development*.

Note that this shows only one iteration through the different steps of a project. In a real case, the steps will be iterated, and the course of events will not be quite so simple.

## A.2.7   Realization of the activity blocks

Implementing the separate activity blocks implies first of all describing how the tasks assigned to them are to be carried out. The interfaces between different tasks will be given by the development cases (interaction diagrams) in which the activity block participates. In other words, we now define how the work is to be carried out in the different activity blocks and with what resources the work will be performed. Resources are personnel, programming tools and CASE tools. Depending on the resources available, the work in the different activity blocks can be done in different ways. In some activity blocks, a great deal of support will be given by CASE tools, which will simplify the manual work. In other activity blocks, most of the work may have to be manual. Owing to the differing amount of resources, the work descriptions of the different activity blocks will therefore be given a different form.

By viewing Objectory from an object-oriented perspective, it becomes easy to adapt Objectory for different implementation environments. When adapting Objectory to a specific implementation environment, it is primarily the activity blocks responsible for implementation that will have to be specialized.

## A.3    From idea to reality

The problems that system development faced when using the prevailing techniques were known even in the 1970s. It was also perfectly clear that the complex systems that were desirable would place greater demands on systems development methods. It is from these demands that Objectory has gradually come into being and been developed.

The idea behind Objectory is the creation of a unified process that will support the activity 'development of software system' throughout the life cycle of the system. Ideally, the process will comprise all the phases of a system, from enterprise modeling, analysis, design, implementation, testing, configuration and installation to maintenance and future changes. Most engineers of today lack this global view of system development: they lack this process thinking. At present it is not possible to formulate such a complete technique in one go. As with any complicated system, Objectory has thus evolved into its present version.

In developing the Objectory technique we started with the architecture and continued with the method, which was a prerequisite for the process and tools (see Figure A.10).

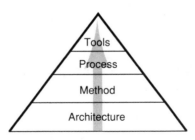

**Figure A.10**   Objectory consists of four levels, which were developed one on top of the other.

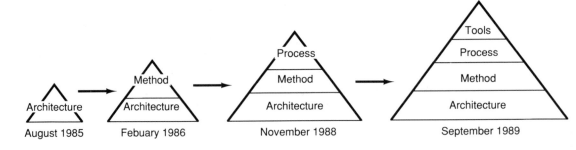

**Figure A.11** Objectory has been developed gradually through the addition of new parts and extension of existing parts.

The technical foundation (the architecture) that Objectory rests on today was formulated as early as 1985. It is published in Jacobson (1985, 1986). Even if this foundation has been developed over time, the basic ideas remain the same. Use cases are still used to describe the essential dynamics of the system. The use case concept has been further developed, however, and its relation to other types of object has been clarified.

The first version of a coherent method description existed as early as February 1986 and it was presented at OOPSLA'87 (see Jacobson (1987)). Like the underlying architecture, the method level has been further developed since then, and has been supplemented by, among other things, criteria for how objects should be formed.

The process description integrates the method description into a framework, stating how the work should be carried out as interacting processes within each phase of the development. The first edition of the process description was ready in November 1988 and covered analysis, construction and testing. At the same time a new version of the method was ready. Since then, it has been developed considerably in the light of experience gained, and the present third edition comprises some 1000 pages. Since the publication of the first edition, the process descriptions have been used in about 20 projects, and the current version of the process description (Summer 1993), which is part of the Objectory product version 3.3, represents the fourth edition.

Even though it may be possible to carry out projects without tool support, the participants in all the projects so far have expressed a strong need for such aid. Above all, they have wanted facilities to keep the information in all documents consistent. Therefore a first version of OrySE (Objectory Support Environment) was ready for customer installation in September 1989. This first version, with support for Objectory analysis, was extended in 1991 to support Objectory design. OrySE is being developed further (using Objectory and OrySE) with one release of new functionality approximately every year. The current product (Summer 1993), Objectory version 3.3, now offers the tool in its third commercial version. The development is illustrated in Figure A.11. Some future directions are indicated in Jacobson (1993).

# References

Abbot R. (1983). Program design by informal English descriptions. *Communications of the ACM*, **26**(11).

Abelson H., Sussman G.J. and Sussman J. (1985). *Structure and Interpretation of Computer Programs*. MIT Press.

Agresti W. W., ed. (1986). *New Paradigms For Software Development*. IEEE Computer Society Press.

Aho A.V., Hopcroft J.E. and Ullman J.D. (1983). *Data Structures and Algorithms*. Reading, MA: Addison-Wesley.

Alford M. (1985). SREM at the age of eight: the distributed computing design system. *IEEE Computer*, **18**(4), pp. 36–46.

Atkinson M., Bancilhon F., DeWitt D., Dittrich K., Maier D. and Zdonik S. (1989). The object-oriented database system manifesto. In *Proceedings of the First International Conference on Deductive and Object-Oriented Databases*, Kyoto, Japan, December.

Backus J. (1977). Can programming be liberated from the von Neumann Style? A functional style and its algebra of programs. 1977 Turing Award Lecture. Reprinted in *ACM Turing Award Lectures*. Reading, MA: Addison-Wesley, pp. 63–130.

Barker R. (1989). *CASE*Method*^TM* – Entity Relationship Modelling. Wokingham: Addison-Wesley.

Barnes J.G.P (1982,1984). *Programming in Ada*. International Computer Science Series.

Barry B. M. (1989). Prototyping a real-time embedded system in Smalltalk. In *Proceedings of OOPSLA '89*, New Orleans, USA, October, pp. 255–65.

Beck K. and Cunningham W. (1989). A laboratory for teaching object-oriented thinking. *Proceedings of OOPSLA '89*, pp. 1–6.

Ben-Ari M. (1982). *Principles of Concurrent Programming*. Englewood Cliffs, NJ: Prentice-Hall.

Bergner S-E. (1990). A CASE Tool for Object-Oriented System Development in an Industrial Environment. *Proceedings of TOOLS 2*. Paris.

Berzins V. and Luqi (1990). An introduction to the Specification Language Spec. *IEEE Software*, March, pp. 74–84.

Bird R.J. and Wadler P. (1988). *Introduction to Functional Programming*. Hertfordshire: Prentice-Hall.

Birrell A.D. and Nelson B.J. (1984). Implementing remote procedure calls. *ACM Trannsaction on Computer Systems*, **2**(1), pp. 39–59.

Birtwistle G.M., Dahl O-J., Myrhaug B. and Nygaard K. (1979). *Simula Begin*, 2nd edn. Lund (Sweden): Studentlitteratur; Goch: Bratt-Institut für Neues Lernen; Bromley: Chartwell-Bratt.

Blaha M.R., Premerlani W.J. and Rumbaugh J.E. (1988) Relational database design using an object-oriented methodology. *Communications of the ACM*, **31**(4), pp. 414–27.

Bloom T. and Zdonik S.B. (1987). Issues in the design of object-oriented database programming languages. *Proceedings of OOPSLA '87*, Orlando, Florida, October, pp. 441–51.

Boehm B.W. (1981). *Software Engineering Economics*. Englewood Cliffs, NJ: Prentice-Hall.

Boehm B.W. (1986). A spiral model of software development and enhancement. *Software Engineering Notes*, **11**(4).

Booch G. (1983). *Software Engineering with Ada*. Menlo Park: Benjamin/Cummings.

Booch G. (1986). Object-oriented development. *IEEE Transactions on Software Engineering*, **12**(2), pp. 211–21.

Booch G. (1987a). *Software Components with Ada*. Benjamin/Cummings.

Booch G. (1987b). *Software Engineering with Ada*, 2nd edn. Menlo Park: Benjamin/Cummings.

Booch G. (1991). *Object-Oriented Design with Applications*. Redwood City: Benjamin/Cummings.

Booch G. and Vilot M. (1990). The design of the C++ Booch components. *Proceedings of OOPSLA '90*. Ottawa, Canada, pp. 1–11.

Brodie M. L., Mylopoulos I. and Schmidt J. W. eds. (1984). *On Conceptual Modelling*. New York: Springer.

Brooks F. (1987). No silver bullet: essence and accidents of software engineering. *IEEE Computer*, **20**(4), pp. 10–19.

Browne J.C, Lee T. and Werth J. (1990). Experimental evaluation of a reusability-oriented parallel programming environment. *IEEE Transactions on Software Engineering*, **16**(2), pp. 111–20.

Bubenko Jr. J. and Lindencrona, E. (1984). *Conceptual Modeling–Information Analysis*. Lund (Sweden): Studentlitteratur.

Buhr R.J.A. (1984). *System Design with Ada*. Englewood Cliffs, NJ: Prentice-Hall.

Buhr R.J.A. (1991). *Practical Visual Techniques in System Design: With Applications to Ada*. Englewood Cliffs, NJ: Prentice-Hall.

Caldiera G. and Basili V.R. (1991). Identifying and qualifying reusable software components. *IEEE Computer*, February, pp. 61–70.

CCITT (1984). *Fascicle vi 12, CHILL*. Recommendation Z.200, Geneva.

CCITT (1988). *Specification and Description Language (SDL)*. Recommendation Z.100. Geneva.

Coad P. and Yourdon E. (1991a). *Object-Oriented Analysis*, 2nd edn. Englewood Cliffs, NJ: Prentice-Hall.

Coad P. and Yourdon E. (1991b). *Object-Oriented Design*. Englewood Cliffs, NJ: Prentice-Hall.

Constantine L. L. (1990). Object-oriented and function-oriented software structure. A revised form of 'Objects, Functions, and Extensibility' in *Computer Language*, **7**, January, pp. 34–56.

Coutag J. (1989). Architecture models for interactive software. In *Proceedings of ECCOP 1989*.

Cox B.J. (1986). *Object Oriented Programming – An Evolutionary Appoach*. Reading, MA: Addison-Wesley.

Cox B. (1990). There *is* a Silver Bullet. *BYTE Magazine,* October, 1990, pp. 209–18.

Dahl O.-J. and Nygaard K. (1966). SlMULA – an Algol-based simulation language. *Communications of the ACM,* **9**(9).

Date C.J. (1986). *An Introduction to Database Systems, Volume 1,* 4th edn. Reading, MA: Addison-Wesley.

Davis J. and Morgan T. (1993). Object-oriented development at Brooklyn Union Gas. *IEEE Software,* January, pp. 67–74.

Dietrich W.C., Nackman L.R. and Gracer F. (1989). Saving a legacy with objects. In *Proceedings OOPSLA '89,* New Orleans, USA, October, pp. 77–83.

Doyle J. (1979). A Truth Maintenance System. *Artificial Intelligence,* **12**(3), pp. 231–79.

Ellis M.A. and B. Stroustrup (1990). *The Annotated C++ Reference Manual.* Reading, MA: Addison-Wesley.

Embley D.W. and Woodfield S.N. (1988). Assessing the quality of abstract data types written in Ada. In *Proceedings of the Tenth International Conference on Software Engineering.* IEEE Computer Society Press, pp. 144–53.

Embley D.W., Kurtz B.D. and Woodfield S.N. (1992). *Object-oriented Systems Analysis – A Model-driven Approach.* Yourdon Press.

Eriksson G. and Holm P. (1984). *Programmering i Simula* (Programming in Simula). Lund (Sweden): KF-Sigma.

Freeman P. ed (1987). *Tutorial: Software Reusability.* IEEE Computer Society Press.

Gibson E. (1990). Objects – born and bred. *BYTE Magazine,* October, pp. 245–54.

Glahn J.E. and Meland C. (1985). Practical tools which give the decision maker clarity of the future. *Proceedings of 8th INTERNET Congress,* Rotterdam.

Goldberg A. and Robson D. (1983). *Smalltalk-80: The Language and its Implementation.* Reading, MA: Addison-Wesley.

Gomaa H. (1984). A software design method for real-time systems. *Communications of the ACM,* **27**(9), pp. 938–9.

Gomaa H. (1989). Structuring criteria for real-time system design. *Proceedings from International Conference on Software Engineering.* Pittsburgh, 15–18 May, pp. 290–301.

Gorlen K.E., Orlow S.M. and Plexico P.S. (1990). *Data Abstraction and Object-Oriented Programming in C++.* Chichester: Wiley.

Grady R.B. and Caswell D.L. (1987). *Software Metrics: Establishing a Company-Wide Program.* Englewood Cliffs, NJ: Prentice-Hall.

Hall A. (1990). Seven myths of formal methods. *IEEE Software,* September, pp. 11–19.

Hartson H.R. and Hix D. (1989). Human-computer interface development: concepts and systems for its management. *ACM Computing Surveys,* **21** (1), pp.5–92.

Hix D. (1990). Generations of user-interface management systems. *IEEE Software,* September, pp. 77–87.

Hoare C.A.R. (1985). *Communicating Sequential Processes.* Englewood Cliffs, NJ: Prentice-Hall.

HOOD (1989a). *HOOD User Manual*. Issue 3.0. WME/89-353/JB. HOOD Working Group. European Space Agency, December.

HOOD (1989b). *HOOD Reference Manual*. Issue 3.0. WME/89-173/JB. HOOD Working Group. European Space Agency, September.

Hull R. and King R. (1987). Semantic database modeling: survey, applications, and research issues. *ACM Computing Surveys*, **19**(3), pp. 201–60.

Humphrey W. (1989). *Managing the Software Process*. Reading, MA: Addison-Wesley.

IEEE (1983). IEEE Std 729-1983. *Standard Glossary of Software Engineering Terminology*.

Jackson M. (1983). *System Development*. Englewood Cliffs, NJ: Prentice-Hall.

Jacky J.P. and Kalet I.J. (1987). An object-oriented programming discipline for standard Pascal. *Communications of the ACM*, **30**(9), pp. 772–6.

Jacobson I. (1985). Concepts for modeling large realtime systems. Ph.D thesis. Royal Institute of Technology: Stockholm.

Jacobson I. (1986). Language support for changeable large real time systems. In *Proceedings of OOPSLA '86*, Portland, Oregon, USA, September, pp.377–84.

Jacobson I. (1987). Object-oriented development in an industrial environment. *Proceedings of OOPSLA '87. SIGPLAN Notices*, **22**(12), pp. 183–91.

Jacobson I. (1991). Industrial development of software with an object-oriented technique. *Journal of Object-Oriented Programming*. March/April, pp. 30–41.

Jacobson I. (1992). Object orientation as a competitive advantage. *American Programmer*, October, **5**(8).

Jacobson I. (1993). Is object technology software's industrial platform? *IEEE Software*, January, pp. 24 – 30.

Jacobson I. and Lindström F. (1991). Re-engineering of Old Systems to an Object-Oriented architecture. *Proceedings of OOPSLA '91*. Phoenix AZ, October 1991, pp. 340–50.

Johnson R.E. and Foote B. (1988). Designing reusable classes. *Journal of Object-Oriented Programming*, June/July, 22–35.

JOOP (1991). Special issue on databases. *Journal of Object-Oriented Programming*, July/August.

Knuth D.E. (1973, 1981). *The Art of Computer Programming*, Volumes 1–3. Reading, MA: Addison-Wesley.

LaLonde W.R. and Pugh J.R. (1990). *Inside Smalltalk*. Vol I. Englewood Cliffs, NJ: Prentice-Hall.

LaLonde W.R. and Pugh J.R. (1991a). *Inside Smalltalk*. Vol II. Englewood Cliffs, NJ: Prentice-Hall.

LaLonde W.R. and Pugh J.R. (1991b). Subclassing≠Subtyping≠IsA. *Journal of Object-Oriented Programming*, January, pp. 57–62.

LaLonde W.R., Thomas D.A. and Pugh J.R. (1986). An Exemplar Based Smalltalk. *Proceedings of OOPSLA '86*, Portland, OR, September-October, pp. 322–30.

Lawson H. (1990). Philosophies for engineering computer based systems. *IEEE Computer*, **23**(12), pp. 52–63.

Lawson H. (1991). *Parallel Processing in Industrial Real-Time Applications*. Englewood Cliffs, NJ: Prentice-Hall.

Lehman M.M. and Belady L. (1985). *Program Evolution. Process of Software Change*. London: Academic.

Levendel Y. (1990). Reliability analysis of large software systems: defect data modeling. *IEEE Transactions on Software Engineering*, **16**(2), pp. 141–52.

Lieberherr K.J. and Holland I.M. (1989). Assuring good style for object-oriented programs. *IEEE Software*. September, pp. 38–48.

Lieberman H. (1986). Using prototypical objects to implement shared behavior in object oriented systems. *Proceedings of OOPSLA '86*. Portland, OR, September-October, 214–23.

Linowes J.S (1988). It's an attitude. *Byte Magazine*, August, pp. 219–24.

Lippman S. (1991). C++ *Primer*, 2nd edn. Reading, MA: Addison-Wesley.

Loomis M.E.S. (1990). Several columns discussing issues on ODBMS. *Journal of Object-Oriented Programming*, May/June and later.

Loomis M.E.S., Shah A.V. and Rumbaugh J. E. (1987). An object modeling technique for conceptual design. *Proceedings of ECOOP '87*, pp. 325–35.

Matsumoto Y. (1987). A software factory: an overall approach to software production. In Freeman (1987).

McCabe T.J. (1976). A complexity measure. *IEEE Transactions on Software Engineering*, **2**(4), pp. 308–20.

McIlroy M.D (1976). Mass-Produced Software Components. In *Software Engineering Concepts and Techniques (1968 NATO Conference on Software Engineering)*. J.M. Buxton, P. Naur and B. Randell, eds. Van Nostrand Reinhold, pp. 88–98.

McMenamin S.M. and Palmer J.F. (1984). *Essential Systems Analysis*. Englewood Cliffs, NJ: Yourdon Press.

Metzger P.W. (1981). *Managing a Programming Project*, 2nd edn. Englewood Cliffs, NJ: Prentice-Hall.

Meyer B. (1988). *Object-Oriented Software Construction*. Englewood Cliffs, NJ: Prentice-Hall.

Meyer B. (1990). Lessons from the design of the Eiffel libraries. *Communications of the ACM*, **33**(9), pp. 68–88.

Mills H.D., Dyer M. and Linger R.C. (1987). Cleanroom software engineering. *IEEE Software*, September, pp. 19–24.

Myers, G. J. (1979). *The Art of Software Testing*. New York: Wiley.

Myers, G. J. (1987). *Software Reliability: Principles and Practices*. New York: Wiley.

Nielsen K. and Shumate K (1988). *Designing Large Real-Time Systems with Ada*. New York: McGraw-Hill and Intertext.

OOPSLA (1990). Structured Analysis and Object-Oriented Analysis. *Proceedings of OOPSLA '90*, pp. 135–9.

Page-Jones M. and Weiss S. (1989). Synthesis/analysis object-oriented method. *DCI Object-Oriented Systems Symposium*, June.

Parnas D. (1972). On the criteria to be used in decomposing systems into modules. *Communications of the ACM*, **15**(2), 1053–8.

Parnas D.L., Clements P.C. and Weiss D.M. (1983). Enhancing reusability with information hiding. *ITT Proceedings of the Workshop on Reusability in Programming*, 1983, pp. 240–47. Also in Freeman (1986).

Partsch H. and Steinbruggen R. (1983). Program transformation systems. *ACM Computing Surveys*, **15**(3), pp. 109–226.

Peckham J. and Maryansli F. (1988). Semantic Data Models. *ACM Computing Surveys*, **20**(3), pp. 153–89.

Perry D.E. and Kaiser G.E. (1990). Adequate testing and object-oriented programming. *Journal of Object-Oriented Programming*, January/February, pp. 13–19.

Peterson J.L. and Silberschatz A. (1985). *Operating Systems Concepts*. Reading, MA: Addison-Wesley.

Premerlani W.J., Blaha M.R., Rumbaugh J.E. and Varwig T.A. (1990). An object-oriented relational database. *Communications of the ACM*, **33**(11), pp. 99–109.

Prieto-Diaz R. and Freeman P. (1987). Classifying software for reusability. *IEEE Software*, January, pp. 616. Also in Freeman (1987), pp. 106–16.

Purchase J.A. and Winder R.L. (1991). Debugging tools for object-oriented programming. *Journal of Object-Oriented Programming*, June, pp. 10–27.

Ramamritham K., Stankovic J.A. and Zhao W. (1989). Distributed scheduling of tasks with deadlines and resource requirements. *IEEE Transactions on Computers*, **38**(9), pp. 938–62.

Rochat R. (1986). *In Search of Good Smalltalk Programming Style*. Technical Report CR-86-19. Tektronix.

Ross D.T. (1985). Applications and Extensions of SADT. *IEEE Computer*, April.

Rubin K. S. and Goldberg A. (1992). Object behavior analysis. *Communications of the ACM*, September pp. 48–62.

Rumbaugh J., Blaha M., Premerlani W., Eddy F., Lorensen W. (1991). *Object-Oriented Modeling and Design*. Englewood Cliffs, NJ: Prentice-Hall.

Scharenberg M.E. and Dunsmore H.E. (1991). Evolution of classes and objects during object-oriented design and programming. *Journal of Object-Oriented Programming*, January, pp. 30–4.

Sha L. and Goodenough J.B. (1990). Real-time scheduling theory and Ada. *IEEE Computer*, April, pp. 53–62.

Shaw A.C. (1989). Reasoning about time in higher-level language software. *IEEE Transactions on Software Engineering*, **15**(7), pp. 875–89.

Shlaer S. and Mellor S.J. (1988). *Object-oriented Systems Analysis*. Englewood Cliffs, NJ: Prentice-Hall.

Snyder A. (1986). Encapsulation and inheritance in object-oriented programming languages. *Proceedings of OOPSLA '86*. Portland, OR, September-October, 38–45.

Sommerville, I. (1989). *Software Engineering*, 3rd edn. Wokingham: Addison-Wesley.

Spector A. and Gifford D. (1986). A Computer Science Perspective of Bridge Design. *Communications of the ACM*, **29**, pp. 267–83.

Stankovic J.A. (1988). Misconceptions about real-time computing. *IEEE Computer*, October, pp. 1–18.

Stankovic J.A. and Ramamritham K. (1988). Tutorial: hard real-time systems. Washington: IEEE Computer Society Press.

Stefik M.J., Bobrow D.G. and Kahn K.H. 1986. Integrating access-oriented programming into a multiparadigm environment. *IEEE Software*, January, pp. 170–8.

Stone C.M. and Hentchel D.(1990). Database wars revisited. *BYTE Magazine*, October, pp. 233–42.

Sudkamp T.A. (1988). *Languages and Machines: An Introduction to the Theory of Computer Science*. Reading, MA: Addison-Wesley.

Taenzer D., Ganti M. and Podar S. (1989). Object-oriented software reuse: the yoyo Problem. *Journal of Object-Oriented Programming*, September/October, 30–5.

Thomas D. (1989) What's an object? *Datamation*, **14**(3), March, pp. 231–44.

Tracz W. (1988). Software reuse maxims. *ACM Software Engineering Notes*, **13**(4), pp. 28–31.

Tsichritzis D. C. and Lochovsky F. H. (1982). *Data Models*. Englewood Cliffs, NJ: Prentice-Hall.

Turner C.D. and Robson D.J. (1993). The testing of object-oriented programs. Technical Report TR–13/92. University of Durham, England.

von Neumann J. (1945). First Draft of a Report on the EDVAC Moore School of Electrical Engineering, University of Pennsylvania.

Ward P.T. (1989). How to integrate object orientation with structured analysis and design. *IEEE Software*, March, pp. 74–82.

Ward P.T. and Mellor S.J. (1985). *Structured Development for Real-Time Systems*. New York: Yourdon Press.

Wasserman A.l., Pircher P.A. and Müller R.J. (1989). Concepts of object-oriented structured design. *Proceedings of TOOLS '89*, pp. 269–80.

Wasserman A.l., Pircher P.A. and Müller R.J. (1990). The object-oriented structured design notation for software design representation. *IEEE Computer*, March, pp. 50–62.

Wegner P. (1987). Dimensions of Object-Based Language Design. *Proceedings of OOPSLA '87*. Orland Special Issue of *SIGPLAN Notices*, **22**(12), pp. 168–82.

Wegner, P. (1989). Learning the Language. *BYTE Magazine*, March, pp. 245–53.

Wegner P. and Zdonik S. (1988). Inheritance as an Incremental Modification Mechanism or What Like Is and Isn't Like. *Proceedings of ECOOP '88*. Springer, pp. 55–77.

Weinberg G.M. (1971). *The Psychology of Computer Programming*. New York: Van Nostrand Reinhold.

Weinberg G. M. and Freedman D. P. (1982). *Handbook of Walkthroughs, Inspections, and Technical Reviews*. Boston: Little Brown Computer Systems.

Weizenbaum J. (1968). *The Fonary Problem Explained*. Unpublished memorandum, MIT Cambridge 1968 as quoted in Allen J. (1978). *Anatomy of Lisp*. New York: McGraw-Hill.

Wing J.M. (1990). A specifier's introduction to formal methods. *IEEE Computer*, September, pp. 8–24.

Wirfs-Brock R.J. and Johnson R.E. (1990). Surveying current research in object-oriented design. *Communications of the ACM*, **33**(9), pp. 104–24.

Wirfs-Brock R., Wilkerson B. and Wiener L. (1990). *Designing Object-Oriented Software*. Englewood Cliffs, NJ: Prentice-Hall.

Yourdon E. (1989a) *Modern Structured Analysis*, Yourdon Press/Prentice-Hall.

Yourdon E. (1989b). *Structured Walkthroughs*, 4th edn. Englewood Cliffs: Prentice-Hall/Yourdon Press.

Yourdon E. (1990). Auld Lang Syne. *BYTE Magazine*, October, pp. 257–63.

Yourdon E. and Constantine L.L. (1979). *Structured Design: Fundamentals of a Discipline of Computer Program and Systems Design*. Englewood Cliffs,NJ: Prentice-Hall.

Zave P. (1984). The operational versus the conventional approach to software development. *Communications of the ACM*, **27**(2), pp. 10–18.

# Index

# NEW TITLE FROM THIS AWARD-WINNING AUTHOR
# AVAILABLE FALL 1994

## BUSINESS PROCESS RE-ENGINEERING WITH OBJECT TECHNOLOGY

The primary aim of this book is to show how object technology can be used in the Business Process Re-engineering (BPR) model; how the requirements of a new software system can be captured as a result of business engineering, and how business engineering and software engineering can be matched in a seamless way. This seamless transition is achieved by using object technology to describe the architecture of an organisation and thus allow developers to use business objects from the business model as objects in the software architecture itself.

* If you would like more information on this book, including ordering information, please send e-mail to: jacobson@aw.com, please write, 'send info' in the subject line.

* Inquiries may also be sent to:

In North America:  Addison-Wesley Publishing Co., Attn: CS Marketing, One Jacob Way, Reading MA 01867

Outside North America:  Addison-Wesley Publishers Limited, Attn: Sales Dept., Finchampstead Road, Wokingham, Berkshire, RG11 2NZ, England

---

* For more information regarding the Objectory products that implement the technology presented in this book, please contact Objectory at one of the following addresses:

Head office:

Objectory AB
Box 1128
S-164  22 Kista, Sweden
Phone: +46 8 703 4530
Fax: +46 8 751 3096

OBJECTORY

North American office:

Objectory Corporation
#4 Greenwich Office Park
Greenwich, CT 06831
Phone: (203) 625 7250
Fax: (203) 625 7272